Great Holiness Classics
Volume 6

GREAT HOLINESS CLASSICS
in Six Volumes

Volume 1
Holiness Teaching—New Testament Times to Wesley

Volume 2
The Wesley Century

Volume 3
Leading Wesleyan Thinkers

Volume 4
The 19th-Century Holiness Movement

Volume 5
Holiness Preachers and Preaching

Volume 6
Holiness Teaching Today

VOLUME 6

Holiness Teaching Today

Edited by
A. F. Harper

Volume Advisors:
Milton Agnew
Leslie Parrott

BꟼH

BEACON HILL PRESS OF KANSAS CITY
KANSAS CITY, MISSOURI

Permission to quote from the following copyrighted versions is acknowledged with
appreciation:

Amplified Bible (Amp.). *Amplified Old Testament*, copyright © 1962, 1964 by Zon-
dervan Publishing House. *Amplified New Testament*, © 1958 by the Lockman
Foundation.

The Bible: A New Translation (Moffatt), copyright 1954 by James A. R. Moffatt. By
permission of Harper and Row, Publishers, Inc.

New American Standard Bible (NASB), © The Lockman Foundation, 1960, 1962,
1963, 1968, 1971, 1972, 1973, 1975, 1977.

New English Bible (NEB), © The Delegates of the Oxford University Press and The
Syndics of the Cambridge University Press, 1961, 1970.

The Holy Bible, New International Version (NIV), copyright © 1973, 1978, 1984 by
the International Bible Society.

Revised Standard Version of the Bible (RSV), copyrighted 1946, 1952, © 1971, 1973.

Good News Bible, Today's English Version (TEV)—Old Testament © American Bible
Society, 1976; New Testament © American Bible Society, 1966, 1971, 1976.

The Living Bible (TLB), © 1971 by Tyndale House Publishers, Wheaton, Ill.

The Weymouth New Testament in Modern Speech (Weymouth), copyright 1929 by
Harper and Brothers, New York.

The New Testament in the Language of the People (Williams), by Charles B. Williams.
Copyrighted 1937 by Bruce Humphries, Inc.; assigned 1949 to The Moody Bible
Institute of Chicago.

Quotations from the *American Standard Version* are coded ASV and from the *Twentieth
Century New Testament* TCNT.

Contents

Foreword   9

Understanding the *Great Holiness Classics*   11

Concepts and Identifying Terms   15

Acknowledgments   18

Editor's Introduction to Volume 6   19

Section I: 20th-Century Thought

CHAPTER 1: H. C. MORRISON   23
     I. Stating the Case
     II. Subsequent to Regeneration
     III. For Believers Only
     IV. Purifies and Empowers Believers
     V. The Holy Spirit Comforts and Teaches
     VI. Results of Rejecting the Holy Spirit
     VII. Many Witnesses
     VIII. How to Receive the Holy Spirit

CHAPTER 2: R. T. WILLIAMS   48
     The Importance of Right Ethics
     How to Improve Our Ethics

CHAPTER 3: THOMAS R. KELLY   57
     The Nature of Holy Obedience
     Gateways into Holy Obedience
     Humility and Holiness
     The Simplification of Life

CHAPTER 4: JAMES B. CHAPMAN   66
     How I Became Interested
     Holiness in the Teachings of the Bible
     The Prerequisites of Holiness

Holiness Defined
Holiness Differentiated
Holiness Obtained
The Way to Holiness
Holiness as a Life Lived
Holiness and Evangelism
Holiness and Practical Living
Holiness and the Second Coming
A Holiness Catechism
The Terminology of the Christian Estate
   Holiness, Perfect Love, Christian Perfection
   Other Terms
   Figurative Terminology

CHAPTER 5: CHARLES EWING BROWN   116
   Sin as Evil Disposition
   The Work of the Holy Spirit
   Entire Sanctification as a Bundle of Possibilities
   Sanctified as a Child

CHAPTER 6: COL. MILTON S. AGNEW   140
   The Way into Holiness
   The Way of Holiness
   The Liberty of Holiness

CHAPTER 7: EVERETT L. CATTELL   161
   The Sanctification of Self
   The Spirit-controlled Life
   The Guidance of the Spirit

CHAPTER 8: J. HAROLD GREENLEE   196
   The Greek New Testament and the Message of Holiness
   Holiness: A Quality
   Holiness: Its Meaning
   Other Significant Terms
   Significant New Testament Passages
   A Final Word

CHAPTER 9: E. STANLEY JONES   209
   Personal Testimony
   Holiness and Human Personality
   Holiness and the Gifts of the Spirit

Section II: Experiencing Christian Holiness

CHAPTER 10: DOCTRINAL ISSUES   225
   God's Holiness
   Carnality/Cleansing
   A Gift of God's Grace
   Atonement
   Perfect Love
   The Holy Spirit
   Empowerment
   Christlikeness
   A Scriptural Doctrine
   For All Christians
   The Second Blessing
   In a Moment
   Names

CHAPTER 11: STEPS TO SEEKING AND FINDING   296
   The New Birth
   Hunger
   Consecration
   Faith
   Assurance

CHAPTER 12: LIVING THE LIFE OF HOLINESS   335
   Growth
   Attitudes
   Wholeness
   Humanity
   Dangers

CHAPTER 13: WITNESSING AND PROCLAMATION   362
   Witnessing
   Preaching
   Teaching
   Writing
   Ethics

Appendix: Holiness in the 20th Century   391

Bibliography   403

Indexes   407

Foreword

John Wesley is acknowledged and acclaimed as the chief architect of the doctrine of entire sanctification or Christian perfection as understood within the Holiness Movement. However, the truth this tenet expresses derives from the very heart of Scripture, and the experience and life it enshrines have been known and exemplified by the saints of every age.

Nor did Wesley give final and complete formulation of this truth. Theology is an ongoing process; it endeavors to interpret truth in language and thought-forms relevant to each succeeding generation. The creativity of the Spirit is evident in the unfolding of the doctrine from Wesley to the present. The truth of Christian holiness is so grand it defies any finality of expression.

Furthermore, since saints within every Christian tradition have found this Kingdom treasure, their witness to holiness reflects the variety of these traditions. The truth of perfect love is like a sparkling diamond—to appreciate its full beauty and brilliance we must view it from many angles.

This series of classics is designed to provide the modern reader a compact library of holiness literature. Herein you will find, along with appropriate editorial introductions and comments, many of the significant primary documents of the Holiness Movement. I commend these volumes as a devotional treasure for those who seek spiritual enrichment as well as a resource library for teachers and preachers who would deepen and enlarge their understanding of this central truth of Scripture.

—WILLIAM M. GREATHOUSE
General Superintendent
Church of the Nazarene

Understanding the
Great Holiness Classics

Holiness

Christian holiness is a scriptural teaching to be understood and a relationship with God to be experienced. God is a holy God, and He asks His people to be like Him in this respect.

In the Old Testament we read, "Ye shall be holy: for I the Lord your God am holy" (Lev. 19:2). In teaching us about our responsibilities to God, Jesus summarized the first chapter of the Sermon on the Mount with the admonition: "Be ye therefore perfect, even as your Father which is in heaven is perfect" (Matt. 5:48).

Every sincere Christian wants to know what it means to be as holy as God asks us to be. Every follower of Christ feels at times yearnings to be more Christlike, to somehow realize the Christian perfection Jesus sets before us.

It is this ideal and goal taught in the Scriptures that has, across the centuries, stirred every devout Christian who has sought and experienced God's sanctifying grace. In John Wesley's *Plain Account of Christian Perfection* he records his own experience of discovering this truth: "I tell you, as plain as I can speak, where and when I found this. I found it in the oracles of God, in the Old and New Testament, when I read them with no other view or desire, but to save my own soul" (*Works,* 11:444).

The Holiness Classics

Following in the tradition of Wesley and other devout persons who have sought and preached Christian holiness, the publishers conceived and launched this series of six volumes of *Great Holiness Classics.* The desire and purpose was, in Wesley's words, to "spread scriptural holiness over these lands" in the 20th century.

The commission given to the editors states that desire.

To provide a representative compilation of the best holiness literature in a format readily accessible to the average minister, thus providing: (1) the preservation of the essential elements of our holiness heritage; (2) an overview of the broad scope of the holiness message; (3) a norm for holiness theology, proclamation, and practice; (4) a succinct reference work on holiness; and (5) a revival of the best of the out-of-print holiness classics.

What Is a Classic?

A classic work comes from the past, but simply being old does not make it classic. To be classic, a work must have enduring excellence. Its content must be so true and persuasive that succeeding generations read it and are moved to accept the truth and to shape their lives by it. Seeking after holiness as taught in a classic, one finds the truths verified both in Scripture and in his own experience with God. A work is classic because its truths are central to revealed and to experiential Christianity.

It is this verifying of previous experience that keeps a classic alive in the consciousness of the Christian community. There is here a principle somewhat parallel to the scientific method. In science we accept as true an experiment that can be repeated under similar conditions with the same results.

Because a holiness classic represents such a verifiable and biblical promise of spiritual fulfillment, it becomes a typical example of true teaching and a dependable model of Christian experience. Other persons who ponder the Scripture and perform the experiment report comparable experiences of God. The accumulating testimony verifies the classic nature of the document.

A classic thus becomes an authoritative commentary on scriptural truth. It contains guidance that can be depended on to result in sound action and blessed results. The work therefore becomes a norm for future generations. It affirms to the reader, "If you approach God as I did and respond to Him, as by His Word and Spirit He led me to respond, you will discover that He works in your life as I testify He has worked in mine."

In a letter to Dr. Middleton, Wesley cites this appeal to holy living as characteristic of the Christian fathers: "What the Scripture promises, I enjoy. Come and see what Christianity has done here; and acknowledge it is of God" (*Works*, 10:79).

Selection of Materials

The editors have been guided by these concepts of classic holiness writings. Works that have spoken to succeeding generations have endured; therefore, we have included them. Writings that present views widely held by other holiness writers are to be considered classic. A work that stimulates the reader to try the grand experiment is classical. In Christian literature, writings that most faithfully reflect biblical teachings are classical in the best sense of being truly Christian norms.

The materials here selected as classic, then, (1) reflect accurately the teachings of the Bible, (2) have a broad and common base of Christian testimony, (3) and are in line with the best thinking of Christian leaders who have enjoyed the experience of God's sanctifying grace.

What we have chosen, we believe, gives a true account of God's plan for holy living. These writings offer a norm for Christian life that reflects God's will for His children. They lead to the greatest personal fulfillment and inspire believers to make their most effective contribution to the extension of God's kingdom.

Truth with Tolerance

Not all sincere Christians understand Bible holiness in the same way. What is here reflected is generally called the Wesleyan interpretation of entire sanctification. Even within the circle of those who follow Wesley there are some differences of interpretation. The statement of "Concepts and Identifying Terms" was drawn up as a way to reflect the widely accepted positions of the Wesleyan, Methodist tradition.

We recognize and appreciate guides to holy living from other traditions as in the Moravian, Quaker, Mennonite, and modern Keswick movements. Much of what is here included crosses all denominational boundaries. It will therefore speak to the spirits of evangelical Christians from most of the historic orthodox communions.

In order to avoid being too restrictive in our selections, we have sought the advice of a broad group of nearly 50 Bible scholars and churchmen whose names appear in the lists of editors, and of members of the editorial advisory boards. These persons have all been involved in a continuing consultation on the choice of materials to be included. We trust that the broad consensus further assures our choice of truly classic materials.

Editorial Policy

The editors were instructed to select writings "judged by the quality of the material and its ability to speak to this generation." Because many of the holiness classics, especially in the first two volumes, come from an earlier period of writing, we were further given "the right to excerpt and edit the materials, updating archaic usage as needed."

Our goal has been, insofar as is possible, to let the writers speak for themselves. In excerpting we have tried to be completely faithful to the writer's views, deleting only dated, irrelevant, or duplicated materials. Our concern has always been to present as clearly as possible what the writer believed, experienced, and taught about Christian holiness.

In order to make our selections as clear as possible for today's reader we have: (1) modernized some spelling and punctuation, (2) divided some long paragraphs for greater ease in reading, (3) prepared brief introductions and analyses of the writings included, and (4) inserted center heads, side heads, and cut-in headings as brief indications of content in order to guide the reader who is looking for specific aspects of holiness teaching.

For the historical scholar who wishes to follow in our footsteps and form his own judgment of our accuracy, we have: (1) indicated our sources by title, date, edition, and page numbers from which the selection is taken (where relevant for accuracy, we have used the earliest editions of the text); (2) retained original paragraph numbers to aid the reader in locating the source of our quotations; (3) used ellipses to indicate where material has been omitted; and (4) retained italics that appear in the originals, to show what the writers sought to emphasize.

To help the reader more easily distinguish editorial comment from the classic materials quoted, we have printed the editor's additions in a slightly darker type.

Our Prayer

The prayer of the editors and publishers is that all who read these classics of holy living may come to understand "the way of God more perfectly" (Acts 18:26).

We pray "that Christ may dwell in your hearts by faith; that ye, being rooted and grounded in love, may be able to comprehend with all saints what is the breadth, and length, and depth, and height; and to know the love of Christ, which passeth knowledge, that ye might be filled with all the fulness of God.

"Now unto him that is able to do exceeding abundantly above all that we ask or think, according to the power that worketh in us, unto him be glory in the church by Christ Jesus throughout all ages, world without end. Amen" (Eph. 3:17-21).

—A. F. HARPER
Executive Editor

Concepts and Identifying Terms

At the beginning of the project the editors were mandated to "strive for balance, reflecting the various facets of holiness—crisis and process, practice and proclamation, etc."

In order to guide us and to test the inclusiveness and balance of materials chosen, it seemed necessary to devise an instrument for reminder and measurement. We therefore developed the following list of concepts and identifying terms.

The statements are designed to indicate the teachings of the church. The identifying terms are planned as a kind of shorthand device for highlighting these truths throughout the set and in the indexes.

We believe the statements faithfully reflect what the Bible teaches and what the Church has believed and taught across the centuries. The terms are biblical and/or classical in the sense that they represent the language the Church has used to describe the various facets of the experience of God's sanctifying grace.

For convenient reference, we have used these code words as cut-in heads on pages where the related concepts are explored.

A. Doctrinal

1. The requirement of entire sanctification is rooted in God's holiness. **God's Holiness**
2. The need for entire sanctification is seen in the remaining presence of inbred sin, or carnality, in believers. The experience of entire sanctification includes cleansing from this original sin. **Carnality/ Cleansing**
3. Entire sanctification is a gift of God's grace. **Grace**
4. God provides the gift in the atonement of Christ. **Atonement**

5. To be sanctified wholly means to receive grace to love God with your whole heart and to love your neighbor as yourself.

Perfect Love

6. At conversion, Christians receive God's Holy Spirit in regeneration, sometimes described as initial sanctification. To be sanctified wholly means to be baptized, or filled with the Holy Spirit, as happened to the disciples in the Upper Room.

Holy Spirit

7. To be filled with the Holy Spirit brings added power to conquer sin, to love others, and to witness for Christ.

Power[1]

8. God offers the ministry of the indwelling Holy Spirit to make us more Christlike.

Christlikeness

9. We believe the doctrine of entire sanctification is taught in the Bible and is consistent with other salvation truths of Scripture.

Scriptural

10. Entire sanctification is God's call to all Christians.

For All Christians

11. Entire sanctification is experienced as a second blessing of grace subsequent to regeneration.

Second Blessing

12. Because entire sanctification is God's gift in response to faith, it occurs in a moment of time, just as God's forgiveness comes in an instant.

In a Moment

13. Entire sanctification is also known as Christian perfection, perfect love, heart purity, the baptism with the Holy Spirit, being filled with the Spirit, the fullness of the blessing, full salvation, the deeper life, Christian holiness, scriptural holiness, the rest of faith, and the promise of the Father.

Names

B. Steps to Seeking and Finding

14. The new birth is a prerequisite to entire sanctification.

New Birth

---

1. Item 7 was omitted from the first printing of volumes 2 and 3. It will appear in subsequent editions of all volumes in the series.

15. Conviction of need is a condition for the personal quest after holiness.   Hunger

16. Full consecration is both a precondition and a gracious fruit of entire sanctification.   Consecration

17. Faith grounded on the full-orbed purpose of Christ's death, and the fullest consecration of which we are capable, is the human condition for entire sanctification.   Faith

18. God gives the witness of His Spirit when we are sanctified wholly.   Assurance

C. Living the Life of Holiness

19. Christians grow in likeness to Christ, both before and after entire sanctification. Successful growth requires obedience, trust, deep devotion, and personal discipline.   Growth

20. Being filled with the Spirit makes a difference in a Christian's attitudes.   Attitudes

21. Holiness tends toward fulfillment of life and wholeness of human personality.   Wholeness

22. Though sanctified wholly, men and women are still limited by their imperfections in judgment, personality, and conduct; they are still subject to all sorts of temptation.   Humanity

23. Dangers to which the sanctified are especially vulnerable include spiritual pride and setting standards too high.   Dangers

D. Proclamation—Witnessing

24. Testifying to God's work of entire sanctification honors God and spreads the truth.   Witnessing

25. The truth of entire sanctification and a holy life is to be proclaimed through preaching.   Preaching

26. Understanding of the truth of Christian holiness and hunger for the experience are communicated through teaching.   Teaching

27. The truth of Christian holiness is spread through written testimony, exposition, and exhortation.   Writing

28. We document and prove holiness by living holy lives and by Christian ethical behavior.   Ethics

Acknowledgments

Sources from which materials have been reprinted are all listed in the footnotes and the bibliography.

We acknowledge permission to reprint the following major sections of copyrighted materials.

Abingdon Press: Chapter 5, excerpted from *A Song of Ascents*, by E. Stanley Jones. Copyright © 1968 by Abingdon Press. Used by permission.

Beacon Hill Press of Kansas City:
Milton S. Agnew, *More than Conquerors*
James B. Chapman, *Holiness, the Heart of Christian Experience*, and *The Terminology of Holiness*
Kenneth Geiger, comp., *Further Insights into Holiness*
R. T. Williams, *Sanctification: The Experience and the Ethics*
William B. Eerdmans Publishing Company: Everett Lewis Cattell, *The Spirit of Holiness*
Harper and Row: Thomas R. Kelly, *A Testament of Devotion*
Pentecostal Herald Press: H. C. Morrison, *The Baptism with the Holy Ghost*
The War Cry: "Something More," by Mrs. Stanley Walters
Warner Press: Charles Ewing Brown, *The Meaning of Sanctification*

I am indebted to my fellow compilers of the other five volumes of *Great Holiness Classics:* Paul M. Bassett, T. Crichton Mitchell, Richard S. Taylor, Timothy L. Smith, and William E. McCumber. As general editor, my horizons have been expanded and my thinking enriched in planning with them and in reading the resources that they have gathered from the literature of the Holiness Movement.

I also owe a debt of gratitude to former colleagues on the faculty of Nazarene Theological Seminary whom I have consulted, and who have contributed to this volume with information and counsel: Alex R. G. Deasley, J. Kenneth Grider, William C. Miller, Harold E. Raser, and Rob L. Staples.

Editor's Introduction
to Volume 6

The work of God in the human spirit is both timeless and contemporary. The Scripture reminds us that "Jesus Christ is the same yesterday and today and forever" (Heb. 13:8, NIV). The Holy Spirit worked mightily in the apostles and the Early Church, at intervals throughout church history, in Wesley's day, and in the 19th century. Today He fills, empowers, and guides His people as they tarry for His coming and receive His fullness.

Volume 6 of *Great Holiness Classics* was planned to include (1) major contributions from 20th-century writers, and (2) some of the timeless devotional experiences and universal insights of holy people across 20 centuries of the Christian era.

In section 1 we have included classic writings from nine 20th-century holiness exponents. These expositions usually appear in the order in which they were published. The voices come from a variety of denominational backgrounds: the Church of God, Church of the Nazarene, Free Methodist, Evangelical Friends, Quakers, United Methodist, and the Salvation Army. Briefer contributions in section 2 reflect the faith in Christian holiness to be found, not only in these groups, but also among Anglicans, Baptists, Congregationalists, the Covenant church, the Episcopal church, Pilgrim Holiness church, Wesleyans, and Methodism in Great Britain. Wherever the message of holiness is preached, God's people feel the call to a deeper Christian life. Many respond to that call and experience God's sanctifying work in their spirits.

Some 20th-century names that informed readers may look for are not included because their contributions appear among the theologians of Volume 3. These include Daniel Steele, Olin A. Curtis, Wilson Thomas Hogue, Solomon Jacob Gamertsfelder, Aaron M. Hills, Albert Frederick Gray, H. Orton Wiley, and J. Paul Taylor.

Also, a number of popular holiness exponents who ministered in the late 19th and early 20th centuries have been omitted from Volume 6 because their writings appear in Volume 4. Among them are: Benjamin T. Roberts, David B. Updegraff, Albert B. Simpson, Samuel Ashton Keene, Joseph A. Beet, Samuel Logan Brengle, and Phineas F. Bresee.

In section 2, "Experiencing Christian Holiness," we have tried to gather a wide range of human responses to the sanctifying work of the Holy Spirit. Most of these experiences fall under the heading of devotional literature. They are expressions of the human spirit in response to the experienced presence of God in His sanctifying ministry.

These responses are always deeply personal and are often expressed in testimonies of acceptance, joy, commitment, praise, or obedience. Such positive responses to the work of the Holy Spirit frequently take the form of poetry—the language of emotion. When poems are set to music we get songs and hymns that express praise to God, and high human joy in response to the wonder of God's presence in our lives.

We release *Great Holiness Classics,* including Volume 6, with the purpose that readers may understand the truth more clearly, respond to our Lord's command to be filled with the Holy Spirit, and learn better how to walk daily in the Spirit.

We join in Paul's prayer for every follower of Christ:

"May God himself, the God of peace, sanctify you through and through. May your whole spirit, soul and body be kept blameless at the coming of our Lord Jesus Christ. The one who calls you is faithful and he will do it" (1 Thess. 5:23-24, NIV).

—A. F. HARPER

Section I

20th-Century Thought

1

H. C. Morrison
(1857-1942)

Henry Clay Morrison was born on March 10, 1857, at Bedford, Ky. When Henry was three weeks old, his mother dedicated him to the ministry at a Methodist quarterly meeting.

Educated at Ewing Institute, Perryville, Ky., and Vanderbilt University for one year, he passed his examinations in all but one subject. Later in life he was given an honorary D.D. by Vanderbilt.

He married Laura Bain in 1888, and they had three children. Mrs. Morrison died in 1893, and he married Geneva Pedlar on April 9, 1895. They had five children. She died in 1914, and he married Mrs. Bettie Whitehead on February 17, 1916. She died in 1945.

Henry was converted at age 13 and licensed to preach 8 years later. From 1879 to 1882 Morrison served four Methodist circuits. He served five pastorates in Kentucky from 1882 to 1890.

As an evangelist from 1890 to 1910 he ministered to audiences numbered by the thousands. During 1908 he preached 471 times. It is estimated that he held 1,200 revivals, preached 15,000 times, traveled 500,000 miles, and had thousands of converts at his altars.

It was during these years of evangelism that Dr. Morrison recalled his own experience of entire sanctification. In an editorial in the *Pentecostal Herald,* July 20, 1904, he wrote:

"From Mountain Lake Park, I came . . . on to St. Louis . . . and went out to the office of the *American Methodist Magazine* to meet my old friend Bro. Cockrill. . . .

23

"More than any other one man, Bro. Cockrill showed me the doctrine of full salvation. He had received the blessing, and letters were passing between us every few days.

"One day as I read a letter from him, the scales fell from my eyes. The truth broke in upon me clear as noonday. I saw it plainly and wept for joy. It seemed that a conversation went on in my breast. 'Yes, I am God's child, but I am not His holy child, but He wants me to be holy. Yes, but I cannot make myself so. No, but He can make me holy, and He will.'

"I wept for joy and felt sure that I should soon receive the grace, and the Spirit came in mighty sanctifying power before night that very day.

"For a time it seemed that my feet scarcely touched the floor. What joy inexpressible, what rest of soul, what a fountain of love sprang up in my heart and rolled forth to all mankind! The man, the letter, the day, the spot in the upper room, I never shall forget. I feel that same love today, not with all the flood tide of that blessed hour, but it abides. Amen."

Founder of the *Pentecostal Herald* about 1890, Dr. Morrison was its editor for 35 years, stressing holiness, and aiding and promoting Asbury College and Asbury Theological Seminary.

Returning from a tour of world evangelism, Morrison accepted the presidency of Asbury College, and served from 1910 to 1925. He served again as president from 1933 to 1940. Accepting the recognition as president emeritus, he continued to hold this title until his death. Founder of Asbury Theological Seminary in 1923, he was its first president, and his administration continued until his death in 1942. (Excerpted from *World Methodism.*)

The Baptism with the Holy Ghost[1]

Dr. Morrison believed in, battled for, and preached the truths of Christian holiness. He served 22 years as president of Asbury

---

1. An eight-chapter pamphlet first published in 1900. The booklet had a wide influence among holiness people, not only in America, but also in the churches of Japan and China. The descriptive chapter titles in the table of contents were inserted, drawn from the subtitles in the pamphlet.

College and founded Asbury Theological Seminary to help preserve and promote the doctrine and life of full salvation.

In presenting these classic positions for entire sanctification, Morrison, like John Wesley, goes to the Bible, expounding clearly the scriptures on which those beliefs rest. With the logic of a lawyer and the passion of an evangelist he presents the case for entire sanctification through the baptism with the Holy Spirit.

PREFACE

It is scarcely worthwhile to say to the reader that in this booklet on *The Baptism with the Holy Ghost*, I have not attempted anything exhaustive, but have tried to set forth an important Bible truth in a plain, simple way. I have often wished for a booklet on this subject so cheap that the poor could buy it, so small that the busy could read it, and so plain that those of the most ordinary learning and intelligence could understand it. I have preached the truth herein contained to many thousands of people, and God has graciously put the seal of His approval on the Word in the conversion of a multitude of sinners, and the sanctification of many believers. I send it out with the prayer that God may make it a blessing to many, and with the request that those who read it with profit will pass it on to others.

Your brother,
H. C. MORRISON

Chapter I
Stating the Case

In discussing the important doctrine of the baptism with the Holy Ghost, I wish first of all, to state the case; then I shall introduce the inspired witnesses and argue the case from the testimony given by them.

(1) In the great scheme of human redemption God has provided that all of His children may receive the baptism with the Holy Ghost.

(2) The baptism with the Holy Ghost is bestowed subsequent to regeneration; not at, but after pardon.

(3) The baptism with the Holy Ghost is for believers only, and is never bestowed upon the unregenerate.

(4) The baptism with the Holy Ghost purifies believers' hearts and empowers them for service.

(5) The Holy Ghost dwells in, abides with, comforts, and teaches those who receive Him.

(6) The rejection of the Holy Ghost is fatal to Christian experience.

It will be appropriate just here to call attention to the fact that the Holy Ghost is a person.

He is the Third Person in the Trinity and is one with the Father and the Son, equal with them in eternity, holiness, and honor.

This fact is plainly taught in the Scriptures, especially in administering the rite of baptism, and in the apostolic benediction. See Matt. 28:19: "Go ye therefore, and teach all nations, baptizing them in the name of the Father, and of the Son, and of the Holy Ghost."

In the closing verse of the last chapter of his Second Epistle to the Corinthians, St. Paul fully recognizes the equality of the Holy Ghost with the Father, and the Son, in these impressive, beautiful words of benediction: "The grace of the Lord Jesus Christ, and the love of God, and the communion of the Holy Ghost, be with you all. Amen."

All of Christ's sayings about the Holy Ghost prove His personality. Take, for example, John 16:7: "It is expedient for you that I go away: for if I go not away, the Comforter will not come unto you; but if I depart, I will send him unto you." Notice here the pronoun—Him. . . .

Let us bear in mind that the Holy Ghost is as essentially a person as is Jesus Christ, and that as certainly as Jesus made His advent into the world in Bethlehem, the Holy Ghost made His advent into the world at Jerusalem, on the Day of Pentecost, and that the times in which we live are especially the dispensation of the Holy Ghost.

We will now consider the first proposition in the statement of the case. *In the great scheme of human redemption, God has provided that all of His children may receive the baptism with the Holy Ghost.*

FOR ALL CHRISTIANS

When John the Baptist came preaching in the wilderness, the burden of his message was the coming Christ, and the baptism He would bestow. Only those who believed John's message received John's baptism, and all of them were assured that when Christ came they should receive from Him another baptism.

"I indeed baptize you with water unto repentance: but he that cometh after me is mightier than I, whose shoes I am not worthy to bear: he shall baptize you with the Holy Ghost, and with fire" (Matt. 3:11). John administered water baptism with the distinct understanding that the baptism he gave was but a preparation for the greater baptism of the Holy Ghost, which Christ would administer when He came. I have never been able to understand how it is that persons can receive John's testimony with regard to water baptism, and reject it with regard to the baptism with the Holy Ghost, for as certainly as John administered the one, he promised that Christ should administer the other.

So far as John's testimony is concerned, the baptism with the Holy Ghost is Christ's prime credential, proving His Messiahship. After John's definite declaration that Christ would bestow the baptism with the Holy Ghost, if Christ had not bestowed Him, John's testimony would have fallen to the ground. Let us suppose that an intelligent, though sinful, Jew attends upon the ministry of the great wilderness preacher. As John speaks his awful denunciation against sin, crying, "O generation of vipers," and declaring that the "axe is laid unto the root of the trees," and that "every tree which bringeth not forth good fruit [shall be] hewn down, and cast into the fire," this Jew is made to tremble because of his sins. He believes the message, the Messiah is coming. He forsakes his sins, and with faith in the Christ that John is preaching, he asks baptism at the hands of John. John baptizes him and says to him, "He that cometh after me is mightier than I, whose shoes I am not worthy to bear: he shall baptize you with the Holy Ghost, and with fire."

Could this Jew ever forget the promise of John? Would he not say to his friends, "John has baptized me with water, but he has promised me another and greater baptism, which I shall receive from Christ who is greater than John!" Would not that Jew naturally believe that in proportion as Christ is greater than John, the baptism with the Holy Ghost, which Christ administers, is superior to the baptism of water, which John administers? When Jesus appears, will not this Jew, if he be a true believer in John, follow Jesus, expecting to receive from Him the baptism with the Holy Ghost? Most assuredly he will. That is exactly what they did do. John fully understood the situation. John willingly gave up his disciples that they might follow Jesus. He said: "He must increase, but I must decrease" (John 3:30).

These disciples of John had been instructed by him that he was only a herald of the coming King, that Jesus was the true Messiah, and He it was that should baptize them with the Holy Ghost and with fire; and they followed Jesus with no other expectation than that they should receive from Him this baptism; and they were not disappointed.

After the promise made by John, if Jesus had said nothing of the baptism with the Holy Ghost, those who followed Him, full of faith and expectation, would have been forced to the conclusion that John was a false prophet, and that Christ was not the true Messiah; but they were not doomed to disappointment.

John was a true prophet, and Christ was the immaculate Son of God, and what John promised, Christ graciously bestowed.

The disciples had not followed Jesus long until He confirmed John's testimony concerning himself. It was on the last day, that great day of the feast, Jesus stood and cried, saying, "If any man thirst, let him come unto me, and drink. He that believeth on me, as the scripture hath said, out of his belly shall flow rivers of living water. (But this spake he of the Spirit, which they that believe on him should receive: for the Holy Ghost was not yet given; because that Jesus was not yet glorified)" (John 7:38-39).

From these scriptures we learn that the Holy Ghost was to be given to those who *believe* on Christ. This gift of the Spirit was not limited to the apostles. Notice the breadth of the promise: "*If any man thirst, . . . He that believeth on me, . . . they that believe on him . . .*" (italics added throughout). This promise takes in all believers. It is a narrow and unscriptural view that limits the baptism with the Holy Ghost to the apostles only. These plain words of Jesus, "*Any man,*" "*He that believeth,*" "*They that believe,*" sweep away all barriers that men would erect between God's children and the baptism with the Holy Ghost, and teach unmistakably that this divine baptism is for all of God's children. We notice that Christ repeats the promise of the gift of the Holy Ghost in John 14:16.

Jesus had just said to His disciples, "Whither I go, ye cannot come." This filled their hearts with sorrow, and He comforted them with those immortal and sure words of promise, found in John 14. "Let not your heart be troubled: ye believe in God, believe also in me. In my Father's house are many mansions: if it were not so, I would have told you. I go to prepare a place for you. And if I go and prepare a place for you, I will come again, and receive you unto myself; that where I am, there ye may be also."

In the 26th verse of the same chapter, Jesus tells the disciples that this Comforter, whom the Father will send, is the Holy Ghost. It was after the Resurrection, and just before His ascension, that Jesus further confirmed the prophecy of John, and the promises which He had previously made to His disciples. See Acts 1:4-5. "And, being assem-

bled together with them, commanded them that they should not depart from Jerusalem, but wait for the promise of the Father, which,
saith he, ye have heard of me. For John truly baptized with water; but
ye shall be baptized with the Holy Ghost not many days hence."

These words are plain and easy of comprehension. *Command*
and *promise* could not be more specific.

HOLY
SPIRIT The pledge of the gift of the Holy Ghost, of which the
disciples have heard so much, in which they are bound to be so
deeply interested, is vouchsafed in unmistakable language.

In obedience to the *commandment*, and with faith in the *promise*,
the disciples tarried at Jerusalem. The protracted waiting in the Upper
Room while 10 days passed by, shows an obedience and faith in the
early disciples which modern, impatient professors of discipleship will
do well to imitate.

No doubt in these long days of waiting by the faithful 120, there
is a valuable lesson for us. There must be in the disciple of Christ a
spirit of genuine submission, obedience, and faith, that will tarry in
patient waiting so long as the Lord may see fit to tarry in His coming.

When Christ gives a commandment to wait and promises a blessing for those who do wait, we must learn to wait, and to wait without
murmur or complaint, until the promised blessing comes. The disciples waited, and not in vain; for, "when the day of Pentecost was fully
come, they were all with *one accord* in one place" (Acts 2:1). . . . No
rebellious spirit or unbelieving heart broke the harmony of that glad,
humble, patient group who waited in the Upper Room.

There is a peculiar blessing in the *mutual* faith of those who love
the Lord. In Rom. 1:11-12, Paul says, "For I long to see you, that I may
impart unto you some spiritual gift, to the end ye may be established;
that is, that I may be comforted together with you by the mutual faith
both of you and me."

Those who do not believe in, or seek for the Holy Ghost, but
rather oppose those who do, will not know the damage they have
done the Church, or the hurt they have been to the cause of Christ,
until the books are opened at the last day.

The inspired record says, "And *suddenly* [reader, mark the word
'*suddenly*.' It is thus that the Spirit comes upon believers] there came
IN A
MOMENT a sound from heaven as of a rushing mighty wind, and it
filled all the house where they were sitting. And there appeared unto them cloven tongues like as of fire, and it sat
upon each of them. And they were all filled with the Holy Ghost"

(Acts 2:2-4). John's prophecy was fulfilled, and Christ's promise was kept, in this wonderful baptism with the Holy Ghost. Without doubt John was a true prophet, and Jesus of Nazareth is the true Messiah, the world's Redeemer. The disciples are confirmed, the world is convinced, sinners are convicted, and 3,000 souls are converted on the spot.

Lest someone should say this baptism with the Holy Ghost was only a temporary gift to the Church, or a special gift to the early Christians, God in His wisdom put into Peter's mouth words that are plain and unmistakable. "Then Peter said unto them, Repent, and be baptized every one of you in the name of Jesus Christ for the remission of sins, and ye shall receive the gift of the Holy Ghost" (Acts 2:38).

These words of Peter were addressed to the 3,000 who, being pricked in their hearts, had said, "Men and brethren, what shall we do?"

St. Peter encourages them with the following words of assurance: "For the promise is unto you, and to your children, and to all that are afar off, even as many as the Lord our God shall call."

FOR ALL CHRISTIANS

Could a promise be stated more plainly, or be more comprehensive?

The baptism with the Holy Ghost was for the 11 apostles, for the 109 [other] persons in the Upper Room with them, for the 3,000 to be bestowed after they had received remission of sins, for the children of the 3,000, for *all* that are afar off, even as *many* as the Lord our God shall call. The word "call" here evidently means convert, or pardon, or regenerate. Even as many as God shall regenerate, have the promise of the baptism with the Holy Ghost.

Beloved reader, with these plain scriptures before us there is but one reasonable conclusion at which we can arrive, and that is, *that in the great scheme of human redemption, God has provided that all of His children may receive the baptism with the Holy Ghost.*

Permit me to close this chapter by addressing to you the words of the Apostle Paul to the young converts at Ephesus:

"Have ye received the Holy Ghost SINCE ye believed?" (Acts 19:2). If not, it is not because there is not abundant provision made in the Atonement, and oft-repeated promises of such a baptism contained in the Scriptures.

Chapter II

The Second Proposition

The baptism with the Holy Ghost is bestowed subsequent to regeneration; not at, but after pardon.

The above statement is not only abundantly taught in the Scriptures, but is strikingly illustrated in the case of the apostles, and those believers who were with them in the Upper Room at the time of their receiving the baptism with the Spirit.

I am aware that some persons are hard pressed in their efforts to prove that the baptism with the Holy Ghost received on the Day of Pentecost was not a blessing received subsequent to regeneration. They have contended that the apostles and their companions were only converted on that occasion. The fallacy of such reasoning is quite plain when we refer to the following scriptures:

I call attention first, to Luke 10:20, where Jesus said to the disciples, "Rejoice not, that the spirits are subject unto you; but rather rejoice, because your names are written in heaven." Now we know that evil spirits are not subject to sinners, but sinners are subject to the evil spirits; however, the evil spirits were subject to the disciples; therefore the disciples were not sinners. We know also that sinners' names are not written in heaven, but the disciples' names were written in heaven. Therefore the disciples were not sinners. Now, when we remember that the words of Jesus quoted above were uttered some months before the baptism at Pentecost, we are forced to the conclusion that the disciples were pardoned, regenerated men, long before they received the baptism with the Holy Ghost.

SECOND BLESSING

We also read in John 17:12, "While I was with them in the world, I kept them in thy name: those that thou gavest me I have kept, and none of them is lost, but the son of perdition." If none of them were lost but Judas, then the 11 disciples were saved; but unpardoned sinners are lost, therefore the disciples were not sinners. Judas himself had once been in a pardoned state, for the Scriptures say that "Judas by transgression fell." Had this unfortunate man not been in a state of grace, he could not have fallen. In the 16th verse of the same chapter, Jesus says, "They are not of the world, even as I am not of the world."

When we remember that all these sayings of our Lord took place some time before Pentecost, we cannot believe any candid mind will ask for further proof that the disciples were regenerated men long before their sanctification by the baptism with the Holy Ghost.

We call attention to the history of the revival at Samaria, held by the Evangelist Philip. This was a genuine work of grace. "The people with one accord gave heed unto those things which Philip spake . . . unclean spirits, crying with loud voice, came out of many that were possessed with them . . . And there was great joy in that city" (Acts 8:6-8). The reader may be sure that the *great joy* was not among the sinners, who rejected Philip's message. Those who rejoiced were doubtless of the number out of whom the unclean spirits had been cast, and others who, believing the gospel message, had forsaken their sins and accepted Christ.

No Bible Christian will question the excellence and thoroughness of the work done in this revival.

"But when they believed Philip preaching the things concerning the kingdom of God, and the name of Jesus Christ, they were baptized, both men and women" (Acts 8:12).

No language will express what followed so well as Luke's own inspired words: "Now when the apostles which were at Jerusalem heard that Samaria had received the word of God, they sent unto them Peter and John: who, when they were come down, *prayed for them, that they might receive the Holy Ghost: (for as yet he was fallen upon none of them)*." There it is, honest reader. They had received the Word, believed in Jesus, the unclean spirits had been cast out of them, they had great joy, and had been baptized. *Who will dare say they were not pardoned?* But they had not yet received the Holy Ghost. However, when Peter and John prayed for them that they might receive the Holy Ghost, and laid their hands on them, they did receive the Holy Ghost. *All must agree that this baptism with the Holy Ghost was subsequent to regeneration.* Nothing could be plainer.

Now, let us take the case of Cornelius. That this man was a pardoned man prior to Peter's visit to him, and the falling of the Holy Ghost upon him, we cannot understand how anyone can doubt. The Scripture says of Cornelius that he was *"a devout man, and one that feared God with all his house, which gave much alms . . . and prayed to God alway"* (Acts 10:2). The angel who visited him said, "Thy prayers and thine alms are come up for a memorial before God" (v. 4).

Can anyone doubt this man's Christianity? Can the reader conceive of a *devout* sinner fearing God, *"with all his house"?* This man's piety had drawn his family with him into the love and service of God.

"The sacrifice of the wicked is an abomination to the Lord: but the prayer of the upright is his delight" (Prov. 15:8).

Had Cornelius been a wicked man his prayer and alms would not have come up for a memorial before the Lord. But his alms were accepted, therefore he was not a sinner.

"He that turneth away his ear from hearing the law, even his prayer shall be abomination" (Prov. 28:9).

But the prayers of Cornelius were pleasing to God, therefore he did not turn away his ear from hearing the law, but was obedient, devout, upright.

Take the testimony of Peter himself, on his meeting and salutation of Cornelius. "Of a truth I perceive that God is no respecter of persons: but in every nation he that *feareth* him, and *worketh righteousness, is accepted with him*" (Acts 10:34-35).

What need have we of further proof that this man is a servant of God, of a very high order?

Sinners do not *fear* God *and work righteousness,* neither are sinners *accepted with Him.* But Cornelius was accepted with the God he feared, obeyed, and worshiped; therefore he was not a sinner but a Christian. His sins had been pardoned, he was justified before God. . . . But he had not yet received the baptism with the Holy Ghost, for this baptism is a blessing bestowed, not before or at the time of justification, but subsequent to it.

While Peter preached to this *devout, prayerful, charitable, righteous, obedient, God-fearing man,* the Holy Ghost fell on him and his God-fearing household, purifying their hearts. We could not wish for a clearer case of sanctification, by the baptism with the Holy Ghost, subsequent to regeneration.

I could give other instances, and quote other scriptures, but if these scriptures given do not convince the reader beyond all doubt and cavil that the baptism with the Holy Ghost is bestowed subsequent to regeneration, not at, but after pardon, it seems to me that with such an one an appeal to Scripture is useless.

To every humble, believing heart, I will say, The Comforter is promised you. Tarry at the mercy seat in faithful prayer until you receive the gift of the Holy Ghost. Through all the history of the **WITNESSING** Church of Christ, witnesses can be found who will gladly testify from personal experience, that the promise was not restricted to the few, but was vouchsafed to "all" that were "afar off, even as many as the Lord our God shall call." "Seek, and ye shall find; . . . ask, and ye shall receive" (see Matt. 7:7-8; Luke 11:9-10).

Third Proposition

*The baptism with the Holy Ghost is **for believers only**, and is never bestowed upon the unregenerated.*

Shortly before Jesus was crucified He promised His disciples that the indwelling, abiding Holy Ghost should be their Comforter. "Even the Spirit of truth," said He, "whom the world cannot receive, because it seeth him not, neither knoweth him" (John 14:17). The term "world" here refers to the unregenerated, and Jesus says of them that they cannot receive the Holy Ghost.

This fully explains the opposition to the Holy Ghost and His manifestations among many professed Christians. They either have never been converted, or they have fallen away into a sinful, cold, formal life, and have ceased to be the true children of the Father. When Jesus came in the flesh to the Jewish church, only those who were Israelites indeed recognized and received Him as the Son of God. The chief priests and scribes could not understand that Jesus was the Messiah even when He healed the sick and raised the dead.

Simeon and Anna, the prophetess, had no trouble recognizing Him, even when He was a helpless babe in His mother's arms. "The secret of the Lord is with them that fear him" (Ps. 25:14). Jesus himself said of the unbelieving Jews: "He that is of God heareth God's words: ye therefore hear them not, because ye are not of God" (John 8:47). Again, in 1 John 4:6, Jesus says: "He that knoweth God heareth us; he that is not of God heareth not us. Hereby know we the spirit of truth, and the spirit of error."

Just as the unbelieving and godless Jews in the church under the old dispensation rejected Jesus, so do the unconverted and backslidden in the Christian church under the new dispensation reject the Holy Ghost.

There is not only the provision in the gospel for the gift of the

HUNGER Holy Ghost to purify and comfort believing hearts, but there is in truly regenerated hearts a crying out for the gift of the Holy Ghost, an inward longing for the Comforter. Jesus calls it "hungering and thirsting after righteousness" (see Matt. 5:6). It was to this class that He addressed himself on the last great day of the feast, when

He said, "If any man thirst, let him come unto me, and drink. . . . this spake he of the Spirit, which they that believe on him should receive: for the Holy Ghost was not yet given" (John 7:37, 39).

Sinners in the church know full well that the Holy Ghost has His place in the Scriptures. They are willing for Him to have a place in creeds and confessions. He may even be alluded to in songs and sermons, but they would shut Him out of the hearts of men. They object to His demonstrations and manifestations. This is so because spiritual things are spiritually discerned, and they have no spiritual discernment. The unregenerated cannot receive the Spirit of Truth, because they see Him not, neither know Him. And now, O reader, if you have not received the Holy Ghost, and have no longing desire for Him, at least at certain periods in your life, without doubt you are in an unpardoned state. And I must close this chapter by addressing you in the language of the apostle Peter to Simon the Sorcerer: "I perceive that thou art in the gall of bitterness, and in the bond of iniquity" (Acts 8:23). May the mercy of God bring thee to a speedy and sincere repentance.

Chapter IV

Fourth Proposition

*The baptism with the Holy Ghost **purifies believers' hearts and empowers** them for service.*

Uncleanness remains in the hearts of pardoned believers. This is clearly taught in the Scriptures and sadly experienced by Christians; not only by the early followers of Jesus, but all who by faith come into the kingdom of God find remaining within themselves a root of bitterness, a strong tendency to evil, a proneness to wander from the God they love.

Paul calls this remaining uncleanness "sin that dwelleth in me," "the carnal mind," "our old man," and "the body of death."

This "filthiness of the flesh and spirit" remaining in believers greatly impedes their Christian growth and hinders their usefulness. It manifests itself in unholy pride, vicious tempers, covetous desires, unclean thoughts and imaginations. The soul struggling with this inward enemy is often made to cry out: "O wretched man that I am! who shall deliver me from the body of this death?" (Rom. 7:24).

CARNALITY/ CLEANSING

Only those who are truly justified, and are striving to live a New

Testament life in *look* and *thought*, are acquainted with these internal conflicts with the "old man."

The unregenerated and the backslidden in the churches are so completely under the dominion of this evil nature, the "old man," that they have no conflict with him but are under the sway of his dominion, humor his whims, gratify his lusts, and feed his appetites. It is those who have passed from death to life, and are striving after holiness in heart and practice, who find within themselves "a law, that, when" they "would do good, evil is present with" them (Rom. 7:21). They learn to their sorrow that the carnal mind is within them, and that "the carnal mind is enmity against God" (8:7). Writing in 1 Corinthians in the first verses of the third chapter, Paul declares the situation very plainly: "And I, brethren, could not speak unto you as unto spiritual, but as unto *carnal*, even as unto *babes in Christ.* I have fed you with milk, and not with meat: for hitherto ye were not able to bear it, neither yet now are ye able. *For ye are yet carnal*"!

The reader will notice that these Corinthians were "brethren." Yes, they were "babes in Christ." But they *yet* had the carnal mind in them. "For ye are yet carnal," says the apostle.

What clearer testimony could the Holy Ghost give . . . that the carnal mind remains in those who have been born again? These brethren could not have been babes in Christ if they had not been born again. But they were babes in Christ, so without doubt they had been born again, born of the Spirit, *yet* they were carnal, *the carnal mind remained in them.*

How true to experience are the inspired statements found in Rom. 7:21-23: "I find then a law, that, when I would do good, evil is present with me. For I delight in the law of God after the inward man: but I see another law in my members, warring against the law of my mind."[2]

Observe here that the inward man *delights in the law of God.* The sinner has no inward man except the "old man," and you may be sure the "old man" does not delight in the law of God. The inward man spoken of here is the regenerated man, the new man, imparted by the grace of God to the penitent sinner by regenerating grace, at the time of his justification. This *new "inward man"* delights in the law of God, but the "old man" remaining in the nature makes war on the new man,

---

2. Some holiness exponents agree with Dr. Morrison's interpretation of Romans 7; others who support the doctrine would disagree with this interpretation.

and when the *new man* would do good, the "old man" (evil) is present with him, to hinder him in carrying out his good intentions.

The Christian reader will at once recognize the undoubted truthfulness of these scriptures, for they are corroborated by the everyday experience of believing souls, who, struggling against the "old man," have often been made to cry out, "O wretched man that I am! who shall deliver me from the body of this death?" The baptism with the Holy Ghost casts out the "old man." And the casting out of **IN A MOMENT** the "old man," the plucking up of the root of bitterness, the destruction of the body of sin, eradication of the carnal mind, the purging out of "the sin that dwelleth in me," are all one and the same thing, which is accomplished by the instantaneous baptism with the Holy Ghost, purifying the heart by faith. *This is entire sanctification.*

This purifying of hearts took place with the disciples on the Day of Pentecost, when they received the baptism with the Holy Ghost. Not only do their after lives, as contrasted with their former behavior, manifest this to be true, but Peter bears testimony to this fact in relating his experience with Cornelius and his household. "And God, which knoweth the hearts, bare them witness, giving them the Holy Ghost, even as he did unto us; and put no difference between us and them, *purifying their hearts by faith*" (Acts 15:8-9). Peter is here referring to the baptism with the Holy Ghost which fell upon the household of Cornelius and the exact similarity between it and the baptism received by the disciples on the Day of Pentecost. The one important feature of the baptism to which he calls attention was the PURIFYING of their HEARTS.

When Jesus was present with the disciples assembled in Jerusalem after His resurrection, and commanded them not to depart out of Jerusalem until they received the promise of the Father, He said to them: "But ye shall receive power, after that the Holy Ghost is come upon you" (Acts 1:8).

This enduement of power was to especially qualify them, not **POWER** only for their lifework, but for personal victory over Satan and sin. This enduement of power, which is to be obtained only by the baptism with the Holy Ghost, is the great need of the Church in the times in which we live, not only for those who stand in the sacred desk, but for those who sit in the pews also. The work of winning souls from sin to Christ is not shut up alone to ministers of the gospel; but it is the duty and privilege of all who are saved to win lost souls to the Savior.

It seems like a dangerous and arrogant presumption to undertake the work of Christ and, at the same time, refuse to apply to Him for that *power* which He has definitely promised, and which we so manifestly need. It is a sad sight to see an institution claiming to be a church of God undertaking to do with organizations, entertainments, and festivals the work that can only be done by the enduement of power which comes with the baptism with the Holy Ghost. No natural gifts, mental developments, or scholastic training can possibly take the place of the divine energy and unction which alone can be imparted to men by the gift of the Holy Ghost. "We wrestle not," says the apostle Paul, "against flesh and blood, but against principalities, against powers, against the rulers of the darkness of this world, against spiritual wickedness in high places" (Eph. 6:12).

Reader, shall we go forth to do battle against these mighty foes in our strength, or shall we tarry in humble, faithful prayer for the coming of the Holy Ghost, and the *power* which His coming brings? If we wait in humble prayer until we receive Him, then doubtless it can be said of us, "Greater is he that is in you, than he that is in the world" (1 John 4:4). If we must go forth to war against devils and mighty evil spirits; if we must meet in combat the prince of the power of the air, let us meet them endued with the power of the indwelling Holy Ghost.

When men enlist as soldiers in the services of the kingdoms of this world, the government for which they fight is expected to furnish them with arms and ammunition. Those who enlist in the services of the King of Kings may be sure that He will not ask them to go to war without equipment, and that equipment will be an enduement of "*power from on high*," received in the baptism with the Holy Ghost.

Chapter V
Fifth Proposition

The Holy Ghost dwells in, abides with, **comforts and teaches** *those who receive Him.*

(1) The baptism with the Holy Ghost inaugurates between the redeemed soul and the eternal Father the most intimate and sacred relations. The human body out of which the carnal mind has been cast, at once becomes the temple of the Holy Spirit. "Know ye not that ye are the temple of God, and that the Spirit of God dwelleth in you?" (1 Cor. 3:16). Again, in the same Epistle, 6:19, we read: "What?

know ye not that your body is the temple of the Holy Ghost which is in you, which ye have of God, and ye are not your own?"

The kingdom of God is "within you" (Luke 17:21). "The kingdom of God is not meat and drink; but righteousness, and peace, and joy in the Holy Ghost" (Rom. 14:17). When our Lord promised the disciples that He would "pray the Father" to send them "another Comforter, . . . *even the Spirit of truth*," He assured them that the world could not receive this Spirit, "because it seeth him not, neither knoweth him: but ye know him; for he dwelleth with you, and *shall be in you*" (John 14:16-17). One of the best preventives against

POWER OVER SIN temptation and sin for those who have received the baptism with the Holy Ghost, is the constant memory that God, in the person of the Holy Ghost, is *dwelling in them*. The thought will keep out all desire for sin and break the power of the tempter. It will constantly gird up the soul with a blessed assurance of victory, knowing that He that is in us is greater than he that is in the world.

(2) I call the reader's attention to the fact that when the Holy Ghost comes into His temples . . . and purifies them, He comes "to abide forever."

Jesus said to His disciples, "Ye shall seek me: and as I said unto the Jews, Whither I go, ye cannot come" (John 13:33). At this their hearts were filled with sadness, and He comforted them with the promise that He would prepare a place for them, and come again and receive them unto himself, that where He was, there they might be also.

He further assured them that if they loved Him and would keep His commandments, He would pray the Father, and He would give them another Comforter, "*That he may abide with you for ever*" (John 14:16).

Christ made it a point to put in this phrase "for ever" for the good reason that He desired the disciples to be encouraged with the assurance that the Holy Ghost would abide. He would live not only in the Church, but in the individual who received Him. The Comforter would remain not for a few brief years, as Jesus had done, and then grieve their hearts by separating himself from them as He, their Lord, must now soon do, but the Comforter would *abide*. There would be no more painful separation like that for which He was now preparing them, which must take place in a few days.

(3) The Holy Ghost should not only be a *purifier* (being sanctified by the Holy Ghost), an *indweller, abiding forever,* but He should

also be a *Comforter.* This is an important office of the Spirit, the comforting of the hearts of God's children. In sickness, in poverty, in trials and persecutions, when deserted by friends and pursued by enemies, when in a strange land, and in all the conflicts and vicissitudes of life, the blessed Spirit abiding in the heart constantly gives assurance of His presence. He assures of the salvation of the soul, of the love of God for us, of the efficacy of the cleansing blood of Jesus Christ, and thus keeps the soul in a state of blessed comfort.

Let those who have cried to God for comfort in times of distress, learn to cry to God for the gift of the Holy Ghost, and then they will have the abiding Comforter within themselves.

(4) Christ not only promised that the abiding Spirit should comfort, but that He should also be our *Teacher.* In John 14:26 He says: "But the Comforter, which is the Holy Ghost, whom the Father will send in my name, he shall teach you all things, and bring all things to your remembrance, whatsoever I have said unto you."

Again in John 16:13-14, our Lord says: "Howbeit when he, the Spirit of truth, is come, he will guide you into all truth: for he shall not speak of himself; but whatsoever he shall hear, that shall he speak: and he will shew you things to come. He shall glorify me: for he shall receive of mine, and shall shew it unto you."

With these scriptures before us, the reader will appreciate something of the importance of the baptism with the Holy Ghost, and the various offices He performs in the redemption of the souls of men.

Chapter VI

Sixth Proposition

The rejection of the Holy Ghost is fatal to Christian experience.

The greatest sin in past history was the rejection of Jesus Christ by the church under the old dispensation. Often our minds have been amazed and our hearts have shuddered as we have read: "He came unto his own, and his own received him not" (John 1:11). We have marveled at the stupidity and hardness of the Jews, who looked in the face of Jesus of Nazareth, heard His words, beheld His miracles, and yet ridiculed and rejected Him.

Reader, think you that those ancient Jews were sinners above all men? I tell you they were not, and without doubt those members of the Christian church under the new dispensation who reject the Holy Ghost, will commit even more grievous and fatal sin than that committed by the Jews in rejecting Christ. In proportion as our light is greater than was theirs, our sin will be more inexcusable than theirs. In the final day of judgment I would as soon stand there an ancient Jew who rejected Jesus, as to stand there a modern Gentile who rejected the Holy Ghost. In fact, to reject the Holy Ghost is to reject the Father and the Son, also. To come to the actual truth, those Jews who really had the Father, did not reject the Son, but like Simeon and Nathanael, they recognized and worshiped Him.

So it is with those who really have the forgiveness of their sins and true fellowship with Jesus Christ. They will, if properly instructed, gladly receive the Holy Ghost for whom the Son prayed, and whom the Father has sent to all those who believe in and love His Son.

All the preliminary steps in grace, all the elementary blessings in Christian experience, are the preparation of the soul for the reception of the Holy Ghost. These are the fitting up and the preparing of the temple for His dwelling place. The reception of God in the Third Person of the Trinity into the soul is a climax in the history of personal redemption. It is a sealing of the heart for eternal glory. It is the reception of the Sanctifier, Comforter, Revealer, Teacher, and Guide, sent by the Father in answer to the prayer of His Son to cleanse, sanctify, and keep His followers from the evil one, and by His incoming and abiding to prepare them for residence in the New Jerusalem.

FOR ALL CHRISTIANS

The willful and final rejection of the Holy Ghost would prove destructive and fatal to all Christian experience.

"I will therefore put you in remembrance, though ye once knew this, how that the Lord, having saved the people out of the land of Egypt, afterward destroyed them that believed not" (Jude 5).

The grace that one receives at justification does not justify that one in the rejection of the additional grace to be bestowed in the development and perfection of experience and Christian character, but it obligates the soul thus justified to go forward searching out, seeking after, and submitting to all the will of God.

"Now the just shall live by faith: but if any man draw back, my soul shall have no pleasure in him" (Heb. 10:38).

Reader, there comes a time in the history of every justified believer, when the Father will answer the prayer of the Son, and send to that believer the Comforter. The Holy Ghost is the promise of the Father, and the promise of the Father shall not fail. He will come suddenly into His temple. Woe will be to the soul that rejects Him when He comes.

God is long-suffering. Patiently He will wait, earnestly will He entreat; the Spirit will knock again and again for admittance and full control of the believer's heart, but God has said: "My spirit shall not always strive with man" (Gen. 6:3). Repeatedly rejected, He will finally take His departure to return no more. Then the poor soul will find its home desolate indeed. Having rejected Comforter, Guide, Cleanser, Empowerer, and Teacher, its condition is sad to contemplate.

The last Person in the Trinity has come, been trifled with, rejected, grieved, and has finally taken His departure from those who would not receive Him in His sanctifying and indwelling power.

The last state of such a soul is worse than the first. May God in mercy help the reader of these pages now to make so complete a consecration, and to exercise so strong a faith, that the Holy Ghost, in His sanctifying and keeping power, may enter into his heart in all His blessed fullness, and never hence depart.

Chapter VII
Many Witnesses[3]

That the reader may understand that the views set forth in the preceding chapters are not peculiar to the author of this booklet, I will give in this chapter several quotations from distinguished Christian scholars, whose views and teachings are quite in harmony with the main thought of what I have written.

First, I will quote a paragraph from . . . sometime vice-chancellor of the University of Oxford, an eminent Presbyterian minister.[4] . . . Under the head of "The Positive Work of the Spirit in the Sanctification of Believers," we find the following:

> We now proceed to the positive work of the Spirit in the sanctification of believers; for He not only cleanses their natures and persons from the pollution of sin, but He communicates the great, permanent, positive effect of holiness to their souls, whereby He guides and assists them in all the acts and duties thereof.
>
> I shall comprise what belongs to this part of His work in the two following propositions:
>
> 1. There is in the soul of believers a supernatural principle or habit of grace, wrought and preserved by the Spirit of God, whereby they are enabled to live unto God, and perform that obedience which He requires and accepts, and this is essentially

---

3. Title added.
4. John Owen, *The Holy Spirit*, 222-23.

distinct from all natural habits, intellectual or moral, however acquired or improved.

2. There is an immediate work of the Holy Spirit required unto every act of holy obedience, whether external or internal . . . (p. 226). We may learn from hence how great and excellent a work this sanctification is, and that it is a greater matter to be truly holy than most persons are aware of. It is so great a work that it must be wrought by "the God of peace himself," by the blood of Christ, and by the influence of the Spirit.

The pious reader will be pleased with the following from the pen of that eminent Methodist preacher, Rev. William Arthur, A.M. We read on pages 62-64 of *The Tongue of Fire:*

> What a labor of expression do we find in 2 Cor. 9:8, where Paul wants to convey his own idea of the power of grace, as practically enabling men to do the will of God. "And God is able to make all grace abound toward you; that ye, always having all sufficiency in all things, may abound to every good work." Here we have "abound" twice, and "all" four times in one short sentence. "Abound" means not only to fill, but to overflow. The double overflow, first of grace from God to us, then of the same grace from us to "every good work" is a glorious comment on our Lord's word: "He that believeth on me, as the scripture hath said, out of his belly shall flow rivers of living water. (But this spake he of the Spirit, which they that believe on him should receive: for the Holy Ghost was not yet given; because that Jesus was not yet glorified)" (John 7:38-39).
>
> The believer's heart, in itself incapable of holy living, as a
>
> **GRACE** marble cistern of yielding a constant stream, is placed like a cistern in communication with an invisible source; the source constantly overflows into the cistern, and it again overflows. Happy the heart thus filled, thus overflowing with the Holy Spirit! Where is the fountain of those living waters that we may bring our hearts thither? "He showed me a pure river of water of life, clear as crystal, proceeding out of the throne of God and of the Lamb" (Rev. 22:1).
>
> There is the fountain, there the stream: the Spirit proceeding from the Father and the Son to the throne of grace! to the mercy seat! and you are at the fountain of all life. Nor seek a scant supply at that source. "Be filled with the Spirit" sounds in your ears, and if you believe, not only will a well "spring up within" you, but rivers shall flow out from you.
>
> The Spirit, as replenishing the believer's heart with actual virtues and practical holiness, is ever kept before our eye in the apostolic writings. "That ye might walk worthy of the Lord unto all pleasing, being fruitful in every good work, and increasing in the knowledge of God; strengthened with all might, according to his

glorious power, unto all patience and longsuffering with joyfulness."

Putting these various expressions together, what a view do they give of the riches of grace! "all sufficiency" "in all things," "always," "abound to every good work," "fruitful in every good work," "strengthened with all might," "according to the power that worketh in us," "filled with all the fullness of God." Eternal Spirit proceeding from the Father and the Son, answer and disperse all our unbelief by filling our hearts with thyself! The expression "filled with the Holy Ghost" places before us the human spirit restored to its original and highest fellowship.

In speaking of how to obtain this experience, Mr. Arthur says . . .

> We have only to recall the lesson of the 10 days—"they continued with one accord in prayer and supplication." Prayer earnest, prayer united, and prayer persevering—these are the conditions, and these fulfilled, we shall assuredly be "endued with power from on high."[5]

Nothing could be more plainly set forth than Mr. Arthur's teaching here that the Holy Ghost is to be sought and obtained in answer to prayer, by believing Christians.

Perhaps no pastor in the United States, in the last quarter of a century, was more widely known and more genuinely beloved than Rev. A. J. Gordon, a Baptist minister of Boston, who walked with God and was not, for God took him up to himself. In an excellent little volume . . . Mr. Gordon says:

> It seems clear from the Scriptures that it is still the duty and
> **FAITH** privilege of believers to receive the Holy Spirit by a conscious, definite act of appropriating faith, just as they received Jesus. . . .
>
> It seems to me beyond question, as a matter of experience, both of Christians in the present day and of the Early Church, as recorded by inspiration, that in addition to the gift of the Spirit received at conversion, there is another blessing corresponding in its signs and effects to the blessing received by the disciples at Pentecost—a blessing to be asked for and expected by Christians still, and to be described in language similar to that employed in the Book of the Acts. Whatever that blessing may be, it is in immediate connection with the Holy Ghost. . . .
>
> It is easy to cite cases of decisive, vivid, and clearly marked experience of the Spirit's enduement, as in the lives of Dr. Finney, James Brainard, Taylor, and many others! And instead of describing these experiences—so definite as to time and so distinct as to accompanying credentials—we would ask the reader to study

---

5. William Arthur, *The Tongue of Fire*, 320-21.

them, and observe the remarkable effects which followed in the ministry of those who enjoyed them. The lives of many of the colaborers with Wesley and Whitefield give a striking confirmation of the doctrine which we are defending.[6]

The late Phillips Brooks, bishop in the Protestant Episcopal church, reaches a beautiful climax in a sermon on Acts 19:2, in these impressive words:

> But here at Pentecost, what was there to call out such prodigies? If what we have said is true, was there not certainly enough? It was the coming back of God into man. It was the promise in these typical men of how near God would be to every man henceforth. It was the manifestation of the God Inspirer as distinct from and yet one with God Creator, and God Redeemer. It was primarily the entrance of God into man, and so, in consequence, the entrance of [God's] spirit and full meaning into every truth man could know. It was the blossom-day of humanity, full of the promise of unmeasured fruit. And what that first Whit-Sunday [brought] to all the world, one certain day [brings] to any man the day that the Holy Spirit comes to him. God enters into him, and he sees every thing with God's vision.[7]

These quotations will suffice. The doctrine of the baptism with the Holy Ghost is not only a Bible doctrine, but is taught and experienced by the most devout men of all the evangelical churches. For the past half a century this great doctrine and experience has been sadly neglected, and most woeful results have come to the Church because of this neglect. But one of the most hopeful signs of the times is a general revival on Pentecostal lines. The Church everywhere is awakening to the fact of her great need of that power which comes only with the baptism with the Holy Ghost upon her individual members.

This awakening is not confined to any one body or denomination of Christians, or to any country or clime; but in the United States, England, Europe, and the Oriental countries, everywhere from the true children of God who search the Scriptures and believe them, there is a cry going up to God for the outpouring of His Spirit, and the Holy Ghost is falling upon multitudes of believers. . . .

"We have yet to learn that any movement, proved as this has been by its fruits, and seeking for clearer views on the doctrines of grace, and richer experience of the life of God in the soul, can emanate from any other source than the Holy Spirit."

---

6. *The Ministry of the Spirit,* 76, 92, 98.

7. At this point Dr. Morrison also cited the experience of Dwight L. Moody, see p. 371.

Let the thoughtful reader ponder these things well. It is said of the Jews, with regard to their treatment of the world's Redeemer, "He came unto his own, and his own received him not" (John 1:11). Will the world again reach the climax of crime by rejecting one of the Persons of the Trinity, sent of the Father to secure the redemption of mankind?

The Holy Ghost is in the world, sent of the Father, in answer to the prayer of the Son, to cleanse, sanctify, fill, keep, and guide the disciples of Jesus into all truth, and into eternal glory. Will you receive Him *now*?

Chapter VIII
How to Receive the Holy Spirit[8]

To my mind this widespread revival of faith in the personal Holy Ghost, and seeking after Him in His cleansing, empowering, and abiding presence, is the most hopeful sign of the times.

As we have seen, this revival is confined to no country or denomination of Christians, but is as widespread as the flight of the gospel on its mission of salvation to a lost world. It is the pouring out of the Holy Ghost upon all flesh. It will be well to close this last short chapter with some suggestions and instructions to those who have not received the Holy Ghost since they believed and now desire to seek Him.

First of all, be sure that you are a child of God. Do not be satisfied with the memory that you were once converted, that you
SEEKING once experienced the forgiveness of sins, and a consciousness of acceptance with God, but be sure that you have not lapsed again into sin. Know that you have the assurance now of your acceptance in Christ.

Second: Believe in the Holy Ghost. Believe that although invisible He is as genuinely a person, and as really in the world as the Son of God was when He moved visibly among, preached to, and healed the people.

Third: Make a complete consecration of yourself to the Father. Keep back nothing. Cast away every unclean thing, and place every clean thing without reserve upon the altar of a glad, complete, and

---

8. Title added.

eternal sacrifice. Be willing to let the Holy Ghost have His way in you and with you, without complaint or hesitation on your part.

Fourth: Seek Him in earnest, constant prayer. Though He tarry, remember that the disciples waited for Him at Jerusalem 10 days in prayer. Do not relax your vigilance, or give over your purpose, or substitute anything else for the baptism with the Holy Ghost.

Mr. Arthur, in his *Tongue of Fire*, says, "As to the way in which this power may be obtained here, we have only to recall the lesson of the 10 days. 'They continued with one accord in prayer and supplication.' Prayer earnest, prayer united, prayer persevering—these are the conditions; and these being fulfilled, we shall assuredly be endued with power from on high. We should never expect that the power will fall upon us just because we happen once to awake and ask for it."

The faith of the disciples in the promise of our Lord was so strong and unwavering, their desire for the baptism with the Holy Ghost so intense, that if He delay His coming for 10 long days, yet without a doubt or a murmur they wait for Him.

So it must be with those who would receive Him today. Wait not in indifference, or with diverted or divided mind, but wait for Him with Bible open at the promise, and in constant and urgent entreaty for Him to come; and wait until He does come.

He will come. His own presence will be a sufficient witness to the glad heart that receives Him.

He will come, and His incoming will drive out from His temple every unclean thing and banish every foe. His coming may be like the rushing, mighty wind, or as the descent of the Dove of Peace, but, oh, reader, "*If thou seek him, he will be found of thee*" (1 Chron. 28:9).

He will purge thy nature, sanctify thy heart, abide in and comfort thee through all the conflicts of this life, and at last, through the blood of Christ, present thee to the Father without spot or wrinkle. AMEN.

2

R. T. Williams
(1883-1946)

Roy Tilman Williams was born in Milam, Tex., February 14, 1883. At an early age he moved with his family to Many, La., attending high school at Fort Jessup.

When 16 years of age, Roy came under the influence of Josh Sanders, a holiness preacher in a Methodist revival meeting. In that first revival he was both saved and sanctified. His biographer tells the story:

> Roy attended the revival meeting each night. Soon Josh Sanders began to preach on entire sanctification. Roy listened with interest to that doctrine of which he was later to be such an able exponent. On a certain evening when the invitation was given to seek the experience, Henry Mitchell, the Sunday School superintendent, went to the altar as a seeker for the blessing of entire sanctification. Roy said to himself, "Henry Mitchell is the best man I know. If he needs this experience I certainly do." He, too, went to the altar, for the second time.
>
> Light had shone upon him, and his hungry heart responded obediently. The girl of his boyish fancy had spoken the kindly word that encouraged him to make his way to the altar and consecrate his life to God for time and for eternity. He reached out his hand of faith, and again God came to him in a never-to-be-forgotten experience, cleansing his nature from all sin and filling him with the Holy Spirit. From that time forward the strength and beauty of his life and the contagion of his

Christlike spirit began to be felt by his family and friends in that community.[1]

In evaluating this experience of Christian holiness, Dr. Williams himself later wrote: "The sanctified man in reality faces but one vital question, namely, What is the will of God for me? To do the will of God when once it is known is the outstanding duty and joy of every consecrated soul."[2]

In the same year that he was sanctified, Roy was called to preach and began his ministry. Soon after, he went to Peniel University, at Peniel, Tex., to prepare himself for Christian service. There he received his bachelor of arts degree. Later, he did graduate work at the University of Chicago.

In 1905, Roy and Eunice Harvey, of Sunset, Tex., were married. To their happy union two sons were born.

Dr. and Mrs. Williams united with the Church of the Nazarene during the General Assembly at Pilot Point, Tex., in 1908. At the same assembly he was ordained by Dr. P. F. Bresee. Thus his membership and ministry dated from the founding of the denomination.

From 1908 Dr. Williams taught at Peniel University and then in 1911 became its president. Resigning in 1913, he served for two years as a full-time evangelist.

Early in 1916, at 33 years of age, Dr. Williams was elected to fill a vacancy in the Board of General Superintendents where he served until his death in 1946.

For more than 30 years the voice and pen of Dr. R. T. Williams roused the militant spirit and rallied the forces of the young Church of the Nazarene. In every great crisis they looked to him for wise counsel and challenging leadership. Richly endowed in qualities of body, mind, and soul, he was mightily endued with the power of the Holy Spirit.

Dr. Williams was the organizing genius during the formative years of the young denomination—and it was a holiness church that he helped to shape. Among his several books, *Sanctification: The Experience and the Ethics* was the most significant in molding the mind of the church.

His own foreword gives the best introduction to the book and to the chapter selected for this volume.

---

1. G. B. Williamson, *Roy T. Williams, Servant of God,* 38-39.
2. *Sanctification: The Experience and the Ethics,* 54.

There is a deep conviction in the heart of the writer that proper distinction has not been made between the experience of holiness and the ethics of holiness in the preaching and writings on this subject. That is why we have ventured to publish this book.

If we can cheer some honest, conscientious person in his fight to give to his neighbors and friends an ethical life that will harmonize with that glorious divine image he has within his soul, our efforts will be well worthwhile.

It is always a consolation to know that God looketh upon the heart, the motives, rather than upon the outward appearance. This, however, does not justify anyone in being careless of his ethics. We need wisdom or ethical knowledge, which will form right relationships—relationships that are profitable and pleasing.

In this there is room for improvement with us all. The Bible urges us to seek and pray for more wisdom that we may better know how to be real examples of believers. Seeing the good works and ethical life of God's children, the world will be more inclined to glorify our Father in heaven. Being a Christian and living like Christ is the greatest achievement possible.

The Importance of Right Ethics[3]

If we want to do good, if we want to be a blessing, we must seek to make our ethics commensurate with that glorious state of divine purity and divine beauty within us.

The importance of right ethics cannot be overestimated, for it determines our relationship to people as holiness determines our relationship to God. If the experience of holiness is not acceptable to God, we cannot be perfectly related to Him. God could not be satisfied to the fullest extent with any of His children who have sin or sinful affections in their hearts. He could not be contented to look upon His children with qualities of heart that would be unlike Christ.

If the ethics of holiness is right, we can be properly related to our fellowmen. The condition of our heart determines the attitude of God toward us, and the standard of our ethics will determine the attitude of people toward us. No man who loves the Lord can be satisfied merely with getting to heaven. If that is the only meaning the Christian life has, the most of us are certainly mistaken in our conception of

---

3. Ibid., chap. 6.

moral obligation. God gives us to understand that we cannot have holiness toward God without peace toward man. Thus the importance of right relationship with humanity is clearly indicated. We are to follow peace with all men in order to have holiness without which no man shall see the Lord. No man can be right with God and yet intentionally wrong with his fellowman. In spite of our wishes the effects of our ethics upon the lives of others will have much to do with their attitude toward religion and Jesus Christ, the world's Savior.

The method of presenting Jesus Christ will determine the influence Christ has in the world. It will also determine the extent of our own influence over the lives of others. Our ethics will draw men nearer to us and to Christ and increase our influence for good over them, or it will drive them from us and tend to discourage them in seeking Bible salvation. If we want to do good, if we want to be a blessing, we must seek to make our ethics commensurate with that glorious state of divine purity and divine beauty within us.

INFLUENCE

"If I be lifted up," said Christ, "I will draw all men unto me" (John 12:32). This expression constitutes the very heart of ethics and influence. We are to lift up Christ because He is to save the world, and not we ourselves. Poor ethics will tend to draw the attention of the world to us, good ethics will tend to center the attention of men upon Jesus Christ himself.

Two women go to the meat market on the same day. They both purchase meat from the same cut. One prepares and serves her meat in an attractive manner so as to arouse the appetite and nourish the body. The other woman is a poor cook and serves her meat on a dirty table, an unattractive plate, and with surroundings that tend to dry up the gastric juices and discourage the guests. . . . It is a wise woman who tries to make her service at the table most attractive and presents the food in the most attractive way possible. It is not enough merely to serve food; it must be properly served.

The same is true of religion as expressed to others through the ethics of our lives. Two men can come upon the platform to preach the gospel. Both may love the Lord and both may carry a passion for lost souls and both may have a great message; but the manner in which they present the truth to the public will have great bearing with the hearers. If one man is uncouth, rough, boorish, untutored in his mannerisms, awkward in his gestures, and faulty in his language, he is likely to attract the attention of the people to himself

PREACHING

and cause them to forget the beauty and value of the message he is presenting. But the man that can present the truth of Jesus Christ without any particular abnormalities or strange mannerisms so that the people hear the truth and see the picture of Christ without looking upon the speaker himself will naturally accomplish greater good. The value of our ethics is seen in the fact that it will make Christ more acceptable or less acceptable.

When is a man or woman well dressed? This is a question which is not easily answered. Perhaps the dress question is one of the most perplexing that has ever confronted the Church of Jesus Christ. What is proper and what is improper? We understand it is easier to tell people what they may not wear than it is to tell them what they may wear. It is the opinion of the writer that a man or woman is well dressed when it is scarcely noticeable how he is dressed. Dress that brings out the beauty and attractiveness of the person himself rather than the peculiarities of the dress is normal. Personality should constitute the attraction rather than the garments one wears.

Men are well dressed when one does not notice how they are dressed. The same is true of women. . . . Ethics is right when it so presents Jesus Christ as to cause the people to see Him rather than the man or the woman presenting Christ. We are to let our light shine and our good works appear that men may glorify our Father who is in heaven. We are not the attraction; Christ is the attraction. . . . The need of the world is not fine clothes, but fine men and women wearing clothes. . . . The world cannot be saved by ethics; but the ethics of a Christian's life will make Christ appear beautiful or unattractive.

Again, the value of ethics is seen not only in the fact that it brings out the beauty of Jesus Christ and His attractiveness, but there is also a reflex blessing upon the character of the man or woman who talks and acts as a Christian should. A wrong impulse that crystallizes in conduct becomes stronger, and if that wrong impulse continues to be yielded to and continues to crystallize in deeds, it will finally become overmastering. On the other hand, if to a right impulse expression is

GROWTH given, and if it is allowed to crystallize in conduct, it will become stronger and stronger, and the inner state of a man will become more and more acceptable. In this sense the condition of the heart produces ethics, and in a reflex manner ethics also has something to do with the forming of the character. Good ethics therefore will not only cause the human to keep in the background and push

Christ to the front, but it will also strengthen and increase those powers that promote one in the battle for Christ's likeness.

Since good ethics is important it should be the desire of every conscientious man or woman to raise the standard of his ethics in every possible way. It has been stated already that the divine image can be worked within us immediately; but the working out of our salvation is to be with fear and trembling, a constant and daily exercise. No builder will become perfect in the execution of his art without careful and conscientious practice. A man does not have the power to take sin out of his heart or to put Christ within his heart. That is the work of God himself. But man does have the power by exercise to improve his building day by day. The ideal within us is to be worked out slowly with pain and care.

After we are saved and sanctified and sin is removed from the heart, we are conscious that our faculties have been twisted and warped by wrong habits, and it takes time to bring those powers back into proper relationship. This calls for improvement, correction, and conscientious effort on our part. We have wrongly expected young converts, or people sanctified only a few days, to reach the standard of ethics in word and deed that one would produce who had been on the road to heaven 40 or 50 years. This is unreasonable. If the young convert is expected to present such a high standard, then the person that has been serving God for many years would certainly be condemned if his standard should not be higher than the one just leaving the world and entering the kingdom of God.

How to Improve Our Ethics

There is room for improvement in us all. Not room perhaps for improvement in our experiences in the forgiveness of our sins or the cleansing of our hearts. God has forgiven us fully; He has cleansed the heart and filled it with His love. . . . But we have power to improve in our method of executing our art before the eyes of men. There is not only room for improvement, but we have the power to improve. And if a man does not improve in the standard of his ethics day by day he is not doing his duty before God and man and could not be justified before the bar of his own conscience. Let us note some ways to improve our ethics.

First. We should realize that the ideal within the heart is far superior to the methods we have employed in executing that ideal. Without this realization one would not advance very fast. One must realize that he can improve and that he should improve. If one has the false notion that he is doing just as well as he could do, he will certainly not put forth much effort to raise his standards.

Second. We must know that the power lies within us to improve our ethics. We are told educationally that there are two great problems every boy and girl faces in college. One is the problem of horizon. Education is supposed to enlarge the horizon of one's life; his vision should be pushed out to include greater space and take in greater sweeps of territory. The second problem he faces is the problem of mastery. He must be made to understand that he is not to become a slave but a master. He is not to be subjected to the environment and influences of life around him, but he is to stand a victor and a conqueror over everything that would hinder his progress and mar the beauty and dignity of his manhood. He must realize that God has given him a power to change his surroundings to his own liking. This is the glory of man. He is not the slave of his environment but the master of it. This same realization must come to every child of God. He must know that the Holy Ghost within him working out through him can change the environment about him, making him an overcomer, or will enable him to adjust himself to conditions. Standards are to be determined and a desperate struggle put forth to reach them within and without.

Third. One can improve his ethics by reading the Bible. God's Word is a lamp to our feet and a light to our pathway, and day by day it should shine brighter and brighter. The Bible is our Chart and Compass. It is the Book that tells us how to live and what to do. Life has two great problems and only two, and the Bible is the only book that can help us to solve those two problems. The first one is what to do. Men must do something; men will do something.

One of the great principles of moral obligation is doing something. What must I do? That is one of life's two fundamental problems. The second one is how to do it. What must I do and how must I do it? These two problems sum up life in its entirety. The Bible answers these questions as no other book can. It tells us what our duty to ourselves is, what our duty to our fellowman is, and what constitutes our duty to God. Then the Bible tells us how to perform the duties and obligations we are under. It tells us how to talk, how to treat our neighbor, how to live in peace with our fellowman, how to be courteous unto all men, that we are to love our enemies, to do good to them that persecute and despitefully use us. The man who lives the best life is the man who reads the Bible most and who reads it conscientiously for direction in the molding of his character and the shaping of his ethics.

Fourth. We should pray earnestly every day. It is the opinion of the writer that no man will be able to live the kind of life the Bible and his own conscience demand of him unless he prays daily for strength, for wisdom, and for guidance. The church has suffered more through a neglect of prayer than any other one thing in the world's history. Worldliness will wreck a church, but worldliness would never be possible in a church if the people prayed. Worldliness in dress, and worldly habits, are not the cause of backsliding; they are the result, and prayer is the only thing that can keep the spirit of the world out of the church and enable church people to live simple, devout, and exemplary lives.

Fifth. We must carry a passionate love for others. The careless word, the unkind deed, the unethical expression are usu-

PERFECT LOVE

ally the result of coolness of heart and indifference of soul toward others. Nothing can assure the home of peace, harmony, understanding, and happiness like love. The more love one has in his heart, the less likely he is to speak the quick or the harsh word. The greater the amount of divine love in the soul the less danger there is in wrong conduct or discourtesy toward others. Of all the needs of the world, the greatest is love: more love in the heart of man for his friends and his enemies. If I were called upon to give in one expression the cure for ethics that injure the cause of Jesus Christ and bring trouble between neighbors I would say the solution is in one thing—a passionate love in the heart for mankind.

Sixth. We should have a spirit of Christian courtesy toward all men. It should be the resolution and the fixed purpose of every heart to treat with kindness and courtesy every person with

COURTESY

whom he comes in contact. Lack of courtesy on the part of Christians toward one another is an outstanding paradox; it is beyond comprehension. How one church member can talk about another, how one preacher can find fault and express that fault about another preacher is beyond belief.

Men should so live that they can have respect for themselves, because a house divided against itself cannot stand. If one's conscience and affections are warring against each other, weakness is bound to follow. If mind and heart do not agree, progress becomes very difficult if not impossible. If a man be in harmony with himself it is probable that he will be kind and courteous toward his immediate family. There should be the greatest degree of Christian courtesy between husband and wife, father and son, between mother and daughter, and brother and sister. The home itself should be an example of beautiful courtesy between the members of the family.

Again, we should seek to be courteous toward one another in the church. We need more warmth, more cordiality, more friendship in the assembling of the people of God in the house of worship. There is a social touch, a human touch, a touch of friendship that cheers and encourages that should not be overlooked in the house of God. The rich should mingle with the poor, the educated with the illiterate. There should be Christian courtesy at all times in every department of the church. The preacher should treat with respect the most humble and the most ignorant members of his congregation and should listen with respect and courtesy to every suggestion from such a one, and God's anointed should be treated with dignity and respect. Criticism should be unknown, and unkind statements should be avoided with the same care that we would avoid murder or adultery. The tongue should be kept in control, and every expression by word, deed, or attitude should be kind, for God has commanded us to be courteous unto all men.

Finally, the Christian should be courteous toward the unsaved, toward the most wicked man in the community, even toward his bitterest and most deadly enemy. A peaceful answer often turns away wrath, and if kindness and courtesy will not win in life's battles, harsh and oppressive methods certainly will not win. Love never faileth, courtesy never faileth; for real courtesy—genuine, unadulterated courtesy—is a natural and spontaneous expression of love.

May God fill the Church of Jesus Christ with divine love and then enable us to realize the importance of a right standard of ethics. And may He give us a desire not only to realize the importance of right ethics, but a determination to strive to find better and more effective ways of expression for the glorious, divine life within us.

3

Thomas R. Kelly
(1893-1941)

Thomas Raymond Kelly was born in a devout Quaker home, June 4, 1893, on a farm near Chillicothe, Ohio. His father died when Thomas was four, and his mother supported him and his sister for six years by working the farm and selling eggs and butter in the village. She then moved to Wilmington, Ohio, so that the children could have a good school, and later the advantages of a Quaker college.

At Wilmington College, Thomas became absorbed in physical science. This dedication continued when he moved to Haverford College for a year of further study in 1913. Here he came into contact with Rufus Jones and the lure of philosophy.

For two years Kelly taught science at Pickering College, a Quaker preparatory school in Canada. During this period he decided to offer himself for missionary work in Japan, and entered Hartford Theological Seminary in 1916 to prepare himself for this ministry.

The day after graduation in 1919 he married Lael Macy. Together they returned to Wilmington College in response to an invitation to teach Bible. But after two years he returned to Hartford to prepare himself for a career in philosophy. There he completed the Ph.D. in 1924.

For the next 17 years Kelly's life was a blend of classroom teaching and service ministries among the Quakers. He taught at Earlham College, and then at Haverford. For a decade his driving passion was hunger for scholarly achievement and professional recognition.

In autumn of 1937, however, a new life direction took place in Thomas Kelly. His biographer writes:

> No one knows exactly what happened, but a strained period in his life was over. He moved toward adequacy. . . . Science, scholarship, method, remained good, but in a new setting. Now he could say with Isaac Pennington, "Reason is not sin but a deviating from that from which reason came is sin."
>
> He went to the Germantown Friends' Meeting at Coulter Street to deliver three lectures in January 1938. He told me that the lectures wrote themselves. At Germantown, people were deeply moved and said, "This is *authentic.*" His writings and spoken messages began to be marked by a note of experimental authority. "To you in this room who are seekers, to you, young and old who have toiled all night and caught nothing, but who want to launch out into the deeps and let down your nets for a draught, I want to speak as simply, as tenderly, as clearly as I can. For God *can* be found. There *is* a last rock for your souls, a resting place of absolute peace and joy and power and radiance and security.
>
> "There is a divine Center into which your life can slip, a new and absolute orientation in God, a Center where you live with Him and out of which you see all of life, through new and radiant vision, tinged with new sorrows and pangs, new joys unspeakable and full of glory."
>
> It was the same voice, the same pen, the same rich imagery, and on the whole a remarkably similar set of religious ideas. But now he seemed to be expounding less as one possessed of *knowledge about* and more as one who had had unmistakable *acquaintance with.*

From the writings of this period come the essays published posthumously in *A Testament of Devotion.* Kelly died very suddenly of a heart attack on January 17, 1941, at the age of 47.

In Thomas Kelly we find the deeper life emphasis of Meister Eckhart and the language of the Quakers George Fox and John Woolman.

Here is the passion for a life entirely committed to God; and here we find the dynamics of personal relationship to God in the Spirit-filled life. Kelly writes: "Double-mindedness in this matter is wholly destructive of the spiritual life. Totalitarian are the claims of Christ. No vestige or reservation of 'our' rights can remain. Straddle arrangements and compromises between our allegiances to the surface level and the divine Center cannot endure."

The distinctive Quaker language for doing the full will of God is for the Christian to find the "Center." The secondness of an experience of holiness is clearly reflected in Kelly's repeated references to "the second half" of our experience with God. Here are the sources of the theology and language of Philip Doddridge's rhapsody:

> *O happy day that fixed my choice*
> *On Thee, my Savior and my God!*
> *Well may this glowing heart rejoice,*
> *And tell its raptures all abroad.*

> *'Tis done, the great transaction's done;*
> *I am my Lord's and He is mine.*
> *He drew me, and I followed on,*
> *Charmed to confess the voice divine.*

> *Now rest, my long divided heart;*
> *Fixed on this blissful center, rest;*
> *Nor ever from my Lord depart,*
> *With Him of ev'ry good possessed.*

But Kelly also sees clearly the ethics of holiness, linking our inner experience of Christ to the solution of world problems. Not content merely to enjoy the presence of God, he discovers that saintliness sends us out to share in the sufferings of the world, and in the suffering of Christ for the world.

From *A Testament of Devotion* we have selected excerpts from essay 3 on "Holy Obedience," and essay 5 on "The Simplification of Life." Both are moving appeals for inward holiness.

I. The Nature of Holy Obedience[1]

Meister Eckhart wrote: "There are plenty to follow our Lord half-way, but not the other half. They will give up possessions, friends, and honors, but it touches them too closely to disown themselves." It is just this astonishing life which is willing to follow Him the other

---

1. *A Testament of Devotion*, 52-62, 65-67. The essay was written against the background of world tensions in the late 30s and the tragedies of World War II in the early 40s.

half, sincerely to disown itself, this life which intends *complete* obe-
CONSECRATION dience, without *any* reservations, that I would propose
to you in all humility, in all boldness, in all seriousness.
I mean this literally, utterly, completely, and I mean it for you and for
me—commit your lives in unreserved obedience to Him.

If you don't realize the revolutionary explosiveness of this pro-
posal you don't understand what I mean. Only now and then comes a
man or a woman who, like John Woolman or Francis of Assisi, is
willing to be utterly obedient, to go the other half, to follow God's
faintest whisper. But when such a commitment comes in a human life,
God breaks through, miracles are wrought, world-renewing divine
forces are released, history changes. There is nothing more important
now than to have the human race endowed with just such committed
lives. . . . To this extraordinary life I call you—or He calls you through
me—not as a lovely ideal, a charming pattern to aim at hopefully, but
as a serious, concrete program of life, to be lived here and now, in
industrial America, by you and by me.

This is something wholly different from mild, conventional religion which, with respectable skirts held back by dainty fingers, anx-
iously tries to fish the world out of the mudhole of its own selfishness.
Our churches, our meeting houses are full of such respectable and
amiable people. We have plenty of Quakers to follow God the first
half of the way. Many of us have become as mildly and as con-
ventionally religious as were the church folk of three centuries ago,
against whose mildness and mediocrity and passionlessness George
Fox and his followers flung themselves with all the passion of a glorious and a new discovery and with all the energy of dedicated lives. In
some, says William James, religion exists as a dull habit, in others an
acute fever. Religion as a dull habit is not that for which Christ lived
and died.

There is a degree of holy and complete obedience and of joyful
self-renunciation and of sensitive listening that is breath-taking. Difference of degree passes over into utter difference of kind, when one
tries to follow Him the second half. Jesus put this pointedly when He
said, "Ye must be born again" (John 3:3), and Paul knew it: "If any man
be in Christ, he is a new creature" (2 Cor. 5:17). . . .

Parents, if some of your children are seized with this imperative
God-hunger, don't tell them to snap out of it and get a job, but carry
them patiently in your love, or at least keep hands off and let the holy
work of God proceed in their souls.

Young people, you who have in you the stirrings of perfection, the
sweet, sweet rapture of God himself within you, be faith-
CHRISTIAN
PERFECTION   ful to Him until the last lingering bit of self is surrendered
and you are wholly God-possessed.

The life that intends to be wholly obedient, wholly submissive,
wholly listening, is astonishing in its completeness. Its joys are ravishing, its peace profound, its humility the deepest, its power world-
shaking, its love enveloping, its simplicity that of a trusting child. It is
the life and power in which the prophets and apostles lived. It is the
life and power of Jesus of Nazareth, who knew that "when thine eye
is single, thy whole body also is full of light" (Luke 11:34). It is the life
and power of the apostle Paul, who resolved not to know anything
among men save Jesus Christ and Him crucified. It is the life and
power of St. Francis, that little poor man of God who came nearer to
reliving the life of Jesus than has any other man on earth. It is the life
and power of George Fox and of Isaac and Mary Pennington. It is the
life and power and utter obedience of John Woolman who decided, he
says, "to place my whole trust in God," to "act on an inner principle
of virtue, and pursue worldly business no farther than as truth opened
my way therein." It is the life and power of myriads of unknown saints
through the ages. It is the life and power of some people now in this
room who smile knowingly as I speak. And it is a life and power that
can break forth in this tottering Western culture and return the
Church to its rightful life as a fellowship of creative, heaven-led souls.

II. Gateways into Holy Obedience

. . . Some men come into holy obedience through the gateway of
profound mystical experience.

It is an overwhelming experience to fall into the hands of the
living God, to be invaded to the depths of one's being by His presence,
to be, without warning, wholly uprooted from all earth-born securi-
ties and assurances, and to be blown by a tempest of unbelievable
power which leaves one's old proud self utterly, utterly defenseless . . .
Then is the soul swept into a Loving Center of ineffable sweetness,
where calm and unspeakable peace and ravishing joy steal over one.
. . . one sighs, like the convinced Thomas of old, "My Lord and my
God" (John 20:28). . . . And one knows what Paul meant when he
wrote, "The life which I now live in the flesh I live by the faith of the
Son of God" (Gal. 2:20). . . .

Do not mistake me. Our interest just now is in the life of complete obedience to God, not in amazing revelations of His glory graciously granted only to some. Yet the amazing experiences of the mystics leave a permanent residue, a God-subdued, a God-possessed will. States of consciousness are fluctuating. The vision fades. But holy and listening and alert obedience remains, as the core and kernel of a God-intoxicated life, as the abiding pattern of sober, workaday living. And some are led into the state of complete obedience by this well-nigh passive route, wherein God alone seems to be the Actor and we seem to be wholly acted upon. And our wills are melted and dissolved and made pliant, being firmly fixed in Him, as He wills in us.

But in contrast to this passive route to complete obedience most people must follow what Jean-Nicholas Grou calls the active way, wherein *we* must struggle and, like Jacob of old, wrestle with the angel until the morning dawns, the active way wherein the will must be subjected bit by bit, piecemeal and progressively, to the divine will.

But the first step to the obedience of the second half is the flaming vision of the wonder of such a life, a vision which comes occasionally to us all, through biographies of the saints, through **HUNGER** the journals of Fox and early Friends, through a life lived before our eyes, through a haunting verse of the Psalms—"Whom have I in heaven but thee? and there is none upon earth that I desire beside thee" (Ps. 73:25)—through meditation upon the amazing life and death of Jesus, through a flash of illumination or, in Fox's language, a great opening. But whatever the earthly history of this moment of charm, this vision of an absolutely holy life is, I am convinced, the invading, urging, inviting, persuading work of the Eternal One. . . .

Once having the vision, the second step to holy obedience is this: Begin where you are. Obey *now*. Use what little obedience you are capable of, even if it be like a grain of mustard seed. Begin where you are. Live this present moment, this present hour as you now sit in your seats, in utter, utter submission and openness toward Him. **KEEP OPEN TO GOD** Listen outwardly to these words, but within, behind the scenes, in the deeper levels of your lives where you are all alone with God, the loving, Eternal One, keep up a silent prayer, "Open Thou my life. Guide my thoughts where I dare not let them go. But Thou darest. Thy will be done." . . .

And the third step in holy obedience, or a counsel, is this: If you slip and stumble and forget God for an hour, and assert your old, proud self, and rely upon your own clever wisdom, don't spend too much time in anguished regrets and self-accusations but begin again, just where you are.

Yet a fourth consideration in holy obedience is this: Don't grit your teeth and clench your fists and say, "I will! I will!" Relax. Take hands off. Submit yourself to God. Learn to live in the passive voice— a hard saying for Americans—and let life be willed through you. For "I will" spells not obedience.

III. Humility and Holiness

The fruits of holy obedience are many. But two are so closely linked together that they can scarcely be treated separately. They are the passion for personal holiness and the sense of utter humility. . . .
. . . God inflames the soul with a burning craving for absolute purity. One burns for complete innocency and holiness **HUNGER FOR PURITY** of personal life. No man can look on God and live, live in his faults, live in the shadow of the least self-deceit, live in harm toward His least creatures, whether man or bird or beast or creeping thing. The blinding purity of God in Christ, how captivating, how alluring, how compelling it is! The pure in heart shall see God? More, they who see God shall cry out to become pure in heart, even as He is pure, with all the energy of their souls. . . .

No average goodness will do, no measuring of our lives by our fellows, but only a relentless, inexorable divine standard. No **YE SHALL BE HOLY** relatives suffice; only absolutes satisfy the soul committed to holy obedience. Absolute honesty, absolute gentleness, absolute self-control, unwearied patience and thoughtfulness in the midst of the raveling friction of home and office and school and shop. . . .

He who walks in obedience, following God the second half, living the life of inner prayer of submission and exultation, on him God's holiness takes hold as a mastering passion of life. Yet ever he cries out in abysmal sincerity, "I am the blackest of all the sinners of the earth. I am a man of unclean lips, for mine eyes have seen the King, Jehovah of Hosts" [cf. Isa. 6:5]. For humility and holiness are twins in the astonishing birth of obedience in the heart of men. So God draws unworthy us, in loving tenderness, up into fellowship with His glorious self. . . .

IV. The Simplification of Life[2]

If the Society of Friends has anything to say, it lies in this region primarily. Life is meant to be lived from a Center, a divine Center. Each one of us can live such a life of amazing power and peace and serenity, of integration and confidence and simplified multiplicity, on one condition—that is, *if we really want to.* There is a divine Abyss within us all, a holy Infinite Center, a Heart, a Life who speaks in us and through us to the world. We have all heard this holy Whisper at times. At times we have followed the Whisper, and amazing equilibrium of life, amazing effectiveness of living set in. But too many of us have heeded the Voice only at times. Only at times have we submitted to His holy guidance. We have not counted this Holy Thing within us to be the most precious thing in the world. We have not surrendered *all else,* to attend to it alone. Let me repeat. Most of us, I fear, have not surrendered all else, in order to attend to the Holy Within.

HUNGER

John Woolman did. He resolved so to order his outward affairs as to be, *at every moment,* attentive to that Voice. He simplified life on the basis of its relation to the divine Center. Nothing else really counted so much as attentiveness to that Root of all living which he found within himself. And the Quaker discovery lies in just that: the welling-up whispers of divine guidance and love and presence, more precious than heaven or earth. . . .

Let me talk very intimately and very earnestly with you about Him who is dearer than life. Do you really want to live your lives, every moment of your lives, in His presence? Do you long for Him, crave Him? Do you love His presence? Does every drop of blood in your body love Him? Does every breath you draw breathe a prayer, a praise to Him? Do you sing and dance within yourselves, as you glory in His love? Have you set yourselves to be His, and *only* His, walking every moment in holy obedience? I know I'm talking like an old-time evangelist. But I can't help that, nor dare I restrain myself and get prim and conventional. We have too long been prim and restrained. The fires of the love of God, of our love toward God, and of His love toward us, are very hot. "Thou shalt love the Lord thy God with all thy heart and soul and mind and strength." Do we really do it?

ABANDONED TO GOD

---

2. Ibid., 116-24.

Is love steadfastly directed toward God, in our minds, all day **POWER** long? Do we intersperse our work with gentle prayers and praises to Him? Do we live in the steady peace of God, a peace down at the very depths of our souls, where all strain is gone and God is already Victor over the world, already Victor over our weaknesses? This life, this abiding, enduring peace that never fails, this serene power and unhurried conquest, inward conquest over ourselves, outward conquest over the world, is meant to be ours. It is a life that is freed from strain and anxiety and hurry, for something of the cosmic patience of God becomes ours. Are our lives *unshakable*, because we are clear down on bedrock, rooted and grounded in the love of God? This is the first and the great commandment. . . .

I think it is clear that I am talking about a revolutionary way of living. Religion isn't something to be added to our other duties, and thus make our lives yet more complex. The life with God is the center of life, and all else is remodeled and integrated by it. It gives the singleness of eye. The most important thing is not to be perpetually passing out cups of cold water to a thirsty world. We can get so fearfully busy trying to carry out the second great commandment, "Thou shalt love thy neighbour as thyself," that we are underdeveloped in our devoted love to God. But we must love God as well as neighbor. These things ye ought to have done and not to have left the other only partially done.

There is a way of life so hid with Christ in God that in the midst of the day's business one is inwardly lifting brief prayers, short ejaculations of praise, subdued whispers of adoration and of tender love to the Beyond that is within. No one need know about it. I only speak to you because it is a sacred trust, not mine but to be given to others. One can live in a well-nigh continuous state of unworded prayer, directed toward God, directed toward people and enterprises we have on our heart. There is no hurry about it all; it is a life unspeakable and full of glory, an inner world of splendor within which we, unworthy, may live. Some of you know it and live in it; others of you may wistfully long for it; it can be yours. . . .

Life from the Center is a life of unhurried peace and power. It is simple. It is serene. It is amazing. It is triumphant. It is radiant. It takes no time, but it occupies all our time. And it makes our life programs new and overcoming. We need not get frantic. He is at the helm. And when our little day is done we lie down quietly in peace, for all is well.

4

James B. Chapman
(1884-1947)

James Blaine Chapman was born at Yale, Ill., August 30, 1884. Early in life he gave his heart to God and was sanctified wholly. Called to the ministry at the age of 15, he began at once, as an evangelist, to proclaim the gospel message of full salvation.

He completed his education at Peniel College, Peniel, Tex. In 1903 he married Maud Frederick, and to this union six children were born. Mrs. Chapman died in 1940, and in 1942 Dr. Chapman was married to Louise Robinson, who had served as a missionary to Africa for 20 years.

Dr. Chapman was a leader in the Holiness Church of Christ in the South, which united to form the Church of the Nazarene at Pilot Point, Tex., in 1908. He held pastorates at Durant and Bethany, Okla., and preached for a number of years as a full-time evangelist.

In 1913 he was called to the presidency of Peniel College, where he served for five years. Then in 1922 he was elected editor of the *Herald of Holiness*, official publication of the Church of the Nazarene. In 1928 he was elected as a general superintendent of his denomination, where he served until his death.

Dr. Chapman's commitment to the message of Christian holiness was best expressed by himself in his response on the occasion of his election as a general superintendent. In his characteristic manner, he started to speak, but tears began to break the flow of his words. He said, "I was converted in a holiness meeting.

The first church I ever joined was a holiness church. My first sermon was preached under the leadership of a holiness ministry. I know nothing but a holiness people and a holiness church. Truly you are my people."

In addition to his duties as a general superintendent, Dr. Chapman wrote a stream of books, sermons, and pamphlets— more than 3 million words in all. We have chosen excerpts from two books as representative of his understanding and exposition of classic Christian holiness.

Holiness, the Heart of Christian Experience[1]

No writer of the 20th century has understood classic holiness teaching more accurately or expressed it more clearly than J. B. Chapman. This compact and precise little book was written to inform and encourage Christian young people in their search for entire sanctification.

The writer begins with his personal testimony and often reflects the spirit of a true evangelist as he urges the reader to experience the truth of which he is learning.

Written as instruction and exhortation to young people, the clarity and appeal of these messages makes them especially helpful for new Christians, and for others to whom the message of Christian holiness comes for the first time.

No important theme is overlooked, and each area treated is adequate to lead the reader into a deeper understanding and a closer walk with a holy God.

Chapter 12, "A Holiness Catechism," is unique in *Great Holiness Classics.* In question-and-answer form, Dr. Chapman gives a clear statement of what the Bible teaches about Christian holiness.

I. How I Became Interested in Bible Holiness

God has been so real and so satisfying to me from that night when

---

1. We have reprinted this entire little classic except for chapter 13, a kind of appendix titled "Correspondence on Holiness."

as a lad of 15 He came into my heart in full sanctifying grace that I can wish for all that they may find Him early, as I did.

My father had removed his family into a new country community. By special appointment, Rev. Albright was preaching at the neighborhood schoolhouse. During the second service I became interested in the man and the message he seemed to have for the people. Addressing my neighbor in the seat beside me, I asked in a low whisper, "What kind of a preacher is Mr. Albright?" The reply, "A holiness preacher." "Wherein do holiness preachers differ from other preachers?" "I cannot answer that. Perhaps you will be able to see the difference if you listen to this man." I listened, but I could see nothing objectionable in what he said, so I set him up as the standard and reasoned that those who differed from him must be just that much aside from the center. So, although not yet a Christian, I came soon to think of myself as somewhat "bent" toward the holiness people.

It was early spring when I heard Mr. Albright. In September the holiness camp meeting came on. The distance from our house was about six miles, and in those horse and buggy days, this was an hour's travel. I went the first night, only to be disappointed by the failure of the evangelist to arrive for that first service. I missed a night, and then came again to find the meeting in good swing. The evangelist was R. L. Averill from Texas. Night after night he chose the plainest texts and expounded the doctrine of holiness. He held up holiness as the demand of God's law, the provision of Christ's atonement, and the special work of the Holy Spirit in the present dispensation. He showed that men must be holy to get to heaven, and that they must obtain this blessing in the world. He showed from the Bible, the hymns of the Church, and the testimony of men that men are sanctified after they are justified, and that we are made holy by being sanctified wholly after we are justified, and that on this account it is, as John Wesley said, "a second blessing, properly so-called."

PREACHING

But it was not the preaching alone that interested me. There was a small but happy band of people ever ready to stand and testify to the marvelous manner in which God had forgiven their sins and subsequently sanctified them wholly. They sang joyfully, gave liberally, and worked incessantly. Their religion was manifestly a great boon to them, and I could not resist wishing I had what they said they had, and what they really seemed to possess.

WITNESSING

One of the favorite songs was No. 100 in old *Tears and Triumph*

No. 2. It was based on the 51st psalm, and the first stanza went as
follows:

> *Wash me throughly, blessed Savior;*
> *Cleanse me from indwelling sin.*
> *Bathe me in the sacred fountain;*
> *Now complete Thy work within.*

Every time this song was repeated it seemed to increase in its meaning
for me until at last I found myself saying, "If I ever get religion, I want
the kind this song represents."

At the end of 10 days the evangelist had to pass on to his next
engagement. But the people felt they had not yet had the results they
desired, so they decided to run the meeting for a few nights more,
such preachers as chanced to come along taking the meetings for them
from night to night. And how thankful I am that they had that extra
week! For it was during that week that I was brought under conviction
for sin and came to the public altar to pray and seek the Lord. That
first time at the altar marked the crisis, and Christ came and forgave
my sins and gave me a new heart. But I had seen the land of Canaan
before I ever left Egypt, and so pressed right on to get sanctification.
So when the camp meeting closed I was clear in the experience of
Bible holiness and was already giving clear and definite testimony to
the fact that I had found what the preachers had preached and what
the Christians had declared.

That was in September 1899. But today, after these passing years,
I am happy in the full grace of heart holiness, and have come to say a
few things about this blessed experience to the young people of this
day. The majority who read these words will no doubt be older in
years than I was when I found this blessed grace, so I feel that I am not
imposing upon them the words of an elder who passed his youth in a
manner he is unwilling to recommend to others. Rather, I come to say
that God has been so real and so satisfying to me from that night when
as a lad of 15 He came into my heart in full sanctifying grace that I can
wish for all that they may find Him early, as I did, and that I am
assured they will have no regrets with the passing years.

I have called holiness the heart of Christian experience because it
is the full realization of what God has promised to us in the way of
crises. Regeneration and entire sanctification are the two crises in
which God deals with the sin problem in us and by which He takes us
out of sin and then takes sin out of us. After that the Christian life is
a way of process and progress, but there are no more crises until

glorification comes at the return of Jesus to this world. There is all room for growth after sanctification, but there is no more place for crises. There is no state of grace beyond a pure heart filled with the Holy Spirit. But from such a heart flow forth the passive and the active phases of Christian life as water flows forth from a spring. Holiness is purity—not maturity. Holiness is the goal only in that it prepares one for whatever there is of Christian life—it is the "enabling blessing" which every Christian needs.

II. Holiness in the Teachings of the Bible

There is a great deal about sin in the Bible, but sin is always condemned and holiness is exalted.

It is a good thing to store the mind with scripture texts. If I were back again in my teens I think I would give more attention to memorizing the Bible and the old hymns of the Church. These become an increasing heritage as the years come and go. But to be fair with the Bible one must take it in its broad sense. That is, one must not get a preconceived idea and then go to the Bible for "proof texts." Rather, he must take the Bible in its general, as well as in its specific, statements.

Dr. Ellyson used to suggest that the name Holy Bible means simply "Book on Holiness." And that is what we find it to be. Of course there is a great deal about sin in the Bible, but sin is always condemned and holiness is exalted. There is a great deal about judgment, but mercy is the outstanding theme. After the first few chapters, which tell of sin's entrance into the world, all the rest of the Bible is given to redemption and salvation—showing how to get rid of sin.

Sin and holiness are moral and spiritual antipodes, and one or the other must finally prevail. Sin and holiness cannot go on in mixed form forever. Either we must be saved from sin, or sin will damn us forever. And this applies to all sin. There is no sin in heaven and no holiness in hell. This world is the place where we must make the abiding choice, and God proposes to allow our choice of sin to become fixed in impenitence or our choice of holiness to become effective by the power of His grace. This is the teaching of the whole tenor of the Scriptures.

Many of the types of the Old Testament are difficult. Some of them seem to us to be involved. But to the people to whom they were first given they were clearer than they are to us—clearer even than straight, unillustrated statements would have been. Take the camp life of the Israelites: They were to keep the camp itself clean by excluding lepers, and by the observance of the most rigid sanitary laws known in the world at that time. They were to keep their houses clean; they were to keep their bodies clean; and their menu included only such animals and birds as were known as clean for food and for sacrifice to God. All these things—insignificant some of them within themselves—united in making clear to the people of those and succeeding times the root idea of purity, so that when it was applied to the heart, men could immediately understand the significance of a heart entirely free from moral defilement. Indeed "the Old Testament is the New Testament concealed, and the New Testament is the Old Testament revealed"—all this with reference to the Bible standard of heart and life.

Take the question of atonement for sin: Even the ancient sacrifices included the idea of cleansing as well as pardon. Sin **CARNALITY/ CLEANSING** was seen to be something deeper than guilt, although it included guilt. David prayed, "Purge me with hyssop, and I shall be clean: wash me, and I shall be whiter than snow" (Ps. 51:7). This purging and washing reached further than guilt for transgression and involved a purity that goes beyond the whiteness of snow. The flake of snow that seems so white may after all have a grain of dust at heart. But David would have a heart with no moral dirt at its center. And the minor prophet sang of "a fountain opened to the house of David and to the inhabitants of Jerusalem for sin and for uncleanness" (Zech. 13:1). Sin is transgression of the law, but uncleanness is the root from which transgression springs. The fountain that flowed from the pierced side of the Lamb of God upon the Cross contained both water and blood, and was for sin as transgression and for sin as uncleanness.

> Rock of Ages, cleft for me,
> Let me hide myself in Thee.
> Let the water and the blood,
> From Thy wounded side which flowed,
> Be of sin the double cure,
> Save from wrath and make me pure.

Pardon of sin saves from wrath, and cleansing from inbred sin makes us pure.

Then take the question of "the finished work"—that is, the change designated as the new birth and the further work designated as sanctification. Here again we meet with duality of process. There is a work of the Holy Spirit by which we are made alive unto God. Then there is a work by which we are crucified to the world and sin dies out within us. There is a work of the Spirit by which we are made new. Then there is a further or second work by which we are made clean. There is a distinction between a new heart in which there is yet contention between the Holy Spirit and the fleshly or sinful nature, and a clean heart in which the Holy Spirit reigns supremely and in which there is no longer any fleshly nature with which we must contend.

And if any man question whether it is possible to attain to such a state of holiness in this world, let him remember that this is our world of probation, and that here the blood of Jesus was **HOLY IN THIS LIFE** shed and here the Holy Spirit is poured out. Here all the conditions are possible and here all the propitiation of Christ and all the efficiency of the Holy Spirit are available. What merit can the future have that we do not have now? We have the blood of Jesus. What more of merit can saints in heaven have? What power to renovate spirit can they have in heaven that we do not have here? We have the Holy Spirit, the infinite Refining Fire; what can they have in heaven that can be more efficient? The world is sinful! That is true, but "greater is he that is in you, than he that is in the world" (1 John 4:4). Our own natures are depraved! True, but "the blood of Jesus Christ his Son cleanseth us from all sin" (1:7). We are too unworthy and weak! True, but "the grace of God that bringeth salvation hath appeared to all men, teaching us that, denying ungodliness and worldly lusts, we should live soberly, righteously, and godly, in this present world" (Titus 2:11-12).

III. The Prerequisites of Holiness

The promise of cleansing is conditioned upon walking in the light. This . . . means simply obeying God to the full measure of our knowledge of His will.

Serious Christians are wont to ask, "Why is sanctification a second work of grace? Why cannot God sanctify at the same instant in which He justifies?" The answer is that the limitations are all on the human side. Stated in simple language, men cannot be sanctified at the time when they are justified because some of the conditions necessary to sanctification cannot be met until after men are justified. This is why we speak of some things as prerequisites to (required before) holiness.

There is a distinction in theology between justification, regeneration, and adoption. Justification, the theologians say, takes place in the heart of God and is accomplished by His gracious act of pardoning the sins of the penitent sinner. Regeneration, the same authorities say, takes place in the heart of man and is the work of the Holy Spirit in implanting the new spiritual life in the soul of the believing penitent. The new birth is just another term for the same experience. Adoption is the gracious act of God by which the alien is made a child, and this act is based upon the fact of regeneration. All this is theology. In actual experience whoever is justified is also regenerated and adopted. So for all practical purposes we may think of these terms as synonyms, and the fact described is a definite prerequisite to holiness.

In His high-priestly prayer recorded in the 17th chapter of John, our Lord prayed for the sanctification of His disciples, and in this connection He definitely said, "I pray not for the world" (v. 9). He could not in the nature of the case pray for the sanctification of the world. He prayed for the world indirectly when He mentioned "them also which shall believe on me through their word" (v. 20). But those who are of the world must cease to be of the world before they are included in the prayer for sanctification.

It is evident, likewise, that backsliders are not in position to be sanctified. First they must be restored to the favor of God and the joy of salvation. Sanctification is by the will of God, and sinners and backsliders are rebels against God and disqualified for sharing in His will. When David sinned he came first and prayed for forgiveness and restoration, and then for cleansing and purity (Psalm 51).

The preaching and testimony of holiness always act as genuine probers of motives and discoverers of state and relation. There is a difference between conviction for guilt and conviction for want. The sinner and backslider have conviction for guilt, but the justified believer has conviction for want. It may seem unnecessarily harsh to say

HUNGER it, but the fact still remains that just as dead people have no desire and sick people are usually wanting in appetite, so likewise the reason many are not set to seek and find holiness is that they are dead in trespasses and sin or sick and ailing in their spiritual lives.

Those who have explained that people who think they received the second blessing were merely backsliders, and when they were restored to the favor of God supposed they had something more than they ever had before, are altogether mistaken in their premises. It is always the Christians who are in the best state of justification who first realize their need of sanctification; and the divine plan, after all, is not to "bless the man who is nearest hell," as sometimes we are wont to pray at the beginning of the revival, but to begin first with the house of God, and by blessing those who are closest up make way for those who are farther back without doing violence to the moral and spiritual consistency and order.

Then the promise of cleansing is conditioned upon walking in the light. "If we walk in the light, as he is in the light, we have fellowship one with another, and the blood of Jesus Christ his Son cleanseth us from all sin" (1 John 1:7). This walking in the light means simply obeying God to the full measure of our knowledge of His will. It implies willing and glad obedience.

So we may summarize the prerequisites of holiness as (1) a clean, definite condition of regeneration, and (2) a heart that is willing to go all the way with God in all His revealed will. And when these two are considered together they become so closely united as to be almost one. It is essential to a clear state of justification to be ready and obedient. Reluctance and hesitation bring defeat and darkness. How is it with you today? Is your witness of sonship and acceptance with God bright and clear? Are you ready and willing to obey God in any and all things in which His will may be made known to you? Can you, as the poet would say, read your title clear to a mansion in the skies? If all this is descriptive of your state and relation, then you should have no hindrance in coming to God with prayer and faith to be "made every whit whole." There is a fullness in God's grace and mercy for you as a child of God. Do not be content without it. Claim your heritage. Lay hold upon the promise. Pray with the poet:

> *Refining Fire, go through my heart,*
> *Illuminate my soul;*
> *Scatter Thy life through every part,*
> *And sanctify the whole.*

IV. Holiness Defined

Holiness is that state of heart which results from being sanctified wholly by the power of the Holy Spirit. Sanctification is the crisis; holiness is the result following the crisis.

We have always to advance to things we do not know in terms of the things we do know. For that reason spiritual truths have usually to be illustrated by natural things. This was the approach Jesus made when He called the change wrought by the Holy Spirit in making a saint of a sinner being "born again," and the approach He made by the use of parables.

What is holiness? Well, holiness is that state of heart which results from being sanctified wholly by the power of the Holy Spirit. Sanctification is the crisis; holiness is the result following the crisis. Such a state is that of moral purity. The will is completely adjusted to the will of God and the affections are purified, alienated from sin and the world, and exalted to a supreme love for God. It is not a negative state, implied simply by freedom from sin; it is also a positive condition in which the heart is filled with the perfect love of God, which enables one to love God with all his heart and his neighbor as himself.

Holiness and *health* come from the same root word in the Anglo-Saxon. That is, holiness is soul health. Holiness is to the soul what
WHOLENESS   health is to the body. Health is that state of the body in
              which there is freedom from disease and in which there is
general and complete soundness of organs and tissues. It is not easy to describe the symptoms of health. Perhaps it is best to think of it as the state in which one is enabled to live from day to day without pain or tormenting weariness and with a minimum of thought and care concerning himself. And holiness is like that to the soul. Sin is abnormal, like disease in the body. It is likened to a thorn in the side or to a broken foot. It brings uneasiness and strain and burden. Holiness removes the thorn, cures the broken foot, and makes the Christian life a joy.

Holiness is the standard of God's Word for all, regardless of what one may profess in the way of personal grace or attainment. So the
FOR ALL   profession of holiness does not make a new standard; it
CHRISTIANS   just enables one to live up to the standard he has always
              tried as a Christian to reach. It differs from the life of a
justified Christian in that it possesses inner power to walk before God in holiness and righteousness. It does not increase the burdens of the Christian life, but does increase the power of the Christian experience. This is why Dr. Rinehart, pressed for a statement as to what sanctification is, replied, "It is regeneration made easy."

Holiness is not an abnormal attainment. It is the normal state in which man was originally created. Sin is inherent in man since the fall of Adam, but holiness was the image man originally wore, and it is the state in which man reaches his real end. That picture that shows a holy man as wearing long hair, enduring some sort of voluntary punishment, holding himself entirely apart from others, straining to reach a goal of character that is always beyond him, following a course at variance to his inner impulses and desires, and purchasing merit by his denial of the things he desires, is a false picture—a caricature of the holy, happy, victorious Christian which God designs to be the pattern saint. With the desire for sin entirely eradicated, the sanctified Christian has come to the place where he can do what he desires and yet do what God requires, because his will and affections are adjusted and purified, his inner life and outer life are balanced, and he is happy in the will of God.

In giving personal testimony it is always best to use forms that exalt Christ and not ourselves. The vast majority of intelligent people **WITNESSING** are offended if anyone says, "I am sanctified," or, "I am holy." This sounds like holiness is an accomplishment bringing merit to the possessor. The proper form is, "God has graciously sanctified me," or, "The abiding Holy Spirit keeps my heart clean from sin." Here the emphasis is on the divine grace, where it actually belongs. Sin differs greatly in its manifestation. So there are Pharisees and publicans in the same community. But whether the manifestation is in a form of pride or in self-abandonment to evil, the fact remains that "all have sinned, and come short of the glory of God" (Rom. 3:23), and that whatever there is that is good in any, it is all of grace and not of us. John Fletcher used to say, "I nothing have and nothing am; / My glory's in the bleeding Lamb, / Both now and evermore."

Pride is a fruit of sin; holiness brings humility. Those who think we must have some sin in us to keep us humble are entirely mistaken in their judgment of the nature of sin. The quintessence of sin is selfishness and pride. This pride may show itself in a brazen abandon that looks like the opposite of itself, but the fact still remains that it is the heart that lifts itself up in opposition to God that dares to choose a course in any way contrary to that chosen by the Lord in His infinite goodness and wisdom. Everyone who refuses to take God's way in the fullest degree must base his choice upon doubt of either the goodness or the wisdom of God.

Surely no one can answer the following question in any but the affirmative: Is God able to save us from all outward and inner sin? Then there is one more question that is not so simply answered, "Why does God not save me from all outward and inner sin and make me free and holy just now?" But the answer to this is, after all, not so far to seek. God is able and willing to save from all sin. If therefore He does not so save me, it is only because I do not this moment submit myself to the divine processes according to the conditions laid down in the Bible. The responsibility for any sin that may yet remain in me is my own responsibility. Christ is able and willing today.

V. Holiness Differentiated

Purity is obtained as a crisis; maturity comes as a process.

A minister sat by me on the train one day and said, "You preach Christian perfection. Please give me a type of the perfect Christian." I replied that I did not have a type ready to hand, and that I would be glad to consider the one he doubtless would propose.

He answered, "I would take good, pure flower seeds and plant them in well-prepared soil and protect the growing plant from the elements until the stalk is grown to full height and the flowers are in full bloom. And when the stalk is grown and the flower full, there is a type of Christian perfection."

But I answered, "You confuse purity and maturity. The perfect Christian is a pure Christian, but not necessarily a mature Christian. The plant of which you speak is a good type of Christian perfection all the way along, if the plant is what it should be at that stage and is perfectly free from disease."

Purity and maturity! The words are similar in sound, but they are very distinct in meaning. Purity may be found in the earliest moments after a soul finds pardon and peace with God. But maturity involves time and growth and trial and development. The pure Christian may even be a weak Christian. For it is not size or strength that is emphasized, but only the absence of evil and the presence of elementary good. Purity is obtained as a crisis; maturity comes as a process. One can be made pure in the twinkling of an eye; it is doubtful that anyone in this world should be listed as really mature. Growth continues while life lasts, and for aught we know, it may continue throughout eternity.

Since all virtues are capable of enlargement, it is easy to fall into the error of attributing degrees of holiness, so that one may easily imagine that he will finally grow into purity. More faith, more love, more hope, and more patience incline one to think that at some undefined time he will have none of the opposites of these. But growth is not a process for purifying. Growth is addition; purifying is subtraction. And even though one may approach holiness by ever so gradual a process, there must be a last moment when sin exists

IN A MOMENT and the first moment when it is all gone, and that means that in reality sanctification must be instantaneous. At this or any given moment every Christian is either free from sin or he is not free from sin. There can be no sense in which he is actually holy and at the same time still somewhat defiled. There can be no such thing as purer than pure or holier than holy. Those who think otherwise have a concept of holiness that is more formal and external than that which is presented as evangelical holiness in the New Testament.

The body is the home of the soul and is subject to it, so that the body within itself is incapable of moral character or responsible action. The body can be sinned against, but it cannot sin. It may be the instrument of sin, but there is no sin resident in it apart from the spirit. Man's personality is inherent in his spirit, and he is either sinful or holy independent of his body. If he is sinful in spirit he will use his body as a tool of unrighteousness. If he is holy in spirit he will use his body as a channel through which to do holy and righteous deeds. Whatever a man is—sinful or holy—in his body, he would be the same out of his body. Those who think they will be holy when they die, and just because they die, are entirely mistaken. Death brings separation of soul and body, but it does not in any way affect the moral and spiritual state or standing of the person involved.

There is a distinction between the mind and the immortal spirit, but this is a distinction exceedingly difficult to make. The Word of God is said to be a two-edged sword that can divide asunder the soul and spirit (Heb. 4:12), but this statement within itself is indicative of the delicacy of the task. However, we must know that the mind, too, as described in the intellectual life, is incapable of moral choice or action except it be directed by the deeper powers of the spirit. There is no moral quality in dreams, because there is no choice of will involved. Passing thoughts of evil have no moral quality until they are given cognizance by the will.

Speaking of the fact that temptation is not sin until we yield to it, and that thoughts of evil are often involuntary, one has said, "We cannot keep the birds from flying over our heads, but we can keep them from making nests in our hair." When thoughts of evil are willingly entertained they become evil thoughts, and then they are blameworthy. But the adjusted will and purified affections of a fully sanctified Christian bring the thoughts and imaginations of the mind and heart into captivity of obedience to Christ, and every willing thought and every entertained imagination becomes the product and servant of good. Insanity is mental disease and has no more moral quality than physical disease; and although holiness of heart may not actually keep one from becoming mentally unbalanced, it will keep him from any choice of will that would be displeasing to God.

And, finally, conduct depends upon light as well as upon grace. Therefore holiness of heart does not imply perfect conduct. The holy HUMANITY do right, "as they are given to know the right," and that is the end of the law. The perfect law of God is based upon the divine character ("Be ye holy; for I am holy" [1 Pet. 1:16]), and is therefore invariable in heaven and on earth. But where no knowledge is, there is no responsibility. Hence the law of love is the law of conduct for holy men on earth as for holy angels in heaven. We know in part and therefore cannot do the whole. But the promise is that we shall be able to walk before God in holiness and righteousness all the days of our lives (Luke 1:73-75). This means that God, who knows how much we know, gives us credit for full obedience when we obey to the full measure of our knowledge of His will. Therefore one who is but a novice in grace, and who is weak in spiritual might, sick or deformed in body, and limited in intellect, can yet be holy in heart. And holiness is the quality without which we cannot see God.

VI. Holiness Obtained

Holiness is not an accomplishment but is a gift received.

Perhaps it is something of a play on words, but usually we speak of a thing as attained when it is reached as a result of human endeavor, and we speak of a thing as being obtained when it comes as the gift of another upon terms that decidedly favor the receiver. And we think it is not an accident that the word "receive" is used in such passages as Acts 26:18, "That they may receive forgiveness of sins, and inheritance among them which are sanctified by faith that is in me." Holiness is not an accomplishment but is a gift received. It is not attained but is obtained from the Lord. It is not to be approximated by endeavor, but is to be accomplished by the divine enablement. It is wrought as an instantaneous crisis, and not possessed by means of a gradual approach.

The *first step* toward obtaining this blessing is to see and ac-

knowledge its desirability. The commands and promises of the Word
of God should help us in this. Knowing our God is infinite

HUNGER
in goodness, we can but know that that which He commands is for our highest good, and that which He so frequently and forcibly promises He is able to perform. Then we have all had sufficient contact with saintly souls to cause us to see the possibility and desirability of being free from sin and holy in heart. It is beside the question for us to recall that there are those who claim it who do not live it. There are some who claim it who *do* live it, and most of us have seen such undeniable demonstrations of the truth of this blessed word. Then we have, practically all of us, found ourselves face-to-face with tasks for which we were spiritually unprepared. This is a challenge to us to go earnestly after the promised blessing that will make us ready to every good work.

The *second step* toward obtaining the blessing is to choose definitely to have it. By every means God appeals to us, but He by no
means compels us. Desire alone is not sufficient. Desire

CHOICE
alone may easily degenerate into a weak wish. Choice is a human faculty and stands for stamina and determination. It is represented by "I will." It first counts the cost and then discounts it in favor of the prize to be won.

The *third step* toward obtaining the blessing is consecration. Consecration differs from repentance in this: Repentance has to do
with that which is wrong; consecration has to do with

CONSECRATION
that which is right. Repentance is forsaking evil; consecration is presenting that which is good to God. A sinner cannot consecrate until he repents and finds pardon, for consecration is the devotion of the life and talents—not the abandoning of transgression. We mentioned once before that this is a condition that must be met before one can be sanctified, and yet it is a condition that cannot be met until after we are justified; therefore this alone would establish the doctrine that we are sanctified after we are justified, and that sanctification is properly called the second blessing. To be valid as a condition for this blessing, consecration must be complete—without hesitation and without reservation. It must be a devotement to God, and not to just some particular work to which one may find himself drawn. The prayer is:

> *Take my life and let it be*
> *Consecrated, Lord, to Thee.*
>
> . . . .
>
> *Take myself and I will be*
> *Ever, only, all for Thee.*

The *fourth step* toward obtaining the blessing is faith—faith for this particular thing. Here you have come as a justified Christian, assured by the inner witness of the Holy Spirit that you are a child of God. You have found by reading the Bible and searching your own heart that God commands you to be holy and that He has provided the means for making you so. You have desired this blessing and chosen it with its cost before you. You have now brought your all to the altar of God in consecration. You have dedicated yourself and all you are and all you ever expect to be to God to be used of Him in any way that He sees best. So far as you are able to do it, you have sanctified yourself by complete consecration. You have asked God to sanctify you by complete purification. He has promised to do it. You have brought yourself to Him in the fullest condition. You believe He is willing and able to make you holy, and that He is ready to do it this very hour.

FAITH

There is nothing more that God can do in promising. There is nothing more that you can do in meeting the conditions of His promises. To hesitate is to doubt and indicate your uncertainty as to whether He will do what He has said. So without fear and without hesitation, you step right out on the promise and announce to three worlds, "I believe that Jesus Christ sanctifies me now."

The steps have been taken. They are like the steps to Solomon's ivory throne. The only one left is the top of the throne itself—the blessing that God has promised. Will it fail? Will He fail? To ask is to answer. He will not fail. He will come in sanctifying fullness and make your heart His throne. He will purge out the dross of inbred sin and make you clean. He will fill and possess and rule and make you "all glorious within." It will henceforth be your delight to tell among men and angels what wonderful things He has wrought for you and in your heart. You have found your Beulah Land, your Canaan, your inheritance that shall never fail. Henceforth you shall walk in the way of holiness, where neither lion nor ravenous beast is found. I join you in praise. I sing, Hallelujah, "the Comforter has come!"

The Comforter Has Come

Frank Bottome, 1823 - 1894

William J. Kirkpatrick, 1838 - 1921

1. Oh, spread the tid-ings 'round, wher-ev-er man is found, Wher-
2. The long, long night is past; the morn-ing breaks at last; And
3. Lo, the great King of Kings, with heal-ing in His wings, To
4. Oh, bound-less love di-vine! How shall this tongue of mine To

ev-er hu-man hearts and hu-man woes a-bound; Let ev-'ry Christian
hushed the dread-ful wail and fu-ry of the blast, As o'er the gold-en
ev-'ry cap-tive soul a full de-liv'rance brings; And thro' the va-cant
won-d'ring mor-tals tell the match-less grace di-vine— That I, a child of

tongue pro-claim the joy-ful sound:
hills the day ad-vanc-es fast!   The Com-fort-er has come!
cells the song of tri-umph rings:
hell, should in His im-age shine!

REFRAIN

The Com-fort-er has come! The Com-fort-er has come! The Ho-ly Ghost from

heav'n, The Fa-ther's prom-ise giv'n! Oh, spread the tid-ings 'round,

wher-ev-er man is found: The Com-fort-er has come!

VII. The Way to Holiness

The Bible is our infallible Guide as to the manner we are to go about it to seek and find this blessing.

In John 17:17 we are told that we are sanctified through the truth, and further we are told, "Thy word is truth." We understand, then, that the Master was describing the place of the Bible as the Word of God in its relation to the blessing of entire sanctification by means of which we are made holy. In Heb. 13:12 we are told that we are sanctified by the Blood. In Acts 26:18 we are said to be sanctified by faith. In Rom. 15:16 we are described as sanctified by the Holy Ghost. But we all know the Bible, the blood of Jesus, faith, and the Holy Spirit are not interchangeable words, and we know also that we cannot be allowed to choose alternate ways of being sanctified. We never expect to find one Christian sanctified by the Bible, another by the Blood, another by faith, and another by the Holy Ghost. It must be that whoever is sanctified at all must be sanctified by all the means mentioned. What then is the explanation?

The theologians tell us we are to be sanctified *instrumentally* by the Word of God, *efficaciously* by the blood of Jesus, *conditionally* by faith, and *efficiently* by the Holy Ghost. By this we understand that the Bible is our infallible Guide as to the manner we are to go about it to seek and find this blessing. The blood of Jesus is the meritorious price paid for its purchase. Faith is the one prime condition we must meet. And the Holy Spirit is the actual Agent for changing, purging, and filling our hearts. Only Spirit can change spirit, and that is why we cannot ascribe the efficient agency to anyone or anything except the Holy Spirit, who was very properly designated by Dr. Daniel Steele as "the Executor of God in the work of salvation."

In a matter so important as our state and standing with God we need a sure word. The opinions of men will not suffice. Creeds and **SCRIPTURAL** statements wrought out in councils are valuable only when they are true interpretations of the divine Word. But God has given us an inspired and infallible Bible. Whosoever speaks contrary to this Word is to be rejected. The Bible is the Touchstone of all doctrine. It is the dependable revelation of the will of God and the way to God. If we get sanctified at all, we must do so according to the terms laid down in the Word. Bible holiness is the only true holiness.

There is no merit in works or words or tears or anything else we can bring. The blood of Jesus alone is the price of our redemption. When we come to be cleansed from all sin, we have no **ATONEMENT** plea but the Blood. No matter how many years we have served God, we have done only that which it was our duty to do. No matter how much we have given of time or money for the advancement of His kingdom, we have given nothing that we did not first receive. The blood of Jesus alone has merit, and by it alone we have entrance into the holy of holies—the Divine Presence—where we find the cleansing we crave.

Faith has its prerequisites, as repentance in asking for pardon, **FAITH** consecration in asking for holiness, and obedience in praying for persevering grace. But faith remains the one and only prime condition. Faith is the one thing without which there is no deliverance, and when it is present there is always deliverance. Prerequisites lead to faith and faith leads to victory. Faith is not a force within itself, but is the means by which the power of God is released upon us. Faith salvation, like faith healing, is a purely human thing. Faith is just the condition. God is the Power.

The Holy Spirit is a Person, but He has different offices. The Holy Spirit comes in convicting office to the sinner. He comes in regenerating office to the penitent believer. He comes in sanctifying **HOLY** office to the consecrating, accepting believer. There is no rea- **SPIRIT** son for confusion regarding whether the Holy Spirit comes in regeneration or only in entire sanctification. He comes in both instances. But in the latter instance He comes in Pentecostal fullness and power. On the Day of Pentecost, He came in tongues of fire, as well as in the likeness of a rushing mighty wind. Fire is the emblem of purifying. There are many symbols of the Holy Spirit and His works in the Bible. In His life-giving power He is like the wind, as Jesus told Nicodemus in John 3. In His regenerating office He is like water (Titus 3:5). In His feeding office He is like milk (Isaiah 55). In His purifying and energizing power He is like fire. The deeper purging represented by fire in contrast with the more outward cleansing effects of water is well known in the realm of natural things, and the Spirit uses this common knowledge to make clear the distinction between the work of regeneration (a washing) and entire sanctification (a purging with fire).

How fully then is the way to holiness set before us! We come as we are taught in the Bible. We bring the blood of Jesus as our merit. We exercise faith as the condition. The Holy Spirit answers to the Blood by coming as the vital Agency of our full purifying.

I once likened the four factors here considered to getting goods from a mail-order house. There is the catalog that describes the goods, states the price, and gives directions for ordering. This is analogous to the place of the Bible in our sanctification. There is the money required, which is in the position of the Blood in our sanctification. There is the act of sending forth the order by mail—an act that passes beyond sight and is analogous to faith. Then there are the goods actually delivered to the door by the postman, and this is like the coming of the Holy Spirit in Pentecostal fullness. Surely none of us should go farther without the blessing. The Word is true and dependable. The Blood has all merit. Faith has every ground. The Holy Spirit waits at the door. Today, even this hour, "Wilt thou be made whole?"

VIII. Holiness as a Life Lived

As a life to be lived, it is from every point of view the best life possible.

Holiness is a doctrine to be believed, an experience to be received, and a life to be lived. As a doctrine, it is the central thesis of the Bible. As an experience, it is the heart of all the verities in the dealing of men with God in the things of the soul. As a life to be lived, it is from every point of view the best life possible.

There are two contrasting evils, toward one or the other of which we all tend to a greater or lesser extent. One is to lower the

DANGERS standard to the point where we can reach it without the grace God proposes to give us, and the other is to hold up a standard impossible even to the best of men. And, strangely enough, the practical results are about the same in both cases. The standard should remain where God puts it. At such a point we shall need all that grace can do for us to enable us to reach it, and yet by the grace of God we shall be able to reach it with joy and gladness. On the principle that the righteous are scarcely saved, and yet they are abundantly saved, when we fail by refusing the grace of God we fail miserably, and when we succeed by obtaining His grace we succeed gloriously. There is, indeed, a twilight zone between outbroken sin and the fullness of grace, where the appeal of the world is still strong and yet the call of God is more or less effective. But that zone should be crossed, not made a place of permanent dwelling.

Division of a subject sometimes helps us in grasping it, so let us think of conduct in three parts: in our relationship to ourselves, in our relationship to others of mankind, and in our relationship to God. Then we shall have a summary in Titus 2:11-12, where it is said "the grace of God" teaches us to "deny . . . ungodliness and worldly lusts," and that "we should live soberly, righteously, and godly, in this present world." To "deny" ungodliness and worldly lusts means to turn away from them, to forsake them, to refuse to indulge in them. "Ungodliness" is a word describing wicked conduct, and "worldly lusts" a term describing unholy thinking and desires. To deny these is to become outwardly and inwardly good in the negative sense. It involves harmlessness. It describes the passive virtues.

But holiness is more than negative goodness. It is positive goodness also. Taken apart, the statement is that we are to live soberly toward *ourselves*, righteously toward our *neighbors*, and godly toward our *Heavenly Father.*

Sobriety is just another word for temperance. Temperance, in turn, is defined as *self-control.* To live by this rule is to refuse tangents.

ETHICS To govern the temper and the will. To think soundly. To speak gently. To eat and sleep and work with neither sloth nor excess. To check the inner conscience sincerely. To face one's limitations faithfully. To speak the truth in word and in heart. To speak no ill of his neighbor. To neither minimize nor exaggerate. To be transparent before the bar of God and one's own moral judgment. To testify faithfully. And to pray unpretentiously.

To live righteously toward our neighbor is to be clean in our social relations. To be honest in our business relations. To be truthful in our communications. To be fair in our judgment of the

PERFECT LOVE deeds, words, and motives of others. The righteous man is a faithful friend, a good husband, son, and brother, an agreeable neighbor, a helper of the needy, a forgiver of enemies, an upright citizen, a supporter of civic well-being, a careful taxpayer, an observer of law and order, and a doer of good deeds.

To live godly is to live in the fear and love of God. To be obedient to all His known will. To worship God *only,* according to the first

GODLY LIFE commandment; to worship Him *spiritually,* according to the second commandment; to worship Him *reverently,* according to the third commandment; to worship Him *statedly,* according to the fourth commandment. It is to worship with the hand by tithing the income and making gifts according to the ability which God giveth. It is to worship with the mind by reading God's Word and meditating upon His power, wisdom, and love. It is to worship Him with the heart by pouring out the heart in prayer, praise, and giving of thanks. It is to live always in the attitude of willingness to give up what you seem to possess and to receive whatever He may choose to give. To live godly is to live in gracious communion, fellowship, and agreement with God.

If any are struck with the thought that we cannot live godly because we are but finite and God is infinite, then let him remember that it is quality and likeness and not quantity and identity that are required. We can be like God in the sense that a drop of ocean water is like the ocean.

A visitor to a clock and watch exhibition saw there a clock so large that the dial was 52 feet across and the minute hand was 26 feet in length. Then there were smaller clocks ranging on down to hall clocks, mantel clocks, and table alarm clocks. Then there were large, heavy watches, smaller gentlemen's watches, large-sized ladies' watches, wristwatches, and on down to one with a dial so tiny that one could not see the position of the hands except by use of a magnifying glass. But all the clocks and watches, great and small, were good timekeepers, and were kept regulated and set by experts, so that they were in perfect agreement. When the big clock up at the head of the line said, "Twelve o'clock," and the clocks and watches along the line said, "Twelve o'clock," the little, tiny one at the very foot spoke up in unison with the others and said, "Twelve o'clock." The little watch was not the big clock, but it was in perfect accord with it. And it is in something of that sense that we can be godly "in this present world." For our present purpose it is superfluous to add those final words, for it is in this sense only that we can be godly even in heaven. And it is to the glory of His grace that God can so save and keep us that we can live truly godly right here, where Satan is loosed and temptation is rife—and that we can live so all the days of our lives (Luke 1:73-75).

IX. Holiness and Evangelism

If you would be a soul winner, seek and obtain a holy heart and then walk in the light of the true Spirit-filled life.

Holiness implies separation from the world, and yet it does not imply the canceling of our debt to the world. We are yet in the world, even though we are no longer of the world. Jesus described His disciples as "the salt of the earth" (Matt. 5:13), and salt is worthless if it is isolated. It must be brought into contact with that which it preserves.

Likewise those who withdraw from the company of men and live in monasteries or in social seclusion have little value as evangelizing agents. Personal separation from the world must be consistent with the Master's command, "Go ye into all the world, . . . and make disciples" (Mark 16:15; Matt. 28:19, marg.).

In Rev. 2:14, "the doctrine of Balaam" is roundly condemned. By reference to the Old Testament account of this prophet's activities and counsels we find that his doctrine was "evangelism by mixing." Balak could not win over Israel in out-and-out conflict, so Balaam said, "Go along and intermarry with these people and win over them by absorbing them." The results were disastrous, not to the heathen, but to the people of God. And yet there are those who still think the way to save the world is for the Church to become worldly. But when the world and the Church mix, it is the world that captures the Church and not the Church that captures the world.

How then can men be holy and still be saving agencies in a sinful world? The answer is that they must be *insulated* but not *isolated*. Our Master's example is in point. He was holy, harmless, and undefiled, and even His enemies reported they found no fault in Him. Yet He met

CHRIST'S
EXAMPLE

them on the streets, in the markets, in their homes, and at their own tables. It is true that some criticized Him as being the Friend of sinners, but He accepted this as a compliment and adopted this as one of His favorite roles. Ordinarily to touch a leper was to become defiled, but when Jesus touched a leper the leper was cleansed. And this is the key to the whole matter. The *healing* touch does not defile. But the *agreeing* touch does defile. And everyone must keep his own soul from the saturating effect of sin and worldliness by keeping alive the inner protest against all that is wrong. Still he must limit his touch only at that point where healing and agreeing meet. It is an honor to eat with publicans and sinners when to do so is to heal and save them, and every man must know and observe his own limits, not to be overcome of evil, even in the sense of prevailing influence, but to overcome evil with good.

Dilution almost always means weakness, and strength practically always requires concentration. This is true whether the subject is a state, a home, a church, or an individual life. Men who are known too well as "good mixers" are seldom also effective soul winners. The nucleus of the individual life must be kept pure if the impact of evangelism is to be effective. We must ourselves be thoroughly evangelized before we can succeed markedly in evangelizing others. Men readily become exercised over the subject of widening their scope of influence, whereas the greater need is to wield an effective influence. When the choice is between influencing many people a little or influencing a few people much, the instant choice should be the latter. Bringing people near to the kingdom of God is not enough; we must bring them in and introduce them to the King.

The principle of soul winning is divinely inherent in all truly born-again people, although the method by which the lost are sought and found varies as much as the number of Christians in the world. The principle is indicated by that early desire to see one's loved ones and friends brought to Christ. One of the first and best evidences of conversion is the desire to see others converted. But it is always a bad thing to be stirred and then do nothing about the stirring. If one does something about it, the stirring will increase until soul winning becomes a passion. And there is nothing more fundamental in the whole task of evangelism than that of burden for the salvation of souls. If that burden is real and heavy, ways and means will be found. And nothing encourages a burden for others more than getting genuinely through for yourself. Holiness of heart is therefore a great boon for soul winners.

The description of a soul winner requires but a few lines: "For he was a good man, and full of the Holy Ghost and of faith: and much people was added unto the Lord" (Acts 11:24). It is as though the cause and the effect were stated. Nothing is said of the pedigree, breeding, education, gifts, or talents of Barnabas, for such things do not enter into the qualifications of soul winners. He was simply a man in the fullness of the blessing of Pentecostal sanctification and, as the oasis gathers about the palm tree, souls followed him into the kingdom of God. There is no indication of strain or effort. He had the blessing and followed the leadings of the Lord, and his work was fruitful.

Dr. A. M. Hills wrote that during four years in college, it being known that he planned to be a preacher, and three years in the theological seminary, although he was told many things that **PREACHING** would help him in the pursuit of his calling, he was never told the simple thing that the baptism with the Holy Ghost is the one indispensable qualification for success in the divine art of soul winning. Much of the intellectual training given to divinity students and those preparing for Christian work has almost as little direct connection with the task to which the students are called as a course in gymnastics would have. For the task is not primarily intellectual but spiritual, and the greatest need is not a full mind but a full heart.

But even if the expressional life in the business of soul winning is to be considered, the great need here is for the anointing of the Spirit upon song, prayer, testimony, and sermon. Even personal evangelism makes heavier demand for immediate inspiration and direction than for knowledge in psychology and sociology. If you would be a soul winner, seek and obtain a holy heart and then walk in the light of the true Spirit-filled life. This is the apostolic way.

X. Holiness and Practical Living

What we all need most is grace to live the common life in an uncommon manner.

No child has any choice regarding his parentage or the place and condition of his birth. So far as the child's responsibility goes, all these things are accidental. There is not much the child can do about the general course of his life during his minor years. At a very early age he can give his heart to God and be saved and sanctified wholly, but in working out his life he is subjected to the conditions around him, even as our blessed Lord was subject to His earthly parents during His minor years. In Christian lands it is unusual to find parents who are unwilling for their children to live the Christian life, even though they may not share fully the children's practical judgment of what is best and wisest.

There are instances, however, in which it becomes necessary for even a young child to bring to bear the full meaning of the scriptural admonition to obey his parents only "in the Lord" (Eph. 6:1). Should a parent insist that a minor child use liquor or tobacco, attend places of worldly amusement that are clearly ungodly, engage in dishonest dealings of any kind, or enter into associations that the child believes firmly are injurious to the soul, the minor child must choose to suffer affliction with the people of God and keep himself within the bounds of his own good conscience. Any demand for choice or action that is in violation of the Ten Commandments or the well-established principles of Christian conduct must be resisted, even though such resistance may lead to punishment, disinheritance, and even banishment.

When the years of responsibility come along, questions like the choice of company, matrimony, vocation, education, and even the place of one's abode should be taken to the Lord in earnest prayer for divine guidance, and in the fullest confidence that God does know and care and will find a way by His providences, His Holy Word, and the Holy Spirit to direct the course of any who are willing to listen diligently to His voice.

SPIRIT GUIDANCE

As a young sanctified Christian I found great help in *Impressions*, a book by Martin Wells Knapp. From this book I learned that in important matters one should not be hasty in his conclusions and should insist on having "two or three witnesses." That is, the providences of God may determine us in many simple things like eating, drinking, sleeping, and the hours of labor. The Word of God, the Bible, is sufficient guide for actions like purity, honesty, veracity, and industry. The inner impressions of the Holy Spirit are enough to direct us in prayer, testimony, and other such matters. But in such matters as matrimony there should be agreement of two or all three of these methods of guidance before we are satisfied. "Impressions," Mr. Knapp said, "may come from our own desires, from the devil, or from the Holy Spirit, and we need always to keep the Word of God before us and to remember that always the Spirit and the Word agree, and that the Holy Spirit will not lead us to do anything that is contrary to the Word—the Bible."

The majority of people do not have great, romantic experiences in life. Their course leads over a more or less undulating plain. Every day is much like every other day. The necessities of economic life drive them to their hours of labor and of rest. Their occupation brings them the large percentage of contacts with others, and hence their opportunities for doing good. And this is equivalent to saying that what we all need most is grace to live the common life in an uncommon manner. We need wisdom to see God in the circumstances of everyday life, and we need grace to do faithfully the myriad of little things which seem to have no particular connection with our religious profession. To be patient where others would become irritable, to be cheerful where others would be possessed of fear, to be kind when others would be resentful, to be pure when others would break under temptation, to reject all price offered for doing wrong, to just exemplify the spirit of the Master in the common places among common people— this, to the great majority of us, is real victory.

It is our common obligation to "attend the means of grace," such

as family and secret prayer, the services of the church, and as many of the gatherings of the people of God as we can profitably afford. It is our obligation, without exception, to maintain a standard of conduct and conversation that will commend the profession we make,
ETHICS
and make it clear to all that we are conscious always that God sees and knows and cares and that we are responsible to Him now and at the judgment and in eternity. Excessive talk and unguarded levity are twin enemies of true spirituality, and carelessness about keeping one's word even in small matters, and about meeting his bills or meeting his financial obligations, will limit, if not actually destroy, the value of a Christian professor's influence.

We are all commissioned of our Lord to evangelize our neighbors and to send the gospel to the uttermost part of the earth. Some are called personally to devote their lives to the public ministry or to some form of Christian service which within itself becomes a vocation. But those who are not so called are yet commissioned to do the same work in a different manner, that is, by supporting with influence, prayers, and money.

In matters of money and goods, Christians are differentiated from pagans in this: Pagans account themselves owners of what they possess, while Christians know and confess themselves to be stewards only—God is Owner of all. Money is a great means of doing good when properly used. But when improperly used it is a snare and a curse. From the days of Abraham, and long before the Old Testament law was promulgated, good men found the tithing plan a useful guide in making acknowledgment of their stewardship of money and goods, and that plan and principle has never been abrogated. The systematic, faithful tither is assured of a good conscience in prosperity or adversity, and this together with a spirit of liberality enables him to share with those who go, and to feel and know that he is a faithful steward of the gospel, as well as of the money and goods with which he is entrusted.

XI. Holiness and the Second Coming

Holiness of heart and life are the only qualifications for meeting Jesus in joy at His second advent.

The Scriptures abound in threats to the world and promises to the Church that Jesus Christ will come back to the world the second time. The hope of the world is in the salvation which Jesus provided by His first coming into the world. The hope of the Church is in the second coming of Christ. This distinction is fundamental. It is no more valid to preach that the second coming of Christ is the hope of everyone than it is to preach universal salvation. When Christ comes the second time He will bring no offering for sin. His coming is more directly connected with judgment than with mercy. There are, of course, blendings of mercy and judgment in connection with His appearing, but starting with what we have now, the changes that are made are all in the direction of judgment, and of decreased mercy.

The prophecies of Christ's second coming constitute a very interesting study, but they are no more saving in their force than the study of the history of the past would be. In fact, prophecy is a miracle of knowledge, comparable to the miracles of power manifest during the days of Christ's earthly ministry. Prophecy is in reality just history written in advance. Prophecy is not a cause. Therefore we are not to suppose that God wills a thing just because His prophets have foretold its occurrence. And we are not to suppose that the mere knowledge that things are coming is preparation for their coming. One may be an apt and accomplished student of prophecy and still be spiritually unprepared for the issue which he has discerned is about to occur.

We all know that we are "born to die," and that unless we are translated by the coming of Christ we shall die, as all except two—Enoch and Elijah—who have lived in the generations of the past have done. But this common knowledge does not prepare us for death and the life beyond death.

It is folly for us to talk of the second coming of Christ as our hope and prospect unless we gladly and fully accept the full benefits provided for us in His first appearing in the world. And in that first appearing, including His life, ministry, death, and resurrection, He provided a complete solution for the sin problem and a full cure for the disease of sin. "Thou shalt call his name JESUS: for he shall save his people from their sins" (Matt. 1:21). "If we confess our sins, he is faithful and just to forgive us our sins, and to cleanse us from all unrighteousness" (1 John 1:9). "Wherefore Jesus also, that he might sanctify the people with his own blood, suffered without the gate" (Heb. 13:12). "The law of the Spirit of life in Christ Jesus hath made me free from the law of sin and death" (Rom. 8:2). What more could be promised? What addition could be made? The Blood was shed in this world and it is available now. If it cannot make an end of sin in us now, it can never do it, unless we are ready to admit that death or purgatory or some other real or imaginary thing is to assist God in doing the difficult thing of ridding His people of sin.

Jesus made the principal call to preparedness for His coming, "Therefore be ye also ready: for in such an hour as ye think not the Son of man cometh" (Matt. 24:44). And to be ready is to be "blessed and holy" (Rev. 20:6), that is, regenerated and sanctified. Holiness of heart and life are the only qualifications for meeting Jesus in joy at His second advent. Surely no one can deny this. But if these are the qualifications and we are to be ready always, then this is evident: We must get the blessing of a clean, holy heart and keep it continually and live out its implications in everyday contacts and conduct. To say that we will be given holiness at the appearing of the Lord is entirely gratuitous, just as is the claim that there will be further opportunity to repent after death. "Behold, what manner of love the Father hath bestowed upon us, that we should be called the sons of God: therefore the world knoweth us not, because it knew him not. Beloved, now are we the sons of God, and it doth not yet appear what we shall be: but we know that, when he shall appear, we shall be like him; for we shall see him as he is" (1 John 3:1-2).

Now if this were the end of the passage we might suppose that being "like him" means being cleansed from sin at His coming. But the third verse is in direct connection and refers to a present accomplishment: "And every man that hath this hope in him purifieth himself, even as he is pure." The hope of seeing Christ as He is and of being in a glorified body and in a glorified world as He is has this practical effect upon all who possess it: they at once apply themselves to the conditions for being made pure from sin, for sin is the one thing that will keep one from entering into that happy state. The claims of those who say they are hoping for His soon coming are validated only by their pressing immediately into the grace of holiness of heart and then by their living holy lives from there on out to the end.

The Church, that is, the Body of true believers who welcome Christ at His second advent, is, according to John of Revelation, like a pure bride adorned in pure, clean, white linen. And for such a Church, Jesus is said to have given himself, "that he might sanctify and cleanse it with the washing of water by the word, that he might present it to himself a glorious church, not having spot, or wrinkle, or any such thing; but that it should be holy and without blemish" (Eph. 5:25-27).

Jesus Christ is coming back to the world in glory and power. The signs of the times indicate that His coming draweth nigh. To many thoughtful observers, it appears that Jesus could come now at any time and do no violence to the prophecies which set forth the conditions that will prevail upon the earth and in the Church when He appears. But the important questions are, Are you ready? Do you have on the wedding garment of Bible holiness? Is your heart clean from all outward and inbred sin? Does the Holy Spirit possess and rule your heart completely? Are you sanctified wholly just now?

XII. A Holiness Catechism

Q. *What do we understand to be the import of holiness as taught in the Bible and set forth in the testimony of thousands who say they are sanctified wholly?*

A. We understand that holiness is that state of the heart which results from receiving the baptism with the Holy Ghost and fire. The full meaning of this blessed experience cannot be described by one word, and so in the Bible and in Christian literature and hymnology **NAMES** we are supplied with a number of words which are more or less synonymous, and yet which serve to present a more complete picture of what the Christian enjoys who has entered into the full inheritance of the gospel. The doctrine of holiness is taught in the Bible. The standard of holiness is the standard for all God's people. The experience of holiness is the full blessing or grace of the gospel which is God's answer to our human need. The process[2] by which we are made holy is called sanctification. The result of being sanctified is called holiness. But from various angles of approach the experience is described as Christian perfection, perfect love, heart purity, and the Spirit-filled life.

Q. *What are the prerequisites of this experience?*

A. To be a proper candidate for this experience one must be definite in his experience as a justified, born-again Christian. The grace of holiness is not directly promised to the world, as we learn from the prayer of our Lord in the 17th chapter of John, but is reserved for those who have forsaken the world and been made alive

---

2. Dr. Chapman was apparently using the term *process* here in a broader sense to mean the experience or procedure in contrast to the results of the experience. He would be in full agreement that God gives the blessing of entire sanctification as a crisis experience, in a moment of time. See his discussion "Holiness Differentiated," pp. 77-79, also his statement under "The Terminology of the Christian Estate," pp. 102-3.

from the death of sin by the regenerating Spirit of God. One who has not been truly converted, or who has drifted into backslidings after having been saved, must seek and obtain the pardoning mercy of God, that he may be numbered among those who "are not of the world," to whom the promise of full salvation is made.

Q. *Why do not people get sanctified wholly at the same time that they get converted or regenerated?*

A. I think we will have to say there are no limitations on God's part. But we know from the Scriptures and from experience that practically all the promises of God are on conditions. Sometimes the conditions are clearly stated; sometimes they are just implied—but we can be sure they always exist. And because there are certain conditions required of those who seek to get sanctified which they cannot meet until they are justified, therefore sanctification invariably comes after justification. For example, to get sanctified wholly it is required of one that he consecrate himself fully to the Lord. But a sinner cannot consecrate until he has repented of his sins, and if he truly repents of his sins and believes on Christ he will be pardoned and born again. And because the conditions are essential to faith for the blessing, it follows without exception that sanctification is subsequent to justification. We do well to remember the old adage, "Man's extremity is God's opportunity," and to think of it in connection with the desire to be sanctified. God takes up where we of necessity leave off. This means that God does not sanctify until we consecrate. In fact, consecration is human sanctification.

But we must not suppose that consecration is all there is of sanctification any more than we suppose that repentance is all there is of justification. In fact there is danger always of interpreting Christianity as entirely human. Some people are so afraid of becoming extremists that they really become humanists and make bold to say that they question the divine response altogether. But such an interpretation demotes Christianity to the level of Pharisaism. There is a divine response to the believing penitent. And this response comes in the form of the clear witness of the Holy Spirit to the sonship of the born-again soul. Likewise there is a divine response to the Christian who prays to be entirely sanctified, and that response is in the form of the fullness of the Spirit, comparable to that which took place in the hearts of those who tarried in Jerusalem for the promise of the Father, which promise was fulfilled on the Day of Pentecost, as recorded in the second chapter of the Acts of the Apostles.

Those who say they have had "a thousand blessings," and therefore do not believe in the "second blessing," are unnecessarily confusing the issue. There are indeed blessings without number in the Christian life, but there are just two "works of grace" involved in the solution of the sin problem for the individual. The first of these works of grace is the one by means of which the sinner becomes a Christian, and the second is the one by which a Christian becomes a sanctified Christian. The first work is called justification and the second is called sanctification. The first experience is called being born of the Spirit, and the second is called being baptized with the Spirit. But all types and metaphors, as well as all direct statements, show that men must be justified before they are sanctified. For instance, one cannot by any stretch of imagination think of a baptism that is not preceded by a birth.

SECOND BLESSING

Q. *How do we know about this blessing of holiness, and about the conditions upon which it may be obtained?*

A. The Bible is our principal Source for knowledge on this subject, and Jesus made reference to this dependable Source of light when He said in His prayer, "Sanctify them through thy truth: thy word is truth" (John 17:17). The Bible requires holiness in its commandments: "Be ye holy; for I am holy" (1 Pet. 1:16). It offers it in its promises, "The very God of peace sanctify you wholly; and . . . [preserve you] blameless unto the coming of our Lord Jesus Christ" (1 Thess. 5:23). It tells how holiness is provided in the atoning work of Jesus Christ: "Wherefore Jesus also, that he might sanctify the people with his own blood, suffered without the gate" (Heb. 13:12).

SCRIPTURAL

And there are numerous testimonies recorded of those who obtained this grace from God. Surely no one will dispute that to be a Bible Christian one must be holy without and within. But most of us have also been fortunate enough to know some people who have this blessing and live the life. I have been thus favored myself, and for this I am devoutly thankful. Those who claim that they never knew anyone that they thought had the blessing are more likely than not speaking from their own prejudices rather than from the reasonable deductions of experience and observation.

And then there is within us all a deep sense of need that never finds satisfaction until we find it in the fullness of the blessing of the gospel. But whatever else we may doubt, we cannot deny the Scriptures, and from these we learn that we should be holy, and the terms upon which the blessing may be obtained.

Q. *What merit do we have to bring that God may see it and make us holy within?*

A. We have no merit except the blood of Jesus Christ, and we

ATONEMENT need no other than this. Men have often been led astray by the supposition that they must be good in order to be made good. To the sinner we have often said, "All the fitness Christ requires is to feel your need of Him." Likewise with the Christian who would be sanctified wholly. Good pedigrees, good works, and meritorious words do not count. "The Blood, the Blood is all my plea." This is what is meant when it is said we are sanctified by the Blood. That is, it is the merit of the blood of Jesus which enables us to come in faith and confidence for the blessing.

Q. *What are the conditions for obtaining the blessing of holiness?*

A. There is just one prime condition, as in justification, and that condition is faith. We must come believing He is able to save to the

FAITH uttermost, that He is willing to save to the uttermost, and finally (having fully consecrated ourselves to Him), that He does now save to the uttermost and at this moment does make us clean and holy within. In coming to the place where such faith is possible, we may find a good many prerequisites, like consecration with all that it involves; but when these are all finally met, the prime condition is faith. No one who believes ever fails to get the blessing, and no one ever gets the blessing without believing. Sometimes people have said they will not believe until they know. But this is confusing. Faith is like the cable over which the electric current comes, in that it makes the way for God's blessing to be received. We must believe that we may know.

Q. *When may we have this blessing of holiness?*

A. It is promised to us right here in this world. We may have it anytime after we are converted—anytime we are willing and ready to

NOW IS THE TIME pay the price. Some people get this blessing very soon—just a matter of weeks, days, or even hours—after they are born again. Others, usually because of a fault in their doctrine and expectation, go on a long time—sometimes for many years—before they enter into this glorious grace. Some do not get it sooner because of the idea that if God wants them to have it He will give it to them without their seeking for it. But, although it is the will of God for all His people to be sanctified, still there is a preparation for receiving this blessing that can be and is met only by those who set their hearts to have it.

Q. *What is required of us after we obtain this blessing as to the manner of life we shall pursue?*

A. It is required of sanctified Christians that they live in all good conscience before God and men. This means that holiness and righ-

ETHICS teousness—holiness with God and righteousness with men— are inseparably connected. We are not made right by doing right, but we do right when we are made right. And we are not made holy by living holily, but we do live holily, having been made holy by the Spirit of God. But this is not to be interpreted as implying that the life of holiness is a strain. The fact is that sin is the irritation. Holiness is soul health and the holy life for a holy man is the normal life for such a man. Since he loves God supremely, he will find prayer and Bible reading and all worship a joy and a delight. Since he loves his neighbors as himself, he will delight to live in peace with them. He will even find joy in serving them. That interpretation of the Christian life which describes it as "a hard road to travel," as compared with other roads, is based upon the assumption that there is want of grace.

But in the sanctified life there is abundance of grace. Sanctified Christians are no better and no different from other people, just so far as natural goodness is concerned. They are also required to live under the same general conditions that others of their vicinity must face. The difference is on the inside. The burdens of the sanctified are just as heavy as the burdens of others, but they are spiritually stronger to bear them. The standard for all men, good and bad, is the standard of holiness. Sinners fall short of this standard, but this does not affect the standard. Justified Christians find the standard often irksome and impractical, but this does not affect the standard. Sanctified Christians

GRACE find grace to enable them to delight in the will and ways of God, and to say, "His commandments are not grievous" (1 John 5:3). In seeking an easier way in the Christian life, some have thought to bring the standard of requirements down to the place where they practically say, "Whatever is, is right." But this is not God's way. He would bring our lives up to the standard and even keep us where we "are not under the law, but under grace" (Rom. 6:14)—and this means that we do God's will because we love Him, and not because of our being driven by fear of judgment.

Q. *If once we get the blessing of holiness, is there any danger that we shall lose it?*

A. Our whole life in this world is a probation or trial life, and the issue is not settled until death. It is wise for us all to listen to Paul who said, "Let him that thinketh he standeth take heed lest he fall" (1 Cor. 10:12). We need to watch and pray and to guard our hearts and lips and lives always. We must always court the Comforter, that He may be pleased to abide with us. We need always to take full advantage of all "means of grace," that we may be strong enough to be overcomers all the days of our lives. Yes, there is always danger that we may fall back into sin, and we must not slacken our vigil until either Jesus comes the second time or calls us home unto himself.

Q. *If we should be overcome of the devil and should yield to temptation after we have obtained the blessing of holiness, and should find ourselves again separated from God, can we be restored to the fullness of the blessing again?*

A. Backsliding in any degree is always a sad thing to contemplate. It is well that we should go on with God from day to day without allowing our peace to be broken with anxious fears. God is able to keep us always, and from the day we are pardoned from sin until the day when we shall see His face in heaven, it is God's plan that we shall be victorious. But there is pardon and restoration for the backslider; and if one should make a mistake by yielding to temptation, he should certainly not follow this with the worse mistake of casting away his confidence and become a hopeless apostate. Yes, there is always pardon for the truly penitent, and there is restoration to the fullness of the blessing for one who has drifted in any degree whatsoever. Just as no state of grace which we can obtain in this world can make us absolutely proof against backsliding, so likewise there is no sin, except the sin against the Holy Ghost, that can bar us from God forever, if we are willing and ready to repent. There are many testimonies of those who fell from the heights of grace to the low pits of sin and then came back again to as good an experience in the favor of God as they had at the beginning, and even better.

Q. *Is this blessing of holiness for all Christians?*

A. Yes, it is for all—ministers, missionaries, laymen, adults, and little children. Anyone who has been born again of the Spirit of God, and who desires to be sanctified wholly, may come in the full assurance that God will not deny his prayer or practice any reluctance in fulfilling to him the promise to make him every whit whole. Many people have an exaggerated idea of the force of chronology or geography. They scruple not to say that the baptism with the Holy Ghost was just for the apostles. Or if they allow for any closer approach to our own time than that, they say this is just

FOR ALL CHRISTIANS

for those who are called of God to some very special service. But the promise of God is without any such limitations. On the Day of Pentecost, Peter said, "The promise is unto you, and to your children, and to all that are afar off, even as many as the Lord our God shall call" (Acts 2:39). We all need to be holy, no matter what the service we are expected to perform. Sometimes the grace of holiness is as much needed by one whose lot it is to be neglected and overlooked as for one whose place is in the limelight. Humility is as much a fruit of holiness as fluency of tongue or any gift whereby men are made to wonder.

Q. *Why should we be so urgent about this matter of holiness of heart and life?*

A. We should be eager to get sanctified wholly because God is eager to have us so. That word "follow" in Heb. 12:14 is a very strong word. The metaphor back of it is the practice of the good **NOW IS** hunting dog which brooks all dangers and endures all hard- **THE TIME** ships to overtake and apprehend the game. We know not the day of Christ's coming or of our own departure from the world of probation. All we know is that today is the day of salvation. We know only that the present opportunity is ours. Tomorrow belongs to God. Delay in seeking to be made holy may easily come to disobedience, and may result in the complete dimming of our spiritual vision. Today is the day of full salvation for the believer, just as it is the day of initial salvation for the penitent sinner. Today if you hear His voice calling you to holiness, delay not to obey.

The Terminology of Holiness

In this series of lectures Dr. Chapman dealt with the question of how we can best communicate our faith in God's plan of entire sanctification for believers. The author's own preface clearly describes his plan and point of view.

PREFACE[3]

The material contained in this book was prepared for delivery in the Nease Lectures at Pasadena College [now Point Loma Nazarene College] and in the Gould Lectures at Eastern Nazarene College. The purpose of the lectures was not to convince anyone of the truth of the

---

3. *The Terminology of Holiness,* 5-6.

Wesleyan interpretation of the theme of Bible holiness but rather to offer assistance to those who hold this doctrine in the matter of describing it as accurately and fairly as possible. The plan was to say what we as a people believe in terms that we ourselves use, and by repetition and explanation help ourselves to use these terms more intelligently, and thereby make ourselves better understood by those who do not hold with us on this central thesis of our doctrinal interpretation of the Christian faith. . . .

We have . . . not made a strong contention for words, although words are involved in the title and subtitles of our subject matter. We have sought rather to confirm the general understanding of accepted terminology which has been used by those who in the past have testified of the grace of God in Christ Jesus to the full deliverance from sin; for it is because of misunderstanding of the import of these words that much of the opposition to the Wesleyan interpretation of Bible holiness has arisen.

Nothing that we have said, however, is intended to suggest any change in the concepts of the fathers of the Holiness Movement of the past. They said what they believed and felt in words that were forceful and true. And there is a surprising uniformity of vocabulary among them, even though they came from many and varied historical communions of the Protestant division of the church. It is ourselves of the present who need to be instructed rather than the fathers who require to be corrected. When it is said that "we need a new holiness vocabulary," the meaning is that we need to have the vocabulary of the fathers revitalized in our own thinking and feeling; for the fathers found their vocabulary a splendid vehicle for the purpose they had in mind.

Words have pedigree, even as men have ancestry. But the meaning of a word involves much more than etymology. The important question is, What do these words mean to the speaker, and what do they mean to the hearers? If they mean one thing to the speaker and another thing to the hearers, they fail of their purpose of being a means for the communication of thought. Either the speaker should learn new words or else he should explain his old words—he cannot expect his hearers to do either of these things.

The Terminology of the Christian Estate[4]

In the promotion of Bible holiness it has been necessary to lay

---

4. Ibid., rev. ed., 1968, chap. 5.

stress on the crises of regeneration and entire sanctification, for these crises are the essentials of the beginnings of spiritual life and of holiness in the heart. There are just the two crises, no more, no less, essential in the attainment of the blessed estate which is designated the "inheritance among them which are sanctified" (Acts 26:18), and which is the goal of grace for the people of God in this world. Regeneration and justification give us the right to fellowship with God here and in heaven above; sanctification gives us preparation for these blessed privileges.

It must not be supposed, however, that the crises of regeneration and sanctification, having been passed as crises, are to remain only in the form of fond recollections. The grace of God bestowed in the crises makes permanent changes and introduces us into a new and blessed estate, an estate that is to be continuous both in confidence and in consciousness.

In the chapter on "Christian Purity," in his book *Purity and Maturity,* Dr. J. A. Wood says:

> Purity is a state or quality of being. It is the inversion of our sinful moral nature—freedom "from all filthiness of flesh and spirit." It does not consist so much in a repetition of good acts, as in a moral condition of the soul from which all good actions proceed; as depravity, or inbred sin, does not consist so much in vicious acts or habits, as in a state or quality which occasions those acts or habits.[5] . . .

Dr. Asbury Lowrey, in *Positive Theology,* says:

> Entire holiness is the extermination of all sin from the soul. It is a pure, unsullied heart; it is "death to sin," a "freedom from sin," a "cleansing from all filthiness of the flesh and spirit." The fountain of thought, affection, desire, and impulse is pure.[6]

Holiness

These quotations are given as tokens of the many which are available, to show that the term holiness is used to describe the estate of those who are entirely sanctified. One has said that "holiness is sanctification perpetuated." It is the word by which the estate of those from whose hearts inbred sin has been destroyed and eradicated by

---

5. *Purity and Maturity,* 23-24.
6. *Positive Theology,* 241.

the sanctifying agency of the Holy Spirit is described. The word holi-

WHOLENESS ness is a synonym for wholeness—for soul health—and is perhaps the clearest of all expressions used in this connection. It is perhaps for this reason that the term holiness has com-
monly drawn the hottest fire from opposers of the grace for which it
stands. Some have opposed because of a misunderstanding of the
term. But many have opposed because they do understand it, and their
opposition is not to the word only, but to the testimony for which it
stands.

While, strictly speaking, the term holiness emphasizes the negative phase—freedom from sin—the term perfection being rather a
necessary complement, it is in ordinary use a description of all that
is implied by the grace and blessings its possession involves. The fact is

HOLY SPIRIT that no one can be just negatively holy. If holy at all, one is made so initially by the agency and incoming of the Holy Spirit,
and is kept so by the administrative work of the Spirit, who
continually sheds abroad the love of God in the heart. He who is
emptied of sin is also filled with love and with the Holy Spirit.

The testimony to holiness should always be given in such form as

WITNESS to give full credit to Christ, and not to bolster our human side of the matter. It is exceedingly unwise for anyone to use
the form, "I am holy." Rather, the form should be, "The Lord gra-
ciously sanctifies my heart." And whatever the term used, the same
order should be observed in giving God the glory. It is a rather curious
inconsistency that many who draw back from the testimony, even
when given by others, to the effect that God has sanctified and
cleansed from all sin do not scruple to say they are fully consecrated
to the will of God. And yet, come to think of it, the latter claim is the
extolling of a human act or virtue, while the former is making one's
boast in the Lord. But the same bent has been observed also regarding
all profession—the world and worldly people honor claims of human
endeavor to be good, but look askance upon one who claims to have
been inwardly transformed by regenerating grace. If therefore the definite tesitmony to initial salvation is cause for stumbling on the part of
those who have not been born again, we should not be surprised that
the profession of full salvation should appear to be incredulous to
those who have not themselves entered therein. And yet, in both cases,
it is the obligation of the redeemed of the Lord to say so; for while
some may be offended by definite testimony, some will be benefited.
But indefinite testimony neither offends nor benefits.

The desire to be spared classification with "holiness people" is historic. There have been and are now many who enjoy the estate of holiness who are not identified by the term holiness. But our concern is for a terminology that will be useful to those who desire to be identified and who strive to let their joy be known. And for such a purpose we commend the term holiness ("sanctification perpetuated") as perhaps the most suited of all. Any who will turn to the blessed Book will find that, far from avoiding the word, the men of the Bible and the blessed Lord himself loved to use the term holiness in describing both obligation and privilege in the truth and grace of God.

Perfect Love

After holiness, perfect love is perhaps the most useful of the terms by which to describe the estate of the entirely sanctified. This was a favorite term with John Wesley. His opposers compelled Wesley to come to the defense of the term perfection, but there is evidence that this was not his choice.

The term perfect love is scriptural, and while involving a high profession, is also becoming in modesty. It indicates much grace, but makes no claim to either superior light or outstanding advancement in growth and maturity. It is a definite and limited term—qualities highly desirable for the purpose at hand. It is definite because it indicates the absence of anything contrary to love, and limited because it describes affections and intentions only, and does not include judgment or conduct. It is just the equivalent of the "great commandment," which underlies all commandments, and which Jesus defined as loving God with all our hearts, and our neighbors as ourselves. Paul also gave the summary in epitome when he said, "Love is the fulfilling of the law," and, "The end of the commandment is [love] out of a pure heart" (Rom. 13:10; 1 Tim. 1:5).

An analysis of perfect love is found in 1 Corinthians 13, where also the relative importance of the grace is presented in comparison and in contrast. This chapter is a summary of the qualities and factors which make up the New Testament grace, just as the Sermon on the Mount is a statement of what the New Testament Christian should be both outwardly and inwardly. These two sections (the Sermon on the Mount and 1 Corinthians 13) must be taken together, if the picture of the New Testament estate is to be full and complete. While the one is the statement of requirement, the other is the summary of enablement.

In the old *Discipline of the Methodist Church* was the statement:

"No man can keep the commandments of God, except the grace of God prevent him." The word "prevent" was used here in the obsolete

GRACE sense, meaning "to go before." That is, no man can keep the commandments of God except the grace of God go before and prepare him to do so. Either intentionally or inadvertently, those who deny the possibility of perfect love as an experience also deny the possibility of keeping God's commandments in such a manner as to be well pleasing in His sight. And it must be admitted that it is consistent for one who denies the one of these to deny the other also. But when these two tenets of our holy faith are forsaken, Christ and the Christian system largely become the logical defenders and countenancers of sin rather than Savior and salvation from sin.

Wesley was always careful to make it plain that it is the grace of God alone, communicated to us by His Spirit, that enables us to love God with all our hearts, and our neighbors as ourselves. He made the ability so to love, the test (subjective as it must always be) of the possession of the grace. Thus the possessor himself is the only human being who can properly judge his estate. Others are dependent upon demonstration, which must contend with so many human and circumstantial factors that one is likely to stand, in the estimation of others, either better or worse than his real estate in the grace of God warrants.

However, it is consistent for one who has the realization in his heart to profess openly that the grace of God enables him to love God

WITNESSING with all his heart and his neighbor as himself. This is just as consistent as for one to profess initial grace upon the basis of the internal witness of the Spirit to his sonship and adoption. Such testimony is an indispensable factor and an effective force in the propagation of the doctrine and the promotion of the experience of holiness among the people of God. For unless there are those who consciously possess the grace, it profits little to preach the doctrine and exalt the ethics.

Christian Perfection

Christian perfection is a term synonymous with perfect love, and is so defined by authentic holiness teachers. Critics have called attention to the fact that the word Christian in this connection is a limitation, rather than an addition, and this we frankly admit. The word perfection standing alone is not unequivocal. It does sometimes mean Christian perfection, but it also sometimes includes the idea of growth and maturity, and sometimes reaches forth to resurrection perfection. The term therefore must be limited to be useful as a means of describing the estate of the entirely sanctified.

A flower, for example, may be said to be perfect at any state or stage of its life, if it is at that particular stage free from disease and as well developed as its age and circumstances of existence require. But there is another sense in which the plant is not perfect until the blossom is in full bloom. And that these two ideas are expressed by the term perfection in the Word of God and in Christian literature, no clear-thinking Christian will deny. In the Scriptures the context is always the explanation, so that it is seldom necessary to be in doubt which kind of perfection is intended. But in the terminology describing the estate of the entirely sanctified, it is necessary to use the word Christian as a limiting word—hence Christian perfection.

In the Christian sense persons are perfect when their affections and purposes are both pure. We are familiar with this idea in practical things. If a parent, in the endeavor to save the life of his sick child, should accidentally give his child deadly poison, no intelligent and fair-minded person would call him a murderer. On the other hand, if a vicious and wicked parent should give his sick child good medicine, when his intention was to give poison, that parent is a murderer, even though the courts of men are unable to place blame upon him by the force of testimony. In that deeper sense, one who loves God with all his heart and his neighbor as himself is a perfect Christian in that his motives and affections are holy, even though his conduct may not meet all the requirements of the highest ethical standards of his contemporaries. Such is the frailty of the "earthen vessels" of which Paul speaks.

But with these qualifying ideas in mind, the term Christian perfection serves our purpose of definition well. The perfect Christian is simply a sanctified Christian, and the sanctified Christian is one who loves God with all his heart and his neighbor as himself, being enabled to do this by the agency and indwelling of the Holy Spirit, who sheds this love abroad in the heart.

Holiness, perfect love, and Christian perfection are, therefore, the three terms in the first rank for describing the estate of those who have been regenerated and sanctified wholly. They can be used without equivocation or detailed explanation. And the order of the force of these words is, I think, just the order in which we have given them in this paragraph. There is no call for any diminishment in the use of these terms, and to forsake them in any degree is to lessen the force by which the facts which they imply are brought to bear upon the minds and consciences of men.

Other Terms

We come now to another class of terms, which, although useful to the purposes of variety and the pointing out of special characteristics, are yet not as fundamental and unequivocal as those already discussed. The list includes: "the Spirit-filled life," "the more abundant life," "the rest of faith," "full assurance of faith," "perfect peace," "fullness of joy," and "abiding grace."

The sanctified life is indeed a Spirit-filled life, and this term is applicable and useful in emphasizing the power and unction which are essential factors in the experience and life of holiness. Dr. A. M. Hills chose a fortunate title when he called one of his books *Holiness and Power.* Literalists have erred in positing a state of holiness which is like the house that was empty, "swept and garnished" (Luke 11:25). In truth, there is no such state that can in any wise be called a state of holiness. We are made holy by the baptism with the Holy Ghost—the incoming of the Spirit in Pentecostal fullness—and we are kept in a state of purity and holiness only by the Spirit's indwelling fullness. Analogies must be used with discretion, but, as we think of it, the Holy Spirit is the Guardian of our purity. If by any means He withdraws himself from us, sin breaks in, like water through the dike, and thus to be without the Spirit is also to be without holiness.

HOLY SPIRIT

It is an error to consider the term "Spirit-filled life" as anything other than a synonym of the sanctified life. To be filled with the Spirit is to be emptied of sin, and the means of our being emptied of sin is itself the infilling of the Spirit. So, then, whoever is sanctified wholly is filled with the Spirit, and whoever is filled with the Spirit is sanctified wholly. However, as pointed out in another instance, there is sometimes a distinction between being baptized with the Holy Spirit as the initial filling of the Spirit is properly called and being "filled with the Spirit" in the frequent outpourings which are mentioned in the Acts of the Apostles and known in the faithfully followed sanctified life. We protest any suggestion that the Holy Spirit can indwell a heart in His fullness without at the same time sanctifying that heart. Such an idea is a compromise that is indefensible.

Some have thought to escape the reproach of holiness profession by saying, "I do not claim simply to have the blessing; I also have the Blesser." Such a saying has no apostolic precedent and savors of sacrilege. It should be avoided. But Paul did say, "I am sure that, when I come unto you, I shall come in the fulness of the blessing of the gospel of Christ" (Rom. 15:29), and that does constitute a precedent for use of the term "the blessing" as a synonym for the grace of holiness.

"The more abundant life," as a term, is derived directly from the words of Jesus, "I am come that they might have life, and that they might have it more abundantly" (John 10:10). And while this presentation of the gift of life in two phases or degrees does quite clearly prefigure the first and second works of grace, it is not an exact equivalent of the sanctified estate. The sanctified life is the more abundant life as compared with the justified estate, but the word "abundant" is so great in scope and indefinite in limits as to make it possible for it to involve both time and eternity for its realization.

"The rest of faith" was a favorite term with A. B. Earle, a sound holiness preacher of the Baptist communion. He was able, during a long and faithful ministry, to lead many into the reality of the grace which he used this term to describe. "The rest of faith" which he emphasized was and is reached only when the Holy Spirit comes in response to faith and gives witness to the cleansing and infilling of the soul with love. Until this stage was reached, Earle and his coadjutors urged seeking Christians to "pray on," and "seek on," until the divine assurance should be given. The estate reached by obedience to this truly scriptural instruction was the grace and experience of holiness, and was so understood by those who applied to it the very wonderful term "the rest of faith." But the term better describes a special characteristic of the state and grace than it serves as a name for the grace itself.

It has been the practice all along to allow for certain provincialisms in the terminology of Bible holiness, as the preferences of people have suggested. Therefore people have used the term that best fitted their denominational experiences, home training, and other factors that served to give content to their words. We would not criticize, but rather commend this liberality; for in the process of giving content to special terminology the truth is preached, and the reality behind all terminology is made clear.

"Full assurance of faith," or "blessed assurance," as Fanny Crosby, the blind, singing saint, called it, is not much distinguished from "the rest of faith," as used by A. B. Earle. In fact, these are but varieties of the same term, and were current in much the same circles in the time of their greatest usefulness. There can be no doubt that Fanny Crosby had in mind the definite estate of the truly sanctified when she sang, "Blessed assurance, . . . born of His Spirit, washed in His blood," but others have followed her words and sentiment without fully discerning the definite meaning that was so clear to her.

"Perfect peace," "fullness of joy," and "abiding grace" are likewise terms that are useful to many, but they likewise describe certain characteristics of the grace of holiness rather than answer as definitions of the whole. For those who speak discriminatingly and with this understanding, these terms are proper and useful.

There are yet other terms by which this estate is designated, and for all these we rejoice. Like the glory of Solomon, so with this blessed grace, the half cannot be told. There are many who are helped by the various terms that make up the full salvation vocabulary, because the words bear special meaning in their own experiences.

Figurative Terminology

And now, in the third place, we come to a consideration of the figurative terminology of Bible holiness. All language is at best but a system of signs and symbols, and its effectiveness depends upon its usefulness in impressing pictures of reality upon the minds and hearts of those who read or hear. Figures are for illustration, not for proof, and for this reason the terminology of this division is not pressed unduly. But after the truth of God's Word is established by plain statement, the figures will be found to agree with and to illustrate the truth. It is never safe to found an important doctrine or to establish an important practice upon a type or figure, even though the figure be in the Word of God. For such doctrines and practices we have a right to expect the Bible to be plain and explicit. But having taken all the Bible says in this direct and explicit form, the types and shadows of the Bible and of Christian life and literature will be found useful for illustration and emphasis.

"Canaan" is the best-known figurative term used for describing the estate of the wholly sanctified. Canaan was the inheritance of God's ancient Hebrew people, and the transference of the idea to the Christian dispensation is natural and easy. There is close analogy between the ancient Hebrews and the Christians of today. Martin Wells Knapp wrote a book called *Out of Egypt into Canaan*, in which he traced these similarities. Egypt was found to be a type of sin and its bondage; Pharaoh was a type of Satan; making brick without straw stood for continuing in sin after the pleasure of sin has turned into bitterness; crossing the Red Sea was likened to spiritual regeneration; life in the wilderness, up to Kadesh Barnea, pictured the justified life in which there are "twelve wells of water" (a well for each month of the year), "threescore and ten palm trees" (a tree for each year of life on earth), "daily manna," and many other graces and blessings in the favor of God. Then the crossing of the river Jordan was found to be strikingly typical of dying out to sin and the world, and Canaan was a prefigure of the Christian's inheritance in perfect love. This general figurative picture has been pretty well adopted by teachers of Bible holiness, and there is uniformity of practice in allowing Canaan to stand for the "inheritance among them which are sanctified" (Acts 26:18).

The word Jordan means death,[7] and with many it stands for physical death. Canaan, of course, stands for heaven. But there are many difficulties to overcome in such a putting, since Canaan was yet a land of conflict and battles, even though it was designed to be a land of victory. "The city foursquare" which is the eternal home of the glorified does not partake of any of these limitations.

Christian literature, and especially Christian hymnology, abounds in references to Canaan as a spiritual experience to be possessed and enjoyed in this world. On the whole, the historic evidence favors this interpretation of the figure. Christians generally sing of Canaan as they extol the joy and peace of full assurance and fellowship with God— such an estate being clearly the blessed lot of the fully sanctified.

[In the early 20th century I. G. Martin wrote a song often sung in holiness meetings, titled "Out of Egypt into Canaan":

> *When I fled from Egypt's bondage*
> *And crossed the raging sea,*
> *I heard about a country*
> *That was prepared for me.*
> *Some said they'd seen its mountains,*
> *Its cool and sparkling streams,*
> *Its hills and vales and fountains,*
> *O'er which the sunlight gleams.*

> Refrain:
> *I'm over the Jordan tide;*
> *The waters did there divide.*

---

7. The Hebrew means to "go down," and so may be understood symbolically to mean go down into the grave.

I'm in the land of Canaan,
Abundantly satisfied.
And now with joy and gladness
I'm singing along the way;
In fellowship with Jesus,
I'm happy night and day.

With old Egypt far behind me,
The Canaan land ahead,
I started on my journey,
By God so strangely led.
He brought me to the Jordan,
With Canaan now in view;
He opened up the waters,
And led me safely through.

I'm in the land of Canaan,
This land of corn and wine.
The atmosphere is pleasant;
The fruit is large and fine.
The streams with milk and honey
Are made to overflow.
Here all the fragrant flowers
In great abundance grow.]

"Beulah Land" is a figurative term for the sanctified estate. This word appears in the Scriptures (Isa. 62:4), where in the marginal reading the idea is given as "married," and is in contrast with the situation of desolation. But it is Bunyan who made Beulah Land so well known. He located Beulah as out and beyond Doubting Castle and the Slough of Despond, but yet this side of the River of Death. He said the sun shines all the time, the flowers bloom perpetually, and the situation is always pleasant in Beulah. Many, he said, looked with longing eyes across the river from Beulah to the Celestial City, and some thought they could see the tower of that blessed place on certain clear days. When the time came for crossing over from Beulah to the Celestial City, Bunyan said many entered the waters with singing, and gave back to friends on the Beulah bank wonderful testimonies of the glory their eyes glimpsed as they themselves were passing on from sight. Beulah Land has therefore become a striking and beautiful type of the highest and best in the Christian experience and life. Being definite in its location and boundaries, it has no actual antitype except in the experi-

ence and life of the wholly sanctified. Every Beulah song that one ever
hears is a misnomer except it be interpreted as a description of the
estate of holiness. An examination of the work of the poets will substantiate this claim.

[We cite the song by Edgar Page Stites as one example:

Beulah Land

I've reached the land of corn and wine,
And all its riches freely mine;
Here shines undimmed one blissful day,
For all my night has passed away.

Refrain:
O Beulah Land, sweet Beulah Land,
As on thy highest mount I stand;
I look away across the sea,
Where mansions are prepared for me,
And view the shining glory-shore—
My heav'n, my home forevermore!

My Savior comes and walks with me,
And sweet communion here have we;
He gently leads me with the hand,
For this is heaven's borderland.

A sweet perfume upon the breeze
Is borne from ever-vernal trees,
And flow'rs that never-fading grow
Where streams of life forever flow.

The zephyrs seem to float to me,
Sweet sounds of heaven's melody,
As angels with the white-robed throng
Join in the sweet redemption song.]

"Soul rest," a term dependent upon the analogy drawn in the
Book of Hebrews between the Sabbath of God's ancient people and
the assurance of the fully sanctified, is a very valid and precious picture
of certain phases of the blessed estate enjoyed by the pure in heart.
Those who would weaken this symbolic use by suggesting that the
Sabbath is really a prefigure of rest in heaven must explain the wording
"labour . . . to enter into that rest" (Heb. 4:11). Especially is the idea
embarrassing when it must be acknowledged that the word "labour"

harks back to the experience of the children of Israel under Joshua, when the word is "hasten." If therefore the rest that "remaineth to the people of God" is heaven, and God's people are to hasten to enter into it, it would seem difficult for one to apply that exhortation to those whose life tenure has not yet been fulfilled. No, the true sabbath is the sabbath of holiness, where the soul is freed from sin and turmoil and strife.

"The heavenlies" or "heavenly places," an expression Paul uses in Eph. 1:3 and in 6:12 (where it is translated "high places"), is undoubtedly a figure representing the sanctified estate. It is not of heaven that the apostle here speaks, but of a spiritual estate that is like unto heaven. We have the idea in the song "Where Jesus Is, 'Tis Heaven There." And the testimony points unfailingly to the life of one who has been delivered from actual and inbred sin and is in the enjoyment of the grace and blessing of full salvation.

"The mountaintop experience" is the experience of Bible holiness. The figure pictures one who has by grace arisen from the plains of the justified life to the holy mount of entire sanctification. This putting is familiar, especially in the sacred songs which have sprung up, in which the poets have tried to help us describe the glories of the sanctified estate.

There are many other figurative expressions both in the Bible and in the literature and hymnology of the Church that sanctified Christians delight to use in their endeavor to share the good news of full salvation. Just as every good person in the Bible is a type of Jesus, the supreme embodiment of all goodness, so every word and every figure which presents a wholesome and satisfying picture of the Christian estate helps to describe holiness of heart and life.

Holiness, perfect love, and Christian perfection are the three unequivocal terms for describing the estate of the sanctified. These words have been given full content by the careful and conscientious labors of "holy men of old" whom the Spirit of God inspired to give us our holy Bible. They have been made familiar by a long list of worthies down the Christian centuries, and now can be used in confidence and clarity by us today. We are thankful for the labors of those who have gone before us, for they have left us a rich and ready vocabulary which is well understood by Christians generally. In this, as in other matters, we "stand upon the shoulders of the fathers," and by such means become "the true ancients," and colaborers with all who have made it their calling to "spread scriptural holiness over the land."

We claim as a heritage that long list of terms which describe in part, or represent in measure, the grace and estate of those who are sanctified, and we pledge ourselves to use these ready instruments in the blessed task of "telling to the world around what a glorious Savior we have found." Even those terms of the second rank, when used understandingly, are capable of both clarifying the theme and enforcing its urgency.

Who is there that does not like pictures? Who is not intrigued by the possibility of obtaining an inheritance in a spiritual Canaan, a land more fruitful by manyfold than that which was given to the tribes of Israel "beyond Jordan"? Who does not thrill to the invitation to "come over into Beulah Land"? Illustrations are windows to let in the light. And while we would not make our walls all of windows, we are thankful for the light that shines through the windows of the history of God's ancient people, and through the examples and testimonies of all the saints of the ages past.

Being sure that ours is a spiritual inheritance, we find consolation in the assurance that no age of the past offered better things to its children than are the possessions of those today who will "follow on to know the Lord" (Hos. 6:3). We do not envy Abraham his dreams, nor Joshua his visions. We know in truth the spiritual meaning of the fire-touched lips of Isaiah. Even the holy apostles who walked with the Master in the days of His flesh were taught to look forward to the fullness of the Spirit's baptism which is the normal heritage of all God's people in this blessed dispensation. To be saved from the guilt and pollution of sin and to be filled with the love of God, to have His love made perfect in our hearts—there is nothing better than this until we shall see His face in heaven.

> *Oh, the joy of sins forgiven!*
> *Oh, the bliss the Blood-washed know!*
> *Oh, the peace akin to heaven,*
> *Where the healing waters flow!*

Even though words cannot express content fully, we are thankful for their help. And when words have done their full part, we are happy still to be able to say of the grace and blessing of Bible holiness, "It is better felt than told."

5

Charles Ewing Brown
(1883-1971)

Charles Ewing Brown was born December 30, 1883, in Eliza-bethtown, Ill., the son of Willis L. Brown, later an early evangelist in the Church of God.

Charles was converted, sanctified wholly, and began preach-ing when only 11 years of age. As a teenager, the boy helped his father hold tent revivals in the Midwest. He was ordained in 1903.

In 1907 Charles married Carrie Becker of Guilford, Ind., and to this union four children were born. Mrs. Brown died only a few months after her husband passed away in 1971.

Even as a youth Charles was an avid reader of the Bible and a wide variety of other books. This eagerness for knowledge eventually gave him the equivalent of a college education, though he received only a few months of formal seminary training. In midlife Anderson College conferred on him the honorary degree doctor of divinity.

Between 1900 and 1930 Dr. Brown pastored congregations in New York City, Philadelphia, Detroit, Chicago, and Huntington, Ind. During these years he became a regular contributor to *The Gospel Trumpet* (now *Vital Christianity*), the weekly journal of the Church of God. In 1930, he was elected as its editor in chief, a position he held until his retirement in 1951.

Along with his responsibilities as editor, Dr. Brown also served as associate professor of theology at Anderson College and Theological Seminary. As editor and teacher, he wrote more than 20 books. His better-known works include a two-volume set on Christian theology, *The Meaning of Salvation* and *The Meaning of Sanctification*. From this second theology text published in 1945, we have chosen three chapters that forcefully present elements of holiness teaching not treated at length elsewhere in this volume. In the following excerpts from the preface, Dr. Brown gives his own rationale.

This book is not written to give battle, but to give light. . . . No effort is made to *prove* sanctification. I have written for sincere Christians sympathetic with spiritual values and sensitive to them. For these I would remove fallacious intellectual obstacles which hitherto have prevented their seeking and finding this fullness of the blessing of the gospel of Christ. I have written also for those who would understand the experience better, both for their own enjoyment and to enable them to help others by leading them to Him who "shall sit as a refiner and purifier of silver" (Mal. 3:3). . . .

It will be a mistake if we neglect the inner experience of sanctification, which has inspired and strengthened the heartbeats of the church through all the ages past. . . .

The doctrine of sanctification is, for Christian people, the most important of all the doctrines because it teaches the way to find and develop faith in Christ as the perfect Healer of the heart, who alone can make it entirely well and fill it with the enduring strength of the Holy Spirit.

Let us, therefore, think of sanctification . . . as the completion of the work of redemption in the heart and soul of the believer. . . .

The doctrine of entire sanctification is an heroic doctrine. It requires a spiritual church and ministry for its acceptance, promotion, development, and successful growth. It always tends to die out in a worldly church, but it will kindle a flame of fire in every community where it is accepted, witnessed to, and lived out in experience.

Sin as Evil Disposition[1]

SOMETHING HINDERS SOCIAL PROGRESS

Four hundred years before Christ, Plato, the greatest of Greek philosophers, dreamed of an ideal state of human happiness. There people would live in temperance and simplicity. . . .

---

1. *The Meaning of Sanctification*, chap. 5.

But then Plato goes on to show how the natural passions and desires of men will multiply and grow. The country will become too small and then the neighbors' lands must be annexed, causing war. Thus one by one, Plato shows how men's desires grow up, and by their feverish demands for more than justice and temperance will admit, they tend constantly to cancel the plans of idealism. The evil passions and the sinful desires of men's hearts turn the dream of earthly Utopias into a nightmare of corrupt and vicious civilization, anarchy, and war.

We have not cited Plato's views because we agree with them in detail . . . , but because they furnish an illustration of the fact that the inborn perversity of human nature has been an insoluble problem for those who have dreamed dreams of human welfare for the last 2,400 years.

Present-day idealistic dreamers base their plans for a bright future upon the present achievement and the promised development of science. It is true that science does point the way by which a race of good, just, and unselfish men could create an earthly paradise, but, unfortunately, science is not able to show how evil men can create such a desirable world; for when evil men obtain the secrets of power that will level the mountains and make the desert to bloom, they use that power to seek to enslave their neighbors, and instead of leveling the mountains they level the fairest cities, and instead of making the desert bloom they destroy the culture and arts and the most precious blossoms of the civilization of mankind which have developed through a thousand years.

We sympathize with all the dreams of a better world. We long for that land of abundant comfort and beauty which science could provide, but we believe we are justified in directing attention to, and spending thought upon, the problem of changing men so that their hearts will be prepared to work together in building a world of peace and justice.

This approach makes it necessary for us to study the nature of man's singular perversities. What is there about him that makes him

DEPRAVITY fiercer than any living animal? Why does he tend to pervert government to despotism and to desecrate high office by the foulest of graft and corruption? Why does he seek to divert the wealth of a state, which would make all of its citizens prosperous, to a demonic effort to enslave neighboring states and peoples? Why does man degrade and defile every high and beautiful instinct of human nature? Why does he defile his own family life with tobacco, liquor, profanity, hatred, jealousy, and marital infidelity? Why does he profane the church with hypocrisy and prostitute its holiest offices to greed? Why does he make the state an instrument of torture for millions of his fellows?

Why has man always acted so perversely? What hope have we that he will cease this manner of life? We believe that the historic Christian Church has always had the answers to these questions. Some of its teachers may have on occasion gone to extremes in expounding the Christian doctrine of depravity, but in the heart of that doctrine there lies a truth so sound and incontrovertible that it deserves the careful study of people of our times.

INDWELLING SIN

Just as there is opposition to the Christian doctrine of individual and personal guilt and sin, so there is also even wider opposition to the accompanying Christian doctrine of sin as inherited depravity, or race sin. Bear in mind that the term sin as used here in such expressions as "inherent sin" is used accommodatively to describe this corrupt and depraved nature as sin, because it comes originally from the act of sin in the beginning of the race and because it is characterized by an active tendency to sin. Paul used it in this connection and so did the Christian teachers of the ages.

It is a common observation of mankind that acts of sin tend to become habit, or disposition to sin, and this habit tends to form a certain, definite sinful character. This tendency toward sin, or personal depravity, is such a common experience of mankind that it needs no argument to prove it. The question now before us is whether such a tendency toward sin is capable of being transmitted by heredity. Is there such a thing as "race sin" or "inbred sin"? Here again we have the testimony of all ages expressing the common belief of mankind that human nature has in it some hereditary element of depravity which tends to propagate itself anew in every social environment which man can devise.

Plato wrote: "But the point which I desire to note is that in all of us, even in good men, there is a lawless wild-beast nature, which peers out in sleep." . . .

Dr. C. E. M. Joad, of the University of London, formerly an atheist, in his book *God and Evil*, says: "Evil is not merely a by-product of unfavorable circumstances. It is so widespread, so deep-seated that one can only conclude that what the religions have always taught is true and that evil is endemic in the heart of man."

Perhaps the modern psychologists have given the strongest scientific testimony to the correctness of the traditional doctrine of original depravity. Sigmund Freud and other profound researchers in this field have, as they believe, uncovered a very nest of unclean and evil beasts in the subconscious mind of human nature, and it is a most fascinating study to follow them in tracing an evil tendency from the cellar of the human soul disguising itself as something good and beautiful in order to thrust its evil face into the daylight of the conscious mind. . . .

Man is undoubtedly corrupt, judged from any elevated moral standpoint. His depravity, like breaches in the stone wall of an ancient castle, runs clear down to the foundations of his life. . . .

All politicians, statesmen, social reformers, philanthropists, and lovers of mankind would do well to understand the [weakness] of human nature as revealed by history, science, psychology, and the study of the Holy Scripture.

The Change Made by Adam's Fall

This teaching on depravity is best understood by a survey of the conditions of Adam's probation, his tragic fall, and the dismal heritage which he left to mankind. The Bible says that "God hath made man upright; but they have sought out many inventions" (Eccles. 7:29). Paul says that "by one man sin entered into the world" (Rom. 5:12).

Everything in that early world, including man, was good (Gen. 1:31). Man lived in a world that knew no sin, and he enjoyed dominion over all the lower animals and over all nature (v. 28). Moreover he enjoyed fellowship and communion with God.

The old-time theologians exalted the intellectual ability of Adam. He was, they said, of a giant mind, more able and mighty than any of his fallen descendants. . . . Adam's intelligence rating must have been a very high and worthy one, living as he did in perfect innocence and holiness and in the very fullness of the powers with which God created him. . . .

The reason his state was so excellent was because he was made in the image and likeness of God: "And God said, Let us make man in our image, after our likeness . . . So God created man in his own image, in the image of God created he him; male and female created he them" (Gen. 1:26-27).

Of what did this image consist? "And have put on the new man, which is renewed in knowledge after the image of him that created him" (Col. 3:10).

Here the distinctive character of this image is the *power to know*. And surely in it does man far transcend the beasts. Again we read, "And that ye put on the new man, which after God is created in righteousness and *true holiness*" (Eph. 4:24).

In these two texts we have the double character of the divine image. It was a reflection in finite form of the infinite character of God. In the first text the image is intellectual knowledge, as of a free and conscious spirit; and in the second text we see the moral nature of God as righteousness and true holiness. These two phases of the divine image are sometimes called the natural and moral image of God. The moral image of God was one that man could and did lose, namely, righteousness and true holiness.

The natural image of God, the capacity for knowledge, by which man became a living soul and attained to human personality, was not destroyed; and it is that image, together with some faint traces of the moral character of God, which makes man capable of salvation. The natural image of God, even to this day, is man's possibility of surmounting his prejudices and passions and rising to a thought which in its broken and finite way is like the majestic thought of God. "I am thinking God's thoughts after Him," declared Kepler ecstatically as he worked out the motion of the planets by the methods of science.

Possessing the image of God, Adam had dominion over the animals, over nature, and over his own natural body so that his emotions, appetite, and instincts were all free from the disease of sin. He also had access to the tree of life. Undoubtedly Adam's body was naturally mortal to some extent, like that of the lower animals. Nevertheless, he lived in the spiritual atmosphere of eternity in such fellowship with God that surely his body would eventually have taken on immortality and enjoyed glorification just as the bodies of the saints will enjoy it at the resurrection. The tree of life was a symbol of this divine medicine of immortality.

This is the sense in which death came upon all men. As a result of sin, man was barred from access to the means of physical immortality. And this consequence of sin was made so sharp that the body was not able to partake of the full benefit of the Atonement in its rescue from physical death until it had fulfilled its appointment to death. Paul said he was waiting for "the adoption, to wit, the redemption of the body," in the glory of the resurrection (Rom. 8:23).

Some have regarded the prohibition against eating the fruit of the tree of knowledge as being a trivial ordinance. It is evident that this prohibition in itself did not fully describe the central law of holiness and mutual love between God and man. It was simply a positive command, reasonable in its purpose, easy to fulfill, and yet furnishing man a very mild and simple test at the beginning of his probation.

The simplicity of the provision may be regarded as being well adapted to the kindergarten stage of man's moral and spiritual education. Undoubtedly, if he had passed that test successfully he would have ascended step by step to loftier and more perilous heights in which, had he proved faithful, he would have advanced to nobler and more complex conflicts out of which, if faithful, he would have emerged a moral and spiritual giant—a worthy son of God. And there is no doubt that he would have transmitted a fine character to his children.

That the natural image of God, meaning the spiritual nature of human personality, cannot be destroyed is the verdict of Scripture: "Whoso sheddeth man's blood, by man shall his blood be shed: *for in the image of God made he man*" (Gen. 9:6). In other words, even the fallen men who live after Adam retain the natural image of God and, consequently, a sacredness inheres in their personality. "Therewith bless we God, even the Father; and therewith curse we men, which are made *after the similitude of God*" (James 3:9). It is the possession of this natural image of God which makes all doctrines of annihilation false and proves the immortality of the human spirit.

THE EFFECT OF THE FALL

When Adam received the prohibition against eating the fruit of the tree of knowledge, he was warned that "in the day that thou eatest thereof thou shalt surely die" (Gen. 2:17). This death was primarily a death of separation from God. In other words, the loss of the moral image of God befell Adam in the day that he ate the forbidden fruit.

It is also evident that the sentence included physical death. But Adam continued to live hundreds of years after that time, therefore we believe that immediate death was suspended on account of the universal grace coming to all men through the atonement of Christ, which instituted for Adam and for mankind another probation. The first probation was for Adam as the head of the natural human race. The second probation was under the Second Adam, Christ.

However, part of the consequences of Adam's sin followed swiftly and tragically. He was excluded from the Garden of Eden and introduced into the toil and sorrow of the lower region of life. If, as we believe, the Scripture teaches the moral image of God was in righteousness and true holiness, then we must see that possession of that image implies a distinct desire and tendency to love and serve God. Just as it is natural for fish to swim in the sea, for birds to fly through the air, and for the wild fowl to move southward in the autumn, so it is an instinct of man's soul to reach out toward God in loving fellowship and humble obedience.

The loss of the image of God planted an opposite tendency in man's soul, and Adam transmitted that tendency to all mankind. After he lost the image of God, "Adam . . . begat a son in his own likeness" (Gen. 5:3). That is, in the image of Adam, and not in the image of God.

THE TEACHING OF THE APOSTLE PAUL

That a sinful nature was inherited by all men from Adam is the plain teaching of the apostle Paul. Remembering that the word sin is here used in an accommodative sense as describing a tendency toward sin, and that death for innocent infants is not a penalty but a consequence of the sin of Adam, we follow Paul's argument: "Death passed upon all men, for that all have sinned" (Rom. 5:12). It came even over them "that had not sinned after the similitude of Adam's transgression" (v. 14).

Thus we see that when man sinned he lost something essential out of his nature; he lost the image of God in the sense of moral likeness to God. This deprivation made it impossible for him to live a good and righteous life, just as the loss of one leg makes it impossible for man to walk. But this loss led also to depravation, just as the loss of teeth out of the jaw of a growing child makes the jawbone grow into an abnormal shape. When human nature lost the image of God and power to live holy, it became depraved and bent into crooked and abnormal forms, contrary to the original intention of the Father.

This doctrine of inherited depravity does not contradict the justice of God and is not inconsistent with sound reasoning. Also, this inherited depravity does not in and of itself involve guilt. Infants are not guilty, but as they grow into adult life they invariably fall into sin through the depraved character of the nature which they inherit from Adam.

CONSEQUENCE AND PENALTY

Here it is necessary to show a distinction between consequence and penalty. Suppose a quarrelsome and contentious man should become involved in a brawl wherein he loses the use of one hand for life and for this brawl the judge sentences him to six months in jail. The sentence of the judge is the *penalty* for the man's crime, but the lifelong disability of being a cripple is the *consequence* of his crime. The judge never appointed the *consequences* and cannot remove them. On account of his being a lifelong cripple the man's children may suffer the disadvantages of poverty, ignorance, and misery. This also is not a *penalty* for them, but a *consequence* of their father's sin.

The apostle Paul shows that in the same way death is the *consequence* of Adam's sin. It passed upon all men even though individuals, that is, infants among them, had not sinned the same sin as Adam himself had committed. However, the consequence of sin becomes a penalty in the child who accepts the transgression and the guilt as his own by an active choice upon reaching the age of accountability. By so doing he likewise accepts the penalty of sin.

Here it could be said that it is not just that an innocent child should suffer death as a consequence, whereas a wicked man suffers death as a penalty; but also the child knows nothing of the misery and pain and fear of death which comes as a penalty to the adult sinner.

Paul compares the first Adam with Christ, who is the Second Adam. "If through the offence of one many be dead, much more the grace of God, and the gift by grace, which is by one man, Jesus Christ, hath abounded unto many. And not as it was by one that sinned, so is the gift: for the judgment was by one to condemnation, but the free gift is of many offences unto justification" (Rom. 5:15-16). . . .

"As in Adam all die, even so in Christ shall all be made alive" (1 Cor. 15:22).

"The first man Adam was made a living soul; the last Adam was made a quickening spirit" (v. 45).

"The sting of death is sin" (v. 56) means that although death is a consequence of Adam's sin upon all men, it is without sting except for those who have the conscious guilt of sin.

THE BIBLE TEACHES THE DOCTRINE OF INBRED SIN

The Jews of Christ's time spoke truly when they told the blind man that he had been "altogether born in sins" (John 9:34), and it was

Jesus who said, "That which is born of the flesh is flesh" (3:6). Soon after man was expelled from the Garden of Eden, "God saw that the wickedness of man was great in the earth, and that every imagination of the thoughts of his heart was only evil continually. And it repented the Lord that he had made man on the earth, and it grieved him at his heart" (Gen. 6:5-6).

This does not mean that God repented as men do, but that since man had changed his attitude toward God, God automatically must change His attitude toward man. After the Flood "the Lord said in his heart, . . . the imagination of man's heart is evil from his youth" (Gen. 8:21). David confessed: "I was shapen in iniquity; and in sin did my mother conceive me" (Ps. 51:5). Christ taught that evil thoughts and a whole long catalog of sins proceed out of the heart (Matt. 15:19). "Ye then, *being evil,* know how to give good gifts unto your children" (7:11), said Christ. In other words, He took it for granted that they were evil in their hearts. Paul said that "we have borne the image of the earthy" (1 Cor. 15:49), meaning that we inherited the image of Adam. Christ told the Jews of His time, "Ye are from beneath; I am from above: ye are of this world; I am not of this world" (John 8:23).

Christ was unique because of the fact that "in him is no sin" (1 John 3:5). James calls this sinful nature lust: "Every man is tempted, when he is drawn away of his own lust, and enticed. Then when lust hath conceived, it bringeth forth sin: and sin, when it is finished, bringeth forth death" (1:14-15).

But for Paul it is "the law of sin and death" (Rom. 8:2); "sin that dwelleth in me"; "the law of sin" (7:17, 23). He also says that "the carnal mind is enmity against God" (8:7) and that the heathen Ephesians before their conversion were "*by nature* the children of wrath" (Eph. 2:3). . . .

Full proof that this sinful disposition is in children before they reach the age of accountability is given by Paul in these words: "I was alive without the law once: but when the commandment came [that means when he became conscious of the commandment], *sin revived, and I died*" (Rom. 7:9). How could sin revive unless it was already in his heart in a latent form? This was the "*sin that dwelleth in me*" (v. 20), the "*law in my members,* warring against the law of my mind, and bringing me into captivity to *the law of sin* which is in my members" (v. 23). "O wretched man that I am! who shall deliver me from the *body of this death?*" (v. 24).

The body of death is the carnal mind, *the inborn nature of sin.*

This fallen man is without God and without hope in the world (Eph. 2:12).

Further proof of the sinful nature of all mankind is furnished by the sweeping statement of Paul, "There is none righteous, no, not one" (Rom. 3:10). And both Jews and Gentiles are all under sin, for, says John, "if we say that we *have no sin,* we deceive ourselves, and the truth is not in us" (1 John 1:8). This undoubtedly refers to the *inbred nature of sin* and *the sinful tendency* which corrupts the lives of all mankind.

The Work of the Holy Spirit[2]

Careless readers of the Bible have attributed to the plan of salvation a simplicity which it does not have. Just as we find depth and complexity when we attempt a close study of nature, so we likewise find many deep truths when we seek to study the Bible and the plan of salvation. One of these truths is that the Holy Spirit has more than one "office work."

This is illustrated by the case of a man who is a judge and a physician. As a physician he would seek to save a criminal's life, and as a judge he might sentence him to death. There is nothing contradictory in the two offices or professions combined in one man. That is the explanation of the problem concerning Christ's promising to send His Holy Spirit when throughout the Old Testament there are numerous references to prove that He has always been in the world. Christ sent Him in the special office work of the Sanctifier to perfect the Church on the Day of Pentecost and to dwell in it in sanctifying power forever. The multiple work of the Holy Spirit in human life is set forth in scriptural symbols, and there is value in them.

AIR AS AN EMBLEM OF THE SPIRIT

When men began to talk about spiritual truths, they had to use physical things to illustrate their meaning. We say we grasp a subject when we mean, not that we take hold of it with the hand, but with the mind. In this way, the word air came to be used for spirit from the most ancient time. In Gen. 1:2 the Hebrew says the *"ruach* of God brooding on the waters." Here *ruach* is literally the "breath of God," and the text means that the Spirit of God brooded over the chaos of

---

2. Ibid., chap. 8.

the ancient world like a bird brooding over her eggs. And this is the way that God's Spirit has brooded over the souls of all men throughout all times, from the dawn of their existence until their death, or until they had grieved Him away forever, if possible. It was this Spirit of God that breathed life into the first man (2:7). The Hebrew here says *chayyim*—lives—not one life, but many, all merging into one personality like many little flames merging into one bonfire.

"The breath of the Almighty hath given me life" (Job 33:4). "Prophesy unto the wind, prophesy, son of man, and say to the wind, Thus saith the Lord God; Come from the four winds, O breath, and breathe upon these slain, that they may live" (Ezek. 37:9). These texts indicate how the Holy Spirit works to create life, and this truth is climaxed by the teaching of Jesus concerning the work of the Spirit in producing the new birth. "Except a man be born of water and of the Spirit, he cannot enter into the kingdom of God. . . . The wind bloweth where it listeth, and thou hearest the sound thereof, but canst not tell whence it cometh, and whither it goeth: so is every one that is born of the Spirit" (John 3:5, 8).

And so we see that the work of the Spirit is not confined to the experience of entire sanctification. In fact, the Holy Spirit begins to work with men long before they are ever converted. It is He who convicts men of sin and makes them have a desire to find God. "When he is come, he will reprove the world of sin" (John 16:8). That reproof produces what we call "conviction of sin," whenever reproof is heeded by the soul.

Some holiness teachers hold that the office work of the Spirit as Breather of life is confined to a preparation for, and experience of, regeneration, having no place in the work of entire sanctification. But I think differently: I believe that the idea of a creative force of spiritual power is conveyed in the first record of Spirit baptism given in the second chapter of Acts. At that time, "suddenly there came a sound from heaven as of a rushing mighty wind, and it filled all the house where they were sitting" (Acts 2:2). . . . that sound . . . denoted the presence of the creative breath of God . . . This must needs be so if our doctrine of the restoration of the divine image is correct; for it is this creative breath of the Spirit which creates anew the perfect image of God in the heart of a redeemed man, just as it created the image of God in Adam at the dawn of his existence. This is what Christ meant when He said, "I am come that they might have life, and that they might have it more abundantly" (John 10:10). This is the abundant life, imparted by the breath of God in the experience of entire sanctification.

THE HOLY SPIRIT AS FIRE

From immemorial ages the wondering eyes of simpleminded men have gazed at the mysterious movement of a flame of fire in a vain effort to explore its hidden secret. And even in this scientific age, when men know the name and meaning of the chemical change involved, they still must feel baffled by the fact that they have only given a technical description of their ignorance. Fire has seemed to all men as a fit emblem of the nature of God. Man's best friend, heating his building, cooking his food, making life possible in cold climates—no wonder St. Francis called it Brother Fire. Fire has, nevertheless, demanded of man certain cautions and respect; for it has always been capable of striking back at him with withering power whenever he treats it lightly.

And it so happens that nearly all men who have ever believed in God have been led to think of Him somewhat in the same paradoxical vein. They love Him, they recognize His friendship and the benefits of His aid, and they fear Him in recognition of the fact that He always holds the power to visit with stern rebuke every lack of respect that might be shown Him. So it happens that throughout the Bible fire appears repeatedly as an emblem of the presence of God. The Old Testament prophets saw God in visions as "a great cloud, and a fire infolding itself" (Ezek. 1:4). Moses saw God in a burning bush of flame (Exod. 3:2-4).

This fire teaches many truths; perhaps the most important is that of cleansing. The baptism of the Holy Spirit fell upon the disciples on the Day of Pentecost as "cloven tongues like as of fire" (Acts 2:3). And the cleansing nature of this fire is set forth by Malachi: "He is like a refiner's fire, and like fullers' soap: and he shall sit as a refiner and purifier of silver: and he shall purify the sons of Levi, and purge them as gold and silver, that they may offer unto the Lord an offering in righteousness" (Mal. 3:2-3).

Nowadays gold is purified by chemical processes, but in Bible times it was purified by fire, which melted the ore together so that the dross came to the top. The dross was then skimmed off and cast aside, leaving only the pure gold, in which the workman could see his face reflected. Such is the work of Christ when He purifies hearts in the baptism with the Holy Ghost and fire. This is the fire promised in the preaching of John: "He that cometh after me . . . shall baptize you with the Holy Ghost, and with fire: whose fan is in his hand, and he will throughly purge his floor, and gather his wheat into the garner; but he will burn up the chaff with unquenchable fire" (Matt. 3:11-12). This was the fire Isaiah experienced when, bewildered and humbled by the stupendous vision of God, he confessed the uncleanness of a religious man and immediately experienced purification by fire: "Then flew one of the seraphims unto me, having a live coal in his hand, which he had taken with the tongs from off the altar: and he laid it upon my mouth, and said, Lo, this hath touched thy lips; and thine iniquity is taken away, and thy sin purged" (Isa. 6:6-7).

Fire not only symbolized cleansing and purity, but it is also an emblem of energy and power: "Ye shall receive power, after POWER that the Holy Ghost is come upon you: and ye shall be witnesses unto me . . . unto the uttermost part of the earth" (Acts 1:8). . . .

Many people misunderstand this power, thinking it ought to be a destructive force that shatters body and mind in some kind of hysterical shaking and insane behavior. The text just quoted will dissipate these misconceptions by showing that the principal function of the power of the Spirit is to enable one to witness for Christ; that is, witness by holy life and by faithful and persuasive words as one whose speech is "alway with grace, seasoned with salt, that ye may know how ye ought to answer every man" (Col. 4:6). "For God hath not given us the spirit of fear; but of power, and of love, and of a sound mind" (2 Tim. 1:7). Some 1,600 years ago, the great scholars of the church began to lay down the principle that the work of the Holy Spirit, purely and of itself, would be to strengthen and tranquilize the mind and reason. It may be that some great saint has on occasion given way to hysterical frenzy; but if so, it was a weakness of human flesh similar to that weakness to which the saints are always exposed. But the highest manifestation of the Spirit's power is in love and a sound mind. . . .

THE HOLY SPIRIT AS WATER

Many passages of the Bible set forth water as an emblem of the Holy Spirit. "I will pour water upon him that is thirsty, and floods upon the dry ground: I will pour my spirit upon thy seed, and my blessing upon thine offspring: and they shall spring up as among the grass, as willows by the water courses" (Isa. 44:3-4). Here water represents the refreshing and stimulating power of the Spirit. "Christ also loved the church, and gave himself for it; that he might sanctify and cleanse it with the washing of water by the word, that he might present it to himself a glorious church, not having spot, or wrinkle, or any such thing; but that it should be holy and without blemish" (Eph. 5:25-27). Here water represents the cleansing work of the Spirit in washing away all the remains of inbred sin.

> The negative side of sanctification is that of emptying, removing, destroying the carnal mind. The positive side of sanctification involves filling the purified heart with light and love and multiplying within it the graces of the Spirit, and enjoying those graces. Now so far as I can discover, this is just the significance of the two sanctifying emblems of fire and water. The fire represents purity with the idea of destruction, of consuming; water represents the idea of purity with the positive upbuilding of the soul in truth and strength and love.[3]

THE HOLY SPIRIT AS OIL

"But the anointing which ye have received of him abideth in you, and ye need not that any man teach you: but as the same anointing teacheth you of all things, and is truth, and is no lie, and even as it hath taught you, ye shall abide in him" (1 John 2:27). Oil had a value to the ancients of Palestine beyond our conception in this modern day. In that age men had not learned how to preserve food for livestock so as to keep them throughout the winter. Consequently, fat meat food was considered a great luxury. Because the olive tree took many years to grow, it was considered an emblem of peace. Such factors as these contributed to make any kind of oil seem much more important then than now. Perfumed oil was also esteemed a great luxury. . . . Priests and kings were anointed with oil in elaborate ceremony to signify the enduement of power and privilege which were granted by their office. Prophets, too, were anointed for the prophetic office. . . . "Oil in the Old Testament appears as the symbol of the communication of the Spirit."[4]

Even the word "Christ" means "anointed," as the Scriptures have said: "The Spirit of the Lord God is upon me; because the Lord hath anointed me to preach good tidings unto the meek; he hath sent me to bind up the brokenhearted, to proclaim liberty to the captives, and the opening of the prison to them that are bound" (Isa. 61:1). "God

---

3. G. D. Watson, *Coals of Fire*, 102.
4. Gustave F. Von Oehler, *Theology of the Old Testament*, 273.

anointed Jesus of Nazareth with the Holy Ghost and with power" (Acts 10:38). The anointing of the Old Testament, therefore, seems to signify the enduement of authority to rule (the king), to minister (the priest), and to teach (the prophet). Translated into the framework of New Testament ideals, this would signify the noble character of divine self-control, the capacity to lead men to God, and joyous insight into the truth; for the New Testament saints are kings and priests unto God (Rev. 1:6), and they have an anointing that teaches them.

Entire Sanctification as a Bundle of Possibilities[5]

The doctrine of entire sanctification has been preached on the American continent in the Wesleyan tradition as the second work of grace, or as a second crisis in Christian experience, for about 200 years; and while doubtless its opponents would admit that it has on occasion produced astonishing results, an unbiased and fair-minded critic must admit that many of its most sincere teachers and professors have felt deep and widespread disappointment with the results in their own individual experience and observation. In many instances there has been a gap in practice between what the best teachers promised and the actual results obtained by the average Christian who claimed the experience. How shall we explain this simple, but undeniable, fact? First of all, it might be said that even if it were a matter of secular discipline of the mind, results would naturally be widely different. . . .

Therefore we make bold to say that even on the lower level of secular psychology we are not justified in condemning a doctrine or mental discipline because it does not produce uniform results in the various types of mind which are subjected to it. But entire sanctification is not a secular doctrine; it is by definition an experience of the introduction of new power and grace into human life. If it be true that many who have sought this experience have failed to realize their expectations, we have a puzzling problem. What is the use of preaching about mountaintop experiences and fullness of joy, when multitudes of those who profess entire sanctification seem to suffer even more than their neighbors? Why preach about inrushing oceans of crystal power and victory when we know so many sanctified people

---

5. *The Meaning of Sanctification,* chap. 9.

who are struggling, perplexed, confused, and anxious, apparently just like other men?

Among [some] teachers the stock answer to this question has been that these suffering people were not really wholly sanctified. Then we have added to the perplexity and sorrow of these earnest people by accusing them of hypocrisy, thus placing them under a strain of prayer and ascetic effort to lift themselves to some imaginary type of blessedness.

To me there seems to be a better way, in which we shall be realistically honest with ourselves and perfectly candid in our report to the outside world.

Many seekers for the experience have misunderstood the meaning of the cleansing of our nature and the destruction of carnality. They have taken this experience to signify that the natural appetites, by which physical life is preserved and continued, will be eradicated and destroyed by entire sanctification. A little thought would convince anyone of the impossibility of the realization of such an experience. Without hunger the body would waste away and die. Without sex appetite the race would cease from the earth. Without fear men would utterly destroy the life of mankind from the earth. It is the exaggeration and feverish poisoning of these impulses which is cured by the baptism of the Holy Ghost.

While it is correct that the instinctive pattern of holy living is restored to the heart by the restoration of the image of God in sanctification, it is important to remember that the possession of human intelligence modifies the deterministic control of instinct in the case of a human being. . . . A hungry bird will carry a luscious morsel of food to deposit in the mouth of its nestling. Now it is easy for the bird to do this, because it has an instinctive pattern of behavior wrought in its very nature, and it has no intelligence sufficient to balance its own impulse of hunger against the instinctive urge to feed its young. But if that bird were suddenly gifted with human intelligence . . . it would begin to think about the comparative advantages of feeding its young or of satisfying its own hunger. And we may be sure that to go hungry to feed its young would be a harder thing for the bird to do if it were possessed of human intelligence. And we may also be sure that many birds would obey the impulse to satisfy their individual hunger rather than the instinctive urge to feed their young.

I emphasize this point, for so far as I know, it has never before been introduced into the literature of the doctrine of entire sanctification. Yet a little consideration will prove that it is true. Further thought will make it very apparent why even a sanctified man, who has the instinctive pattern of holiness restored to his heart, will often, if not always, find a tension between his simple physical impulses and the organized pattern of religious instinct implanted into his nature by the grace of God. . . .

Too many people have neglected the *continuous response* which a sanctified man must make to the indwelling grace of God. Jesus explained it all in the parable of the sower. The seed sown **GROWTH** represents the whole work of grace in the heart, and thus could be applied to the baptism of the Holy Ghost, the enduement of spiritual power; although the seed is all very much alike, it does not produce anything like uniform results. Jesus explains carefully that its historical outcome shows returns of 30-fold, 60-fold, and 100-fold. (See Matt. 13:8.) Here Jesus inferentially rebukes the expectation that the baptism of the Holy Spirit would produce uniform results in all who experience it. And it is important to remember that the field which produced only a 30-fold increase was not condemned as an apostate and useless piece of ground. It was in its way an example, if not of the best, at least of the satisfactory Christian experience. Notice that Christ teaches with crystal clearness here that the returns are not in any wise limited by the goodness of the seed or the generosity with which it is sown; they are limited by the nature of the soil itself. It is a great mistake for teachers of the doctrine of entire sanctification to infer that all its possessors will realize its possibilities 100-fold. Doubtless that is a goal to be sought, but failure to realize it should not be condemned as apostasy. . . .

A great deal depends on how the individual uses the gift of the Spirit so freely given. Undoubtedly the possibilities are great, but those who receive should bestow more thought and prayer upon the realization of the vast potentialities of the gift.

Seek Not the Gift but the Giver

No apologies need to be made for presenting the baptism of the Holy Spirit, the experience of entire sanctification, as a gift. This is scriptural language. Moreover, it is borne out by numerous spiritual analogies in the parables of our Lord. It is of great importance that all who are concerned with this great truth should understand clearly and emphasize fully the fact that this is a very peculiar and unique gift. The gift of the Holy Spirit is not the gift of a thing, such as a bushel of wheat or a ton of dynamite or $1 million. Such figures are not entirely inaccurate, because they do represent the truth that the gift of the Holy Spirit is an enduement of power that puts the soul in possession of enormous potentialities.

But we have never realized the meaning of entire sanctification so long as we think of it merely as a thing which does certain things. Rather, it is a man's personal experience in which he receives the gift of a person, not given as an ancient slaveowner would give away one of his slaves, but given as today a lover gives himself to his bride, or as a great man gives himself in warm and confiding friendship to another man whom he regards as morally worthy of that friendship.

Throughout this whole discussion we have found that most of our difficulties are relieved by thinking of our relationship to God as a personal one. Here the parables, analogies, and figures of religion come nearest to the absolute truth and are freest from the possibility of misunderstanding. If we think of the baptism of the Holy Ghost as the special, kindly, loving presentation of the Third Person of the Godhead to its recipients in the wealth of a rich and enduring friendship, we have solved most of the problems raised regarding the lack of uniformity in the results of this experience.

Here is a helpful illustration. Take the great industrial leaders and men of vast fortune. Although they are compelled to guard themselves against infringement upon their time by thousands of idle hangers-on and beggars of every description, it will generally remain true that each of them has a considerable number of friends to whom he continues to give himself throughout life. Let us study these friends as illustrations of the lack of uniformity in the sanctified experience. Among them, here and there, will be men who through this friendship have risen to places of enormous power and prestige in the American industrial world. The head of the great corporation has smiled upon them, and they have become powerful executives and multimillionaires in their turn.

But this head of the corporation also has humble friends, some of whom perhaps are shabby men who have never known much success in life and whose only boast is that they are personal friends of the head of the corporation. They have the gift of the captain's friendship, but they have never been able to utilize the possibilities of that friendship to anything like the extent which other men have. Doubtless, like all other parables, this one can be misconstrued. We can say that the captain of industry was unfair to his humble friends. Ruling out that possibility, is it not reasonable to believe that many of his humble friends were well known by him to be incapable of the heavy burdens of responsibility which his power made it possible for him to bestow, but which his wisdom and friendship would not allow him to impose upon a weak friend?

If the possibilities of friendship . . . are so vast and yet so variously realized in practice, is it any wonder that the baptism of the Holy Ghost, the gift of the Comforter, also presents a bundle of possibilities which few men have ever realized in anything but the smallest way? Lack of this complete realization should not be construed as apostasy from the faith, or hypocrisy in the life. As a sanctified man surveys the possibilities of a life in holiness, it should be an encouragement to possess the land.

FEATURES OF THE VICTORIOUS LIFE

Having shown clearly that not all sanctified people realize the possibilities which the experience holds, and guarding against fanaticism and pharisaism on the one hand, and doubt, anxiety, and self-condemnation on the other, it is well to make an optimistic view of the glorious possibilities of faith in the life of holiness opened up to the believer in the experience of entire sanctification. Remember, these are possibilities whose lack of realization should inspire one to more ardent zeal, rather than create a sense of failure and guilt. As we unfold a map of the mountains of Canaan, it is not for anyone to ask who lives on such a high plane as that, but rather to say, "By the grace of God that is my inheritance, and I will realize it more and more as long as I live."

THE BAPTISM OF THE HOLY GHOST GIVES POWER

. . . One of the most outstanding features of the promised baptism of the Holy Spirit was an enduement of power: "Tarry ye in the city of Jerusalem, until ye be endued with power from on high" (Luke 24:49). "Ye shall receive power, after that the Holy Ghost is come upon you" (Acts 1:8).

Perhaps this "power" has created more confusion of thought than any other word in the teaching of the doctrine. First of all, we should remember that it is certainly not power to do just anything a man might wish to do. It is not power to make money; it is not power to avoid suffering; it is not power to bend others to our own will; it is not power to conquer our enemies nor to amass wealth. It is not intellectual power, which makes a man a scholar or a brilliant genius. It is not necessarily power to speak with eloquence and invincible persuasion. It is certainly not such power as Samson had, which made him able to carry the gates of Gath upon his back and to push the temple of Dagon over by physical force.

To define the power is by no means to deny it. A suggestion as to **WITNESSING** the kind of power it is may be seen in the text cited from Acts . . . : "And ye shall be witnesses unto me both in Jerusalem, and in all Judaea, and in Samaria, and unto the uttermost part of the earth" (1:8). That seems to answer our question. The power received by the soul at Pentecost is the power to witness for Christ. Eventually this involves a good many things. It involves the power to live an upright, moral, and worthy life; for this is the first requisite to witnessing. The witness who appears in God's witness chair must be a man with clean hands and a pure heart and a reputation of honor and integrity before the world.

Furthermore, in such a life there must be power to overcome **COURAGE** hatred, discouragement, bitterness, and the melancholy and gloom of life. "Great peace have they which love thy law: and nothing shall offend them" (Ps. 119:165). The exterior fabric of an honorable and noble life must constantly be rebuilt within by the beauty of a clean, courageous, and pure experience. This takes power.

This is a power which exalts a man above the baffling, frustrating circumstances of life. Undoubtedly this is a high claim, but nearly all of the great saints have testified to its reality. Madame Guyon, when in prison for Christ's sake, maintained a serene and cheerful heart and wrote a beautiful poem of herself as Christ's songbird shut up for Him. That takes power.

Incidental to this witnessing for Christ, there might be times when the Spirit's power would take the form of the prophetic gift of inspired preaching, in which the soul is caught up in rapture, filled with strange, lovely, bright, and beautiful thoughts which are uttered with a passionate fervor that the oratory of trained speakers can never approach.

In all cases, this power is simply the manifestation of the Spirit to aid us in witnessing for our beloved and exalted Lord. How foolish to think that this power should mean hysterical jumping and jerking and falling into trances. The apostle Paul taught differently: "God hath not given us the spirit of fear; but of power, and of love, and of a sound mind" (2 Tim. 1:7). The power that accompanies Pentecost would rather strengthen the mind, quicken the intellect, warm the heart, elevate and intensify the intellectual capacity of its possessor. . . .

The greatest of all the Old Testament prophets, if we except John the Baptist, was Moses. He was the prophet whom the Messiah should most resemble (Deut. 18:15). Yet Moses never had one moment when his intellect was darkened by hysterical emotional excitement. He talked to God "face to face, as a man speaketh unto his friend" (Exod. 33:11), but always in the full blaze of a brilliant and clear-seeing intellect. Jesus is the Supreme Prophet of all time, both in ancient Israel and the Christian Church, and He was the One of whom it was said, "He shall not strive, nor cry; neither shall any man hear his voice in the streets" (Matt. 12:19). Never once did He become hysterical or unduly excited. Never once did He fall in unconsciousness. Always His mind was clear under the anointing of the Holy Ghost.

Perhaps we cannot too much exalt the blessed work of the Spirit, sending streams of healing, of peace, and of joy through what was once the wilderness of the human heart and making the desert blossom as the rose. Nevertheless, all Christians must be on guard against loving our Lord for His gift, rather than loving Him as the Giver. We love Him for what He is, rather than for what He does for us. . . . Thomas à Kempis, who died in 1471, wrote:

> Many love Jesus so long as adversities happen not.
> Many praise and bless Him, so long as they receive any consolations from Him.
> But if Jesus hide himself, and leave them but a little while, they fall either into complaining, or into too much dejection of mind.
> But they who love Jesus for the sake of Jesus, and not for some special comfort of their own, bless Him in all tribulation and anguish of heart, as well as in the state of highest comfort.
> And although He should never be willing to give them comfort, they notwithstanding would ever praise Him, and wish to be always giving thanks.[6]

Sanctified as a Child[7]

The covenant that the farmer boy made with the High Priest of

---

6. *The Imitation of Christ,* 104.

7. The testimony of Charles Ewing Brown, in B. Smith, *Flames of Living Fire,* 13-17.

our redemption, kneeling in the grass on the hillside of southern Illinois 50-odd years ago, holds, and shall hold, forever.

Before a man testifies to the blessing of Christian perfection experienced by a child . . . perhaps he ought to recognize some of the greatest objections to such a form of witnessing.

First of all, we find that those who tremble most with doubt regarding the possibility of any experience of Christian perfection are the very ones who hold a granitelike conviction that, even if there were such an experience, no Christian should ever give testimony concerning its reality in his own being. . . .

In answering this objection, we would say that the same line of reasoning would prevent a Christian's making any testimony to the power of Christ's ability to save; but the whole course of Christian history is witness to the fact the major part of the Church's missionary and evangelistic progress is based upon such personal testimonies by Christians everywhere and throughout all time. If it is good to testify about the power of Christ to forgive sins, it is also good to testify about His power to give victory over original sin itself. . . .

WITNESS

Another objection regarding a child's experience of entire sanctification is that a few of the great holiness theologians have restricted that experience to adults only; and of course if that is true, a child who thought he received such an experience could only be self-deceived. . . .

I can only say that as the doctrine has developed in the Church, I believe the majority of holiness theologians today admit that the experience of entire sanctification is not measured by the capacity of the recipient, either in mental ability or maturity, provided only that he be mature enough to know himself as standing accountable before God.

And such indeed was the condition of the farmer boy who prayed for the baptism of the Spirit in the fields on the hillsides of southern Illinois in that momentous springtime. . . . Frankly, I do not know why the thought of God hung so constantly over my childhood, sometimes like the perfume of a flower garden, and again like the cold of a winter night . . . I never saw my mother read the Bible until after I myself was converted. . . .

Among the early memories of my father before his conversion, I recall that he was an infidel who even forbade me to read the Bible under any circumstances. . . . I went only occasionally to Sunday

School and hardly ever to church, and yet I read the Bible a great deal in spite of my father's prohibition—perhaps partly on account of that prohibition—and the thought of God comforted and tormented me through the passing years.

Then there came a miraculous spiritual movement in our community in which my infidel, drunken father was converted in January of 1895. I followed him in a few days, and some months later my mother entered into the fellowship of the faith.

Our spiritual leader . . . taught the doctrine of entire sanctification, and I began to pray earnestly and seek for that blessing in the latter part of the winter and into early spring. I was only 11 years old and knew merely the barest outlines of the teaching . . . But I felt such a burden of yearning on my heart that I can remember it yet as a pain, a longing, a depression of spirit, a heaviness of soul, a cry to God. . . .

HUNGER

Down on my knees in the orchard at the foot of the hill in an agony of yearning desire and struggle with doubt, I passed along the road trampled by Elijah when he heard the strong wind . . . There in the silence, with only the winds rustling the grass and the trees, the thunders of eternity came to me from the distance as a soft whisper of God: "It is done. This is Pentecost. This is the baptism of the Holy Spirit. This is fire and lightning and healing power. This is heart purity. This is fellowship with the gentle Jesus, the country Preacher who loved children; and this is the call to go and minister the healing of His Word and works wherever you can help others."

It has been a long time since I heard the whisper of Jesus in the old orchard on the hillside. . . . The boy has become a youth; the youth has become a man; the man is past middle age and has begun to turn his face toward the setting sun. But the covenant that the farmer boy made with the High Priest of our redemption, kneeling in the grass on the hillside of southern Illinois 50-odd years ago, holds, and shall hold, forever.

6

Col. Milton S. Agnew
(1905—)

Colonel Agnew, now retired in Santa Ana, Calif., served a long and distinguished career as a Salvation Army officer. The colonel held several posts of key influence in the Army, the last as principal of the School for Officers Training in New York City.

In the tradition of Gen. William Booth and Commissioner Samuel Logan Brengle, Colonel Agnew has been deeply committed to the doctrine and experience of entire sanctification. For many years he was active in the Christian Holiness Association and the Wesleyan Theological Society.

Holding degrees from the University of Chicago, the Salvation Army School for Officers Training, and Northern Baptist Theological Seminary, Colonel Agnew maintained a deep interest in biblical exposition. This longtime interest has led to four books in the area of Bible holiness: *The Better Covenant; Transformed Christians; The Holy Spirit, Friend and Counselor;* and *More than Conquerors.*

For *Great Holiness Classics* we have chosen Colonel Agnew's exposition of Romans 6 from *More than Conquerors.*

Sanctification Presented[1]
AN EXPOSITION OF ROMANS 6:1-23
Romans is unique in the exactitude of its definitions and of its

---

1. Milton S. Agnew, *More than Conquerors*, 66-92.

distinctions between one doctrine and another. No other book in the Scriptures, no other of Paul's Epistles so clearly establishes such a definition and distinction. In particular, as in no other section of the Bible, this Epistle distinguishes between "sin" and "sins," that is, between man's nature and the fruit of that nature.

In addition, throughout this section (5:12—8:39), Paul identifies sin with the definite article "the," unfortunately not translated into the English text. This "the" is a continual finger identifying something particular, something important, something exact. Is that sin the sin of murder? of uncleanness? of unbelief? No, it becomes apparent that this is the sin *principle,* introduced by Adam, sometimes known as original sin or Adamic sin, and inflicted upon all mankind. And so, throughout this section, "the" should be inserted before "sin"—"the sin"—to gain the full significance of Paul's thesis.

THE SIN PRINCIPLE

Christ, the believer's Justification and Sanctification, releases him in turn from the doom of sins and from the dominion of sin, from the penalty of sins and from the power of sin.

The first section of the book sets out Christ's work *for* the believer, and the second, Christ's work *in* the believer. The first section declares God's action in forgiving "sins," the second section His action in delivering from "sin," that which is the root of sinning. The first is justification, the second is sanctification. God can forgive *sins,* but *sin* He can never forgive nor tolerate. It must be removed, cleansed.

Furthermore, it will be instructive to note that both the forgiveness of sins and the deliverance from sin, both the justification and the sanctification of the believer are transactions, acts completed at a specific time.

This is identified by the tenses. In English, tense indicates the *time* of the action—past, present, future. In Greek, tense indicates not only the time but the *type* of action.

Present tense indicates a continued or repeated pattern of action and may be represented by a line of undefined length (———). The Greek aorist tense, on the other hand, speaks of an event completed at a given time, and may be represented by a point (·). . . .

Thus our justification is marked as an event defined by the aorist tense: "Therefore, *having been justified* by faith" (Rom. 5:1, NASB).[2]

Thus our sanctification, as we will see, is also marked again and

---

2. Unless otherwise indicated, all references in this chapter are from NASB.

again as an event defined by the aorist tense. For example, "For the law of the Spirit of life in Christ Jesus *has set* you *free* from the law of sin and of death" (Rom. 8:2).

These mark the two crisis experiences of the Christian's life as he pursues the full plan laid out for him by God through Christ.

This chapter (6) opens with a pointed question (v. 1), "Are we to continue in sin that grace might increase?" . . . Without doubt . . . it refers back to the 20th verse of the previous chapter, "But where sin increased, grace abounded all the more." Paul foresaw the question in the minds of his readers. Does that not then give us liberty? Cannot we continue in whatever sin we please since God's grace is so abundant? Does not that remove from us the responsibility of moral standards and of obedience to law? Such a question in the minds of his readers needed immediate answer.

But before looking to the answer, the reader may well look to the exact question. Paul does *not* ask, "Shall we continue *to* sin that grace might increase?" Rather, "Are we to continue *in* [the] sin?" Thus the question is not, Shall we continue to practice sin? but, Shall we continue in the principle of sin, under its dominion? . . .

Paul's answer to the question in verse 1 is forthright—"May it never be!" He used as strong a negative as was available in the Greek language.

Now this exclamatory denial of the necessity of the believer's continuing in sin serves as an introduction to a masterly chapter, which deals in turn with the *way into* holiness (1-7), the *way of* holiness (8-14), and the *liberty of* holiness (15-23).

The Way into Holiness

6:1-7

Using the two figures of speech of baptism and crucifixion as illustrative of the same truth through differing viewpoints, Paul says that there is a clearly defined way *into* this experience of holiness.

1. Through Baptism

1 What shall we say then? Are we to continue in sin that grace might increase?

2 May it never be! How shall we who died to sin still live in it?

3 Or do you not know that all of us who have been baptized into Christ Jesus have been baptized into His death?

4 Therefore we have been buried with Him through baptism into death, in order that as Christ was raised from the dead through the glory of the Father, so we too might walk in newness of life.

5 For if we have become united with Him in the likeness of His death, certainly we shall be also in the likeness of His resurrection.

He who is so baptized does not continue in *the* sin. Such a believer is baptized into Christ's death. By such a baptism this believer shows the death of his Lord, and himself becomes dead to sin, "baptized into His death . . . buried with Him through baptism into death." But the person who is so baptized into Christ is not only baptized into His death, but also into His resurrection—into newness of life, "so we too might walk in newness of life . . . in the likeness of His resurrection." This is not just a negative experience of death, but it is also a positive experience of living a continuous life, in the sense of "walking about"—a daily experience. This is for them who are "baptized into Christ."

But what baptism is this? Some would maintain that it is water baptism. Indeed, the phrase "buried with Him through baptism" is commonly associated with the baptismal fount. However, to accept this *merely* as water baptism is to subscribe to sacramental grace. For it would say that a man dies to sin by being immersed. He is saved through water. But water is not a *means* of grace. It can only be a symbol. Although water baptism, signifying the dedication of oneself to Christ, may indeed be a picture of the spiritual experience, it is not the *reality* of that experience. It is only a testimony to it.

Paul is talking about a real spiritual identification with Christ in life and death, which can only be *symbolized* by water baptism. And, as Talbot has expressed himself, "I know many people who have obeyed the teaching of the Lord in water baptism who do not know of this baptism *with* Christ unto death."[3] This is not a baptism into water, but "into . . . death" (v. 3).

Then, what baptism is this? Paul answers: "There is one body and one Spirit, just as also you were called in one hope of your calling; one Lord, one faith, one baptism, one God and Father of all" (Eph. 4:4-6). When considering eternal issues, whether for Jew or for Gentile, for slave or for free, there is the same baptism which is a means of grace,

---

3. Louis T. Talbot, *Addresses on Romans.*

and that is the baptism of the Spirit: "For by one Spirit we were all
baptized into one body, whether [we are] Jews or Greeks,
whether slaves or free, and we were all made to drink of one
Spirit" (1 Cor. 12:13).

HOLY
SPIRIT

But John also answers. He declared: "As for me, I baptize you
with water for repentance, but He who is coming after me is mightier
than I, and I am not fit to remove His sandals; He will baptize you with
the Holy Spirit and fire" (Matt. 3:11).

And what of Jesus himself? His answer, too, is forthright and
clear: "For John baptized with water, but you shall be baptized with
the Holy Spirit not many days from now" (Acts 1:5).

That effectual, transforming baptism into Christ, that baptism
which delivers from the sin principle, that baptism which is uniquely
Christian, is the Pentecostal experience, the baptism with the Holy
Spirit. No other religion offers this cleansing, empowering, transforming experience. It is the only uniquely Christian baptism.

Who, then, is thus baptized? If water baptism is but a symbol,
then what Christians are included in the classification? "All of us who
were baptized into Jesus Christ" (v. 3). There are those, like Ironside,
who affirm that *every* baptized Christian is included.[4] However, the
pronoun *hosoi*, translated "all of us who," is more than a relative
pronoun. It is a pronoun of characterization, of quantity, of measure
and degree. It refers to a certain number as contrasted to another
certain number. Actually the KJV probably is more accurate in trans-
lating it as "*so many of us as* were baptized." Matthew 14:36 reads,
"*As many as* touched [Him] were made perfectly whole" (KJV). There
were quite evidently those who did *not* touch Him, and therefore were
not made whole. This selective use of *hosoi* is consistent. Mark 3:10:
"For he had healed many . . . *as many as* had plagues" (KJV); and Rom.
2:12: "For *as many as* have sinned without [the] law shall also perish
without [the] law: and *as many as* have sinned in the law shall be
judged by the law" (KJV).

Hosoi, then, is a selective pronoun. It would truly say here that
there are some of "us" (believers) who have *not* been so baptized. It
would indicate that there is not necessarily given to every Christian the
baptism of the Holy Spirit as an unsought gift. It would remind us that
Jesus said the Holy Spirit, in His fullness, was available "to those who

---

4. Indeed there are unfortunate translations that erroneously indicate this. *The
Living Bible* says, "When we became Christians and were baptized." And both NEB and
TEV imply such with "*When* we were baptized."

"wait for the promise of the Father" (Acts 1:4, KJV). It should remind us that while all Christians "have the Spirit of Christ" (Rom. 8:9) through His convicting them of their sin (John 16:8-9) and through bringing them into the new birth (3:5-6), yet all Christians are not filled with the Spirit. As Billy Graham has expressed it, "All Christians possess the Holy Spirit; but not all Christians are possessed by the Holy Spirit."

Thus Paul declares that those "of us" who have been so baptized in the Holy Spirit do not continue to be ruled by the principle of sin, for "we have been buried with Him through baptism into death" (v. 4).

John Lawley caught something of the significance of such a baptism when he wrote:

> *Wanted, hearts baptized with fire,*
> *Hearts completely cleansed from sin,*
> *Hearts that will go to the mire,*
> *Hearts that dare do aught for Him;*
> *Hearts that will be firmer, braver,*
> *Hearts like heroes gone before,*
> *Hearts enjoying God's full favor,*
> *Hearts to love Him more and more.*

2. Through Crucifixion

6 knowing this, that our old self was crucified with Him, that our body of sin might be done away with, that we should no longer be slaves to sin;
7 for he who has died is freed from sin.

He who is crucified does not continue in *the* sin. This is not so much a new statement as a restatement—a different figure of speech illustrating another facet of the same experience. In each, the result is the same as to sin—we should not "still live in it" (v. 2); "we should no longer be slaves to sin" (v. 6). But now Paul likens the experience not to baptism but to crucifixion—when the old self, the old man is crucified with Christ. Now "our old self" is the unregenerate person of the past. It is our inherited nature infected in consequence of the Fall. It **THE OLD MAN** is all we were before we were Christians when we were men in the flesh, the "man of old," the unsaved man with all his habits and desires. That man was crucified with Christ. When Jesus died, he died, too. So untold millions were seen by God as hanging there with Christ. The old man is the "I" of Gal. 2:20, "I have been crucified with Christ; and it is no longer I who live, but Christ lives in me." The old self is crucified, is slain, is dead with Christ. It is a new man who lives.

Now, we may then well ask, who is crucified with Christ? Potentially, every believer is crucified with Him. He died with Christ on the cross of Calvary. Judicially he was crucified with Christ at his Lord's passion. *Potentially* he was delivered from the sin principle at Calvary. But *experimentally* this is only accomplished at the time of entire sanctification, the crucifixion of self. Jesus had called for it: "If anyone wishes to come after Me, let him deny himself, and take up his cross, and follow Me" (Matt. 16:24). Paul now experiences it and expounds on it.

It is just at this point that many a Christian falters. After conversion he discovers in himself a new nature that does "joyfully concur with the law of God" (Rom. 7:22). But he learns to his distress that he *also* has an old nature, an "old self," aroused and battling for supremacy. There occurs a profoundly disturbing struggle between the two natures, the two "I's" of 7:14-25. . . . Oh, that the believer might at that time discover the deliverance that is possible by crucifying the old man—the old I! If all Christians are potentially crucified with Christ on the Cross, they are there in fact *only when they place themselves there.*

A helpful statement is made in The Salvation Army *Handbook on Doctrine:*

> Believers must do more than associate themselves with Calvary as those who look upon the Sin-bearer who suffers there *for* them. They are called to identify themselves wth Him *on* the Cross, as being crucified *with* Him and fully united with Him, and He with them, so that His death means the death of their old nature, leading to a new life in the power of the Resurrection.

How many thousands of Christians have never faced the fact of the necessity of being crucified with Christ! They remain self-centered, shallow, defeated Christians.

In considering the three crosses on the hill we find a great throng who identify with the cross to His left, with the cursing, unrepentant thief. These are the lost multitudes, dying in their sins, to whom we must ever go in urgent compassion, pointing them to the Savior who really loves them enough to die for them.

There is also a great throng identified with the cross to His right, with the repentant thief whom our Lord assured with the gracious words: "Today you shall be with Me in Paradise" (Luke 23:43).

But it is another thing to identify yourself with the center cross, to find yourself crucified with Christ. And this remains the great challenge to God's people everywhere. To this He calls His people with gentle urgency.

As Talbot states, "It is a blessed experience to kneel in wonderment and adoration at the Cross, the place of salvation. But it is another thing to see yourself *on* the Cross beside your Lord." He then relates a very telling incident recounted by the late Dr. F. B. Meyer concerning his coming into this truth. Dr. Meyer says, in part:

> My soul was saturated with the message of the sixth chapter of Romans; therefore I prepared a sermon on the subject to be delivered the following Sunday. When the day came, as I stood before the mirror to adjust my tie before going into the pulpit, I thought of my sermon. I began to enumerate the points, thinking of the Cross.
>
> **A TESTIMONY**
>
> Then I said to myself, "Have I ever been on that Cross? Potentially I was there with Christ, but in experience have I ever been there? Have my pride, my hunger for popularity, my greed—have these ever been put there? Have I felt the loneliness, the sorrow, the agony Christ felt on Calvary?"
>
> This humbled me, and I fell to my knees, trying to pray. But I could not. Something seemed to say, "Have you been on that Cross?" I got up from my knees and walked to my mirror and said, "O God! Nail my pride, my love of self, my desire for popularity, my greed, all the lusts of the flesh to the Cross." Then, *then* I actually could see myself hanging there, dying *with Christ.*
>
> Instead of preaching the sermon, I told my congregation of the experience and made an appeal that every Christian get on his knees and stay there until he saw himself on the Cross.

This experience of that great man of God was the beginning and the secret of his great success. His "old man," everything that was according to Adam, was put upon the Cross, crucified with Christ. And when the "old man" was crucified, he was baptized into the death of Christ as well.

As Laurin has so aptly stated, "If self is on the Cross, Christ is on the throne; but if self is on the throne, Christ is on the Cross."[5]

The poet has given us a challenging verse which the worshiper must consider carefully when he sings:

> *Come, O Spirit, come to sanctify*
> *All my body, mind, and will;*
> *Come, oh, come, and self now crucify;*
> *Let me henceforth be like Jesus.*

---

5. Roy L. Laurin, *Romans, Where Life Begins.*

And to what purpose shall the "old man," our "old self" be crucified? The answer is twofold: in order that "our body of sin might be done away with," and in order that "we should no longer be slaves to [the principle of] sin." The second is quite plain—that the lordship of sin might be broken. The first deserves some examination. What is this "body of sin"? And what does it mean that it should "be done away with"?

Let us first examine the verb, which is *katargeō*. The translation here given ("might be done away with") is out of step with other renderings of the verb in the NASB. Take Rom. 3:3, "Their unbelief will not *nullify* the faithfulness of God, will it?" Or Heb. 2:14, "That through death He might *render powerless* him [the devil] who had the power of death." Or Rom. 3:31, "Do we then *nullify* the Law through faith?" In the light of this, and indeed the true meaning of the verb, we will accept the margin translation of "made powerless." As Vine has so aptly put it, "The word *katargeō* never means to annihilate. The general idea is that of depriving a thing of the use for which it was intended. It implies not loss of *being,* but loss of *well-being."* [6]

Now consider the "body of sin." Some would equate this to the "totality of the sin principle." In that case the "totality of the very principle of sin" shall, as far as I am concerned, be made powerless, be made of none effect, unfruitful, ineffectual. This is an acceptable interpretation.

On the other hand it is held by some that *soma* always is used by Paul for the human body, literally or in a figurative and a spiritual way. And this is the body of which sin has taken possession. Laurin explains it: "The old man refers to our old spiritual nature; the body of sin, to our physical body. One is the *source* of sinfulness, the other, the *place* where sin operates." The one is "crucified," the other "made powerless," ineffectual, unfruitful as far as being an instrument of sin. That is what *The Amplified Bible* apparently has in mind when it says: "In order that [our] body, [which is the instrument] of sin, might be

THE HUMAN
BODY NOT
DESTROYED

made ineffective and inactive for evil." And this, of course, would make our bodies acceptable as the temple of the Holy Spirit. This second is an acceptable alternate interpretation.

At this point it is well to note that it is "we who died to sin" (v. 2). Sin as a principle remains very much alive, though not in us. Rather *the old self is to be crucified in order that the body shall no longer be*

---

6. W. E. Vine, *The Epistle to the Romans.*

used by Satan for the operation of sin. An understanding of this is most essential to a true comprehension of God's plan for scriptural holiness. A misunderstanding can be the basis of much bewilderment and false doctrine.

Thus, "He who has died is freed [or acquitted] from sin" (v. 7). In the light of the preceding verse, this clearly refers, not to physical death, which is *not at all our savior,* but to the death of "our old self," to the crucifixion of the old man. This, and this alone, brings freedom from the very principle of sin. Talbot expresses himself on the subject: "Some Christians who realize their justification before God are still under the power of sin. Every believer has been saved from the *guilt* of sin, but how few have been saved from the *power* of sin. God's plan is that we die out to sin."

3. By an Act of Decisiveness

We have already noted that, like justification, the entrance into holiness is a crisis act, marked by the Greek aorist tense, the tense of the simple occurrence of an action. This is emphasized here with the aorist tense governing the several verbs "have been baptized" (v. 3), "was crucified" (v. 6), "made powerless" (v. 6, margin), and "has died" (v. 7). Thus the scripture does *not* say that we are *progressively* or *repeatedly* to put away something within us called the old self, but to crucify him *as an act,* as an event at a point of time.

Simpson pointedly observes, "There is a moment when we consent to die, and pronounce sentence of death upon ourselves, and then God executes it. . . . We must not everlastingly be getting crucified over again." Then he adds, "Calvary is not only for sins, but sinfulness. To be crucified with Him it is necessary that we make this an actual fact in our experience and yield ourselves unto death with Christ."[7]

IN A MOMENT

*   *   *

Now there are in general three possible attitudes toward the principle of sin:

a. There is the *fatalistic approach,* that, because of a continual warring of the flesh against the spirit (Gal. 5:17), sin must be indulged, and that the more we sin the more grace there is to meet it (Rom. 6:1). But Paul cries out against that, "May it never be!" Furthermore he

---

7. A. B. Simpson, *Christ in the Bible,* vol. 2, *Romans.*

declares (Gal. 5:24), "Now those who belong to Christ Jesus have crucified the flesh with its passions and desires."

b. There is the attitude of *sinless perfection,* that in this life it is possible to live with Adamic perfection. But this would involve the annihilation, the destruction of the very sin principle in the world so that it can never rise again. This, however, is supported neither by Scripture nor by experience. Sin remains very much alive in the world. It is we who must die to sin.

WE DIE TO SIN

c. There is the attitude of *Christian perfection* which is offered to the believer as an act of deliverance and as a life of continuous victory, as presented in this chapter of Romans. Sin has been rendered unfruitful and of none effect in the life of the sanctified believer. This may also [show] that God's plan for the believer's victory over the sin principle is not *suppression,* which speaks of an endless struggle, as in chapter 7. Rather it is deliverance (v. 6), it is freedom (v. 7), it is the experience of being "dead to sin, but alive to God" (v. 11). As someone has well declared, "To say that I *must* sin is to deny the foundation of Christianity. To say that I *cannot* sin is to deceive myself. But to say that I *need not* sin is to state a divine privilege."

Again we look to our songwriters for helpful expression. James Nicholson, the Methodist minister, expresses confidence in the final verse of his searching song:

> *The blessing by faith I receive from above.*
> *Oh, glory, my soul is made perfect in love!*
> *My prayer has prevailed, and this moment I know*
> *The Blood is applied, I am whiter than snow.*

And what says Gen. Albert Orsborn of The Salvation Army regarding this orderly life of Christian perfection?

> *Spirit of eternal love,*
> *Guide me, or I blindly rove;*
> *Set my heart on things above,*
>   *Draw me after Thee.*
> *Earthly things are paltry show,*
> *Phantom charms, they come and go;*
> *Give me constantly to know*
>   *Fellowship with Thee.*
>
> *Come, O Spirit, take control*
> *Where the fires of passion roll;*
> *Let the yearnings of my soul*
>   *Center all in Thee.*

Call into Thy fold of peace
Thoughts that seek forbidden ways;
Calm and order all my days,
    Hide my life in Thee.

It is Charles Wesley who gives us this delightful prayer of faith.

Be pleased to keep me, Lord, this day
    Without committing sin,
And with me let Thy Spirit stay,
    And ever dwell within.

Thou canst from every sin secure;
    And is it not Thy will
Still to preserve Thy servant pure
    From every touch of ill?

My soul on Thee, O Lord, relies,
    Thine arms are my defense;
My soul hell, earth, and sin defies
    To come and pluck me thence.

The Way of Holiness

6:8-14

Having outlined in the first seven verses of the chapter the way *to* or *into* holiness, Paul takes occasion now to speak of the way *of* holiness, or the art of possessing holiness. He bases his argument in these several verses on the first phrase of verse 8, "Now if we have died with Christ."

In Greek there are three "ifs," all found in John 8: the if of contrary to fact, verse 42; the if of condition, verse 36; and the if of fact, of reality, verse 46. It should be noted that this "if" *(ei)* in verse 8 is the if of reality. The *20th Century New Testament* translates it, "Now *since* we are dead with Christ." Paul thus addresses himself to *those who have been crucified with Christ,* and therefore to those who have been freed from sin.

To such sanctified believers he then gives these three thoughts: "Believe" (v. 8), and the commands "consider" (v. 11) and "present" (v. 13). These words express three *characteristics* of the Christian mind which make real a life of spiritual sanctification.

    8 Now if we have died with Christ, we believe that we shall also live with Him,

9 knowing that Christ, having been raised from the dead, is never to die again; death no longer is master over Him.

10 For the death that He died, He died to sin, once for all; but the life that He lives, He lives to God.

11 Even so consider yourselves to be dead to sin, but alive to God in Christ Jesus.

12 Therefore do not let sin reign in your mortal body that you should obey its lusts,

13 and do not go on presenting the members of your body to sin as instruments of unrighteousness; but present yourselves to God as those alive from the dead, and your members as instruments of righteousness to God.

14 For sin shall not be master over you, for you are not under law, but under grace.

1. By Faith

"We believe" (v. 8). Holiness or sanctification is a life of faith: "an inheritance among those who have been sanctified by faith in Me" (Acts 26:18). But during the centuries the church has gone through the experiment of seeking to live the life of holiness by works rather than by faith. For example, the second century saw an acceptance of *persecution* and even *martyrdom* as the true signs of a holy life. There were even those who sought out the martyr's death that they might be known as among the saints of the church.

A following period gave accent to *monasticism* as the main source of Christian perfection. Forgetting Christ's words, "I do not ask Thee to take them out of the world, but to keep them from the evil one" (John 17:15), the church felt that the recluse in the monastery was the true saint. Soon the church added *asceticism,* on the premise that all evil is of the body, and that men who withdrew from normal bodily life, who mortified the flesh, and who refrained from marriage, received the particular blessings of the Lord. *Sacramentalism* early made its entry, with the church declaring that men were saved by baptism and forgiven of their postbaptismal sins by the Eucharist or Mass. Even *ceremonialism* and *ritualism* have had their place among some as the chief source of imparting or marking holiness in the worshiper.

It was John Wesley who sensed in these several methods their inadequacy, their shortcomings, their unscripturalness, and who proclaimed again the scriptural, first-century doctrine of sanc-**FAITH** tification, not by works, but by an act of faith, and that a practice of sanctifying faith must be the cornerstone for a holy life.

Now this faith, based on the finished work of the resurrected

Christ who "died to sin, once for all; but the life that He lives, He lives to God" (v. 10), is the faith that "we shall also live with Him" (v. 8), both here and hereafter. This faith accepts man's inability to live a holy life by self-resolve, by good works, but accepts the absolute sufficiency and finality in the death of Christ for all purposes for which He died—our regeneration, our justification, our sanctification.

Such is sanctifying faith.

2. By Acceptance

"Even so consider yourselves to be dead to sin, but alive to God" (v. 11). If faith makes *real* the life of holiness, an active acceptance of the fact makes *practical* this life. Paul terms this the act of "considering." Now such a consideration must be done on the basis of what transpired in Christ—"Even so," or, in like manner. After He died, all relation to sin ceased. Sin could never make Him its victim again at the Cross. Similarly, while we lived, that is, before we died with Christ, we also had relation to sin. But these relations must cease with our death with Him. Thus, "Even so," or, in like manner accept the fact that you are "dead to sin, but alive to God in Christ Jesus."

This verse is an application of all that precedes. The death with Christ and the life with Christ are real. The calling of the Christian is to live up to them.

Now the word "consider" has an interesting connotation. Translated "reckon" by KJV, "count" in the NIV, and "regard" by NEB, it means "to take account" of something which is a fact. What is true in itself should be true in our convictions and consciousness. Don't "consider" "as though it were true," as a child makes believe that he is a fairy or goblin. Not as though it were so, but *because it is true.* God says so; we too may say so. Consider is a product of logical, careful thought, and not an exercise of the imagination or of wishing it could happen. In commenting on the KJV, Laurin has aptly pointed out that "reckon" means "to take account" as an accountant takes account of the figures from which he gets his balance. While Ironside comments, "Count as true what God considers true."[8]

The Living Bible has aptly translated this verse: "So look upon your old sin nature as dead and unresponsive to sin, and instead be alive to God, alert to him, through Jesus Christ our Lord."

This death is an act, a crisis. Godet has remarked, "The believer

---

8. H. A. Ironside, *Lectures on the Epistle to the Romans.*

does not get disentangled from sin gradually. He breaks with it in
Christ, once for all."[9] So a man who is dead to sin, when
DEAD TO SIN temptation comes his way, can say, "I am dead." When injury
comes, he can reply, "But I am dead." When insult comes, he
can produce the death certificate and remind himself that he is dead
unto this. To one who asked him the secret of his distinguished service
for Christ, George Müller replied, "There was a day when I died, died
utterly, died to George Müller, his opinions, preferences, tastes, and
will; died to the world, its approval and censure, died to the approval
or blame even of my brethren and friends, and since then I've studied
only to show myself approved unto God."

Conversely, if one is dead to sin, he must be alive to God. Holiness is not just negative. Holiness is positive, being alive to God's
standards, alive to His fellowship, alive to His will. It was
ALIVE TO GOD Jesus who said, "I came that they might have life, and might
have it abundantly" (John 10:10).

If death is a crisis act (in the aorist tense)—and it is—"consider,"
"reckon" (in the present tense) is a daily practice, a constant assurance,
a state of life.

Of this dual experience Clarke has stated, "Die as truly unto sin
as He died for sin. Live as truly unto God as He lives with God."[10]
While Simpson has commented, "The death is for a moment, but the
life is for evermore. The death is one act, but the life is a perpetual
succession of acts and experiences. Sanctification is not merely the
death of the old, but the resurrection of the new."

Of this the sanctified Christian will constantly take account, because it is true. He died . . . he is alive.

3. By Surrender

"Present yourselves to God" (v. 13). According to the present
tense in the Greek the first two acts which we have reviewed are really
practices—that is, the daily practice of believing, and the continuous
practice of considering or accepting. But this, the act of yielding, is a
single act, a crisis. "Present" is in the aorist tense as a call to an act of
surrender, just as specific as the single act of being crucified, of dying.
Interestingly it immediately follows the present tense warning not to
"go on presenting" the members of one's body to sin as instruments of

---

9. *Epistle to the Romans.*
10. Adam Clarke, *Commentary*, vol. 6.

unrighteousness, a practice formerly followed when we were alive to sin.

But now, to yield yourselves to God, and then to withdraw, and then to yield again, and again withdraw makes for enfeeblement of decision and contributes to tragic weakness of character. Too many Christians practice just that. God's plan is that in every area of decision we yield once to His will in that area. In such a decisive act,

SURRENDER ONCE FOR ALL tempations are met at once. There need not come a *new* decision every time the same testing and temptation faces the believer, though there may be frequent recurrent dedications to reemphasize the fact of *the* surrender.

Some have to argue and dispute and decide anew every time a certain temptation arises. That is unnecessary. The only way to live the life of holiness is to live it on a once-for-all decision of surrender to God. Holiness *can* be and holiness *must* be an experience of growth. But such growth must be based upon a foundation of lasting decisions. As indecision and decision mark the difference between the fluttering butterfly, ever changing his course and never arriving anywhere, and the soaring eagle who sets his course by the distant landmark and holds resolutely to it, so they mark the difference between the vacillating child of God, halting "between two opinions" (1 Kings 18:21), and the resolute Christian whose final act of surrender has been made.

Now this yielding is twofold: first of all, yielding yourself, that is your renewed self, "a living . . . sacrifice" (12:1); and, secondly, yielding your "members." By members Paul may have meant members of your body—the eyes, the feet, the ears, the hands; or he may have meant the talents which are related to those parts of the body—the thoughts, the service, the skill, the sight, the voice. In either case the body and its members are usable by God as "*weapons* of righteousness" (6:13, margin). What a stirring thought: the warring Son of God using your members, your very nature as weapons in His eternal warfare with the powers of darkness. There is a sobering counterthought. They are "weapons" either "to sin" or "to God"—one or the other. The choice is ours.

And, finally, the surrender is not to service, not to work, not to obedience, not a surrender to sacrifice, to the church, to the ministry, but rather a presentation to God himself. It is under these conditions, then, that verse 14 states, "Sin shall not be the master over you."

This then is the *way* of holiness, the art of unbroken possession by the Holy Spirit, the continuous pattern of full salvation.

Again the songwriters give us vehicles of expression . . . We are indebted to Ruth Tracy for the searching lines:

> *Lord, Thou art questioning: Lovest thou Me?*
> *Yea, Lord, Thou knowest, my answer must be;*
> *But since love's value is proved by love's test,*
> *Jesus, I'll give Thee the dearest and best.*
>
> *How couldst Thou smile on me if, in my heart,*
> *I was unwilling from treasures to part?*
> *Since my redemption cost Thee such a price,*
> *Utmost surrender alone will suffice.*
>
> *All in my heart, Lord, Thou canst read;*
> *Master, Thou knowest I love Thee indeed.*
> *Ask what Thou wilt my devotion to test,*
> *I will surrender the dearest and best.*

Or consider the verses by Lowell L. Mason:

> *Lord, I make a full surrender,*
> *All I have I yield to Thee;*
> *For Thy love, so great and tender,*
> *Asks the gift of me.*
> *Lord, I bring my whole affection;*
> *Claim it, take it for Thine own,*
> *Safely kept by Thy protection,*
> *Fixed on Thee alone.*
>
> *Lord, my will I here present Thee*
> *Gladly, now no longer mine;*
> *Let no evil thing prevent me*
> *Blending it with Thine.*
> *Lord, my life I lay before Thee;*
> *Hear this hour the sacred vow;*
> *All Thine own I now restore Thee,*
> *Thine forever now.*

Or, finally, be blessed by the words penned by Brindley Boone, written in a time of doubt regarding God's will for him.

> *I would be Thy holy temple,*
> *Sacred and indwelt by Thee;*
> *Naught then could stain my commission,*
> *'Tis Thy divine charge to me.*

Seeking to mirror Thy glory,
Living to answer Thy call,
Each faithful vow now renewing,
Gladly I yield Thee my all.

Take Thou my life, Lord,
In deep submission I pray;
My all to Thee dedicating,
Accept my offering today.

The Liberty of Holiness

6:15-23

The chapter now is punctuated by a second . . . question. But it is worded differently from the question in verse 1. This one says, "What then? Shall we sin because we are not under law but under grace?" (v. 15). As Robertson explains, these are occasional acts of sin, as opposed to the principle of sin mentioned in verse 1.[11] The questioner muses, Surely we may take a night off now and then and sin a little bit, since we are under grace.

Godet is quoted as saying, "Will this death to sin be strong enough to banish sin *in every particular case?* Should we not be allowed to commit an act of sin now and then?" To this Paul again gives the horrified response, "May it never be!" What a contrast this to the creed which teaches that we sin daily in thought, and word, and deed. If the Bible teaches anything, it teaches that sin is not a necessity. John in his first letter advises, "My little children, I am writing these things to you that you may not sin [Gr., "at all"]" (2:1), that is, that you do not commit *even one* sin. This must continually be God's standard for His children.

This leads to a consideration of the *liberty* of holiness.

15 What then? Shall we sin because we are not under law but under grace? May it never be!
16 Do you not know that when you present yourselves to someone as slaves for obedience, you are slaves of the one whom you obey, either of sin resulting in death, or of obedience resulting in righteousness?
17 But thanks be to God that though you were slaves of sin, you became obedient from the heart to that form of teaching to which you were committed,

---

11. A. T. Robertson, *Word Pictures in the New Testament,* vol. 4.

18 and having been freed from sin, you became slaves of righteousness.

19 I am speaking in human terms because of the weakness of your flesh. For just as you presented your members as slaves to impurity and to lawlessness, resulting in further lawlessness, so now present your members as slaves to righteousness, resulting in sanctification.

20 For when you were slaves of sin, you were free in regard to righteousness.

21 Therefore what benefit were you then deriving from the things of which you are now ashamed? For the outcome of those things is death.

22 But now having been freed from sin and enslaved to God, you derive your benefit, resulting in sanctification, and the outcome, eternal life.

23 For the wages of sin is death, but the free gift of God is eternal life in Christ Jesus our Lord.

Paul, after giving his horrified denial, exclaimed, "That's slavery" (v. 17). Then, in deference to the "weakness of your flesh" (v. 19), that is your being human, he put his answer into a parable, the parable of a love slave.

Paul had introduced this figurative expression of the love slave for the first time in his writings in the opening verse of this letter when he declared himself to be "a bond-servant of Christ Jesus." It was a Jewish, not a Roman, pattern. But undoubtedly there were enough Jews in Rome to interpret it to the uninstructed. According to the Scriptures a Jew could become a slave because of indebtedness or through war. He might be redeemed from his slavery by a friend, or released because of illness. The year of jubilee meant freedom for all slaves, and none served more than seven years.

However, there was also provided a love service which was entered into voluntarily, and which was to be for life. The practice is outlined in Exodus 21. "If you buy a Hebrew slave, he shall serve for six years; but on the seventh he shall go out as a free man without payment. . . . But if the slave plainly says, 'I love my master, my wife and my children; I will not go out as a free man,' then his master shall bring him to God, then he shall bring him to the door or the doorpost. And his master shall pierce his ear with an awl; and he shall serve him permanently" (vv. 2, 5-6). Thus, the love slave came to be known as "the slave with the pierced ear." It was to something of this nature that Paul referred when he said, "I bear on my body the brand-marks of Jesus" (Gal. 6:17).

It is to this Jewish custom that Paul again makes reference in this chapter. But now he expands the figure. He says that the slave of sin can be freed from his evil master, turn to a new Lord, and, attaching himself with the bonds of devotion, become a love slave to this new Master, even to God.

Supported by this entire section, verses 22 and 23 are the heart of the passage and contain three glorious truths.

1. There Is a Freedom from (the) Sin

The first requirement for freedom from sin is the awakening of the justified person to the fact that *sin is a master.* There is freedom only when sin is recognized as lord (vv. 16-17*a*). Newell has said, "Many people who have been convicted of the guilt of sin and rely on the blood of Jesus Christ for putting away that guilt have not yet seen the state of sin as abject slavery." That Paul had seen this state of slavery is apparent from his terrified cry as he reflected on his previous unsanctified state: "Wretched man that I am! Who will set me free from the body of this death?" (7:24).

A second step toward freedom from sin is the necessity of a *choice* between two masters (vv. 18, 22*a*). Paul found himself beset by two masters, claiming his obedience and his loyalty (7:19). This he found an untenable position.

Jesus recognized this impossibility when He declared, "No one can serve two masters" (Matt. 6:24). Or did He say just that? Not exactly. More particularly Jesus said no man can *continue* to serve two masters (Greek present continuing tense). He was not speaking to sinful people. He was speaking to disciples in the service of their Lord. He was not giving a declaration as to how to be saved. He was rather giving an outline of how to live a godly life. Examination of the Greek verb tenses will show that Jesus continued, "Either he will [in the future—eventually] hate the one and love the other, or he will [future—someday] hold to one and despise the other." Then He concluded by saying, "You [who are now My disciples] cannot [continue to] serve God and mammon."

There is a pointed example in Demas, who, as companion to Paul, tried desperately to serve two masters, but finally ended up by forsaking his Christian duty and clinging to the world (2 Tim. 4:10).

Paul was here getting to the very heart of the sin question. Laurin, in connection with this verse, has commented, "Most people deal with the problem of sin outside, at the place of its commission, whereas we ought to deal with it inside, at the place of its temptation."

Paul further presses the solution by saying that not only must you choose between two masters, but you must attach yourself to the one. There is no absolute independence for man. His nature requires him to serve some master. You must become a "love slave" to God (vv. 18, 22). The only true freedom from sin, from the principle of sin, is an attachment as a love slave to a new master—to One "who loved [us], and gave himself for" us (Gal. 2:20, KJV). . . .

2. There Is an Immediate Benefit and a Final Assurance

The Amplified Bible expresses the thought of verses 22-23 well: "But now since you have been set free from sin and have become the slaves of God, you have your present reward in holiness and its end is eternal life. For the wages which sin pays is death; but the [bountiful] free gift of God is eternal life through (in union with) Jesus Christ our Lord."

The reward indeed is holiness. And that isn't future or distant, it is present. There is a "now" in the Greek, indeed a strengthened or sharpened form, *nuni,* meaning according to Robertson, "right now" or "just now." This is caught in the KJV with the word "now," and expressed by *The Amplified Bible* with the word "present." All this emphasizes the fact that holiness is a *now* experience. We are reminded that physical death indeed is not our sanctifier. Paul elsewhere emphasizes this in Titus 2:11-14: "For the grace of God has appeared, bringing salvation to all men, instructing us to deny ungodliness and worldly desires and to live sensibly, righteously and godly *in the present age,* looking for the blessed hope and the appearing of the glory of our great God and Savior, Christ Jesus; who gave Himself for us, that HE MIGHT REDEEM US FROM EVERY LAWLESS DEED AND PURIFY FOR HIMSELF A PEOPLE FOR HIS OWN POSSESSION, zealous for good deeds."

3. The Final Assurance Is Life Eternal

Eternal life stems from holiness of life, as indicated in verse 23. This verse has been honored again and again by the Holy Spirit as a gospel text to the unsaved. And it will continue to be so honored. But this line is directed, not to the sinner, but rather to the justified man, to the child of God who is still trying to serve two masters. To such a man Paul gives the warning that persisting in the principle of sin as master will bring wages, the wages of death. But to him who will make Jesus, not only his Savior, but also his Lord and Master, there is a gift. That gift is eternal life.

7

Everett L. Cattell
(1905-81)

Everett Lewis Cattell was born September 16, 1905, into a Friends home belonging to the Ohio Yearly Meeting. In the preface to *The Spirit of Holiness* he writes: "During the last 100 years large sections of American Quakerism have been deeply influenced by the Wesleyan emphasis of the National Holiness Association of America. Hence, I was brought up on holiness."

As a Friends minister Dr. Cattell served nine years pastoring churches in Ohio—Columbus, Springfield, and Cleveland. During the Cleveland pastorate he also taught as a part-time professor at Cleveland Bible Institute.

From 1936 to 1957 Dr. Cattell served overseas with the Friends Missionary Society in India. His services there included ministries in Bible conferences and churches of many denominations. During those years he also served as executive secretary to the Evangelical Fellowship of India.

In 1957, at the call of his denomination, he returned to the United States to become its general superintendent. Then in 1960 he was inaugurated as the seventh president of Malone College, Canton, Ohio, where he served until his retirement in 1972.

Dr. Cattell wrote three books: *The Self-giving Missionary, The Spirit of Holiness*, and *Christian Mission: A Matter of Life*, published the year that he died.

From *The Spirit of Holiness*, published in 1963, three chapters were chosen. These sections were selected because in them Dr. Cattell gives such a clear and accurate statement of holiness theology in terms of our human experience of God's grace. He seeks to help us understand the truths of cleansing and empowering in terms of our own conscious experience.

Dr. Cattell especially wishes to help Christians live the sanctified life. In his preface he speaks of concern for the multitudes who have passed through the crisis and who need help in going on from there to living out the holy life.

Throughout, the author emphasizes the goal and essence of entire sanctification as Christlikeness. His key descriptive phrase, borrowed from Paul, is: "Your life is hid with Christ in God" (Col. 3:3).

In the preface below, Dr. Cattell gives his own rationale for the book.

PREFACE[1]

It has been my happy privilege for many years, both in America and in India, to preach across the lines that divide Christians in their views of the deeper spiritual life. This book contains the gist of what I have preached, now from one passage of Scripture and now from another.

I was brought up in the Friends church with its traditional emphasis upon the work of the Holy Spirit. During the last 100 years large sections of American Quakerism have been deeply influenced by the Wesleyan emphasis of the National Holiness Association of America [now Christian Holiness Association]. Hence, I was brought up on "holiness." As a young Christian trying to live the sanctified life, I found problems in correlating the teaching I heard with my own experience. This drove me to a deeper study of the actual teaching.

Here I found that much confusion was being caused by the fact that the Holiness Movement was emphasizing certain truths or facets of truth to the neglect or near exclusion of others. For example, the valid truth about crisis experience had been so emphasized GROWTH as to leave the development of the holy life neglected. The average preacher was out in every sermon to catch one more soul for the crisis—and showed little concern for the multitude who had passed through the crisis and needed help in going on from there to the living out of the holy life. Another weakness was the failure to distinguish between the carnal nature to be eradicated and the purified human nature which needs to be disciplined. Many were afraid of

---

1. *The Spirit of Holiness*, 6-7.

discipline for fear of being guilty of "suppression." Nor was temptation in the life of holiness given adequate treatment.

By studying the writings of the really responsible leaders in the movement and particularly by going back to Wesley himself, I found the answers to these questions given, but usually tucked away out of the light of major emphasis. Moreover, I found that the doctrine of holiness squared better with Scripture when it was kept in balance. And so I began to preach with an effort to clarify the confusions I had experienced. The result, as it has developed over the years, is contained in the following pages.

Before I went to India I had only slight association with people in the Victorious Life movement, but nevertheless I came to feel that the differences between "Holiness" and "Victorious Life" were more a matter of definition than of reality. In India I met, perforce, all kinds of people. We missionaries, thank God, are not able to live in the splendid denominational isolation of the West. As doors for ministry opened to groups of varying background, I was driven to a more scriptural and elemental expression of truth than is required in a circle where shibboleths reign. I have tried to understand what differing views of the deeper spiritual life, or life of holiness, really are, and to give a clear statement of what I believe all views have in common.

It remains for the reader to discover whether this presentation is helpful or not. I am impressed from study that life in the Spirit is hard to express, just because it is life. Words, at best, are "frozen thought" and inadequate fully to express life. Even the apostle Paul struggled to find adequate language for the paradoxes he experienced. It is therefore of the essence of bigotry for any of us to claim finality for our way of expressing the deeper spiritual life. May God help us past words to the reality of what Phillips calls "the holiness which is no illusion" (Eph. 4:24).

The Sanctification of Self[2]

In this chapter Cattell seeks to make clear the distinction between carnal self-centeredness and the essential human self. God proposes to crucify the self-centered spirit, but our essential human self He intends to shape more and more into the image of Christ.

---

2. Ibid., chap. 2.

The Holy Spirit is given to the redeemed person at his conversion. It is proper, however, to distinguish this from what is often referred to as the "fullness of the Spirit." What is meant by the "fullness of the Spirit" is that He now fully possesses us. We only have Him in fullness when He fully controls us. Theoretically and scripturally there is no reason why this could not happen simultaneously with conversion, but in actual practice it seems for nearly everyone to happen later. This receiving of the Holy Spirit is expressed by Paul in Rom. 5:5, "The love of God is shed abroad in our hearts by the Holy Ghost which is given unto us."

I was preaching from this text once under very uninspiring circumstances. The Christmas holidays were over and we evangelists were back in camp. It was rainy and cold as we sat on the mud floor of an Indian mud-walled house, trying to have a Sunday morning worship service. There were less than a dozen of us. We had just passed through some bitter experiences of rejection, and everyone felt something less than inspired, if not positively low. I was trying to bring a little message from the Word when suddenly came one of those experiences, which preachers understand, of being given something from above. It was a thought about the expression "shed abroad." Of course God is love and so shedding His love abroad is synonymous with shedding abroad himself in the person of His Holy Spirit. But shedding abroad is a term best figured in light. Press the button, the bulb is illuminated, and instantly light is shed abroad throughout the room. So far as the light is concerned it is ready instantly to occupy every nook and corner of the room. The only reason for its not arriving is the presence of things which cast shadows—boxes, furniture, people, and the like.

Then I pictured to my Indian friends a *Diwali* preparation. This is a Hindu holiday in the fall after the rains have stopped. It is preceded by a thorough housecleaning, fresh whitewashing, and decorating with lights. I reminded them of how boxes and furniture and all movable things are put out of a room before it is swept and whitewashed. I told them also of the boxes and furniture and things that clutter up our hearts and cast shadows and keep the Holy Spirit from penetrating to the corners so that He might occupy in fullness. These things I labeled jealousy and bitterness and wrath and evil speaking and gossip and standing up for your family members when they are wrong, the love of money, and the like.

I do not think my picture made much impression on the

preachers—it was too simple and not very theological—but there was a village man present who listened, for a change, with rapt attention. **ATTITUDES** Although he was a recent convert, he was not altogether satisfactory. He had fixed his eyes on other Christians and their shortcomings. He was both jealous and bitter over their preferment in jobs and positions in the church. Much of his feeling had grown to ugly proportions.

For some weeks after my preaching I did not know just what had happened that morning. The fact was that this simple villager had a housecleaning. He could not have labeled it theologically nor have given a very satisfactory testimony about it. But the cleaning was real. Weeks later we were talking together as a group about the fullness of the Spirit when suddenly light dawned, and he told us that this was what had happened to him that Sunday morning. And, as we observed, the change in his life from that Sunday morning was as marked as it had been at his conversion.

It is not enough that we should receive the Holy Spirit. We must **HOLY SPIRIT** have Him in fullness—He must have us fully. He is not holding out on us. He does not have to be begged and coaxed to come in. Long seasons of groaning and struggling are not necessary to make Him willing to enter. Jesus' word for it is: "Behold, I stand at the door, and knock: if any man hear my voice, and open the door, I will come in to him" (Rev. 3:20). He stands and knocks at our heart's door. It is impossible to ignore Him with impunity. To fail to open the door is to refuse Him. That is disastrous. But if we open, He comes! It is not written, "If any man struggle, or cry, or plead, or labor to be good"; no: "If any man hear my voice, and open the door." It is as simple as that. He is as ready to fill us instantly with His Spirit as light is ready to occupy every corner of a room in which it is shed abroad.

If there is any delay, any struggle, any begging and coaxing, it is due not to His unwillingness but to our difficulty in getting the door open. Roughly speaking, the older we grow, the longer we postpone commitment, the dirtier our hearts, the more entrenched our habits, the more difficult it is to open the door. Furthermore, we must not confuse His simple entry in fullness with any particular way we may feel about it. To some folk it is an immense thrill, to others an overmastering emotional tide, while to others it is simple peace. None of this is normative—the essential is simply the cleansing.

My poor old grandfather first heard of this experience from a man who declared that when the Holy Spirit filled him it struck him like an electric shock going from head to foot. He was sure Grandfather ought to get the shock also. So for six months Grandfather went about seeking for an electric shock which, fortunately, he was unable to get. What a pity it would have been if he had merely gotten a shock! As it was he at last realized that what he needed and wanted was not a shock nor any other phenomena, but just the Holy Spirit himself.

"If any man hear my voice, and open the door, I will come in to him." It is only our unsurrendered will that can keep Him out, and there need be no further evidence than the witness of His Spirit to our cleansed conscience that the door is open, to claim by faith His promise of entrance. One need not have the testimony of his senses in any phenomenal way to *know* that the Holy Spirit is in the house.

If this be true, then why is it that so many struggle so long before fullness of the Spirit is accomplished? Seeing that the delay is not the fault nor the will of God, we must examine more closely what it is in us that holds Him off. Unfortunately our refusal to open the door is no mere ephemeral ugly mood but rather a consistent state of rebellion. That is an ugly word, but it has to be said because it is true. Sophistication does not change it. Paul says that "the carnal mind is enmity against God" (Rom. 8:7). We sometimes hate to admit it, but there are definite areas in which we resent God's interference in our lives. That is the carnal mind.

Paul's fuller explanation is to be found in a lengthy passage in Romans 6, where he uses the master-slave relationship, pointing out **FREE FROM SIN** that sin may be our master unto death, or righteousness may be our master unto holiness. The choice of masters is ours, but we cannot serve both. "When ye were the servants of sin, ye were free from righteousness." Again and again in the passage he refers to "being made free from sin" (v. 22, cf. 18) and indicates that then and then only can we become the servants of righteousness. So it is which master we acknowledge that determines our being "after the Spirit" or "after the flesh" (8:1, 4-5, 9, 12-13).

In Ephesians 4 Paul talks of the "old man" (v. 22) and the "new man" (v. 24) and thereby further clarifies his meaning. It may help us to think of these as two patterns of life, one revolving around self as center—that is sin (the old man), and the other revolving around God as center—that is holiness (the new man). All of the events and stuff of which life is made fall into one or the other of these two patterns. Indeed, in some measure these patterns exist simultaneously in most incompletely surrendered hearts, overlapping so that, pictured geometrically, there is an ellipse where a circle ought to be.

This may be illustrated by passing a horseshoe magnet under a sheet of paper on which have been sprinkled iron filings. Looking from above one cannot see the magnet, but one can tell the location of its poles by the behavior of the filings, which instantly arrange themselves around the poles and form two overlapping patterns. In the lives of converted men there are still two great poles—self and God. All of the particles that go to make up life group themselves around these two poles in patterns of life which are partially self-centered and partially God-centered. It is conceivable that the particles where the patterns overlap have a hard time making up their minds as to which pole to obey. James has this conflict in mind when he speaks of the "double minded man" who is "unstable in all his ways" (1:8). Now the carnal mind is precisely the mentality whose center is self, and the pattern it forms in life is displeasing to God just because it is enmity against Him.

What then is to be done? The apostle uses strong language. His common terms are "crucify," "mortify," "put to death," "strip off," and like terms. We must be careful here to understand correctly. Paul wants the old man crucified. It is this pattern which stands off-center from God, which must go out of existence as definitely and decisively as death. But we must be very clear as to just what goes out of existence and what becomes of it, for it is at this point that so much misunderstanding has arisen over the terms "eradication" and "suppression" and "counteraction." Obviously there is confusion here, for those who object most strenuously to eradication still insist upon the crucifixion of the old man (which of course is the scriptural term), while those who stress eradication are usually no more certain or clear as to just what it is that is to be eradicated than their opponents are as to what it is that is to be crucified. It is clear that everyone agrees that *something* has to be dealt with and eliminated decisively. And of course there are words and phrases—the "old man," the "carnal nature," the "sinful nature," the "bias to evil," the "corrupted nature." But what both camps lack is a clear translation of these terms into language psychologically comprehensible so that, in terms of everyday experience, we can recognize just what is to be eliminated, and what is left, and what is to be done with what is left.

The answer to the problem lies in the position of the self. To return to our illustration of the magnet: We saw a double pattern created by the fact that self stood off-center from God. Now the crucial point for understanding is that this doubleness of pattern must go out of existence, but *not the self* which is its center. Those who are striving for the deeper life in the Spirit often call for the death of self. One realizes what is meant, but nevertheless the language is inaccurate. The self can never die. It is eternal. It is the center of the soul and must live forever. God created it and has no desire that it should be eradicated. It is inaccurate to speak of the death *of* self, but it is entirely proper to speak of death *to* self. There is a world of difference. *Self* must live but *selfishness* must die. There, too, is a world of difference. Selfishness is that pattern of life which inevitably results when the self stands apart from God in any degree. The self as such is holy and good, for it was made by God. The self is made unholy by choices which are at variance with God's will.

To show what should be done with the self we need another text. Paul in Col. 3:3 says: "Ye are dead, and your life is hid with Christ in God." If we have our difficulties in expressing the deeper life in words, it is some comfort to realize that Paul himself again and again finds words failing him as he tries to make it clear. He usually resorts to paradoxical language. So he does here—"Ye are dead . . . your life." How can there be life where there is death? It is a paradox. Something has died. Something also is very much alive and living on. It may be useful here to continue our illustration. The self as a pole apart from God must yield up its aloofness, its separateness, its enmity against God, its independent sovereignty, by an act of utter surrender; it must move over and become "hid with Christ in God." The self then continues to live, but it lives in God. The poles are now, so to speak, identical, and the pattern of life is one. This integration, however, cannot take place without something going out of existence. Not the self, but the pattern of life created by the self when it is not hid with Christ in God is the thing that must be destroyed.

Now actually this destruction of the "old man" is difficult only as, and in the measure that, our self-will or enmity toward God is strongly fixed. For some, surrender appears simple and easy; for others it is a fight. Sometimes it occurs in an instant of decision; sometimes it occurs only after long struggle. It never happens by accident. No one ever just drifts into it. Nothing can be assumed about it. No mere pious hope will do. Decision is called for. Moreover, surrender must be absolute and final; every last reservation must go. One cannot bargain nor make terms. Paul uses terms like "crucifixion" and "death" to emphasize the decisiveness and absoluteness of the action.

A DEFINITE
CHOICE

These terms, "crucifixion" and "death," are of course figurative, referring to the pattern and not to the self as such, and, like all figures of speech, they must not be pressed beyond their intended use. After they have served to emphasize the way we must deal with the rebellion, we must drop them. Otherwise we shall get into another common misunderstanding. For some who have experienced such a surrender and such a deliverance feel that the carnal nature is crucified, dead, and buried, and that dead things do not return to bother us. They assume, therefore, that the carnal nature will never appear again, that there is no use guarding that front any longer. But Paul never intended his figure to be pressed to that point. He had finished with it in the moment of full surrender. Then a new figure must be taken up. The self is then "hid with Christ in God." Whatever else this text may mean, it is clear from the context that we have a right to take as its primary meaning its application to the Spirit-filled life. Now the chief weapon of temptation used by the devil against the surrendered and holy heart is to try to draw the self out of its hidden place and, in some particular at least, get it to set up again in independence from God.

The self carries with it all the equipment of human nature with which God endowed us by creation. All of the factors, physical and mental, the drives, urges, instincts (or whatever terms your psychology requires) which are part of normal human nature are instruments controlled by and used for the glory of the dominant center in life. That center may be self hid with Christ in God, or self standing on its own. In the latter case these factors become warped and in ugly fashion reveal the self-centeredness of the life. When they are cleansed, they reveal the glory of God. This is what Paul means when he says that God "shall also quicken your mortal bodies by his Spirit that dwelleth in you" (Rom. 8:11). This means that any of our capacities, our urges, our abilities, physical and mental, all that God made to reside in our bodies, shall, when cleansed, be free from its self-centeredness, its bias to self and evil, its enmity against God, and shall be free, quickened and enlivened, until it shall then really begin to function as God intended it should when He created it. Note that no part of this equipment is to be eliminated, any more than the self is to die. Rather it, like the self, is to be cleansed and hid with Christ in God, where it can at long last function to the glory of God in true holiness as He had originally intended.

George Fox described this very quaintly in his own experience when he said that it seemed as though "all the creation gave another smell unto me than before." This is to say that when enmity against God is cleansed from our hearts, our whole being—every sense, every desire, every instinct, every part of our nature—is more sensitive, more alive, and more vigorous than ever before, ready now for the first time to be a vessel for the expression of the glory of God.

Upon arrival at a convention in India where I was to preach, I unpacked a new pearl gray suit to wear in the pulpit. To my dismay I found I had left the trousers on a wire hanger throughout the rainy season. There was now a long streak of rust across one leg. This posed a problem: how to remove the rust without, at the same time, taking out the delicate gray color of the suit. There are many chemical substances which could easily have taken out the rust—but they go too far; they would have taken out the color in the cloth and thus have traded a white streak for a rust streak. I am very grateful to a woman who had just the right thing, which took out the rust and left the color as it was originally. Too many views of salvation prescribe cures which would destroy normal human nature along with sin. This we do not want. Thanks be unto God He has provided, through His Son, cleansing which leaves human nature completely intact, including its liability to temptation.

This latter must be recognized as a part of normal human nature—a part of that which God made and saw that it was "good." It **TEMPTATION** is wrong to include our liability to temptation as a part of **IS NOT** our fallen or sinful or depraved human nature. The capac- **CARNALITY** ity to be tempted is part of our holy moral nature—it was true of Adam and Eve before the Fall, and it was true of the sinless Christ. It is not right to bewail our sinful nature just because we are subject to temptation. God wants voluntary love and service, and to get these He made us with the power of choice. This is good, not evil. The sinful nature is the attitude of enmity, and this in turn warps and colors every phase of normal human nature. Until that attitude dies, it is proper to bewail our bias or propensity to evil. Deliverance from enmity against God puts us on the victory side of temptation, even when it is intensified by the scars of sin.

For instance, a drunkard may be forgiven and obtain complete victory over his evil habit. But there may still remain impressed upon the very cells of his body something that makes the smell of liquor an enticement. Some will call this his sinful nature. In a broad sense this is possible, since these scars are the result of sin. But we must make a radical distinction between these scars, which are quite involuntary and amoral, . . . and that attitude of enmity against the will of God which is distinctly voluntary, immoral, sinful, and to be legitimately called the sinful nature. If this enmity should be readmitted to the heart, it will of course find a strong and probably winning ally in the scar-tissue taste for liquor.

When we speak of deliverance from our sinful nature, it is necessary to keep this distinction clear. We may be delivered from our inherited attitude of conscious enmity against God, and that is enough. Moral scars may remain. Our bodies, our minds, and our spirits may have twists which will open doors of temptation. But [even though these] persist for life, the case is not hopeless. God's grace is sufficient to give victory provided we have been delivered from the root enmity which we consciously harbor until we consciously and fully surrender it for destruction and cleansing.

In the old days of British rule in India I saw a curious thing at the investiture ceremony where the maharajah of Chhatarpur received, on coming of age, his ruling powers. The guests were assembled in the Darbar Hall of the Palace when, with great pomp and ceremony, the maharajah entered and occupied one of two thrones at the end of the hall, the other being occupied by the British resident. Thus was symbolized the dual sovereignty under which the Indian states functioned and which always posed a nice point in law known as paramountcy. The maharajah was fully sovereign—and yet within the limits of British paramountcy. This has its own spiritual lesson, but I am now concerned with another part of the proceedings. It was that moment when the nobles of the court came to pledge their fealty to the British Crown as they had doubtless done earlier to the maharajah. Each one in turn came slowly to the throne, bowed low, and extended his hand draped with a silk handkerchief on which was a quantity of gold. It was the right of the resident on behalf of the Crown to take this gold as a pledge of the loyalty of this Indian nobleman. But instead, he touched it slowly, symbolizing his acceptance of the man's fealty, then withdrew his hand, allowing the man to return to his seat with the gold in his possession. He was free to use that gold in any way he chose so long as it was consistent with his loyalty to the Crown. To use it in any subversive way would be criminal.

Seeing this, I was reminded of our crisis experience in which we bring our *all* to King Jesus. He has a right to take it from us, to keep us from misusing it, but that is not His choice.

CLEANSING

Rather He touches us with the cleansing of His precious blood and then leaves our cleansed human nature in our control as a stewardship. But every use must be consistent with loyalty and such as will glorify Him. He removes from us no particle of our legitimate human nature which He created. He removes only the taint of rebelliousness and purifies our love for Him until it becomes holy obedience.

This truth is so important that it needs to be seen in some detail, and we can do so by taking up several items of human nature in turn to see how it works out. In doing so we must see how the devil makes his attacks, and how he tries to worm us out of that hidden place "with Christ in God."

Everyone knows that hunger and eating are essential to life and therefore to the glory of God. Fasting may have value as an ascetic discipline (and certainly for weight reduction), but no one asks for a spiritual experience which would "eradicate" hunger. Still, it is perfectly true that eating to the glory of God and being a glutton are two different things. Where then does one cross the line, in eating, from the glory of God to gluttony? Obviously, the answer is not simple. We shall come to that later, but let it suffice for the present to say that there is a "line," and that eating on one side of it is consistent with a self hid with Christ in God and on the other side consistent with a self out on its own.

Now the solution of this problem does not lie in eliminating the joy from eating. An emotional or feeling tone accompanies every act we perform. God made us that way, and to try to eradicate feeling is not only impossible but wrong. The Stoics tried to do so. When a plate of fried fish was brought before a Stoic he was to stifle his impulse to say, "Just look at this wonderful meal; I will certainly enjoy it." Rather he was to say, "See, here is the carcass of a dead fish; I shall consume it to keep body and soul together." The message of the Bhagavad-Gita runs in the same vein. But all such teaching ends in hypocrisy or ruin. No, the Christian's task is more difficult. He is to eat to glorify God, and he is also to enjoy that which is to the glory of God.

I have used this illustration because it is so simple and because it is universally taken for granted that there is nothing wrong with the satisfaction of hunger. Yet the very matter-of-factness with which this is taken for granted means peril. Why do we hear so few sermons on the sanctification of eating? There are multitudes of overweight gluttons who claim to be filled with the Spirit to whom it has never occurred that sanctification has anything to do with eating. We need to see that hunger, like every other bit of our human equipment, is a possible servant of self or of God. Just how this is so will be clearer as we proceed.

Another and less obvious God-given item is sensitiveness. God made us so that we could feel the sufferings of others and enter sympathetically into their need. But when sensitiveness is turned in upon self and produces self-pity, it becomes a reprehensible and a carnal thing. . . .

SELF-PITY

Now it is not the will of God that sensitiveness should be "eradicated." But it must be cleansed of its self-centeredness and set free to express the glory of God. Where this capacity has been carnal and has constituted a real problem in one's life, the cleansing of the self-centeredness out of the sensitiveness often constitutes a very remarkable deliverance.

I know a Spirit-filled Indian brother who is blessed with an unusual capacity for being sensitive to the suffering of others. It drives him to endless labors, and he has a passion for souls which is rare. But the devil always attacks us on the points of our greatest strength, and this brother frequently has terrific spiritual battles over feeling sorry for himself. Why should he give so much of himself for others when other preachers who get more money give so little of themselves and suffer so little inconvenience? How easily these qualities given to us as instruments for the service of God may be twisted into instruments for self, and how easily can the devil create situations where the legitimate use of an instrument becomes the occasion of the withdrawal of self from its hidden place in God and of its setting up in independence again.

This may be clearer from a study of envy. No one will suggest that envy has a legitimate side, but that is because our English word is limited to only the bad side of a twofold experience. In 1 Cor. 13:4 we are told that love "envieth not." But actually the Greek word is *dzēloi,* meaning excitement of mind, ardor, fervor of spirit. This is capable of being exercised in both a good and a bad way. In the good way it is zeal for, ardor in embracing, pursuing, or defending a good thing. "The *zeal* of thine house hath eaten me up" (John 2:17) is a case in point. The Corinthians responded to Paul's exhortations with "what clearing of yourselves, yea, what indignation, yea, what fear, yea, what vehement desire, yea, what *zeal,* yea, what revenge! In all things ye have approved yourselves to be clear in this matter" (2

ENVY

Cor. 7:11). Yet on the other hand this quality may be exercised in an evil way. In this evil way it is envy, contentious rivalry, jealousy (as in Rom. 13:13, "Let us walk . . . not in strife and *envying*").

On the surface, zeal and envy seem to have little in common, but an illustration will make plain their relationship. Suppose some election is to take place in your church—perhaps it is the Sunday School superintendent. Two names are before the people, and yours is one. You like Sunday School work. In fact, you feel very responsible toward it and can give yourself to the work with zeal. You have abilities which will enable you to do the job creditably and to the glory of God. The other name represents a good man, but candidly you suspect he has less love for this work than you have, and not quite the same ability. The election takes place. The people are not always as wise as they ought to be. The other man is elected!

You protest to your friends that this is much the better thing, and you congratulate the new superintendent and tell him you will pray for him. But down in your heart of hearts you wonder: *Was* it God's will? How zealous you had been to serve in this way. Then you begin to watch your brother carefully. It is your zeal for the Lord's work. You want him to make good, you tell yourself. He makes some blunders. Then some carelessness is in evidence. How you wish you could help. You do not want to see the Sunday School suffer. Your zeal is intense. Then more blunders. You try to forget. But it keeps bothering you. You just can't forget. And to make a long story short, you wake up one day to the fact that you have a full-blown case of envy on your hands.

Now just when does one cross the line between zeal and envy? How can one tell when he crosses or is in danger of crossing? And what happens to his sanctification if he should cross? These are important questions which must be answered after we look at additional illustrations.

The tongue seems to be the chief problem of some folk, and a real problem to us all. Now obviously there is no "eradication" of the tongue. But it is equally obvious that one cannot let it run without control, even in the life of holiness.

I was once attending a convention for the deepening of spiritual life in India. A friend of mine in that mission had a very exacting spirit.

A SANCTIFIED TONGUE He was virtually always right in what he said, but the manner he used had left a long train of heartache and wounded spirits. He had sought deliverance, claimed victory, and there had been great improvement. Then on the opening day of the convention he spoke to an Indian brother about that brother's conduct. Again he was right, but again his manner set off tempers, and the resulting explosion threatened to blow the convention right off the calendar. The missionary went into seclusion. The next morning I found him in his tent packing his suitcase, in the depths of discouragement. It was no use. He had failed again, he was unworthy as a missionary, and he intended to go home. After a little talk and prayer he entered the next meeting with a new victory. There he rose before his Indian brethren, humbly apologized, and then said an interesting thing. "If my trouble were something like liquor or tobacco, it would be easy to deal with. I could simply throw them away and be done with them. But my problem is my tongue. I know that I cannot cut it out to the glory of God. I have committed my all afresh, including my tongue, to God, trusting that the Holy Spirit will cleanse and help me to use it to His glory."

There are two common errors with regard to the use of the tongue. The first is to suppose that we are helpless in the hands of our CLEANSING sinful nature, that an offensive tongue is something about AND which God's grace does nothing in this life, and that we DISCIPLINE must control it as best we may, but with little hope of acquiring anything better than our nature provides. The other error is to suppose that the eradication of the carnal nature leaves the tongue so cleansed as to need no discipline. The truth is that the cleansing of the heart—the elimination of our willful enmity against God—does provide a cleansing within every part of our equipment, including our tongues, and makes every part ready to speak to God's glory. The tongue is then ready for intense discipline, as James faithfully testifies.

God does something for us. He cleanses us and gives us power to do something for ourselves. There is much left for us to do. Cleansing and discipline are two watchwords, two apparent contradictories, which must be caught up in a living paradox if we want God's best. Then we can say that He does for us something which we could never do for ourselves. No amount of discipline would ever control the tongue if it were still expressing the abundance of a heart in which there was enmity against God. While God does something for us which we could not do *by* our disciplining, yet He does it in order to make it possible *for* us to discipline our lives to His glory.

Every once in a while we hear someone say, "Well, I just told him off—you know I'm made that way—I just have to say what comes to my mind!" There is no doubt that many people do say what comes to their mind, but it is a lame defense to say that they *have* to. What we all have to do is to control sternly our tongues, and we cannot hope to get on well with this unless we submit our hearts to the cleansing which leaves our selves hid with Christ in God.

It is entirely consistent with our hidden place in God that we should still be subject to much of human infirmity. We shall often, with the best of intentions and with much of discipline, give a word of offense. The Spirit-filled heart is not evidenced by at-taining a state of grace in which we never are caught off guard and say a wounding word, but rather by the quickness and fullness with which we find ourselves ready to make amends when it comes to our consciousness that offense has been taken. Here it is not enough that we should feel clear in our intentions when we speak. "If . . . thy brother *hath aught against thee,*" go to him (Matt. 5:23-24). A disposition to apologize, to come quickly to terms, to heal a wound, to satisfy an offended brother: this *disposition* is the test for holiness, not the elimination of every offending word.

A DISPOSITION TO APOLOGIZE

Jesus was before the high priest when an officer struck Him with the palm of his hand. Jesus replied: "If I have spoken evil, bear witness of the evil: but if well, why smitest thou me?" (John 18:23). If you will ponder this answer for an hour you can think of no possible im-provement. Under the greatest provocation, Jesus gives an absolutely perfect answer.

At a later date, the apostle Paul found himself in an identical situation (Acts 23:1-5). When the high priest's servant smote him on the mouth, Paul said, "God shall smite thee, thou whited wall: for sittest thou to judge me after the law, and commandest me to be smitten contrary to the law?"

Now this is something else. One does not have to think long to be able to improve on this speech. Not but that it was mostly true. Per-haps it was all true—even to the "whited wall" if that phrase were properly interpreted. But the spirit of it is not the spirit of Christ's remark. Calling names, using epithets, throwing labels at folk is not of the Spirit of Christ. It is true that Jesus once called the Pharisees "serpents" and a "generation of vipers" (Matt. 23:33). But as in the case of the reference to the Syrophoenician woman as a "dog," we need to understand the connotation of "serpent" in His day. Further-more, whereas our name-calling is usually a sudden burst of temper, this word of Jesus comes as a climax to a long denunciation of the hypocrisy of the Pharisees, the whole tenor of which, while exceedingly penetrating, is yet so restrained that one does not feel the flash of self in His words. Our indignation is rarely as righteous. No matter how true or right may have been Paul's words, the total impression they gave to the hearers was that he was reviling the high priest.

Now what about Paul? Was he Spirit-filled? Was he fully surrendered? Was he hid with Christ in God?

We must make clear that all these questions concern disposition rather than outward or absolute perfection. There is proof that Paul was surrendered, that he was Spirit-filled. But the proof lies not in any experience which would make his answers, his words, the use of his tongue as perfect as those of Jesus. Rather the proof lies in the *disposition* which he manifested as soon as his error was revealed. Instantly, upon the rebuke of the bystanders, Paul came through with an apology. That indicated more truly the real heart of the man.

And so it will with us. Caught off guard, a word is spoken, an attitude taken, or a spirit shown for which we receive the Spirit's rebuke. If, in that situation, we allow self to reaffirm its independent stand, if we slip out of our hidden place in God, if a bit of enmity against God creeps back in, that spirit will be manifest by an unwillingness to heed the check of the Spirit and a stubborn decision to go right on. Usually there is something more cutting still ready to be said, and one says it. But if there is love for Christ above all else and a desire to be altogether His, that disposition will show itself, even in so stern and tempestuous a nature as Paul's, with complete readiness to apologize and make right the incident. Note also that Paul's action was instant— he did not wait for three or four days to cool off and then come around and merely try to act pleasant as though nothing had ever happened! The Spirit-filled heart does not hold grudges.

We are far from exhausting the phases of human nature which must be cleansed and regulated to the glory of God in the sanctified life. But before proceeding to further illustrations we must give answer to the questions we have been holding over until now. How can we know when we have crossed the line from legitimate hunger to gluttony, from sensitiveness about the condition of others to self-pity, from zeal to envy, and from holy to unholy speech?

CROSSING
THE LINE

The answer is simple. No man can tell me when I cross the line, nor can I tell another when he crosses his line. *We are shut up to the guidance of the Holy Spirit.* It is a living way and nothing short of the living Spirit of God dwelling within us can solve our problem. *But He does guide us!* There is never a time when we are in danger of crossing one of these lines but that He faithfully speaks! Yet never thunderously —only with a still small voice. We can always hear—*if we listen!*

I have spoken of "crossing the line." Actually there is an area between that which is clearly and wholly for the glory of God and that which is clearly and wholly for the glory of the isolated self—a sort of twilight zone. As one enters it, the Spirit begins to whisper words of caution. These grow more intense as we approach the line. Crossing, there is a feeling of condemnation and guilt which intensifies the further we go. It is not simple, partly because of our dullness of hearing and perception, and partly because of the complex nature of the situation—the intertwining of the legitimate with the sinful in the shaded area. It is something like sunset. On shipboard I have watched the sun set into the sea in a cloudless sky. The horizon is a sharp line, and there is not an instant's doubt when the sun has gone. But often sunset is complicated by the presence of clouds and an irregular horizon or skyline. Sometimes we are aware, especially on cloudy and drizzly days, only of a gradual loss of light when twilight turns to dark. So too in Christian living. It is impossible to reduce the matter to simple rules or to define exactly the line in all cases. We are shut up to the voice of the Spirit as our only guide.

And suppose we fail. Suppose we cross the line and do the thing the Holy Spirit rebuked. What then is our condition and what can we do about it?

First of all, let us recognize our condition as sinful. It must not be covered up by reference to the wonder of our original crisis experience of surrender and cleansing or sanctification. Too many have thus accumulated a lot of unforgiven sin by assuming that since we had such a glorious experience back there, and carnality was eradicated, surely nothing now can be wrong. Whatever eradication means—or crucifixion, or putting to death the old man—it is not a chunk of something *material* that is done away. Rather, it is a wrong *relationship* between us and God that is destroyed. But just because it is a relationship, an immaterial rather than a material something, it can as quickly be reinstated as destroyed. The cure, then, is fresh repentance and forgiveness and cleansing as we put the relationship right again. And happy is the one who has learned to make this adjustment instantly and quickly.

The Spirit-controlled Life[3]

Here Cattell explores the human experiences of pride, temper, and sex. He explains how Christians who are controlled by the Holy Spirit manage these human urges in Christlike ways under the guidance of the Holy Spirit.

Pride is something reprehensible in its self-centered form, and yet it has a counterpart which is glorifying to God. What we call self-respect may be a thing which God can bless. God takes no particular pleasure in our looking sloppy—even when the styles are that way—in our failing through carelessness, in our being satisfied with the bottom of the ladder. Yet it is perfectly obvious that our dress and our ambitions may be, and very often are, clear evidences of pride.

PRIDE

We Quakers once tried to curb pride in the hearts of our members by legislating the precise length of skirts and sleeves and the exact style and cut of coats and dresses. Buttons were sinful, for they were decorative rather than merely useful. Gray was the standard color. Men could not wear neckties, and their coats could not have lapels— for these, too, were merely decorative. Collars were square and coats were fastened together by invisible and, therefore, nondecorative hooks and eyes. The minutes of business meetings of that period were full of rules and regulations and of disciplinary action taken against offenders.

Principles of modesty and simplicity are clearly set forth in Scripture. But there still remains the problem of applying these and reducing the general principle to the specific instance. There are two false methods of handling this situation. One is to forget it all on the assumption that clothes have nothing to do with the gospel. The other is to pass regulations prescribing a uniform, with strict measures covering every detail of one's outfit. These are the ways of death. We must find a living way.

How then can we tell when we have crossed the line from a legitimate, God-honoring self-respect to a pride which is carnal and selfish? How can we know which clothes are consistent with self-respect and which ones minister to pride? It should be noted that merely being colorless or ugly does not eliminate pride. Some folk are proud of their ugliness. It is so distinctive! And John Wesley wrote a

---

3. Ibid., chap. 3.

sermon on the subject of dress in which he said that he hoped some day to see a Methodist congregation as plainly clad as Quakers, but mind you, he said, that there be no "Quaker linen."[4] The reference is to the practice of wealthy Quakers who went to Paris to find materials of the prescribed shade of gray that would be sufficiently elegant to show their wealthy station in life.

A wildfire young Indian evangelist came into our church once and suddenly ordered everyone present to take off their shoes and put them outside the door—not only to conform with Indian custom but to observe some obscure Old Testament passage. No one moved. A missionary protested that we were not living in the Old Testament. But the young fellow was insistent that only pride made people wear their shoes in the church. I found the confused congregation looking in my direction, so I spoke. I told the brother I hoped I was not proud of my shoes, and to prove it I would put them outside the door—which I promptly did. Then I proceeded to stand in my socks and **LOVING THE WEAK** give a message on the subtlety of pride, which may be just as evident in a minister in his supposed power to lord it over a congregation as in anyone's dress.

Indeed this is important, for there is a legitimate field for ambition which may be used for the glory of God. Ministers and servants of God are by no means exempt from ambitions, particularly the ambition to be at their best in the service of the Lord. Every preacher wants to preach a good sermon. But it is one of the subtlest fields of the devil's work to pull a man across the line from wanting to preach a good sermon for God's glory to the point where his inner satisfaction becomes pride. Can he keep a sense that it was all the gift of God, or does he begin to "recognize" his own considerable ability? Every Spirit-filled heart may be encouraged by words of appreciation. But when does this become a love of flattery? Does that situation just take care of itself when one is Spirit-filled? Decidedly not! The sanctified life is an intensely disciplined life, or it soon ceases to be sanctified. And one occasion that calls for drastic discipline is when the preacher meets his admiring parishioners at the door after he has done tolerably well.

One of my best missionary friends in India, now retired, tells of a time when as a student he was sent out to be the evangelist for a revival meeting. Another student was sent along as song leader. After

---

4. *Sermons on Several Occasions,* "On Dress," 26-27.

a few days he noticed that more people came forward to shake hands with the song leader than with the preacher. In another day or so he knew that he had to do something about this or lose victory. So he went to the song leader and arranged to have him preach the next night, and by this self-abasement he won the victory. His action was part of that discipline of the cleansed human nature which is necessary to keep it from reverting to carnal nature. Every preacher needs something better than a book of rules to show him through the maze of temptations which are directed at him in particular to push his legitimate ambitions for the advancement of the Kingdom across the line into the field of personal pride. In fear and trembling he needs to hang across his conscience like a banner of fire that word of the Lord from ancient times: "My glory will I not give to another" (Isa. 42:8).

To exercise authority while recognizing that all authority is derived from above is a most exacting spiritual test. Someone said that supervision ought to be 90 percent "vision" and not more than 10 percent "super." Obviously nothing short of the living presence of the Holy Spirit whispering His little checks will save us from reinfecting our holy self-respect with carnal pride. As Oswald Chambers well said: "One of the outstanding miracles of God's grace is to make us able to take any kind of leadership at all without losing spiritual power."[5]

Another most troublesome item of human nature is the temper. No part of our equipment is more necessary, and no part more easily prostituted to selfishness. There is a common misconception that

SANCTIFIED TEMPER

temper is eradicated by sanctification, or should be. Awful confusion attends this error, which results either in hypocrisy or loss of confidence. Temper is no more eradicated than is the self. But it must be cleansed and, along with the self, be hid with Christ in God. Temper is part of God's creation. Without it we would be worthless. It is simply a phase of the emotional life. If we had no temper we would placidly stand in the path of an oncoming car, unmoved by the sound of the horn and unable to escape death.

Temper enables us to react to wrong situations in ways which tend to change and redeem those situations. This is particularly true where the wrong is moral in character. God wants us to feel stirred and stirred deeply by the sight of evil. Spineless Christianity, temperless in the face of grave wrongs, is not of God. We sometimes forget that one of the commands of Scripture is, "Be ye angry" (Eph. 4:26). But with

---

5. *The Message of Invincible Consolation,* 19.

the command goes instantly the recognition that in actual practice it is more difficult to keep the temper hid with Christ in God than any other part of our equipment. This is because the temper along with our whole emotional life is reflexive in character and is controlled by the involuntary autonomic nervous system.

Psychologists have noted that a baby is born with innate responses such as fear of a loud noise near the head, and anger at having its movements restrained. As life goes on, these elemental emotions become conditioned by ever more complex situations. And into the complexity comes, as a further complicating factor, the bias of the carnal mind. Since emotional reactions are involuntary, they form an excellent mirror of the heart. If the heart is impure it will be revealed in flashes of selfish temper. After cleansing, the temper will still work involuntarily, but it should reflect the new and holy condition of the heart. Furthermore, those feelings which rise involuntarily must be subjected to rigid discipline.

ATTITUDES

"Be ye angry, and sin not." To this is then added good practical advice for the disciplining of righteous anger so as to keep it from being the instrument of the return of that mind which is enmity against God: "Let not the sun go down upon your wrath." It is as though one said, Take off this righteous anger before you go to bed at night, and hang it up like a coat. The next morning scrutinize it carefully and very prayerfully before putting it on again, to see whether it is really righteous and worth taking up again.

We must recognize clearly the distinction between emotional impulses which are controlled by the autonomic nervous system and which arise quite involuntarily, and emotional states which are permitted to continue voluntarily. There are great individual differences in the speed and strength of involuntary impulses. Indeed, we call some people "impulsive," meaning that by nature they react more suddenly and violently than others to situations.

There is a sense in which these strong sudden feelings do indicate the inner nature. Selfishness may thus be revealed. But it does not necessarily follow that the slow and steady person is unselfish because he does not suddenly show temper. What is more important is to look at the area of emotional states which we voluntarily permit or condone. For instance, on the good side, the joy of the Lord as our strength is an emotional attitude deliberately maintained by a choice independent of circumstances. On the bad side are feelings of resentment, bitterness, or anger which are tolerated, nursed, and perpetuated over a period of time.

Not all of the wrong situations which stir us deeply are great moral issues. Take the matter of orderliness. Disorderliness in the home, in business, or in the work of the Lord bothers an orderly mind. God intended it to be so. He himself is a God of order. He wants us to feel strongly about disorderliness, else we would never do anything about it. But if we are blessed with a sense of order, we shall have to exercise patience with those who are not, while they must strive to be **PATIENCE** orderly just because God is orderly. Our problem arises in that it is so easy in this field for our sense of the wrongness in a disorderly situation to arise not from the fact of God's orderliness but from a personal and selfish frustration or inconvenience. The children are having a romp around the house. It is raining, so they cannot play outside. We want to read or write or listen to the radio. By what scale can we determine whether our concern for quiet is for the children's good and the glory of God or merely for our own personal comfort?

The answer to this question, along with those raised above, is simply a deep sensitiveness to the voice of the Holy Spirit, which cautions us as to the impure character of the temper we are about to indulge. It should be clear that there is a legitimate temper and that God is not pleased with disorder, but that one easily crosses a line where this legitimate temper becomes an instrument of self in a selfish state.

In Paul's Hymn to Love he states that love "is not easily provoked" (1 Cor. 13:5). The word translated "provoked" is, like all of the terms used in this passage to define the characteristics of love, usable in two senses, a good and a bad. The word here is *paroxunetai*, which comes over into English as *paroxysm*. Literally it means "to make sharp." To illustrate its two senses we may see two incidents in Paul's life. In Athens he walked the streets, saw the innumerable idols, and "his spirit was stirred in him" (Acts 17:16). In other words, he had a paroxysm. The idolatry around him made sharp his sense of wrong. This sense obviously was consistent with divine love. But there was another time when the contention grew so sharp (paroxysm) between Paul and Barnabas that they separated. Probably this paroxysm was of the sort which Paul later conceded was not of love. Both incidents show Paul's temper stirred, the one time righteously, the other of doubtful indignation. Yet we cannot judge finally, and that is true of all this line crossing which I have tried to set forth. We cannot finally judge another as to when the good becomes the evil. We can only say, If I were in that case, I should be convicted. The only righteous judge is Christ himself. Thank God, for He is entirely faithful. And He is prepared to speak, passing judgment on every involuntary flash of temper, if we discipline ourselves to listen.

To go much further would be wearisome. But it should be clear that any part of our human nature can be looked at in the same way. Reason itself may be useful to save us from error—or it may stoop to rationalizing, where our selfish wishes are made respectable to ourselves. Imagination is valuable for formulating plans for the furtherance of the Kingdom, for producing useful inventions, and for solving difficult problems—or it may be prostituted to the level of idle daydreaming which feeds our vanity, picturing us in situations which get us much applause for passing for far more than we are worth, or causing us to imagine meanings and motives in the actions of others which are not there.

I started with the urge to hunger. All our urges can be treated likewise. At times there crops up in circles stressing the deeper life in the Spirit a misconception that sex is wrong, carnal, and selfish. Some

SANCTIFICATION OF SEX

even think it ought to be eradicated. A great need in our day is to set forth an adequate message on the sanctification of sex. There seems to be a supposition that all the attendant pleasures of the sexual life are vaguely but somehow carnal. This reminds one of the Stoic eating fish. What we need to see is that God created the pleasures of eating and sex just as surely as He created the urges themselves, and that their enjoyment can be sanctified to His glory. Quite obviously these may likewise be made ends in themselves and prostituted to the low level of selfishness and sin. Sex outside wedlock is of course an instance of this. No rationalizing can make it right. It is sin.

But our borderline difficulties lie on a different plane. It is where sexual attraction works in those mild, preliminary ways which are subtle. Here again, the attraction is a God-given thing. The biological fact that male and female attract one another like the negative and positive poles of magnets is entirely holy. Without that attraction there would of course be no love, courtship, or marriage. Nor can we suppose that either sanctification *or marriage* removes it. This is not eradicated. But when cleansed and hid with Christ in God, it can be effectively disciplined. The sanctified apostle said, "I maul and master my body" (1 Cor. 9:27, Moffatt). Before marriage this impulse in those sanctified will be disciplined so as to save them from improper liberties in courtship and from giving their affections to partners outside the Lord.

It is a mistake, of course, to suppose that this attraction in itself is the sufficient ground for choice of a life partner. Just because two young people feel they love each other is no adequate reason for marriage. Such pathetic things happen when a young person who has claimed to be a Christian accepts a partner who is not, and justifies it with the inadequate reason that they love each other! This attraction is to be disciplined even to denial, when it cannot be satisfied in the Lord.

It is also a mistake to suppose that this attraction operates only between two people entirely meant for each other by God. Sexual attraction works pretty generally as a biological fact, and because this is true, married couples who have plighted their troth must exercise discipline as well as the unmarried. In our modern pagan civilization these biological urges have been accepted as masters, and our modern pagans expect neither to give nor receive faithfulness for any length of time. When the newness wears off there is an increasing number of new attractions. This is a fact. Pagans yield to it. Christians discipline themselves in the Lord.

Now there are certain simple features of this attraction which are constantly at work. Indian society pretty well admits no middle ground between initial attraction and sexual consummation. That is why their society permits no free mingling of the sexes, no courtship, and in its extreme forms puts its women behind a curtain or a *burkha*. The theory is that what a man cannot see he will not desire. Western civilization looks upon the matter differently. In India there is no thought of inner controls—they must all be external. No
INNER CONTROLS man is trusted; rather he is restricted. But Western civilization owes a great debt to Christ for the idea of inner control—that a man in Christ may be trusted even in the dark, and that impulses may be felt, even enjoyed, under a discipline which restrains and controls them. We do not feel it necessary to hang a veil over a pretty woman's face in order to keep men from being tempted to immorality. We assume that there is a place where a man in Christ may see, admire, and feel pleasure in such a face, having the doors of his mind closed to further satisfactions of the sexual attraction which lies implicit in the experience.

From the pretty face it is a short step to notice the beautiful form. To women this same element of sexual attraction is present but in altered form. A dashing personality may be just as devastating to a woman as a beautiful form to a man. Women may be in more danger because personality is so much more subtle than physical form. Now the important fact to bear in mind is that this attraction in itself is not sin; it is not carnal; it is definitely present in the Spirit-filled. But while it is a thing of real beauty which puts zest in life without jeopardizing marital faithfulness or real holiness, yet sexual attraction is as dangerous as it is subtle, and it calls for rigid discipline.

The lustful look condemned by Jesus is not necessarily so. The fact of attraction, appreciation, and pleasure regarding a woman's beauty is not sin or carnal in itself. But it is extremely easy to cross the line where this legitimate exercise of God-given impulse becomes an occasion for self to slip out into independence again, and for the look to become carnal. Probably when one becomes aware of his look taking on aspects of improper desire he is crossing over and must exercise discipline. But this question of crossing the line, in this as in so many other areas which we have set forth, leaves us utterly dependent upon the still small voice of the Holy Spirit for its answer.

What is said here applies not only to men. Women, too, have their moments of great attraction to men for reasons which they could scarcely explain. Some have felt this to be a carnal surge within them. If there has been no full surrender maintained to that moment, this might be so. But even in the Spirit-filled heart these moments of attraction, of extreme awareness of the presence of the well-liked man or of a specially attractive woman, may mean no more than the presence of this God-created urge, may indicate no disloyalty either to one's spouse or to Christ, and may be in keeping with the general enjoyment of free commingling of the sexes allowed in our civilization and indeed in the Christian Church of all time and everywhere.

Yet it is obvious that the devil's way into the hearts of many men and women is to begin to pull on this natural and legitimate element and to cause momentary enjoyment to grow into a pleasure demanding more and more satisfaction. If the heart is truly pure, there will be an instant willingness to apply discipline, to have done with the pleasure, putting it from oneself when the realization comes that it is becoming dangerous or unholy. But the very pleasure of free commingling will be used by the enemy to set up an insistent clamor for more and more satisfaction, and if the self yields to this clamor and comes out of its hidden, surrendered place in God, it will become insistent on having a little more pleasure instead of obeying the checks, and thus it gives way to a carnal, selfish state again.

It must be clear by now that the sanctified life is basically life lived utterly under the control, moment by moment, of the Holy Spirit. How can we know when we have crossed the line from legitimate hunger to gluttony, from holy sensitiveness or anger to that which is carnal, from zeal to envy, from holy to unholy speech, from self-respect to pride, from pleasure in beauty to the lustful look, and from the holy to the unholy use of sex?

The first element in the answer is that none of us can tell each other when he has crossed the line. My friend's conversation about a third friend may impress me as being more of envy than of zeal, but I cannot possibly know just what are his inner light and motives. Nor can I know just when, *for him,* the line has been crossed. I may observe that his conduct in this particular is a lesson to me and that I could not under similar circumstances do the same thing without being convicted. Whether it would actually register in that way in my consciousness if I were actually in the same circumstances, is another question, but it ought to be so. *Obviously, I must not judge my brother.* I may judge myself severely the next time I am caught in similar circumstances; but I cannot know what light has come to my brother.

An infinite amount of trouble and misunderstanding among Christians arises out of this persistent temptation to judge others, **DANGERS** imputing motives which we have no right to impute. It is true that we are to exercise righteous judgment and that the power to weigh evidence and choose the good and reject the bad, the critical faculty, is a part of the equipment God has given us. With this, evil may be cut off from the church. But here is one more case where a legitimate God-given quality can become the agent of self. What is there which is so ready to Satan's hand with which to pull at the vanity of our minds as the pride of our opinions and judgments?

It has not yet dawned in the minds of many Christians that the pride of opinion is just as damning and must be dealt with just as **PRIDE OF OPINION** decisively as any other sin. Of course the answer always is, "But I am right!" That is the way we always feel about our judgments. It is in the very nature of judgment that it should carry with it an emotional tone which we call conviction or certainty. But suppose two sanctified people hold opposite judgments. Each feels the other is wrong. Actually both are wrong if there is not a disposition to yield! So I must stop passing judgment on whether my brother is sanctified when he wears things I cannot wear without pride, or speaks more explosively than I would let myself under provocation, or seems too sensitive about the criticisms I have given for his good. I just do not know whether he has crossed his line in these matters or not, and he is not judged before God by my line.

But I have a line. *And I know when I cross it!* God sees to that! Life in the Spirit does not operate by sheer momentum of inertia, nor by rules and regulations, nor yet again by the judgments of men, good

THE SPIRIT GUIDES US and helpful though these may be at times. The sanctified life is *life!* And it can only be lived in the Holy Spirit. He it is who, when put in full control of our hearts, stands ready to whisper whenever we approach the line. His checks and promptings are absolutely faithful. He will always whisper—and we shall hear if we listen. The sad part is that we so often fail to listen. One missionary, who had precipitated an ugly situation by a certain speech, told me, when I asked whether he really felt led to make that speech: "No. I felt I must say it quickly for fear I would be checked before I got it said." That was more honest than most of us care to be, but how often that has been our experience.

The Holy Spirit's guidance, then, is our only answer. Most folk want a sanctification that will work itself. Human nature is essentially lazy. People want spectacular experiences which will give them in an instant a sanctification like a chunk of something all wrapped up and labeled and ready to be shipped through to glory without further attention. Not so, however, for Christ offers *life.* Many have been attracted to the doctrine of "eradication" in the hope of having all their problems and particularly the need for effort and discipline eradicated from their lives. This is not scriptural holiness. On the other hand, to try to discipline one's life without first having the pattern of life which revolved around self as a center eradicated by a surrender which brings cleansing and the hiding of the self with Christ in God, is futile and doomed to defeat. Only the living of a life disciplined by the guidance and control of the Holy Spirit brings knowledge of the path of continual victory.

Sanctification is both a crisis and a process. Neither is possible without the other. It should be clear by now how easy it would be to lose what one received in the crisis—to leave one's hidden place with Christ in God and slip back to the easy old self-life again. There is no way to victory except a walk of carefulness under the constant guidance and in instant obedience to the Holy Spirit. Whether this seems hard or not depends largely on whether we have made the great committal or not. If we love Jesus Christ as we ought to love Him, with all there is of us and without reservation, then this will seem not arduous but a glorious, victorious life of love and service for Him. To the unsurrendered it will seem irksome and dreary indeed.

The Guidance of the Spirit[6]

This chapter highlights our experience of the guidance of the Holy Spirit in the sanctified life. Dr. Cattell's unique contribution is his discussion of the Spirit's specific guidance to us in times of temptation when, in the experience of legitimate human emotions, we are in danger of crossing the line into carnal thoughts and responses.

Every high spiritual privilege carries with it immense peril. The greater the privilege the greater the peril. Divine guidance is a precious privilege fraught with peculiar peril. Yet we dare not neglect it, for "as many as are led by the Spirit of God, they are the sons of God" (Rom. 8:14).

As a boy trying to be a Christian, I was greatly puzzled by the testimonies of adult Christians who would say that God had spoken to them and told them to do thus and so. I listened intently but no voice broke on my ears. As a Quaker boy my heritage included the remarkable stories of people who in spectacular ways received direction from God. There were those two women who in the beginnings of Quakerism felt impressed of the Spirit to carry a gospel message in person to the sultan of Turkey. It was difficult for anyone to see the sultan in those days, and for two single women to make the journey alone was quite unthinkable. But God told them to go. They were not only given audience, but their message was kindly received. The sultan, realizing the dangers attendant upon single women traveling through Turkey, offered them an armed guard from the capital to the border. This they refused, saying that they felt safer in God's keeping than in that of soldiers.

Then there was Stephen Grellet, French nobleman who missed the guillotine, escaped to America, and became a leading Quaker preacher. Amid his arduous travels in America he was once led of the

---

6. *Spirit of Holiness*, chap. 4.

Spirit to go and preach in a certain logging camp. Although he found the camp deserted he was so sure of his leadings that he stood up and preached in an empty dining hall. Years later in London a man approached Grellet, reminded him of the incident, said that he was the cook of the camp and the only man around that day. Seeing a preacher come, he hid, and listened outside the window. He was so impressed by the sermon, given without an audience, that, although at the time remaining concealed, he was convicted and converted, and from then on did a large Christian service.[7]

Again, there were the remarkable and often discomfiting insights into individual spiritual needs by the late Amos Kenworthy. And in my own yearly meeting there was Esther Butler, who 50 years ago founded our mission in China. When called of God to that pioneer work, she saw a crowded Chinese street in a vision, the faces and places of which she later clearly recognized upon arrival in Nanking.[8]

How could I get God to speak to me like that? Many young friends were in those days claiming calls of God to service in foreign lands. I wanted to go desperately, but for the life of me I could not honestly say that I had any experience which I could label a call from God. I interviewed preachers, missionaries, and church officials, but mostly I got only the instruction to be sure to obey when the will of God was revealed. I had settled that long before. What I needed now was instruction as to how to hear the voice of God. One good pastor comforted me somewhat by relating an incident. Some new convert asked Amos Kenworthy how it was that Christ had said, "My sheep hear my voice" (John 10:27), yet he couldn't hear Christ's voice. The aged saint replied, "Yes, it is true that His sheep hear His voice, but it is also true that the lambs have to learn it." That helped some. But if only I could know how to begin to learn, how happy I would be.

Later I found two very helpful books, Upham's *Inward Divine Guidance* and Knapp's *Impressions*. Then came simple little experiences in which I applied the tests as best I could. Most of my earliest experiences were in the form of guidance to speak to boyhood companions about becoming Christians. I found in almost every case where I was truly led that the person was prepared by the Spirit to receive my invitation. It worried me a bit that I could not describe that guidance to myself in any more substantial terms than that when my fear reached a certain stage of nervous tension, then I knew it was time

---

7. William Wistar Comfort, *Stephen Grellet*, 42-43.
8. Walter R. Williams, *Ohio Friends in the Land of Sinim*, 21.

to go and speak to the one on my heart. If it was not of God, the fear subsided. Later I recognized that the voice of God did not consist of an experience of being scared but rather in the growth of an inner conviction. In those days that particular conviction carried an emotional tone of fright for me, but I gradually came to **A GROWING** realize that it was the sense of conviction that counted **CONVICTION** rather than any emotion, pleasant or unpleasant, with which it might be associated.

About that time I heard another helpful thing from some preacher. He said that the devil moves people on sudden impulse but that God always gives us time for consideration, the application of tests, and the growth of conviction. He went so far as to say that whenever we were seized with a sudden impulse to do something odd and to do it quickly, we could be practically sure that the impression had come from the devil. In the main this has proved true in my later experience. God is love; He does not give us guidance as a form of punishment but rather as a loving expression of His interest in the affairs of our lives. He is therefore patient, and glad to have us assured of His will before we act. God does speak when we listen, and it works out in experience. It is a glorious privilege.

We must have done with fear—even fear of making mistakes—if we would learn to know the voice of God. In a quiet time it is possible **TEST THE** to receive impulses from Satan or merely from one's own **SPIRITS** desires, as well as from God. One will need to apply some simple tests by which to screen these impulses.

First, *Is the impression scriptural?* God never violates His written Word. The Holy Spirit can always be depended upon to be consistent. Any impression which is not consistent with the Scriptures did not originate with Him. One of the most profound reasons why a Christian should be a constant and consistent student of the Word is that thereby he comes better to know the mind of Christ. The first, and primary, test must be constantly applied. Word and Spirit go together.

Second, *Is it right?* God never requires immoral acts. I knew a married man who approached a single lady and asked for her hand in marriage, saying that the Lord had revealed this as His will. Evidently the wires were crossed. So were they when the mother of several small children felt that she should leave her family and go alone to Africa as a missionary.

Third, *Is it providential?* Do circumstances, all of which we may believe are either in the active or the permissive will of God, converge to open the doors for the accomplishment of the object about which we have been impressed? If God is calling, He will always open the doors—we need not force them.

Fourth, *Is it corroborated by trusted and Spirit-led friends?* This is a necessary check against unbridled individualism. It is conceivable that the individual may be right in standing against a group of Christians, but it is most dangerous. I think there is a better way. The late Amos Kenworthy, who is known for his instant revelation and spiritual insight, was a man whom most folk regarded as next to infallible. Nevertheless, I am told that he faithfully adhered to the Quaker principle of submitting his concerns to the fellowship of the elders and overseers of the meeting, and went on his errands of ministry only when they united with him. Usually they endorsed his concern, granting, according to the custom of Friends, a written "minute" expressing their unity with him in this service. This credential he was careful to carry with him in the discharge of his concern. But occasionally the "select meeting" did not concur with his guidance. It was then that he left the responsibility for that service with the fellowship of the group and submitted to their judgment. This to me is the deepest proof that he was led of God. The fellowship is of extreme importance—granted of course that it is a true fellowship in the Spirit.

Finally, *Does the impression become an ever more weighty conviction?* For me this has been the heart of guidance. Many an idea has seized me with great enthusiasm. Then to my surprise it faded out over a short period of time. But the voice of God is in a conviction which grows with the passing of time and becomes inescapable and compelling.

I must hasten to guard against two wrong impressions which I may have given. First, it must not be assumed that knowing God's will for life service is only for preachers and missionaries. I thank God for a host of young Christians in business and professional **GUIDANCE FOR LAYMEN** life who are just as sure of God's will for their lives as any preacher could be for his. Second, it must not be supposed that divine guidance is only for great crisis decisions of life. The Holy Spirit is interested in the detailed conduct of our daily lives to the end that they should be Christlike. Much He leaves to the realm of our sanctified judgment. But there is possible to us an ever-deepening and conscious dependence upon Him for direction in the small matters. Neither must it be supposed from my extended discussion of the tests of guidance that obtaining the mind of the Lord must always be a lengthy and labored process. Rather, it is true that with experience one can soon discover that same quality of conviction attaching itself to impressions concerning small details of the daily program. . . . Weightier matters about which there is some uncertainty may well be held over for another day or more extended periods of time to allow for the crystallization or the fading of the conviction as the case may be.

Life is terribly inadequate unless caught up into the vital, adventurous realm of daily divine guidance where the Holy Spirit controls, not in some vague deistic sense, but in an intimate rela-
A DAILY
FELLOWSHIP tionship where our losing ourselves in Him is so real that He becomes our intelligence, our heart, our will, our very life. In this intimate relationship the discipline of the early morning quiet time is supplemented by the discipline of momentary, conscious recognition of His presence and Headship in all the affairs which come and go throughout the day. We become thus more and more sensitive to His gentle pressure upon our hearts that prompts us here, checks us there, as to conduct, as to what we say in our conversation, as to where we go, as to what we buy, as to where we are seen, as to whom we turn to give help, as to which beggar is worthy, as to when to answer and when to keep silent, as to what recreations are wholesome, as to whether to leave the TV on this station or turn to another—and when to turn it off!—as to when to go with an apology for a misspoken word or an act that hurt another.

This is the essence of spiritual-mindedness. There is no end to the room for development here in ever-increasing sensitiveness to the Spirit's pressure as a momentary guide through every day. It helps me to think of His guidance as a pressure rather than a voice in my soul. Indeed, it is necessary to recognize that the guidance of the Spirit is meant to assist us primarily with moral judgments. It is not concerned with the prudential thing to do but with the *right* thing to do. It is not concerned with giving us, for their own sake, infallible answers about how to make money in business, or whether it will rain tomorrow, or whether the stock market will go up or down, or the like. It is not a species of necromancy or palm reading by which our curiosity may be satisfied about things which we need not know, or we may be spared the labor of using our reason and judgment in their sanctified form. But it is given to show us the moral aspect of all such. The Spirit is interested in helping a man to conduct his business on strictly Christian lines, whether or not that means financial success. Financial success concerns the Spirit only indirectly as it bears on the businessman's moral standing in the will of God. This fact gives us our clue as to how to learn the voice of the Spirit.

It is precisely in the matter of "crossing the line," which was treated in the last chapter, that guidance begins. People want spectacular guidance—to avoid taking the train that is going to be wrecked or to choose the right occupation or companion—but they forget that these extraordinary experiences come to those who have built well the foundation of sensitiveness to the Spirit's pressure in the soul in small matters. The increase of sensitiveness to the voice of the Spirit is in direct proportion to the implicitness of obedience moment by moment.

No man can tell another when he is becoming a glutton, but the Holy Spirit will. No man can tell another when his sensitiveness is becoming self-centered to the point of enmity against God, but the Holy Spirit always does. One may be confused in his own thinking as to when religious zeal becomes envy, when the encouraging words of others are being accepted by an inordinate love of praise, when righteous anger gives way to an ugly temper, but into that confusion will come, if we listen, the "still small voice," that gentle pressure of the Spirit in tones of conviction: "This is the way, walk ye in it" (Isa. 30:21). To know when we are exercising leadership for the thrill of power, or when the enjoyment of the presence of one of the opposite sex is becoming a thing of danger or disloyalty, or when the admiration of beauty has shifted to the lustful look—all this is possible only by the guidance of the Spirit. Our Christian experience will be barren and merely historic unless it is made a living thing through the guidance of the Holy Spirit. "As many as are led by the Spirit of God, they are the [children] of God" (Rom. 8:14). . . .

As Sangster said, "*God does guide us.*" And the result is blessed. If one never had a spectacular experience in his life, it would be worth everything just to have the kind of guidance that covers these day-to-day matters. Yet constant obedience in this field brings a growing sensitiveness to the voice of the Spirit, and the larger experiences then become occasionally in order.

The word about guidance in Romans 8 is followed by a word on the witness of the Spirit. The voice of the Spirit is the same in both instances. Just as He has a way of making us individually assured of salvation with an inner conviction that leaves no room for doubt, so

He speaks in all His guidance with that same inner voice in conscience, giving a conviction of certainty. Guidance and conscience are not the same thing, but guidance uses conscience. . . .

Once I was evangelist for our Young Peoples Conference held on the shores of Lake Erie. One night, after the scheduled service, a spirit of praise came upon the group, and one after another **OBEDIENCE IS BLESSED** began to give words of testimony and thanksgiving. In the course of the praise some girl emphasized deep assurance in her testimony. I felt impressed to start a chorus the author of which had been a remarkable minister in the Friends church. It had been my honor to follow him in the pastorate where he died. I had seen his widow and two small children through the depression. Then I went to India and had not seen the family for 10 years. I understood they had gone east. I hesitated about starting the chorus, for it was old, I had not heard it for a long time, and I did not know whether the young people knew it or not. Three more testimonies passed, but the pressure increased. I started the chorus and we sang it twice.

During the second time a great, strapping fellow rose, came forward, and gave himself to Christ. I had no idea who he was. Later he testified: "This is the first time I have been happy for two years. I had not thought of my father for a long time until tonight you sang the chorus he wrote. I began to wonder what he would think if he knew the way I had been living." It broke him, and he found Christ. How easy it would have been to have brushed aside that gentle pressure to sing, especially since singing is naturally rather hard for me. But how thankful I have been for obedience at that point.

8

J. Harold Greenlee
(1918—)

Jacob Harold Greenlee, an ordained United Methodist minister, was born in Charleston, W.Va., in a devout Methodist home. He graduated from Asbury College in 1939, then earned his B.D. at Asbury Theological Seminary and his Ph.D. from Harvard University. His training includes postdoctoral studies at Harvard and Oxford universities.

Mrs. Greenlee, Ruth Olney, comes from a Minnesota Methodist pastor's family. She was a nurse at Asbury Theological Seminary when she and Harold met. They have three grown children, two daughters and a son.

Dr. Greenlee served as professor of New Testament Greek at Asbury Theological Seminary from 1947 to 1965 and in a parallel role as research associate for the United Bible Societies, 1955-65. He was professor of New Testament Greek at Oral Roberts University Graduate School of Theology, 1965-69. Since 1969 Dr. Greenlee has been on the staff of the Oriental Missionary Society International (OMS). He has served as visiting professor or lecturer on 12 fields where OMS maintains seminaries or other schools of theology. He is also currently serving as a translation consultant to Wycliffe Bible Translators, and as adjunct professor of linguistics, University of Texas at Arlington.

Dr. Greenlee is the author of more than 100 articles, primarily dealing with the Greek New Testament. His six published books all reflect biblical language studies as they affect our understanding of the Scriptures.

In 1961 and 1962 the National Holiness Association (now the Christian Holiness Association) sponsored a series of lectures on 13 seminary and Christian college campuses. The purpose was to present contemporary thought in the field of Wesleyan-Arminian theology.

Dr. J. Harold Greenlee, professor of New Testament language at Asbury Seminary, was invited to discuss the biblical base for the church's message of Christian holiness. That presentation was preserved, along with 33 other lectures, in a two-volume series, *Insights into Holiness* (1962), and *Further Insights into Holiness* (1963).

Dr. Greenlee here presents some of the fundamental lines of exegesis upon which Wesleyan Bible scholars base their understanding of entire sanctification as a work of God's grace available to Christians in this life. It was John Wesley himself who wrote: "I tell you as plain as I can speak, where and when I found this [truth of entire sanctification]. I found it in the oracles of God, in the Old and New Testaments, when I read them with no other view or desire but to save my own soul."

The Greek New Testament and the Message of Holiness[1]

There is only one morally adequate basis for the requirement that Christians be pure and holy in heart and life. . . . Christians are to be holy because, and only because, God is holy.

Since the New Testament is the one basic Textbook of Christianity, anything that can properly be said concerning the Christian faith must find its basis in the Greek New Testament. Furthermore, whatever can be said about the Christian faith can be said about holiness; because the quality of holiness is coextensive with whatever is Christian.

1. Holiness: A Quality

Let us examine this latter statement. By "holiness" I do not mean a particular doctrine *about* holiness; I mean holiness with a small *h*—holiness as a moral and spiritual quality of life. This *quality* of holiness permeates everything that is Christian. Holiness is the dis-

---

1. Geiger, comp., *Further Insights into Holiness*, 73-88.

tinctive quality of whatever is Christian: the Christian's God, the Bible, heaven, conduct—make your own list! Indeed, there is nothing that is truly Christian that is not holy, and there is nothing that is holy that is *non-Christian.* Therefore, while sincere Christians may feel obliged to reject or even oppose certain *doctrines about* holiness, for a person to be a Christian and yet oppose holiness as a moral and spiritual quality is a contradiction of terms—it is to claim to be a Christian and yet oppose its distinctive characteristic.

This paper, therefore, while it has a doctrinal purpose—we are concerned with the historic Wesleyan doctrine of holiness—yet is first of all concerned with holiness as a quality and with laying a foundation upon which any doctrine about holiness must rest. I suspect that the superficiality of too much holiness preaching in Wesleyan circles is due to the fact that the preacher fails to ground his message in this basic fact of holiness as a quality, and as the characteristic quality of Christianity.

2. Holiness: Its Meaning

a. Its Basic Idea. Before someone suggests that we are reasoning in a circle, however, or assuming the thing to be proved, we would do well to define the principal term which we are using. What does "holiness" mean, after all? We probably assume that we know what we mean when we say that God is holy, but what about the word as used of a Hindu "holy man" who sits on a bed of spikes? Is it simply a misuse of the term to call such a man "holy"?

The English words "holy," "holiness," "sanctify," and other words of these families are translations of the Greek word *hagios* and its word family. The Liddell-Scott lexicon gives as a basic definition of *hagios,* "devoted to the gods." *Hagios* is in turn derived from another adjective *hagos,* "any matter of religious awe."

The Greek word "holy" is therefore basically not a word of moral quality. Its emphasis is upon *separation.* At the same time, it is not ordinary separation, as when two little boys divide a bag of candy, saying, "One for you and one for me." The New Testament knows this kind of separation and expresses it with such words as *aphorizō* and *chorizō. Hagios,* on the other hand, means a separation between a lower and a higher, between a common and a special, between objects destined for ordinary use and those destined for the service of a god. It is therefore inadequate to say, as some have said, that biblical holiness is merely separation; for to the average English listener "separation" implies no more than the separation of equals.

There is a second fallacy involved in saying that holiness is "merely separation." It is true that the Greek word "holy" has no moral quality in itself. It can therefore be predicated of a person or object which is dedicated to the service of any god or religion. The Hindu who spends his days lying on a bed of spikes and accepting money from passersby is indeed a "holy man," because he is set apart from ordinary occupations and is dedicated to his god or gods. Yet in any given instance the word "holy" takes on a moral connotation, for the reason that *an object or person dedicated to a god must have qualities which are appropriate to that god.* This is a principle which we take for granted in other areas of life. What, for example, is the basic question which we ask when we want to purchase a gift for someone? ... Is it not ... "What would be *appropriate?*" Thus we buy a teething ring for the Smiths' new baby, but not for Johnny's high school graduation gift; or a party dress for daughter Susan in college, but not for Uncle Henry. ...

Holiness, then, *does* have a moral connotation; it *always* has a moral connotation; for whatever is holy must have qualities which are commensurate with the god to whom it is dedicated. In an immoral religion, whose gods are degraded and debasing, a temple prostitute would appropriately be designated "holy." To a god of war, weapons of violence could be holy. Holiness always has a moral connotation, but what that moral connotation is depends upon the moral character of the god who is being worshiped. Since we are concerned with

GOD'S HOLINESS Christian holiness, we must simply ask what is the moral character of the Christian God. The answer is, of course, that the Christian God is a God of absolute moral purity and perfection of character. It follows that anything which is holy in a Christian sense must have qualities which are appropriate for the presence and service of a God of moral purity and perfection of character. This does not mean that anything which is holy must be as perfect as God is. It means that it must partake of qualities which for the thing involved are analogous to the moral perfection of God's person and nature.

Over and over in the Old Testament, for example, God pointed the Israelites to His own holiness by such analogies. An animal has no moral qualities, but an animal acceptable for sacrifice to God had to be free from physical blemishes. Priests were likewise required to be free from physical defects. These lessons helped point the people to the greater lesson, which was that they themselves were to be morally pure and without blemish before a God of moral perfection. In summary, holiness always implies qualities appropriate to the god who is being worshiped, and Christian holiness means moral purity.

b. Its Levels of Meaning. Yet another problem is often encountered. Granted that holiness in the biblical sense has moral overtones, is not the level of meaning sometimes so low that little emphasis upon it is justified? This is an argument which is fallacious in general, not merely as regards the word "holiness." In many instances—in Greek, in English, and in other languages—words may have different levels of meaning, and the existence of one level of meaning does not preclude the existence of other levels of meaning. English words such as *drink, mistress,* and *desire,* for example, are words which may have either a neutral or an undesirable meaning. Let us therefore see what levels of meaning the *hagios* family of words has in the New Testament.

In 1 Cor. 7:14, Paul uses the verb of the *hagios* family, *hagiazō,* to describe the effect of a Christian husband or wife upon an unbelieving spouse: "For the unbelieving husband is made holy in the wife, and the unbelieving wife is made holy in the husband"; and adds that the children of such a mixed marriage are "holy."[2] Paul is certainly not teaching that an unconverted wife or husband is automatically made spiritually pure simply by being married to a Christian, or that children of such a marriage possess Christian holiness without ever being born again. He apparently means that an unbelieving husband or wife, married to a Christian, is to some extent drawn out of the pagan influence of a city like Corinth and brought under the influences of righteousness and godliness by sharing a home with a believer; and that the children are likewise to some extent separated from pagan influence. Here, then, is a distinctly lower level of meaning of *hagios.*

The Israelites of the Old Testament are referred to as a "holy" nation, although many of their deeds could lay no claim to the quality of moral purity. It is also clear that Paul uses the term "holy ones" (*hagioi,* "saints") to designate Christians in general in the churches to whom his letters are written, although the same Epistles reveal that the lives of some of these Christians were not morally pure. Here is a level of meaning higher than that of 1 Cor. 7:14, for these Christians were converted, and in a definite sense any such believer was separated from the old life of sin and separated to God in Christ.

Yet there is a still higher level of holiness than that which char-

---

2. Note that the author throughout this chapter makes his own translations of the scripture quotations.

acterizes all born-again Christians; for these Christians, called "holy ones" or "saints," are summoned to *become* "holy": 2 Cor. 7:1, "Let us cleanse ourselves from every defilement of flesh and spirit, **SECOND BLESSING** bringing holiness to completion"; and 1 Thess. 5:23, "May the God of peace himself make you completely holy"—to mention two such passages.

We must therefore let each context help us decide which meaning of "holy" is intended; but we should certainly not permit the instances in which "holy" has a lower level of meaning in the New Testament to blind us to the fact of a high level of meaning in other instances. On the other hand, another caution may be appropriate here. Anyone of any theological persuasion should avoid the temptation to assume that such words as "holiness" and "sanctification" always mean specifically his own doctrine of holiness or sanctification.

Holiness, then, as a quality of life, is the Christian standard and the Christian distinctive. This is not so, however, *merely* because certain passages in the Bible can reasonably be interpreted to mean that Christians should be pure and holy—and many such passages can thus be interpreted; nor even because this is an underlying assumption throughout the Bible—and it is. It is not so *merely* because we are convinced of the correctness of a certain doctrine relative to holiness, nor even because John Wesley taught such a doctrine. There is only one morally adequate basis for the requirement that Christians be pure and holy in heart and life. I believe that too much holiness preaching has been superficial because it is not grounded upon this one foundation.

This one basis is expressed in God's command, repeated over and over throughout the Bible in various forms, "Be ye holy; for I am holy." Christians are to be holy because, and only because, God is holy. **GOD'S HOLINESS** Perhaps, since God is all-powerful, He could require His people to be holy even if He himself were not holy, and we would have no choice but to obey or suffer the consequences. Even so, this would be neither a rational nor a morally adequate basis for such a requirement. On the other hand, since God is holy, and since we are His people, living in His presence in this life and destined to live in His presence forever, it is unthinkable that we should not be pure and holy, in the very nature of the case and even if such a demand were nowhere mentioned in the Bible. The fact that the holiness of a Christian is at best immeasurably below the perfection of God does not affect the case. The Christian can be pure and holy, as a human being, in a sense which is acceptable to a holy God, as was the sacrificial animal in the Old Testament, which had no moral qualities whatever but which was free from physical blemish.

3. Other Significant Terms

a. Words. So much for *hagios,* which I trust has given us a basic orientation for our concept of Christian holiness. There are other Greek words which are significant in the concept of Christian holiness, and we may note some of these more briefly.

Katharos means "clean." This word and other words of its family occur frequently in the New Testament: in John 15:2 to mean "pruning" a productive grapevine; in Matt. 23:25-26 to mean washing leftover particles of food from dishes; in 8:2, and indeed in every such New Testament instance, to refer to the healing of leprosy; in Heb. 9:22 and elsewhere, to refer to making something clean in a ceremonial sense. The common denominator in all of these meanings is the cleansing away or removal of that which would hinder or defile. This **CLEANSING** sense may then be applied to the instances in which words of the *katharos* family are used in a spiritual sense: for example, verse 14, "How much more shall the blood of Christ, . . . cleanse our conscience from dead works to serve a living God?" 1 John 1:7, "the blood of Jesus . . . cleanses us from all sin"; and verse 9, "He is faithful and righteous . . . to cleanse us from all unrighteousness." Spiritual cleansing, then, refers to the washing away of sin and whatever would defile or hinder spiritually.

The word *teleios* and its family are translated "perfect," "perfection," and the like, and might seem to be particularly appropriate in a holiness vocabulary. While *teleios* is to be distinguished from *telos,* which means merely "an end," yet the *teleios* family generally emphasizes more the aspect of full growth or maturity rather than flawlessness: for example, 1 Cor. 2:6, "But we speak wisdom among the mature ones *[teleioi]*"; and Heb. 5:14, "But solid food is for mature people *[teleioi]*"; although freedom from defect may also be implied: for example, Matt. 5:48, "You shall be perfect *[teleioi]*, as your Heavenly Father is perfect"; and Col. 1:28, "That we may present every man mature *[teleion]* in Christ."

We might point out here that, although we should be discriminating in our use of terms, we should not be afraid of using the word "perfect" in contexts where it is appropriate to do so. **CHRISTIAN PERFECTION** "Perfect" has several levels of meaning. In one sense, nothing in this human world is perfect. Yet if we accept such terms as "a perfect day," "a perfect baby," and "a car in perfect condition," when sufficiently close inspection would reveal imperfections in all of these, it ought to be reasonable to accept such terms as "perfect love" and "Christian perfection" to mean, not absolute perfection, but Christian character which meets the approval of God.

Katartizō and its word family have the basic meaning of making a thing all that it was intended to be, either by outfitting and equipping or by mending what has fallen into disrepair. The verb is used of mending nets in Matt. 4:21 and Mark 1:19, and of a servant "equipped as his teacher" in Luke 6:40. Passages of spiritual significance for our study include 1 Thess. 3:10, "Praying that we may see your face and *supply* what is lacking in your faith"; Eph. 4:12, "For the *equipping* of the saints"; 2 Cor. 13:9, "And this we pray for, that you may be *completely equipped*"; and 1 Pet. 5:10 and Heb. 13:21.

Katargeō is a negative word whose etymology gives the meaning "completely not working." It refers to the nullifying of faith (Rom. 3:3) or a law (7:2), to the abolishing or doing away with knowledge and prophecies (1 Cor. 13:8) or a promise (Gal. 3:17), to the doing away with the offense to which the Cross gives rise (5:11), and to the destruction of death (1 Cor. 15:26). Its emphasis is upon the doing away with something so as to remove it completely from the picture. The passage which is particularly significant for our study is Rom. 6:6, "Our old man has been crucified with him, in order that the body of sin might be *done away with*." In this passage Paul is giving a figure which emphasizes the completeness and finality with which God can deal with the sin problem, to set the Christian free from his enslavement to sin.

At the same time, the illustration should not be taken for more than Paul intends. The figure of crucifixion might seem to suggest that the spiritually "crucified" person could never sin again. The figure ceases, however, with the emphasis upon death. Paul is here showing how effectively God can deal with the sin problem; he is not saying that sin will thereafter be impossible to the Christian. Indeed the apostle goes on, not to tell these "crucified" Christians that their sin problem is now automatically settled, but rather to *urge* them to act in accordance with such a crucifixion: "*Let not* sin reign in your mortal bodies" (6:12), and, "Do not yield your members as instruments of unrighteousness" (v. 13).

b. Suffixes. In addition to specific words, the suffixes on these words are significant, just as they are in English words. There are two suffixes which mean "having the quality of," as "-ness" does in

English—"holiness," "softness," for example. In the *hagios* family, *ha-giōsynē* and *hagiotēs* therefore mean "having the quality of being holy," as in Rom. 1:4, "according to a spirit of holiness"; and 1 Thess. 3:13, "to establish your hearts blameless in holiness." Similarly, with the *katharos* family one of these suffixes produces the word *ka-tharotēs,* "having the quality of being clean," as in Heb. 9:13, "If the blood of bulls and goats . . . makes holy as regards the quality of ceremonial cleanness of the flesh."

Another suffix has the basic meaning of action or process, like the English *-ing* in *painting* or *-sis* in *catharsis.* With the *katharos* family this suffix gives the word *katharismos,* "the process of cleans-ing," as in John 2:6, "six stone water jars for the Jews' cleansing rites"; and Heb. 1:3, "having performed the action of cleansing sins away." With the *hagios* family this suffix gives the meaning, "the action of becoming or of being made holy," as in 2 Thess. 2:13, "God has chosen us . . . for salvation by the sanctifying action of the Holy Spirit." This suffix of action sometimes carries over into the meaning of the state which results from the action, and it is the resulting state of holiness rather than the action of being made or of becoming holy which is dominant in such passages as 1 Thess. 4:4, "to possess his own vessel in a condition of holiness"; 1 Tim. 2:15, "if they continue in faith and love and holiness"; and perhaps other instances.

4. Significant New Testament Passages

There was a time when I was concerned over the fact that I could not honestly use as proof texts for the Wesleyan doctrine of holiness some of the texts which I heard others use in this way. This matter no longer worries me, not because I now have so many more proof texts, but because I have come to see that holiness is not a matter of mere proof texts but of the whole message of the Bible. Paul does not seem to place major emphasis upon the distinction between the experience of conversion and the experience of heart cleansing. His emphasis is upon the facts and fruit, as well as the necessity, of forgiveness and of holiness rather than upon the mechanics of the experiences. Yet, just as when the ground in a given locality is rich in underlying ore there will often be outcroppings which appear on the surface, so also holi-ness, which underlies the whole of Scripture, stands in specific clarity in numerous passages. These passages, moreover, reveal various significant facets of this great truth. We may profitably "sample" some of these passages, anticipating that one passage may reveal a **SCRIPTURAL** facet which another passage does not make clear, and that the consensus of all the passages will give a good representation of the whole underlying stratum of holiness.

Thus there are New Testament passages which seem to imply that the divine bestowal of a pure heart is to be distinguished from the bestowal of the forgiveness of sins. Let us examine some of these.

First John 1:9 reads, "He is faithful and righteous to forgive us our sins, and to cleanse us from all unrighteousness." The verb "forgive" is in the Greek aorist tense, which describes an action as a completed act. Forgiveness here is described as something which can be done and completed. The verb "cleanse" is likewise in the aorist tense, and therefore the cleansing is also an action which takes place and can be completed. The fact, moreover, that the two verbs are connected by the word "and" prevents us from interpreting "forgive" and "cleanse" as being the same action. In other words, the verse conceives of forgiveness and cleansing as being separate acts, both of which God will faithfully complete.

The Greek aorist tense, to which we have just referred, deserves a further word. In contrast with the Greek tenses which describe an action as continuing,[3] the aorist tense describes an action as completed. The action may be instantaneous, or it may take a longer or shorter time to occur. The aorist tense is not merely, as some have wanted to say, the "lightning tense." The aorist tense is not concerned with the length of time which is required for an action to occur. What the aorist tense *does* emphasize is that the action is conceived of as *completed.* Thus in 1 John 1:7, "The blood of Jesus . . . cleanses us from all sin," the verb "cleanses" is a Greek present tense and refers to a continuation of cleansing. In 1:9, however, the aorist tenses emphasize that God's forgiveness and His cleansing from unrighteousness are acts which God *completes* in such a way that the believer can say, "The work has been done."

We referred earlier to the familiar 1 Thess. 5:23. We point out now that the two verbs in this verse are in the aorist tense: "May the God of peace himself *make* you completely *holy;* and may your spirit and soul and body *be kept.*" In many passages in his Epistles, Paul urges Christians to grow, to abound, and to make spiritual progress. In

---

3. The imperfect tense in the indicative mood, and the present tense in the other moods.

the verses immediately preceding verse 23 the apostle uses present tenses, urging continuous actions: "Make a habit of not quenching the Spirit, and of not making light of prophecies; make a habit of testing all things, and of holding to what is good, and of abstaining from every form of evil" (vv. 19-22). The present passage, however, does not speak of continuation. The tense is aorist, and the emphasis is therefore upon an event, an action which is to take place and become completed. "May God make you completely holy" does not imply that they were not holy at all before, nor does it imply that this action will make them as perfectly holy as God is.

IN A MOMENT

It does emphasize that God's action in making them "completely holy" was in Paul's mind an event which could take place and be completed, and was distinct from their previous state of holiness. Likewise, while the "keeping" in the second part of the verse presumably would be continued over a period of time to the coming of the Lord, Paul's use of the aorist tense here puts the emphasis, not upon the continual keeping, but upon the completion of the "keeping" on the day when the Lord returns.

In 2 Cor. 7:1, on the other hand, we have both a present and an aorist tense. The first verb, "Let us *cleanse* ourselves," is aorist, emphasizing that the Christian's action in cleansing himself is to be completed and not merely begun or progressed toward. The second verb, "*completing* holiness in the fear of God," is a present tense, emphasizing the process; but the word "completing" itself obviously means that the holiness referred to is to become complete. The combined meaning is therefore that the quality of holiness is to be brought to completion in these Christians' lives.

From the point of view of tenses, Paul's prayer for the Ephesian church (Eph. 3:14-21) is striking. Much of the significance of the tenses is lost in the common English versions. This passage contains one aorist tense after another, and I cannot avoid the conclusion that the apostle here is praying that an *event* may take place in the hearts of these Christians, not mere continued progress. The use of present tenses in this passage would properly have referred to a continuing growth and progress—and the apostle often makes just such an emphasis in his letters. Yet in the present passage Paul does not pray that God may "continue to grant" that they may "continue to be strengthened by a power" and that they may "continue to be more and more able to grasp" the dimensions of divine love. Let me give a paraphrase of these verses that I trust will reflect the tenses involved:

I pray that God may grant to you [as a completed action] that you may receive, through the agency of His Holy Spirit, the strength of a power coming [as a completed event] into your inner being. This power will consist in Christ's taking up a settled dwelling in your hearts in a definite way which has not been the case before now. When this occurs, an accompanying fact will be that you will be found to be firmly rooted with your spiritual foundations solidly established in the divine love.[4] One purpose of all this is that you may receive [as a completed event] the strength to grasp with your mind, along with all of the saints, the full range of the dimensions of Christ's love—or, rather, to comprehend the fact that His love is so great that it is impossible to comprehend it!—so that God may so fill you [as a completed fact], that you will be, so to speak, a vessel which God himself has filled. Does this seem an exaggerated wish? Remember that our God is constantly able to accomplish things which are exceedingly and above measure beyond everything which we ask or even think, and these things He accomplishes according to the divine power which is constantly at work in us.

There is one rather popular holiness text, on the other hand, which I feel should be used only in a qualified sense in preaching
PREACHING entire sanctification. This passage is 1 Thess. 4:3, which begins, "For this is the will of God, your sanctification." In the first place, the syntax of the first two clauses is not as clear as some sermons assume it to be; there are several alternative possibilities. In the second place, "holiness" here is related to one specific area of moral conduct, which is sexual purity. There is no doubt, of course, that holiness of life is the standard here (cf. v. 7). At the same time the emphasis in verses 3-6 is not so much, "Be ye holy," but rather, "Holy people will, among other things, be pure in matters of sex and marriage." It therefore seems safer to take this passage as pointing out that holiness includes sexual and marital purity rather than to take it primarily as an exhortation to seek the experience of entire sanctification.

5. A Final Word

Let me close, however, with a final word of caution and admonition. First, the message of holiness does not rest solely upon the exegesis of small points or single passages, as though holiness were a biblical secret which must be carefully sought if it is to be detected at

---

4. "Rooted" and "established" are perfect tenses, describing a state resulting from a prior action.

all; it is rather the all-pervading quality of the Christian faith, the reflection of God's moral purity in the lives and hearts of His people. In the second place, holiness is not merely something to be spelled with a capital *H* and equated with the doctrines on this subject which John Wesley taught; it is rather a quality of heart and life, and John Wesley's doctrines are a human effort (in my opinion, a very good effort) to explain certain facts concerning this quality of life. In the third place, let us remember, on the one hand, that all preaching on the Christian message is the preaching of holiness; and let us remember, on the other hand, that while holiness is always implicit in a Christian message, we ought also to make it an explicit emphasis in such a way that people will know it not only as the characteristic quality of the Christian message but also as a specific reality in their individual hearts and lives, imparted through asking and accepting, by faith in the cleansing power of the blood of Christ.

9

E. Stanley Jones
(1884-1973)

Dr. E. Stanley Jones was one of the world's best-known religious leaders of the 20th century—in the words of a biographer, "one of the greatest Christian missionaries."

Born in Clarkesville, Md., January 3, 1884, Eli Stanley grew up in a Methodist home. At 15 years of age, he went to hear an overseas evangelist from John Bunyan's church in England. Convicted by the Holy Spirit, Stanley went forward and took his place among the seekers at the altar. In his own words he evaluates the experience.

"I fumbled for the latchstring of the kingdom of God, missed it, for they didn't tell me the steps to find." Dr. Jones continues: "The real thing came two years later. An evangelist, Robert J. Bateman, came to Memorial Church. . . . The third night . . . before going to the meeting I knelt beside my bed and prayed the sincerest prayer I had prayed so far in my life. My whole life was behind that simple prayer: 'O Jesus, save me tonight.' And He did!"

A student of Baltimore City College, Stanley was influenced by Evangelist Bateman to transfer to Asbury College in Wilmore, Ky. There he was sanctified wholly and called to missionary work. He graduated from Asbury with an M.A. degree in 1912, and was later honored with a D.D. from Duke University, and the S.T.D. from Syracuse.

Dr. Jones first went to India in 1907 as a missionary of the Methodist church. For eight years he served in various assignments: pastor of the English church in Lucknow, superintendent of the Lucknow District, and principal of the Sitapur Boarding School. In 1917 he was the evangelist for the North India Conference.

For these first years he labored chiefly among the low-caste people. But playing tennis in the evening after work, he made contact with the high-class Muslims and Hindus. One of the Hindus asked him, "Why do you work only among the low castes?" That seed began to germinate, and in 1924 he wrote, "I was strangely drawn to work among the educated high castes, the intelligentsia." Thus he began his lifelong ministry to the high caste, the educated, and student groups.

In 1928 Dr. Jones was elected a bishop of the Methodist church but resigned after 24 hours, choosing to continue his work in India. In the foreword to Dr. Jones's autobiography his son-in-law writes: "Always at heart . . . he has been an evangelist; this has been at the center. Beyond this has been the real center—his commitment to Jesus Christ as Lord."

Dr. Jones's first book, *The Christ of the Indian Road*, was published in 1925. At intervals of about two years, he wrote 25 others, translated into many languages. His message of the Spirit-filled life permeates all that he wrote. It is the dominant theme of *The Christ of Every Road, Abundant Living, Victorious Living*, and *Victory Through Surrender.*

A New Crisis Ensues[1]

In this chapter from Dr. Jones's autobiography, he gives his personal testimony to being filled with the Holy Spirit. The experience occurred about one year after his conversion. In addition to the personal witness, he gives his own interpretation of the experience of entire sanctification as the "conversion of the subconscious."

In the debate over eradication or suppression, Dr. Jones's theology calls for eradication of sin and evil, but suppression of the natural human urges.

Regarding the gift of the Holy Spirit and speaking in tongues, Dr. Jones recognizes the miracle at Pentecost as a special ministry of the Early Church but not known today. He distinguishes clearly Pentecostal tongues from Corinthian tongues.

---

1. *A Song of Ascents*, chap. 3.

But now, in the words of Dr. Jones's son-in-law, who wrote the foreword to *A Song of Ascents*, we will "let him tell his own story."

"The soul gets on by a series of crises." I've found it so. In conversion there is the sudden, or gradual, rise to a new level of life, a life as different from the ordinary man as the ordinary man is different from the animal. Then after the rise life is on a permanently higher level. But on that new level there usually ensues an experience of ups and downs, of alternate encouragement and discouragement, of victory and defeat.

It was so with me. For a year I lived under cloudless skies. The sun of my happiness seemed to have risen in the heavens to stay there forever. But after a year of unalloyed joy I found something alien began to rise from the cellar of my life. I felt there was something down there not in alignment with this new life I had found—ugly tempers, moodiness, deep-down conflicts. The general tenor of life was victory, but there were disturbing intrusions from the depths. I was becoming a house divided against itself. I was puzzled, confused, hurt with a tinge of disappointment. Was this the best that Christianity could do—to leave me wrestling with myself, or with something alien to myself? What was this dark something within?

Theology has described it as the "old man," the "flesh," "innate depravity." Perhaps it can best be described in more understandable terms as the "unconverted subconscious." The subconscious is like the submerged portion of an iceberg, one-tenth above and nine-tenths below. Freud says we are determined by lower drives in the subconscious. We think we consciously determine our conduct, but these basic drives in the subconscious actually determine us. These basic drives can be roughly described as self, sex, and the herd. These drives come down through a long racial history; hence they have bents, bents toward evil. The self has been asserted so much in racial history that it becomes dominant and demanding: "I want what I want when I want it." Sex has played such a part in a long racial history that it now demands the leading role, as it does in modern life. The herd, or social instinct, urge bids for a dominant place and often occupies it. Think of the things that we do because "everybody does it." We usually do not act, but only react to what other people do. We are not voices; we are echoes.

Which of these urges is the dominant urge it is hard to say, for there are moments when each seems dominant for that moment. But if I were to pick out the most decisive and dominant urge, I would say the self urge is. For beside having its own peculiar manifestations, the self is manifested in the sex urge as the self's desire for pleasure and in the herd urge as the self's desire for protection through conformity. So "innate depravity" is the self surrendered to nothing except itself—the self become God.

In conversion a new life is introduced into the conscious mind as we consciously accept Christ as Savior and Lord. A new love and a new loyalty flood the conscious mind. The subconscious mind is stunned and subdued by this new dominant loyalty to Christ, introduced into the conscious mind by conversion. Sometimes it lies low for long periods, subdued but not surrendered. It waits for low moments in the conscious mind and then sticks up its head and, when it sees an opportunity, takes over the conscious mind. Then we are a house divided against itself. Paul puts it this way: "If you are guided by the Spirit you will not fulfil the desires of your lower nature. That nature sets its desires against the Spirit, while the Spirit fights against it. They are in conflict with one another so that what you will to do you cannot do" (Gal. 5:16-17, NEB).

This was my condition after a year of almost unalloyed joy and victory. I was in a crisis. I was stymied by this inner conflict. And then **WRITING** a door out of the conflict opened through a book. When I took that book out of a Sunday School library, I felt a sense of destiny in reaching for it. A kind of tingle went through me, a tingle of expectancy. There was destiny in taking that book, for it changed my life and helped me solve the crisis I was in. I began to read *The Christian's Secret of a Happy Life,* by Hannah Whitall Smith, a Quaker. It told of complete victory for the total person. My heart was kindled with desire as I read it. I wasn't reading it; I was eating it. I got to the 42nd page when God spoke to me: "Now is the time to find." I pleaded: "Lord, I don't know what I want. This book is telling me. Let me read the book first, and then I can intelligently seek." But the Voice was imperious: "Now is the time to find."

I tried to read on, but the words were blurred. I saw I was in a controversy with God, so I closed the book, dropped on my knees beside my bed, and said: "Now, Lord, what shall I do?"

And He replied: "Will you give Me your all?"

And after a moment's hesitation I replied: "Yes, Lord, of course I will. I will give You my all, all I know and all I don't know."

Then He replied: "Then take My all, take the Holy Spirit."

I paused for a moment: my all for His all; my all was myself, His all was himself, the Holy Spirit. I saw as in a flash the offer. I eagerly replied: "I will take the Holy Spirit." I rose from my knees with no evidence save His Word. I walked out on the naked promise of that Word. His character was behind that Word. I could trust Him with my all, and I could trust Him to give me His all. I walked around the room repeating my acceptance. The doubts began to close in on me. I did what Abraham did when the birds came to scatter his sacrifice—he shooed them away. I walked around the room pushing away with my hands the menacing doubts. When suddenly I was filled— IN A MOMENT filled with the Holy Spirit. Wave after wave of the Spirit seemed to be going through me as a cleansing fire. I could only walk the floor with the tears of joy flowing down my cheeks. I could do nothing but praise Him—and did. I knew this was no passing emotion; the Holy Spirit had come to abide with me forever.

He had been with me, with me in the conscious mind in conversion. Now He was in me, in me in the subconscious. When He was with me in the conscious, it was conversion limited, for the subconscious was not redeemed; cowed and suppressed, but not redeemed. Now the subconscious was redeemed. These drives which reside in the subconscious—self, sex, and the herd—were cleansed; the self-urge cleansed from selfishness, the sex urge from sexuality; the herd urge from being fastened on society was now refastened on the kingdom of God, the ultimate society. With these drives redeemed it was conversion unlimited, nothing left out of its sway.

Holiness and Human Personality

Note, these drives were not eliminated; they were still there. It is impossible to eliminate them; they are an integral part of us and cannot by any known process be eliminated. But they can be CLEANSING cleansed from personal and racial bents and can be consecrated to Kingdom purposes. The self instead of belonging to its self and trying to be God now belongs to God and seeks His glory and not its own. Sex cleansed from sexuality, no longer an end in itself, is now dedicated to creation: within the home dedicated to procreation and fellowship, outside the home sublimated to creativity, creating new hopes, new movements, newborn souls, new creative activities—creative on a higher level. The herd urge, hitherto fastened on the futilities of allegiance to society around, is now cleansed from that enslaving bondage and fastened on the fruitfulness of the kingdom of God. You do not become unsocial, but loving God supremely you can love others subordinately—subordinately, but with a love intensified, you love others with His love.

These urges are cleansed, consecrated, and coordinated. They are no longer pulling in all directions, making you a civil war, a divided personality. They are under the one control of the Holy Spirit, so they are now a team working together for Kingdom ends. This is true of the conscious mind as well. The conscious mind and the subconscious mind are now under one redemption and one control, and "according well, they beat out music vaster than before."

That the subconscious mind can be redeemed is good news. For the area of the work of the Holy Spirit is largely in the subconscious mind. So if we surrender "all we know"—the conscious mind—"and all we don't know"—the subconscious—then the Holy Spirit takes over areas in the subconscious which have hitherto been "enemy territory" and now makes them friendly territory. The subconscious works with you, a friend and ally. And an important ally of the new life.

Jesus said: "A good man out of the good treasure of the heart bringeth forth good things" (Matt. 12:35). Is a redeemed subconscious a "good thing"? Yes. For we are producing a "good thing" in the subconscious by adding to it good attitudes, good deeds, good thoughts, good purposes, good victories day by day, hour by hour, minute by minute. We pile up reserves. Then, when in a moment of temptation and pressure we bring these moral and spiritual reserves in the subconscious into action, we come through with flying colors, a surprise to ourselves. The "good thing" was the hidden ally.

So the Creator created the subconscious for security purposes. Without it we would be living from hand to mouth; with it we are living from resource to resource.

This interpretation of what happens with the coming of the Holy Spirit may make possible a reconciliation of two views about the "deeper life." One view says there is complete eradication of the "old man of sin," and the other says there is suppression but not eradication. Obviously we cannot believe that in the Christian redemption we must provide for suppression of inner evil only, but not for eradication. That would be a half-redemption, a coming to terms with evil, if only it lies low. Sin and evil must be eradicated. So we say with the coming of the Holy Spirit both the conscious and the subconscious minds are cleansed from sin and evil

ERADICATION

bents. This is eradication. But the driving urges, self, sex, and the herd, are still there. Since they are part of you, you can't get rid of them. Hence they have to be suppressed, lest they try to climb **SUPPRESSION** back into dominance; this is suppression. So eradication and suppression are still facts of the Christian life—eradication of sin and evil and suppression of natural urges. These natural urges can be the source of temptation; self, deposed in surrender and cleansing, may try to climb back into the saddle and become dominant again; sex, surrendered and cleansed, may try to depart from procreation and fellowship and may try to become an end in itself; the herd urge, surrendered and cleansed, may gradually listen more to society than to the Savior. These urges are still alive and have to be watched. So there is a truth in suppression.

But it is a half-truth. For the real Christian remedy is not suppression, but expression on a higher level. The self, dedicated to Christ, now expresses itself as the servant of all, thus becoming the greatest of all; sex, now dedicated to the creative God, becomes creative, creating procreation and fellowship within the home and, sublimated, outside the home, creating new movements, new hopes, newborn souls. The herd urge, now emancipated by surrender to God from subservience to society, can serve and love society—"delivering thee from the people . . . unto whom now I send thee" (Acts 26:17). Delivered from the people, you can now serve them—and only then!

So instead of sitting on a lid in suppression, you now take off the lid and bid these urges, now emancipated, to go forth and love and serve in the name and power of their Master and Lord. And you guide them by watchful prayer.

But even this watchful prayer has to be modified. It would mean tense anxiety about the urges. There is a corrective: Instead of our trying by tense, prayerful anxiety to keep these urges consecrated, there is the fact that the Holy Spirit himself consecrates them. He keeps them "on the altar." "It falls to me to offer the Gentiles to him as an acceptable sacrifice, consecrated by the Holy Spirit" (Rom. 15:16, NEB). The Holy Spirit consecrates the sacrifice. That is important, for the usual idea is that through consecration we receive the Holy Spirit initially. That is true, but there is the further truth: the Holy Spirit keeps the gift consecrated. When we fully surrender ourselves and our urges to the Holy Spirit, He receives and cleanses them. But He also consecrates them and keeps them consecrated. That is a part of His redemptive work. That takes the strain, hence the drain, out of our Christian life. We are no longer nervously tying the sacrifices of our urges on the altar of consecration. We surrender them to the Holy Spirit, and He keeps them consecrated as a part of His job. So we can go about our jobs released and relaxed, knowing that He will attend to His.

A man introduced his wife to me: "Here is one of your wrestlin' Christians." She was wrestling hard to be good and to be consecrated. But she was tied in knots. She believed in the Holy Spirit, but not in the Holy Spirit as One who receives the consecrated gift and keeps it consecrated—with our consent. Ours is consent, not constraint.

As I look back, I find my experience coincides with the experience of the Early Church as to the permanent elements in the coming of the Holy Spirit. There seem to be two permanent facts in the coming of the Holy Spirit. Peter, speaking of what happened in the Gentiles' Pentecost at the house of Cornelius, said: "God, which knoweth the hearts, bare them witness, giving them the Holy Ghost, even as he did unto us; and put no difference between us and them, purifying their hearts by faith" (Acts 15:8-9). Both Jew and Gentile received the Holy Spirit, and both of them had their hearts purified in the coming of the Holy Spirit. This seemed a permanent element—purity of heart.

The other permanent element was in what Jesus said: "But **POWER TO WITNESS** ye shall receive power, after that the Holy Ghost is come upon you: and ye shall be witnesses unto me both in Jerusalem, and in all Judaea, and in Samaria, and unto the uttermost part of the earth" (Acts 1:8). Something would persist from Jerusalem to the uttermost parts of the earth, namely, the power to witness effectively for Jesus. Not "power"—full stop; but power of a certain kind, the power to witness to Jesus Christ. When we witness to our group, our denomination, our particular brand, it is not power—it is powwow. So the Holy Spirit means power to witness effectively for Christ.

Two things, then, are permanent in the gift of the Holy Spirit: purity and power. Purity for myself and my own inner needs, and power to witness effectively to others. These two things comprehended their needs then, and they comprehend my needs now.

Holiness and the Gifts of the Spirit

But a new complication is brought in: You have the Holy Spirit if you have the gift of tongues. The gift of tongues, they say, is an integral part of the gift of the Holy Spirit. It is true that in the Acts the gift of tongues was associated with the coming of the Holy Spirit in three places—Jerusalem, Caesarea, and Ephesus; the centers of Hebrew culture, Roman culture, and Greek culture. The question was very acute in those early days as to whether if you became a Christian you would also have to adopt the Hebrew culture and language, become a Jew. That pattern was broken at Pentecost. Men were gathered from all that ancient world—Asia, Africa, Europe—and when the apostles began to speak, every man heard in his own language "the wonderful works of God" (Acts 2:11). What did that mean? It meant that God was going to use every language, every culture, every nation to express the wonderful works of God.

The Jewish mold was broken at Jerusalem. The Roman mold was broken at Caesarea, and the Greek at Ephesus. Over the head of Jesus on the Cross were the words: "THIS IS JESUS THE KING OF THE JEWS" (Matt. 27:37). It was written in Hebrew, Latin, and Greek. Here in essence was the same thing—this new message was not to be confined to the Hebrew, Latin, or Greek. All the molds were broken. This, I believe, was a special miracle performed for a special purpose and a very necessary one. That power to speak directly in the language of a people *without an interpreter* and without learning the language has not reappeared in our day as far as I know. Many have come to India, hoping to be able to repeat the miracle of Pentecost, but the wreckage of those hopes is strewn across India. It hasn't happened. The Corinthian type of tongues has appeared, but not the Pentecost type. The Corinthian type was one of the gifts of the Spirit, an unknown tongue which needed an interpreter. At Pentecost no interpreter was needed.

The gift of the Spirit is for all, but the gifts of the Spirit He is "dividing to every man severally as he wills" (1 Cor. 12:11). Paul puts it: "Are all apostles? Are all prophets? Are all teachers? Do all work miracles? Do all possess gifts of healing? Do all speak with tongues? Do all interpret?" (vv. 29-30, RSV). The answer is no. Then can we have the gift of the Holy Spirit without the gift of tongues? The answer is simple: Did Jesus have the Holy Spirit? Yes. Did He speak in tongues? And the answer is no. Then I can have the Holy Spirit CHRISTLIKENESS without the gift of tongues. For He is my Pattern. "The Spirit had not yet been given, because Jesus had not yet been glorified" (John 7:39, NEB). Why? For the pattern of what constitutes spiritual power had to be fixed in Jesus—He had to live, teach, die, rise again, and go to the right hand of the Father before the Spirit could be given. The Holy Spirit is a Christlike type of character and produces Christlike persons when He comes within.

Paul evidently found that the emphasis on the gifts of the Holy Spirit was divisive, creating more division than direction, so he dropped that emphasis. He mentioned the[se] gifts of the Spirit in 1 Corinthians 12—14, but [some of these] never again in all his Epistles. Nor did John mention the gift of tongues in his Epistles, nor did Peter or James or Jude. The working emphasis in the Early Church became the fruits of the Spirit: "love, joy, peace, patience, kindness, goodness, fidelity, gentleness, and self-control" (Gal. 5:22-23, NEB). All of them were moral qualities. So the emphasis shifted from the nonmoral, semimagical gifts, which were divisive then, and are today, to the fruits of the Spirit, the moral qualities beginning with "love" and ending with "self-control," which are nondivisive and uniting.

Some quote the passage in Mark 16:17 (RSV): "And these signs will accompany those who believe: in my name they will cast out demons; they will speak in new tongues; they will pick up serpents, and if they drink any deadly thing, it will not hurt them; they will lay hands on the sick, and they will recover." But all the modern versions tell us that the Gospel of Mark was lost from verse 8 on, and this passage was put in as a second- or third-century attempt to fill out the lost portion. It is exactly the kind of list that man, unaided by inspiration, would make out. Not one of the five "signs" is a moral quality. Every one is a semimagical power.

Suppose the Christian movement had gone out into that ancient world with these five signs upon their banners. It would have died as a "wonder cult," tossing off miracles. Instead, it became a moral and spiritual movement remaking and redeeming character. So it lived on. If you take one of these "signs"—"new tongues"—you have to take them all. You have to pick up serpents, and you have to drink deadly poison without hurt. Only two of these so-called signs were in Jesus. He cast out demons and He laid hands on the sick. What kinds of "signs" are these when three of them were not in the Lord and Savior?

Apparently, speaking in tongues occurs today, and it is real to some, but they cannot connect their type with Pentecost; it is Corinthian and one of the "gifts" of the Spirit. The "gifts" of the Spirit are not to be confounded with the gift of the Spirit. The gift of the Spirit is for all. The gifts of the Spirit He divides "severally as he will" (1 Cor. 12:11).

So we say in the fellowship of our Ashrams: "We welcome the immersed and the unimmersed, those who do not speak in tongues and those who do, provided they do as Paul suggests, 'He that speaketh in tongues speaketh to himself.' Let him speak to himself and not make it a public issue, for it will divide any group it comes into. The basis on which we come together is this: If you belong to Christ and I belong to Christ, we belong to each other." We do not let any side issues divide us.

I said above that after mentioning the gifts of the Spirit, Paul dropped the emphasis on them. There is one exception: "We recommend ourselves by the innocence of our behaviour, our grasp of truth, our patience and kindliness; by gifts of the Holy Spirit, by sincere love, by declaring the truth, by the power of God" (2 Cor. 6:6-7, NEB). Here he mentions the gifts of the Holy Spirit but defines them as "sincere love," "declaring the truth," "the power of God," but no gift of tongues. He redefined the gifts of the Holy Spirit in terms of moral qualities and then dismissed them, never mentioning them again.

So I'm grateful that I received the Holy Spirit without complications or "riders." The Holy Spirit brought me purity, and He brought me power, for He brought me himself. I need and want no more.

"He on whom you see the Spirit descend and remain [Pattern], this is he who baptizes with the Holy Spirit [Giver]" (John 1:33, RSV). So Jesus is not only the Giver of the Holy Spirit; He is the Pattern of the Gift. If you surrender to the Holy Spirit, He will make you into His image, a Christlike type of person. Jesus was infinite sanctity, and He was also infinite sanity. There was nothing psychopathic

WHOLENESS about Him. He went off into no visions, no dreams; every virtue was balanced by its opposite virtue and all held in a living blend; He was the most balanced character that ever moved through the pages of history. So I can pray for and receive the Holy Spirit with the stops out—with no reservations. I can ask for and receive the Spirit "without measure," for I cannot have too much of purity, nor too much of power, nor too much of Christlikeness—too little, but not too much.

So a year after I met Christ, I had been led into two vital things—a new birth and the fullness of the Holy Spirit. One brought me into the Kingdom, and the other brought the Kingdom into me. The first beatitude was fulfilled in me: "How blest are those who know their need of God; the kingdom of Heaven is theirs" (Matt. 5:3, NEB). Here blessedness is pronounced upon those who know they are poor—poor enough to receive. The verse could be translated, "How blest are they who are surrendered and receptive; the kingdom of heaven belongs to them." They belong to the kingdom of heaven, yes, but— more breathtaking—the kingdom of heaven belongs to them; all its resources are at their disposal; they could have all they could appropriate and use. And the only qualification was to be poor enough to receive.

There are those who believe that the Sermon on the Mount is another law, more spiritual, more inward, but still a law. You can't do this; you must do that. Therefore it is not a part of the gospel. Therefore it is impractical, for it means a vast whipping up of the will—try harder! A theological professor asked his students: "Is the gospel you preach a demand or an offer?" With one accord they said it was a demand. "Think again," he suggested. "Well, it is a demand and an offer," they replied. "Think again," he persisted. And they finally came to the conclusion that if it is the gospel, it is an offer.

If that be true, then the Sermon on the Mount is an integral part of the gospel, for its opening emphasis is not on the whipping up of the will but on a surrender of the will. Be poor enough to receive, and the kingdom of heaven is yours; all its resources and power are yours. This strikes a dart at the heart of self-sufficiency, at self-salvation; it asks self-surrender! If you are poor enough to receive, the kingdom of heaven is at your disposal—all yours. Then the impossible "demands" of the Sermon on the Mount become possible accomplishments— possible through an "offer"; the kingdom of heaven and all its powers and resources belong to you if you're poor enough to receive!

Here within a year after I put my feet upon the Way, I had made a major discovery, at least for me, that I could be born again and I could be filled with the Spirit—all for the taking! Too cheap? No, very expensive. For if you take the gift, you belong forever to the Giver! He binds you to His heart by cords of love and gratitude, but you wouldn't have it otherwise for worlds.

So I was on the Way. And the only qualification was receptivity, to be poor enough to receive.

But as I look back, I can now see that I came near adopting an emphasis that would have dimmed the emphasis on receptivity as the keynote of my life. I became interested, passionately interested, in the Second Coming. In my eagerness to absorb everything in the Christian life I got hold of three volumes of *Lectures on the Apocalypse*. I devoured them. I felt the author knew the key to the future and was unlocking it. I became absorbed in this Coming calendar, became intolerant of those who dared disagree with it. Then I found a subtle change taking place in my emphasis. I was living on expectancy, expectancy of the coming Christ, instead of living on experience—experience of the present Christ. I saw that the First Coming was the working center of the gospel, the Incarnation, the Atonement, the coming of the Holy Spirit, the evangelization of the world.

The Second Coming was marginal and not my area now: "It is not for you to know the times or the seasons . . . But ye shall receive power, after that the Holy Ghost is come upon you: and ye shall be witnesses unto me in Jerusalem, and in all Judaea, and in Samaria, and unto the uttermost part of the earth" (Acts 1:7-8). My area of emphasis was the First Coming. I believed in the Second Coming, but I was told that we knew little or nothing about it, about times and seasons; no one knew, only the Father. So I would put up a question mark about the future. He came once; He will come again. But I would preach and emphasize what I knew—the First Coming. And I hope to fulfill the statement of Jesus when He said: "Happy that servant who is found at his task when his master comes!" (Matt. 24:46, NEB). Note "at his task." Not skygazing, but "at his task," the task of preaching the good news of the present, saving Christ.

(I recently met a man who was emphasizing "revival" by emphasizing the Second Coming. He said to me: "You will not see the Second Coming in your lifetime. You are 82. I will; I'm younger." But he had the jitters at the thought of getting on a plane; cold perspiration stood on his brow. He was living by expectancy instead of by experience. He was not appropriating the living Christ now, but approximating the time of the coming Christ. His experience of the living Christ was thin—so thin it didn't save him from fear *now*.)

So I pulled my feet back from the bypaths of speculation about this event or that event as the precursor of the Second Coming. I would preach the event—the living Christ now. I had no map or timetable about the future, but my feet were on the Way. And my heart was singing my Song of Ascents.

The amazing thing is that these basic changes and attitudes were gained within a year. Evidently, human nature is infinitely plastic and capable of great changes in a short time. I need not depend on the calendar, but on Christ, this living Christ, for further and infinite changes.

But my lyre had two very important strings with which I was to begin my Song of Ascents—first, the string of reconciliation; I was forgiven, converted, born again, with the past blotted out or transformed. Second, the string of adequacy—I was cleansed by the Holy Spirit in both conscious and subconscious minds and unified within, and given power by that same Holy Spirit to witness for my Lord. And **GRACE** the amazing thing was that I did nothing to merit all this. I did nothing but receive; the initiative was His. Love invaded me, and now love pervaded me as I began my pilgrimage from what I was to what He is making me. I was at once humbled to the dust and lifted to the highest heaven. It was all of grace!

In addition to the two strings of forgiveness and cleansing was a third and an important one—the string of knowing personally and at first hand my Heavenly Father. God was no longer a name. He was a fact, a living fact—within me, around me, above me. I could drop into the silence of my heart and commune with Him there, in a wordless communion; but not always wordless, for He is a God who speaks. He speaks and I speak to Him—we talk together. I can never be alone again; hence I can never be lonely again.

With these three strings in my lyre I set out a happy pilgrim. More strings would be added, for what I had set me on fire for more.

Section II

Experiencing Christian Holiness

In this section we have tried to gather a wide range of human responses to the sanctifying work of the Holy Spirit. Many of these witnesses come from the 20th century, but we have not limited selections to the modern period. Most of such experiences fall under the heading of devotional literature. They are expressions of the human spirit in response to the experienced presence of God in His sanctifying ministry.

These responses are always deeply personal, and often expressed in testimonies of acceptance, joy, commitment, praise, or obedience. Such positive responses to the work of the Holy Spirit frequently take the form of poetry—the language of emotion. When poems are set to music we get songs and hymns that express praise to God, and high human joy in response to the wonder of His presence in our lives.

We have used the list of "Concepts and Identifying Terms" (see pp. 15-17) as a way to organize this variety of devotional materials.

Under each of the 28 headings we have listed
>   The identifying term
>   The description of the concept
>   Selected scriptural supports

Following the Bible texts we have included relevant items from the list below:

Brief Expositions	Poems
Illustrations	Exhortations
Testimonies	Appeals
Songs and Hymns	Prayers

We have grouped these selections under four chapter headings:

Doctrinal Issues

Steps to Seeking and Finding

Living the Life of Holiness

Witnessing and Proclamation

10

Doctrinal Issues

All valid Christian faith rests on our understanding of truth. Thus all teachings about the holy life must be based on an understanding of holiness as it is revealed to us by God in the Scriptures.

What is the nature of God? What is the character of man? What is God's plan for human life—here and hereafter? These are the questions to which we first turn in exploring the meaning of Christian holiness.

God's Holiness

The requirement of entire sanctification is rooted in God's holiness.

Consecrate yourselves and be holy, because I am the Lord your God. Keep my decrees and follow them. I am the Lord, who makes you holy (Lev. 20:7-8, NIV).

Therefore, prepare your minds for action; be self-controlled; set your hope fully on the grace to be given you when Jesus Christ is revealed. As obedient children, do not conform to the evil desires you had when you lived in ignorance. But just as he who called you is holy, so be holy in all you do; for it is written: "Be holy, because I am holy" (1 Pet. 1:13-16, NIV).

THE HOLINESS OF GOD[1]

What kind of God have we? This question is presented often to the minds of thinking people. Another question closely related is also

---

1. D. Shelby Corlett, *The Meaning of Holiness*, 9-21.
D. Shelby Corlett (1894-1979) was born in Homestead, Pa., but when only a child

asked frequently: What does God expect of us?

We have no need to grope about blindly to seek an answer to these questions, for the answer is found easily in the Bible, God's Book, in which is given a revelation of God and of His will for man. The Apostle Peter epitomizes the answer to these questions as found in the Scriptures, and states in a few words what is the moral character of God, also what God expects of man: "Because it is written, Be ye holy; for I am holy" (1 Pet. 1:16). God answers man's query about Him in the statement "I am holy."

THE BIBLE REVEALS GOD'S CHARACTER

Throughout the Scriptures numerous statements are given which stress the moral character of God or emphasize His holiness. Among these may be found the statements: "I the Lord your God am holy." "I the Lord am holy." "I the Lord, which sanctify you, am holy." "He is an holy God." "This holy Lord God." (Cf. Lev. 19:2; 20:26; 21:8; Josh. 24:19; 1 Sam. 6:20.) In frequent places in the Old Testament God is called "The Holy One of Israel." The great prophet Isaiah was granted an unusual vision of God as the thrice Holy One: "Holy, holy, holy, is the Lord of hosts" (6:3).

The idea of the holiness of God permeates the writings of the New Testament also. Not only do the New Testament writers stress the truths presented by men of old, but also they emphasize greatly the holy God as the Holy Spirit and magnify His work in the world today.

The greatest revelation of God is given, not in words nor in statements made about Him; it is given in a Person, in our Lord Jesus Christ. Of Him it was said: "No man hath seen God at any time; the only begotten Son, . . . he hath declared him" (John 1:18). Also John

---

moved with his parents to southern California. Reared in a godly home, he early answered a call to preach.

Following pastorates in California and the state of Washington, Shelby was elected as the first general secretary of the Nazarene Young People's Society (now Nazarene Youth International). After 12 years in this position he served 14 years as editor of the *Herald of Holiness*, official paper for his denomination. From 1948 to retirement in 1973 Dr. Corlett ministered as college teacher, pastor, and evangelist.

During the middle of the 20th century, through his preaching, editorials, and six books promoting the Wesleyan message, Shelby Corlett was a key force in shaping the life of the Holiness Movement in America.

The Meaning of Holiness (1944) was first developed as a lecture series delivered at Eastern Nazarene College.

says of Him: "The Word was made flesh, and dwelt among us . . . full of grace and truth" (v. 14).

In Jesus is given a living revelation of the holy God. He lived a normal physical life, possessed all essential qualities of the human **CHRISTLIKENESS** nature, contacted people of all stages of moral living, and experienced all conditions of our human existence; yet He was "holy, harmless, undefiled, separate from sinners" (Heb. 7:26). Jesus revealed the holiness of God to be a practical holiness. He lived among sinners but was separate from them in moral character. To Jesus we must come for our highest and most practical conception of the holiness of God. He is the living embodiment of that holiness in the world in which we must live. . . .

WHAT IS HOLINESS IN GOD?

The Scriptures speak but little of the holiness of God as something in the abstract, something to be taken to pieces to be analyzed and understood; rather they speak much more of "The Holy One," a Person to be known, a God to be worshiped and adored. . . .

Holiness in God is more than an attribute, it is the sum total of all of His moral characteristics. Holiness is the moral excellency of the Divine nature, that quality which permeates all of His nature and binds together all of His moral attributes to make Him the God that He is—a holy God. Holiness emphasizes His absolute purity, His freedom from all moral imperfections; it comprehends the perfection of His wisdom, His righteousness, His faithfulness, His goodness. To say that God is holy includes the perfection of all of His moral qualities, His blessedness, His glory. . . .

Because God is holy, His holiness permeates His whole being, His wisdom is entirely consistent with His moral nature, His justice is marked with mercy, His sovereignty with love, His truth with grace, and His power is free from oppression. . . .

GOD'S SEPARATENESS FROM SIN

The primary meaning of the scriptural teaching of holiness as it relates to God is God's separateness from sin. The Bible pictures the holy God as being absolutely sinless, possessing infinite purity; He dwells in a holy place, is absolutely removed from and opposed to all sin, and therefore no sin can be admitted into His immediate presence. The question was asked by one of old, "Who shall stand in his holy place?" The reply given was, "He that hath clean hands, and a pure heart; who hath not lifted up his soul unto vanity, nor sworn deceitfully" (Ps. 24:3-4).

There is something awful and overpowering about the thought of the holiness of God and its separateness from sin. As the holy God, He is not only separated from sin, but He is eternally opposed **OPPOSED TO SIN** to sin; sin is the very opposite of His nature. . . . He wills and seeks the destruction of sin from His universe. The very thought of this holiness as opposition to sin brings fear and dread to the sinner. The holy God is separated from him, He is opposed to his sin, He will punish and destroy sin. . . .

The awfulness of God's holiness is pictured in the experience of the prophet Isaiah. The prophet, God's spokesman to Judah, was prostrated in the Temple before Him. He was mourning the death of King Uzziah. The throne of David was vacant, the king was dead. He was anxious about the new ruler who would ascend the throne. Thus prostrated before God, he was privileged to see "the Lord sitting upon a throne, high and lifted up." . . . But what particular aspect of God did that vision stress? The holiness of God! The seraphim—the burning ones—cried one to another, saying: "Holy, holy, holy, is the Lord of hosts: the whole earth is full of his glory" (Isa. 6:1, 3).

What was the effect of this vision upon . . . the man of God? It acted like a mighty X ray upon his own heart. The vision of the holiness of God gave to him a deep consciousness of his own uncleanness; his impurities became so apparent that he cried, "Woe is me! for I am undone; because I am a man of unclean lips, and I dwell in the midst of a people of unclean lips: for mine eyes have seen the King, the Lord of hosts" (v. 5). What was he saying? He was saying, "I am conscious of uncleanness in my life. How can I live? I have seen the holy God, the one who is absolutely pure, the one who is absolutely separate from and opposed to sin!" Terrible! Awful! Overpowering! was the vision of the holiness of God to the prophet. Little wonder he said, "Woe is me! for I am undone."

A look at Calvary will give another view of this phase of God's holiness. There is a dark side to Calvary. We think so much of its glory and of the beauty of its redeeming love that often we overlook its darker aspects. But Calvary shows a holy God bringing judgment upon sin. A holy God, separate from sin, could not spare His own Son when that Son, who knew no sin, was made sin for us and suffered the punishment for our sins, the sins of the world. Why the darkness for the space of three hours? Why did the sun hide its face? Why did the earth quake? Why were the rocks rent? Why did the cry come from that innocent Sufferer's heart, "My God, my God, why hast thou forsaken me?" (Matt. 27:46; Mark 15:34). WHY? It was the scene of a holy God bringing judgment upon sin. A holy God was in such opposition to sin that He could not spare His Son when that Son bore upon himself the sins of the world. Thus Calvary pictures the terrible, awful aspect of the holiness of God. . . .

HOLINESS AND MORAL GOVERNMENT

The characteristic of the nature of God which makes Him absolutely consistent in all moral and righteous matters is His holiness. This holiness of God is active particularly in His moral government.

God's holiness provides the absolute standard of right and wrong. Whatever is in accord with His holiness is right; what is not in accord with His holiness is wrong. Such a standard runs consistently throughout God's whole moral universe. There is rigidness, absoluteness, something demanding about the righteousness thus required.

The requirements of the moral law with their consequent penalties pronounced upon those breaking that law are a manifestation of the holiness of God. "The soul that sinneth, it shall die" (Ezek. 18:4), and similar statements of Scripture indicate the holiness of God in its requirements of righteousness among men. The requirement of character is stressed by the apostle Peter in these words: "As he which hath called you is holy, so be ye holy in all manner of conversation" (or conduct; 1 Pet. 1:15).

It has been said that there is no absolute standard of right and wrong, that each succeeding generation establishes its own standards, that the practices of the group provide the moral code **GOD'S MORAL STANDARDS** for all. But there is an absolute standard of righteousness—it is the holiness of God; and it runs consistently throughout God's moral universe. It may be granted that interpretations of that absolute righteous standard have differed throughout the centuries, that some generations have had clearer perceptions of it and have lived closer to it than others; but the standard remains the same—it is God's fixed, eternal standard, the revelation of His holy character. What is in accord with His holiness is right; what is not in accord with that holiness is wrong. . . .

Would we judge ourselves as to our own righteousness? Let us not judge ourselves by ourselves. Let us not judge ourselves by the standards of others. Let the standard of our judgment be the holiness of God. Where do we stand in character as we square ourselves with the requirement God has made: "Be ye holy in all manner of conversation"—in all manner of human relationships, or conduct? Where do we stand in our inner nature? In our attitudes toward others? In our judgments of people? Are we right? Are we wrong? We must determine that in the light of the holiness of God. How greatly that righteous standard stresses our need of a Savior and Divine Helper! . . .

There is an awfulness to the holiness of God when viewed in the light of His opposition to sin; but there is a majesty in that holiness as we think of His righteousness and of the consistency of His moral government. . . .

HOLINESS AND REDEMPTION

The positive aspect of God's holiness is not His absolute purity, His separateness, and His opposition to sin, nor is it fully portrayed in the majesty of His moral government. The positive aspect of the holiness of God is His infinite love actively manifested in His willingness to save the sinner and exhibited in the sacrifice He made on Calvary for man's redemption. A holy God could not be indifferent to man, the creature of His own hands made in His own image, even though that man had become polluted by sin. A holy God would destroy sin, but He would save the sinner. A holy God is gracious. A holy God would redeem man.

The holiness of God manifested in redemption takes us to Calvary. . . . There the holiness of God is revealed in that great act of redemption in which His heart was laid bare in an act of love providing redemption for sinful and unholy mankind. There at Calvary, God, the holy God, "was in Christ, reconciling the world unto himself" (2 Cor. 5:19). The holy God could not be indifferent to man; He could not be inactive toward his sin. He who was absolutely opposed to sin and willed its destruction, would make men holy even though it brought great suffering to His own loving heart, even though He in Christ must taste death for every man.

HOLINESS IS LOVE

In redemption the holiness of God is manifested as the grace of God. "Grace means that Divinity dwells not in the iron will that never yields but in the holy Love, stronger than iron, that yields, and in yielding saves to the uttermost" (James Robert Cameron in *God the Christlike,* 41). Grace is love, holy love, that bleeds for its object, and for love's sake endures the Cross, despising the shame. Grace is the moving of a holy, righteous God, intolerant of sin, bending low with a tender heart of love to save, showing in an act that it is not the will of the Heavenly Father that any should perish, but that all should come to repentance (2 Pet. 3:9). Grace denotes the merciful kindness of God by which He exerts His holy influence upon sinful men to turn them to himself, to bring them to repentance and forgiveness, to make them His children, to purge their hearts from the pollution of sin and make them holy, and to continue the reign of grace in the redeemed heart, through righteousness unto eternal life, by Jesus Christ our Lord (Rom. 5:21).

The primary purpose of redemption is to bring into existence through the grace of Christ a redeemed or holy manhood with a character in the spiritual likeness of God. This is the purpose of a holy God revealed in His redeeming love.

There is a beauty in that holiness; something attractive which draws the heart of the sinner, something which inspires **THE BEAUTY OF HOLINESS** the deepest expression of devotion and worship to a holy God. . . .

The beauty of His holiness as revealed in His holy love dying to save an unholy people from sin, pronouncing judgment upon the sin He abhors, preserving His righteousness by the gracious atoning act of the Lamb of God, and bringing His grace to redeem and save unworthy and unholy people, touches the hearts of men deeply; it draws them to himself and makes them exclaim: "I can love a God like that. I will accept Him as my Savior and Lord."

What is God like? Peter revealed Him as saying of himself, "I am holy." Yes, God is a holy God, perfect in all of His moral characteristics, absolutely sinless and separate from sin, opposed in His nature to sin, ever seeking its destruction. He is a holy God, rigid and demanding in His requirements for righteousness and in the consistent preservation of His moral government. But also He is the loving, gracious Heavenly Father; a holy God who would redeem and save the sinner and through grace bring man's character to conform to His own: "Be ye holy, for I am holy."

Holy, Holy, Holy, Lord God Almighty

NICAEA

Reginald Heber, 1783-1826   John B. Dykes, 1823-1876

1. Ho-ly, Ho-ly, Ho - ly, Lord God Al - might - y! Ear - ly in the
2. Ho-ly, Ho-ly, Ho - ly! All the saints a - dore Thee, Casting down their
3. Ho-ly, Ho-ly, Ho - ly! Tho' the darkness hide Thee, Tho' the eye of
4. Ho-ly, Ho-ly, Ho - ly! Lord God Al - might - y! All Thy works shall

morn - ing our song shall rise to Thee. Ho - ly, Ho - ly, Ho - ly!
gold - en crowns a - round the glass - y sea; Cher - u - bim and ser-a-phim
sin - ful man Thy glo - ry may not see, On - ly Thou art ho - ly;
praise Thy name in earth, and sky, and sea. Ho - ly, Ho - ly, Ho - ly!

Mer - ci - ful and Might - y! God in three Per-sons, bless-ed Trin - i - ty!
fall - ing down be-fore Thee, Which wert, and art, and ev - er-more shalt be.
there is none be-side Thee Per - fect in pow'r, in love, in pu - ri - ty.
Mer - ci - ful and Might - y! God in three Per-sons, bless-ed Trin - i - ty!

Carnality/Cleansing

The need for entire sanctification is seen in the remaining presence of inbred sin, or carnality, in believers. The experience of entire sanctification includes cleansing from this original sin.

I will sprinkle clean water on you, and you will be clean; I will cleanse you from all your impurities and from all your idols. I will give you a new heart and put a new spirit in you; I will remove from you your heart of stone and give you a heart of flesh. And I will put my Spirit in you and move you to follow my decrees and be careful to keep my laws. . . . you will be my people, and I will be your God (Ezek. 36:25-28, NIV).

I, brethren, could not speak unto you as unto spiritual but as unto carnal, even as unto babes in Christ. . . . For ye are yet carnal: for whereas there is among you envying, and strife, and divisions, are ye not carnal, and walk as men? (1 Cor. 3:1-3).

The mind of sinful man is death, but the mind controlled by the Spirit is life and peace; the sinful mind is hostile to God. It does not submit to God's law, nor can it do so. Those controlled by the sinful nature cannot please God.

You, however, are controlled not by the sinful nature but by the Spirit, if the Spirit of God lives in you (Rom. 8:6-9, NIV).

*   *   *

Call it what you will—carnality, sin, inherited depravity, or just a bad attitude—if you have it, you ought to get rid of it (*Holiness and High Country*, 60).

THE TESTIMONY OF THOMAS À KEMPIS[2]

Still, alas! the old man doth live in me, he is not wholly crucified, is not perfectly dead.

Still doth he mightily strive against the Spirit, and stirreth up inward wars, and suffereth not the kingdom of my soul to be in peace.

For the love of God thou oughtest cheerfully to undergo all things, that is to say, all labor, grief, temptation, vexation, anxiety, necessity, infirmity, injury, detraction, reproof, humiliation, shame, correction, and contempt. . . .

There is need of Thy grace [O Lord], and of great degrees thereof, that nature may be overcome, which is ever prone to evil from her youth.

For through Adam the first man, nature being fallen and corrupted by sin, the penalty of this stain hath descended upon all mankind, in such sort, that "nature" itself, which by Thee was created good and upright, is now taken for the sin and infirmity of corrupted nature; because the inclination thereof left unto itself draweth to evil and to inferior things.

---

2. *Imitation of Christ* (15th cent.).

The Cleansing Wave

Oh, now I see the crimson wave,
The fountain deep and wide;
Jesus, my Lord, mighty to save,
Points to His wounded side.

Refrain:
The cleansing stream, I see, I see!
I plunge and, oh, it cleanseth me!
Oh! praise the Lord, it cleanseth me!
It cleanseth me, yes, cleanseth me!

—PHOEBE PALMER KNAPP, 1839-1908

SARX, FLESH, CARNALITY[3]

Our purpose in pointing out the offending thing is not to bring fruitless embarrassment. Rather our purpose is to define the disease that we may the better know and apply the remedy which will effect a cure.

Sarx

The Greek word *sarx*, which is invariably translated "flesh" in the English, comes the nearest to being a word of mathematical exactitude as a symbol for sin as a state of corruption. But this word has almost the same limitations as its English equivalent, "flesh," and its use requires a consideration of the context. There are times when this word *sarx* (flesh) means simply meat (of the human body, of fish or birds or animals). Sometimes it means human nature as distinguished from divine nature, and again it means simply the race of man without any suggestion of moral implication. Occasionally it means material as contrasted with spiritual, or it may mean kinship (as in Rom. 11:14). Sometimes it serves only to emphasize human frailty.

But in such instances as the word is used to contrast physical living in opposition to the spiritual, it certainly does mean the sinfully carnal. . . . Whenever it is clear that this word means something evil as distinguished from that which is good, we should always understand it as referring to the corrupt, carnal, sinful nature, and not to the essential human nature in which man was originally created. The flesh, as meat, is neither good nor bad. As it always was, it is of neutral moral significance, being simply a form of existence that it pleased God to

---

3. Chapman, *Terminology of Holiness*, 34-36.

give to man. To say, then, that we must sin or be sinful so long as we are in the flesh (the meat) is to indict the Creator for folly and complicity with evil. When it is said, "They that are in the flesh cannot please God," we are not left to guess at the meaning, for the very next verse (Rom. 8:9) explains, "Ye are not in the flesh, but in the Spirit, if so be that the Spirit of God dwell in you." This certainly does not mean that the human personality is dual, and that one may be "in the Spirit" in his heart and "in the flesh" as to his body at one and the same time. The meaning of the Scriptures plainly is that when the life is permeated by the Spirit of God, and ruled, indwelt, and directed by Him, that person (spirit, soul, and body) is not in the flesh (the carnal, sinful flesh), but in the Holy Spirit.

It should be observed that our English word "carnal" and its variations are but translations of the Greek word *sarx,* and that no particular light is thrown on the general subject by use of the detached words "carnal" or "carnality." The context must always be considered before exposition is possible. But when the context clearly shows that the reference is to something evil, and not simply to something corporeal or natural, these words may be used as approximate symbols for the sinful state, or sin within the heart.

Besides the terms that speak in accuracy and discrimination, we have in the Bible and in Christian literature a considerable vocabulary of metaphorical terminology which is exceedingly useful for illustration and emphasis. But these terms, like parabolic language in general, suffer if pressed too far. Examples from this category are: "sin of the world" (John 1:29); "root of bitterness" (Heb. 12:15); "our old man" (Rom. 6:6); "the sin which doth so easily beset us" (Heb. 12:1); "the stony heart" (Ezek. 36:26); and "dross" and "chaff" (see Mal. 3:2-3 and Matt. 3:12). All these and many more of their kind often clearly point to a spiritual state and condition that is undesirable, and from which prayer is made for deliverance. And while there are sometimes more literal meanings in given passages, the presumption of the moral and spiritual is also often there.

Theologians have spoken of inbred sin, inherited sin, original sin, depravity, pollution of nature, corruption of nature, self, sin that remaineth in believers, indwelling sin, moral inability, and besetting sin. Poets have sung of enemies in the castle; allegorists have described enemy reservations in the city of Mansoul; and saints have prayed for purging from "the clinging remnants of sin." But beneath all terminology, both accurate and metaphorical, is the fact of the sinful nature—which, not being guilt, is not the subject of pardon, but being pollution, demands purging and cleansing. There is no disputing the fact that men and women who are truly born of the Spirit do long for deliverance from this foe within that wars against them in their efforts to "live soberly, righteously, and godly, in this present world" (Titus 2:12). Our purpose in pointing out the offending thing as clearly as we can is not to bring fruitless embarrassment to such as would know the way of true holiness. Rather our purpose is to define the disease that we may the better know and apply the remedy which will effect a cure.

ERADICATION[4]

In our time the special prejudice has been directed against the term *eradication* and against the idea expressed by this term. Some urge that we discontinue the use of this term on the ground that it is not found in the Scriptures. But many who raise this objection seem to have no scruples against such words as *suppression, repression,* and *counteraction*—words which are neither scripture nor scriptural. But although the word *eradication* is not found in our English Bible, the idea contained in the word is there in bold type. Note such passages as those which exhort that your old man may be crucified, "that the body of sin might be destroyed," that "the old man" may be "put off," that we might be made "free from sin," and that the Christian may "purge himself from these," and others (Rom. 6:6; Eph. 4:22; Col. 3:9; Rom. 6:18, 22; 2 Tim. 2:21).

Dr. Asbury Lowrey . . . says: "A critical knowledge of any doctrine, duty or privilege of the New Testament requires an examination of the language in which it was first promulgated."[5] Such a study, followed without prejudice, will serve but to substantiate the following observations:

1. Although there are words in the Greek language that mean suppression, not one of them is ever used in connection with the disposition to be made of inbred sin. Invariably the word used (and there are a number of them) signifies to "loosen," to "unbind," to "disengage," to "set free," to "deliver," to "break up," to "destroy," or to "demolish." If it were the plan of God that sin should be suppressed or counteracted, is it not reason that the use of the Greek would indicate this purpose? If it were not God's plan to eradicate sin from

---

4. Ibid., 66-68.
5. *Possibilities of Grace*, 35.

the hearts of believers, is it not beyond explanation that a Greek word carrying this meaning was invariably used in indicating what the disposition was to be?

2. The tense of the Greek verbs used in all passages like Rom. 6:6 where the death-stroke to sin is described is always aorist, which indicates an act as being completed at a definite time and continuing as complete until the present time. And when the energy of the Holy Spirit in the work of entire sanctification is described, the verb is never in the imperfect tense, the tense which the Greek uses to describe a gradual process.

On this basis we conclude that the word eradication is permissible, and the idea it involves is essential. Those who use terms which imply that inbred sin is to be suppressed or counteracted are using words which are not permissible, and holding views that are altogether erroneous. Dr. A. M. Hills quotes from an unnamed writer as follows: "Repressive power is nowhere ascribed to the blood of Christ, but rather purgative efficiency."[6]

Then Dr. Hills goes on to say:

"The truth is, we have the most critical and scholarly commentaries and Greek exegetes, the lexicons and grammars, on our side in this matter. If the Greek New Testament can teach anything by nouns, adjectives, and verbs, and even adverbs and prepositions, about a spiritual experience, our doctrine of sanctification, as a heart-cleansing work, is taught by the Word of God."[7]

INNER CLEANSING—WESLEY'S DOCTRINE ILLUSTRATED[8]

It will help us all, probably, if I can give a concrete illustration of Wesley's view. Here is a man, a Christian preacher now, who has from infancy been naturally jealous. He is not only converted but is a noble Christian man, ready to sacrifice for his Lord, and equally ready to serve his brethren. But he is still jealous in disposition. Yesterday he heard another preacher's sermon receive large commendation, and, like an uprush of mercury in the heat, that old feeling of jealousy rose into consciousness. His volition, his personality, had no more to do with it than his will had to do with the coming on of night. But the

---

6. *Scriptural Holiness*, 75.
7. Ibid.
8. Olin A. Curtis, *The Christian Faith*, 373. For biography see 3:280.

moment our preacher realizes that he is jealous he makes Christian battle and forces the disposition back, back into its cave.

Now we have here an exceedingly strange psychological situation, for the man's struggle is plainly Christian in its revelation of the moral ideal, and yet the struggle reveals a motive life that no Christian ought to have at all. Or we can say this: The victory is truly that of a Christian man—but as a Christian man he should have been without the possibility of that kind of battle.

Now comes a pivotal inquiry. As our preacher grows, what does his growth in grace accomplish? According to Wesley, the growth does not affect the inherent disposition of jealousy at all; but it does bring the regenerate man himself to a more potent attitude, both of intolerance toward the disposition and of trust toward Jesus Christ. With this more potent personal attitude the man dares to believe that his Lord can and will take that jealousy, and every wrong disposition, out of his life. In full, simple faith he asks Christ to do it; and, precisely as when he was converted, *it is all done at one stroke.*

Now what is the man's condition? On the one hand, he never is conscious of jealousy. Rather does he spontaneously rejoice in another man's success. On the other hand, he never comes to self-consciousness without being filled, like the prodigality of a freshet, with the love of God. This, as I understand him, is what John Wesley means by the conquest of inbred sin through supreme love. And if there is one man here to whom Wesley's view of inbred sin suggests no reality, no point in kindred experience, he most surely is to be regarded as extremely fortunate.

THE TESTIMONY OF D. I. VANDERPOOL[9]

Two or three times within 10 days I had upsets because of my quick temper, but after prayer and repentance I found forgiveness, and the joy bells would ring again in my heart. I loathed the thing within my heart that constantly strove to upset me.

My father and mother were separated and our home was broken up when I was about six years of age. I remember Father taking us to

---

9. *Flames of Living Fire,* 114-17.

Dr. D. I. Vanderpool (1891—) was a native of Missouri. He pastored in Denver; Pasadena, Calif.; and Walla Walla, Wash. An effective evangelist, he was often called for revivals and camp meetings. Dr. Vanderpool served as district superintendent from 1937 to 1949. He was elected as a general superintendent in the Church of the Nazarene in 1949 and served until his retirement in 1964.

live with him, and my grandmother coming to keep house. Neither my father nor my grandmother was inclined toward religion. The family was without any religious training whatsoever.

A Methodist minister came through the country where we lived and stopped at our house for a short call. Before he left he prayed for our home, a prayer that made a lasting impression on my youthful mind. When he had left, Grandmother said, "I believe that was a good man." With the preacher's prayer still ringing in my ears, I prayed at nightfall and promised God that I would try to be a good boy. A strange peace came into my heart, but it was gone by noon the next day.

Soon after this my father bought a sawmill and moved the family near it, where my three brothers and I were surrounded by a group of very wicked men. This environment caused me to lose ground rapidly. Having a quick temper and a feeling that I was quite important, I kept in trouble most of the time. My life of sin was brought to an end when I was converted at age 17. I never saw anyone converted at an altar until I went to one myself. I knew nothing about the Bible or Christian doctrine. However, my conversion was clear and definite. . . . I was supremely happy in my newly found joy.

I had been converted only a few days when a fellow with whom I had had trouble insulted me. My first impulse was to fight, but something reminded me that I was now a Christian . . . I was filled with fear when I considered how near I came to doing something which I would have always regretted.

Knowing that I had that vicious something still in my heart alarmed me and put me on my guard. Two or three times within 10 days I had upsets because of my quick temper, but after prayer and repentance I found forgiveness, and the joy bells would ring again in my heart. I loathed the thing within my heart that constantly strove to upset me.

An elderly lady who heard of my conversion spoke to me one day and inquired how I was getting along spiritually.

I said, "Oh, fine! I only wish I could get victory over my quick temper."

Then she said, "Well, son, you do not have all the Lord has for you."

I asked, "What do you mean?"

WITNESSING

Her answer was, "You need to be sanctified."

My next question was, "Do you mean I can get rid of that inward uprising?"

She quickly replied, "Yes, and you ought not to put it off."

I hastened to ask with all the earnestness of my soul, "How do you get sanctified?"

I still remember her answer; it was clear and simple: "Give God everything you have, pray earnestly, and trust Christ, and He will meet your need."

From that moment I became an earnest seeker, desiring to be sanctified. I prayed when I worked. I prayed in my bedroom. A prayer was sent up from my heart almost night and day, crying out for this experience that would give deliverance.

One afternoon, I had such a calm rest in my heart that I decided I must have the experience I had been seeking. I went to the water tank with my horses. While they were drinking, I was meditating on how pleasant it was to be sanctified. I was so engrossed in thought that I did not notice old Bill raise his head and look around. I was taken by complete surprise when he opened his mouth and let about a quart of water on my head and down my neck. . . . Like a flash, I jerked him and kicked him several times. Then I caught myself. I shall never forget the sorrow that came over my whole spirit as I realized that I had been mistaken in thinking that I was sanctified; and, too, now I must seek pardon and forgiveness for my unchristian feeling and actions. I found peace before I slept that night and renewed my seeking for deliverance from this quick temper.

A few days afterward I sent word to a man who was having a cottage prayer meeting that I wanted him to make an altar call the next Tuesday night, for I wanted to be sanctified.

I did not know that he did not believe in people getting sanctified. Tuesday night I started for prayer meeting with my heart bubbling over with joy because I believed I was going to get sanctified that night.

The man gave a little talk at the prayer meeting and finally set out a chair and said, "I understand there is a fellow here that wants special prayer." I quickly knelt at the chair and began to pray for God to sanctify me. A fellow who knew the way came and knelt by me and began to probe my consecration, uncovering several things of which I had not thought. One was being a preacher; the other was going to Africa as a missionary. Both were high hurdles; but after much earnest prayer for about an hour, I got over them. Everything else was easy.

He further instructed me that the same Christ that gave me pardon also purchased my cleansing. My faith reached up; I trusted Him to sanctify and cleanse the gift I had brought Him. A quiet assurance came into my heart that Christ was faithful and that the work of cleansing had been wrought in my heart. From that day to this I have never questioned or doubted that I was sanctified that Tuesday night. . . .

I have thanked God a thousand times that I met the little old lady who said, "You do not have all the Lord has for you." I feel certain I would not have continued on the Christian way and have climbed the hills and journeyed through the tunnels thus far had I not found the way of holiness in my early Christian life.

Cleanse Me

J. Edwin Orr, 1912-

Maori Melody

1. Search me, O God, and know my heart to-day._____ Try me, O
2. I praise Thee, Lord, for cleans-ing me from sin._____ Ful-fill Thy
3. Lord, take my life, and make it whol-ly Thine;_____ Fill my poor
4. O Ho-ly Ghost, re-viv-al comes from Thee._____ Send a re-

Sav-iour; know my thoughts, I pray._____ See if there be some wicked
Word, and make me pure with-in;_____ Fill me with fire, where once I
heart with Thy great love di-vine._____ Take all my will, my pas-sion,
viv-al— start the work in me._____ Thy Word de-clares Thou wilt sup-

way in me;_____ Cleanse me from ev-'ry sin, and set me free._____
burned with shame.___ Grant my de-sire to mag-ni-fy Thy name._____
self, and pride._____ I now sur-ren-der; Lord, in me a-bide._____
ply our need._____ For bless-ing now, O Lord, I hum-bly plead._____

Grace

Entire sanctification is **a gift of God's grace.**

And, behold, I send the promise of my Father upon you: but tarry ye in the city of Jerusalem, until ye be endued with power from on high (Luke 24:49).

For the grace of God that brings salvation has appeared to all men. It teaches us to say "No" to ungodliness and worldly passions, and to live self-controlled, upright and godly lives in this present age, while we wait for the blessed hope—the glorious appearing of our great God and Savior, Jesus Christ, who gave himself for us to redeem us from all wickedness and to purify for himself a people that are his very own, eager to do what is good (Titus 2:11-14, NIV).

LIFE OF DEPENDENCE[10]

The life of holiness must be considered as a life of dependence upon God and upon His grace.

The source of all grace, of all life, and of all power is God. Only as the Christian constantly relies upon God can he maintain a satisfactory relationship with Him. Holiness is a gift from God, GRACE for a holy man is a partaker of God's holiness, and to have holiness continue as a state of life man must depend constantly upon the holy God. Holiness is not a deposit given to man to be kept independent of God; a holy life is maintained moment by moment through active faith and obedience to God. "For God does not give them a stock of holiness," says John Wesley, "but unless they receive a supply every moment nothing but unholiness will remain" (*Plain Account*, 33).

There must be also the constant reliance upon the cleansing power of the blood of Jesus to be kept pure and clean in a sinful world. This is emphasized by the apostle John in the statement, "The blood of Jesus Christ his Son cleanseth us from all sin" (1 John 1:7). Note the word, "cleans*eth*"; it means a present and continued cleansing. "Cleanseth"—the blood of Jesus continues to cleanse or keep clean as one walks in the light. "It is only as and while a soul is under the full power of the blood of Christ that it can be cleansed from all sin. One moment's withdrawal from that position and it is again actu-

---

10. Corlett, *Meaning of Holiness*, 89-92.

ally sinning. It is only as and while kept by the power of God himself that we are not sinning against Him. One instant of standing alone is certain fall" (Frances R. Havergal).

A necessary element in this life of holiness through dependence upon God is an attitude of penitence expressed in a feeling of our unworthiness of being the recipients of God's grace and holiness, in a realization of the weaknesses and limitations of the "earthen vessel" which houses this spiritual "treasure" and of our consequent coming short of God's ideal for us, in a readiness to confess our blunders and mistakes and failures, and in an eagerness to make any necessary adjustments with others in order to "keep the unity of the Spirit in the bond of peace" (Eph. 4:3).

This attitude of heart is expressed beautifully by Henry Brockett:

> By virtue of the fact that we are still in a fallen condition so far as our bodily and mental powers are concerned, we **HUMANITY** are subject to many infirmities, we lack perfect knowledge of God's will in all things (this has to be learned by degrees), we are liable, therefore, to errors of judgment, and various other faults which may not be known to ourselves but are seen by God. Hence the holiest Christian, from this point of view, may daily pray that humble prayer of confession, "Forgive us our debts, as we forgive our debtors." . . . Yes, every moment we need the cleansing efficacy of the precious blood of Christ and the high-priestly intercession of our Lord Jesus if we are to enjoy unclouded fellowship with God who is infinitely holy. Hence we see that the holding of the truth of entire sanctification by faith produces an attitude of self-abnegation and deep humility in the presence of the Lord. And yet, all the time, we can have a deep joy because we know that we have been set free from our greatest inward enemy, namely, indwelling sin, and possess the glorious blessing of an indwelling Christ, i.e., we truly know the blessing of entire sanctification.[11]

Always there must be a ceaseless drawing from God for all of the necessities of the spiritual life. This fact is pictured by Jesus in the analogy of the vine and the branches. The holy Christian is a branch, a purged branch of that true Vine, and as such he must constantly draw from Christ all of his spiritual sustenance and also the ability to bear fruit. No person realizes the truth of Jesus' statement, "For without me ye can do nothing" (John 15:5), and the absolute necessity of abiding in Christ always, more than does the person who has been entirely sanctified.

In all of this life of holiness there is ever the realization that it is

---

11. *Scriptural Freedom from Sin*, 42.

"not by works of righteousness which we have done, but according to his mercy he saved us" (Titus 3:5); and, it is not by our works of righteousness that He keeps us saved, or keeps us living a holy life. It is only by our constant reliance upon His grace. The life of holiness, like the experience of heart purity, is "not of works, lest any man should boast. For we are his workmanship, created in Christ Jesus unto good works, which God hath before ordained that we should walk in them" (Eph. 2:9-10).

An active and consistent practice of the exercises of devotion is essential to holy living, such as the reading and meditation upon the Word of God, the giving of oneself to prayer and communion with God, seeking to know and to do the will of God, the cultivation of spiritual-mindedness, faithfulness in matters of personal relationship to God and in service, and always a consciousness of "walking in the Spirit."

This consciousness of dependence upon God in the life of holiness safeguards against spiritual pride and boasting, against a feeling of **DANGERS** self-sufficiency, and against Pharisaism in any of its forms. On the other hand, it encourages a spirit of humility and trust. The life of holiness is a life of dependence upon God.

*   *   *   *   *

Grace Greater than Our Sin
MOODY

Julia H. Johnston, 1849-1919   Daniel B. Towner, 1850-1919

1. Mar - vel - ous grace of our lov - ing Lord, Grace that ex - ceeds our
2. Sin and de - spair, like the sea waves cold, Threat-en the soul with
3. Dark is the stain that we can - not hide. What can a - vail to
4. Mar - vel - ous, in - fi - nite, match - less grace, Free - ly be-stowed on

sin and our guilt, Yon - der on Cal - va - ry's mount out - poured,
in - fi - nite loss. Grace that is great - er, yes, grace un - told,
wash it a - way? Look! there is flow - ing a crim - son tide;
all who be - lieve! You that are long - ing to see His face,

There where the blood of the Lamb was spilt!
Points to the ref - uge, the might - y Cross.
Whit - er than snow you may be to - day.
Will you this mo - ment His grace re - ceive?

Grace, grace,

Mar - ve - lous grace,

God's grace, Grace that will par-don and cleanse with - in!
in - fi - nite grace,

Grace,
Mar - ve-lous

grace, God's grace, Grace that is great - er than all our sin!
grace, in - fi - nite grace,

* * * * *

Atonement

God provides the gift of entire sanctification through the atonement of Christ.

Christ also loved the church, and gave himself for it; that he might sanctify and cleanse it with the washing of water by the word, that he might present it to himself a glorious church, not having spot, or wrinkle, or any such thing; but that it should be holy and without blemish (Eph. 5:25-27).

Wherefore Jesus also, that he might sanctify the people with his own blood, suffered without the gate. Let us go forth therefore unto him without the camp, bearing his reproach (Heb. 13:12-13).

Augustus M. Toplady (1740-78) understood the teaching of these scriptures when he wrote:

Rock of Ages, cleft for me,
Let me hide myself in Thee.
Let the water and the blood,
From Thy wounded side which flowed,
Be of sin the double cure,
Save from wrath and make me pure.

Q. *What merit do we have to bring that God may see it and make us holy within?*
A. We have no merit except the blood of Jesus Christ, and we need no other than this. Men have often been led astray by the supposition that they must be good in order to be made good. To the sinner we have often said, "All the fitness Christ requires is to feel your need of Him." Likewise with the Christian who would be sanctified wholly. Good pedigrees, good works, and meritorious words do not count. "The Blood, the Blood is all my plea." This is what is meant when it is said we are sanctified by the Blood. That is, it is the merit of the blood of Jesus which enables us to come in faith and confidence for the blessing.[12]

SANCTIFICATION IN THE ATONEMENT[13]

The emphasis of the provision in the atonement for purity or entire sanctification for the Christian is as definite as the provision made for the forgiveness of the sinner. Let us note a few of the statements of the Scriptures emphasizing this deeper benefit: ". . . our Saviour Jesus Christ; who gave himself for us, that he might redeem us from all iniquity, and purify unto himself a peculiar people [a people for his own possession—ASV]" (Titus 2:13-14). "Christ also loved the church, and gave himself for it; that he might sanctify and cleanse it with the washing of water by the word, . . . that it should be holy and without blemish (Eph. 5:25-27). "How much more shall the blood of Christ, who through the eternal Spirit offered himself without spot to God, purge your conscience from dead works to serve the living God?" (Heb. 9:14). "Wherefore Jesus also, that he might sanctify the people with his own blood, suffered without the gate" (13:12).

These scriptures stress a deeper benefit and emphasize a deeper experience than . . . the benefit provided in the atonement for sinners. These scriptures state primarily the provision for cleansing, for entire

---

12. Chapman, *Holiness, the Heart of Christian Experience,* 59.
13. Corlett, *Meaning of Holiness,* 43-45.

sanctification, for the purifying of the heart, for making holy the child of God.

There are scriptures which give another emphasis to this deeper benefit of redemption, scriptures that teach that Jesus in His death dealt as definitely with the nature of sin, the old sin principle, in the heart of the child of God, as He did with the actual sins of the sinner. Let us note several of these scriptures: "Knowing this, that our old man is crucified with him, that the body of sin might be destroyed, that henceforth we should not serve sin" (Rom. 6:6). "God sending his own Son in the likeness of sinful flesh, and for sin, condemned sin in the flesh" (8:3).

There is a marked contrast between the terms used here to indicate the deeper benefits of the provisions of redemption and those used in stressing the benefits for sinners. For the sinner, the words used were "justify," "forgiveness," "brought nigh to God." But concerning this deeper benefit the words used are "crucified," "destroyed," "condemned," all of which emphasize the destruction of the sin principle or nature remaining in the heart of a justified
CLEANSING PROVIDED believer or child of God. These latter terms specifically refer to that phase of the provisions of redemption made for the removing from the nature of the child of God those inner conditions which keep him from being holy in the scriptural sense of that word.

The terms used in these scriptures, namely, "the old man," "the body of sin," "sin in the flesh," and other terms such as "carnal," "the carnal mind," "the flesh," and the like, designate sin in the nature, the impure or unholy condition remaining in the heart of a person after being born again. Whatever may be the interpretation given these terms, we must recognize that the destruction of that state is provided in redemption: "the old man is [was, ASV] crucified with him [Christ], that the body of sin might be destroyed"; and, "God . . . condemned sin in the flesh." Here is emphasized a wonderful and complete provision of redemption to meet the deepest needs of man and to make him holy.

CLEANSED BY THE BLOOD[14]

Many of God's children, I know, find it hard to understand in what sense we are made holy by the blood of Christ. The atoning

---

14. A. Paget Wilkes, *The Dynamics of Redemption*, 80-81.

work for our justification and the indwelling of His Spirit for our sanctification are easy to comprehend, but in what sense can we be made holy in heart by the shedding of His blood? This difficulty arises partly from ignorance of the nature of sin. In the minds of many, sin is regarded merely as an act of wrong doing, wrong thinking, or wrong speaking. According to this view, the Holy Spirit can of course keep us from yielding to temptation and thus "free from sin" in the above sense, while the blood of Christ avails to remove all stain of guilt and condemnation, if we do so transgress. This, however, is a very defective view of sin, and in consequence, of sanctification. The truth is that in the Word of God, sin (as distinguished from sins and sinning) is spoken of as a spiritual entity, e.g., "the body of sin" and "the carnal mind." Sanctification, then, in its principal meaning is the destruction of that entity, a moral cleansing of our nature from that defiling presence and power, a real healing of the soul and a removal of inward depravity. A further difficulty of understanding in what sense we are made holy by the blood of Christ is due to our failure to recognize the use of figurative language. The late Thomas Cook writes thus:

"But some cannot understand how this cleansing is through the blood of Jesus; we need to explain that we are obliged to use figurative language. We sing of a 'fountain filled with blood,' but we know there is no such fountain. When we speak of the blood of Jesus cleansing from sin, we do not mean that the blood of Christ is literally applied to the heart. What is meant is that through the great atoning work, Christ has procured or purchased complete deliverance from sin for us exactly as He has made forgiveness possible for us. But while Christ is thus through His death what may be called the procuring cause of sanctification, the work itself is wrought in us through the agency of the Holy Spirit. He comes to the heart in sanctifying power, excluding the evil and filling it with love (when we believe the blood cleanseth us from all sin) just as He comes in regenerating power when we believe for forgiveness and are adopted into the family of God."

Perfect Cleansing

MRS. L. B.   MRS. LOYD BURPO

1. Lord, I come in full sur - ren - der; Let Thy blood for
2. I am trust - ing, bless - ed Je - sus, In Thy sac - ri -
3. Now by faith I claim the bless - ing Of Thy Spir - it's

*   *   *   *   *

Perfect Love

To be sanctified wholly means to receive grace to love God with your whole heart and to love your neighbor as yourself.

Thou shalt love the Lord thy God with all thine heart, and with all thy soul, and with all thy might (Deut. 6:5).

Love is patient, love is kind. It does not envy, it does not boast, it is not proud. It is not rude, it is not self-seeking, it is not easily angered, it keeps no record of wrongs. Love does not delight in evil but rejoices with the truth. It always protects, always trusts, always hopes, always perseveres. Love never fails (1 Cor. 13:4-8, NIV).

CHRISTIAN PERFECTION[15]

Although we should be discriminating in our use of terms, we should not be afraid of using the word "perfect" in contexts where it is appropriate to do so. "Perfect" has several levels of meaning. In one sense, nothing in this human world is perfect. Yet if we accept such terms as "a perfect day," "a perfect baby," and "a car in perfect condition," when sufficiently close inspection would reveal imperfections in all of these, it ought to be reasonable to accept such terms as "perfect love" and "Christian perfection" to mean, not absolute perfection, but Christian character which meets the approval of God.

PERFECT LOVE[16]

In the New Testament there are two words for love. One is *philos,* which is the word used to express natural human affection. This exists in greater or less degree throughout the entire animal kingdom, including all natural affections of human nature apart from divine grace. The other word, *agapē,* is invariably used to express a divine affection, imparted to the soul by the Holy Ghost. Natural love existed within us before we were regenerated, as it exists until we were born into the kingdom of God. "The love of God" was then "shed abroad in our hearts" (Rom. 5:5), and by this alone can we claim the title of children of God, as partakers of His nature. "The love of God here means not our love to God, nor exactly the sense of God's love to us, but *God's love itself for us.*" "Behold, what manner of love the Father hath bestowed upon us" (1 John 3:1), not manifested or demonstrated, but *bestowed,* imparted, given to us as a gift. . . .

Was this not what our Lord asked for when He prayed "that the love wherewith thou hast loved me may be in them, and I in them" (John 17:26)? The truth declared is that God gives us His love to love with; He has made His love our property, absolutely given it to us, so that it is now ours. Who can tell all that this means? Inspiration itself

---

15. Greenlee, in *Further Insights into Holiness,* 80.

16. Thomas Cook, *New Testament Holiness,* 52-56.

Thomas Cook, a British Methodist evangelist of the late 19th and early 20th centuries, conducted holiness crusades in many countries.

In 1903 Cook was appointed principal of Cliff College, a British Methodist school for laymen. Under Cook and his most distinguished successor, Samuel Chadwick, Cliff College has been the chief center in Britain of the Methodist holiness tradition.

Cook is best known in the English-speaking world for his classic work, *New Testament Holiness.* First published in 1902, the book had gone through 12 editions by 1950.

can only find relief in adoring gratitude. "Behold, what manner of love."

Perhaps we shall now better understand the "new commandment [to] love . . . as I have loved you" (John 13:34). On Calvary we see love stronger than death. There we learn what love really is, and what it can do. When that same love drives our chariot wheels, we shall be ready to do as He did. It is where sacrifice begins that the proof of love begins. We must not offer, either to God or man, what costs nothing. The noblest thing in God's world is a lavished life. Carnal, selfish men cannot understand the service and sacrifice of those

> *Who spend their lives for others,*
> *With no ends of their own.*

But when our love is in *kind* like His, we cannot help doing it. Our *"must"* then is like the *"must"* of God. God must give His love, whether souls accept it or not. Let the love of Christ, the most sublime of all motives, and the glory of Christ, the most sublime of all ends, become the ruling principle of action, and who can help living magnanimously for man and for God?

More of Christ's love in our hearts means always increased sympathy with His dominant passion, the salvation of the lost. **LOVE GIVES** There is a grave mistake somewhere when a person imagines that he has mounted up to the plane of the "high life" and yet feels no quickened impulse toward those who are perishing in their sins around him. Zeal in soul winning is our love on fire. Give us more of the hidden fire, and all the rest will follow.

In serving the poor, the suffering, and the lost, we serve Him, and nothing is counted too good for Him by those who are filled with His sanctifying love. We prove our love to Christ by what we do for our fellow creatures. Love cannot treat its Lord meanly. She will not give Him the remnant, the drift, and the dregs of life. Giving of our surplus is no proof of love at all. She always offers the most that is possible, and the best. The one motive that has the power to lift us out of self, and to exalt life to its highest and loftiest phase, is a heart brimful of love to Christ. "For Christ's sake"—these three little words are the touchstone of love. . . .

Love service is the spontaneous, glad offering of a grateful heart, like that of the woman who broke the box of ointment and poured it on the feet of Christ. It is not clearer views of our duty to God that will win us over to new obedience; but as the love of Jesus floods our souls, a deeper, fuller, and ever-augmenting stream, the life of duty becomes transformed into a life of liberty and delight.

"Perfect love casteth out fear" (1 John 4:18). The two words "love" and "fear," placed in contrast in this scripture, represent the two different motives that may actuate us in Christian service. Some serve from love . . . and some from fear. . . . Mrs. Pearsall Smith puts the difference well; it is simply the difference between "may I" and "must I," between enjoyment and endurance. . . . Perhaps in most Christians the two motives exist together, the pure gold of love is mingled with the dross of fear in service; but when our love is "made perfect," our will elects God's will with unspeakable gladness. We shall keep the law then, not from dread of its penalties, but from love for the law itself, and the Lawgiver. Filled with divine love, we love what God loves, and in this condition the will of God is no longer as a yoke upon the neck; Christ's service is perfect freedom. Faber sings:

> He hath breathed into my heart
> A special love of Thee,
> A love to lose my will in His,
> And by the loss be free.

This is not freedom from law; that would be license. Nor is it being under law; that would be bondage. It is being inlawed, God putting the law into our love, so that we keep it from our very love of it, by a glad assent as naturally as water runs downhill. Before we reach this experience we are often like a man carrying a burden toward a hill, but when we reach it the burden and the hill suddenly disappear, and we can joyfully appropriate the words of the Son of God, and say, "I delight to do thy will, O my God: yea, thy law is within my heart" (Ps. 40:8).

MY LAW IN YOUR HEART

The old covenant was an outside, coercive force, a law written in stone. The new covenant is written in the heart, rectifying and inspiring all the springs of action. God fulfills the promise of the new covenant, "I will put my law into your hearts" (cf. Heb. 8:10), when His love is so fully shed abroad in the heart of the believer as to effect a complete release from the fear of the law as a motive to obedience. . . .

When every faculty is energized, every capacity filled, and the whole nature pervaded with this transcendent gift, the bondage, the irksomeness, the subtle legalism which more or less characterize the service of incipient believers, are entirely removed. The yoke of Christ no longer chafes, the last trace of servile feeling is gone, and the will of God becomes our free, spontaneous, delightful choice. We can sing then, not as mere poetic fancy, but as a glorious experimental reality:

> *I worship Thee, sweet will of God,*
> *And all Thy ways adore;*
> *And every day I live, I seem*
> *To love Thee more and more.*

But do you ask, "How am I to enter into this blessed experience? We brace our wills to secure it. We try to copy those who have it. We lay down rules about it. We watch, we pray; but these things do not bring the fullness of love into our souls." Love is never produced by straining and struggling, or by any direct action of the soul upon itself. . . . We receive love when we receive God. If we would have love we must seek Him. God is love and love is God. More love means more of God. Perfect love means that we have opened all the avenues of our being, and that He has come and taken possession of every chamber. Some writer has said, "Take love from an angel and you have a devil, take love from a man and you have a brute, take love from God and there is nothing left."

SEEKING AND FINDING

When Sir James Mackintosh was dying, a friend saw his lips move, and when the ear was put down it caught the whisper, "God— Love—the very same." Yes, love is the only word convertible with God. It is not His mere name but His nature, His being, himself. When He comes to the heart, He comes not empty-handed. He brings His love with Him, and that, consciously received, produces a corresponding and answering love in our hearts to Him. Says Lange, "When God's love to us comes to be in us, it is like the virtue which the loadstone gives to the needle, inclining it to move toward the pole."

There is no need to ask whether the perfect love of which John speaks means Christ's love to us, or our love to Christ. It is both. The recognition of His love, and the response of ours, are the result of His entering and abiding in the heart. "He that has made his home in love has his home in God, and God has His home in him."

*   *   *

In only three things is the child of God expected to be perfect: obedience, faith, and love.—E. S. Dunham.

Love Divine, All Loves Excelling

BEECHER

Charles Wesley, 1707-1788   John Zundel, 1815-1882

1. Love di - vine, all loves ex -cel-ling, Joy of heav'n, to earth come down!
2. Breathe,oh,breathe Thy lov - ing Spir - it In - to ev - 'ry trou-bled breast!
3. Come, Al-might - y to De - liv - er; Let us all Thy life re - ceive.
4. Fin - ish then Thy new cre - a - tion; Pure and spot - less let us be.

Fix in us Thy hum-ble dwell-ing; All Thy faith - ful mer - cies crown.
Let us all in Thee in - her - it; Let us find that sec - ond rest.
Sud - den -ly re - turn, and nev - er, Nev - er -more Thy tem -ples leave.
Let us see Thy great sal - va - tion, Per - fect - ly re - stored in Thee:

Je - sus, Thou art all com - pas - sion; Pure, un-bound-ed love Thou art.
Take a - way our bent to sin - ning; Al - pha and O - me - ga be.
Thee we would be al - ways bless - ing, Serve Thee as Thy hosts a - bove,
Changed from glo - ry in - to glo - ry, Till in heav'n we take our place,

Vis - it us with Thy sal - va - tion; En - ter ev - 'ry trem-bling heart.
End of faith, as its Be - gin - ning, Set our hearts at lib - er - ty.
Pray, and praise Thee with - out ceas - ing, Glo - ry in Thy per - fect love.
Till we cast our crowns be - fore Thee, Lost in won - der, love, and praise.

The Holy Spirit

At conversion, Christians receive God's Holy Spirit in regeneration, sometimes described as initial sanctification. To be sanctified wholly means to be baptized, or filled with the Holy Spirit, as happened to the disciples in the Upper Room.

I baptize you with water for repentance. But after me will come one who is more powerful than I, whose sandals I am not fit to carry. He will baptize you with the Holy Spirit and with fire (Matt. 3:11, NIV).

On one occasion, while he was eating with them, he gave them this command: "Do not leave Jerusalem, but wait for the gift my Father promised, which you have heard me speak about. For John baptized with water, but in a few days you will be baptized with the Holy Spirit" (Acts 1:4-5, NIV).

When the day of Pentecost came, they were all together in one place. Suddenly a sound like the blowing of a violent wind came from heaven and filled the whole house where they were sitting. They saw what seemed to be tongues of fire that separated and came to rest on each of them. All of them were filled with the Holy Spirit and began to speak in other tongues as the Spirit enabled them (Acts 2:1-4, NIV).

SANCTIFIED BY THE BAPTISM WITH THE HOLY SPIRIT

Most writers of the Holiness Movement have identified entire sanctification with the baptism with the Holy Spirit. John Fletcher was the first to give major emphasis to this interpretation of the Scripture; John Wesley allowed the view, though not endorsing it. Most writers of the 19th and 20th centuries have agreed with Fletcher at this point. Dr. J. B. Chapman writes:

The sanctified life is indeed a Spirit-filled life, and this term is applicable and useful in emphasizing the power and unction which are essential factors in the experience and life of holiness. . . . We are made holy by the baptism with the Holy Ghost—the incoming of the Spirit in Pentecostal fullness—and we are kept in a state of purity and holiness only by the Spirit's indwelling fullness. Analogies must be used with discretion, but, as we think of it, the Holy Spirit is the Guardian of our purity. If by any means He withdraws himself from us, sin breaks in, like water through the dike, and thus to be without the Spirit is also to be without holiness.

It is an error to consider the term "Spirit-filled life" as anything other than a synonym of the sanctified life. To be filled with the Spirit is to be emptied of sin, and the means of our being emptied of sin is itself the infilling of the Spirit. So, then, whoever is sanctified wholly is filled with the Spirit, and whoever is filled with the Spirit is sanctified wholly.[17]

FILLED WITH THE SPIRIT[18]

We must recognize the fact that to possess the Holy Spirit is one thing, but to be filled with the Spirit is quite another. Before Pentecost the Holy Ghost was given to the disciples. Christ had breathed upon them and said, "Receive ye the Holy Ghost" (John 20:22). But Pentecost made an unspeakable difference to them. The visible tongues of fire were only emblems of what had passed within. What new creatures they then became! How their gross conception of Christ's kingdom was purged away, and how they were raised from earthliness to spirituality! Their intellects were flooded with divine light, their souls throbbed with divine sympathy, and their tongues spoke so wonderfully of the things of God that all who had known them previously were amazed, saying, "What meaneth this?" They were all raised to a new altitude; a new energy and force possessed them. . . . They met together as the sincere but timid and partially enlightened followers of Christ, but they left the Upper Room full of light, and power, and love. They were now filled with the Holy Ghost as an all-illuminating, all-strengthening, all-sanctifying presence. The baptism of fire had consumed their inward depravity, subsidized all their faculties, and filled to the full each capacity with divine energy and life.

"Baptized with" and "filled with the Holy Ghost" are often convertible terms in the Acts of the Apostles, but it is instructive to note that they are not always so. The apostles received but one baptism, but they were "filled" with the Spirit over and over again. The baptism of the Holy Ghost was, and still is, a sort of initiatory rite to the life of Pentecostal service, and fullness, and victory. Christian life begins at Calvary, but effective service begins at Pentecost. Before Pentecost there was not much service rendered by the apostles that was worth the name. But with the Spirit's baptism they entered upon a new phase of service. The analogy of the sacrament of baptism connects the

---

17. *Terminology of Holiness,* 169-70.
18. Cook, *New Testament Holiness,* 75-76.

baptism of the Spirit with a new era in Christian life. Pentecost and the visit of Cornelius, when the baptism of the Spirit is spoken of, were not only historical events but great representative occasions, which may be held to typify and signify the beginning of the Spirit-filled life.

JOHN FLETCHER'S EXPERIENCE

The fullest account of how Fletcher was filled with the Holy Spirit is given in a letter written by the famous Spirit-filled Hester Ann Rogers.[19] Describing a meeting held in 1781, she says:

When I entered the room, where they were assembled, the heavenly man (Fletcher) was giving out the following verses with such animation as I have seldom witnessed—

> *Near us, assisting Jesus, stand;*
> *Give us the opening heavens to see;*
> *Thee to behold at God's right hand,*
> *And yield our parting souls to Thee.*

> *My Father, O my Father, hear,*
> *And send the fiery chariot down;*
> *Let Israel's famous steeds appear,*
> *And whirl us to the starry crown.*

> *We, we would die for Jesus too;*
> *Through tortures, fires, and seas of blood,*
> *All triumphantly break through,*
> *And plunge into the depths of God.*

After this Mr. Fletcher poured out his full soul in prayer, or praise, or spiritual instruction; and every word that fell from his lips appeared to be accompanied with an unction from above. . . .

He insisted now that believers are called upon to [experience] the same baptismal fire that on the Day of Pentecost was the opening of the dispensation of the Spirit—the great promise of the Father; and that the *latter day glory*, which he believed was near at hand, should far exceed the first effusion of the Spirit. Seeing then that they, on the Day of Pentecost, bare witness to the grace of our Lord, so shall *we*; and, like them, spread the flame of love.

After singing a hymn, he cried, "Oh, to be filled with the Holy Ghost! I want to be filled! Oh, my friends, let us wrestle for a more

---

19. E. Davies, *Life and Journal of Mrs. Hester Ann Rogers*, 82-91.

abundant outpouring of the Holy Spirit!" To me, he said, "Come, my sister, will you covenant with me this day, to pray for *the fullness of the Spirit?* Will *you* be a witness for Jesus?" I answered with flowing tears, "In the strength of Jesus I will." He cried, "Glory, glory be to God! Lord, strengthen Thine handmaid to keep this covenant, even unto death!"

He then said, "My dear brethren and sisters, God is here! I feel Him in this place; but I would hide my face in the dust, because I have been ashamed to declare what He has done for *me.* For many years, I have grieved His Spirit; I am deeply humbled; and He has again restored these words, '*Reckon yourselves to be dead indeed unto sin, but alive unto God through Jesus Christ our Lord.*' I obey the voice of God; I now obey it; and tell you all, to the praise of His love—*I am freed from sin.* Yes, I rejoice to declare it, and to be a witness to the glory of His grace, that *I am dead unto sin, and alive unto God, through Jesus Christ,* who is my Lord and King! I received this blessing four or five times before; but I lost it, by not observing the order of God; who has

WITNESS told us, '*With the heart man believeth unto righteousness; and with the mouth confession is made unto salvation.*' But the enemy offered his bait, under various colors, to keep me from a public declaration of what God had wrought.

"When I first received this grace, Satan bid me wait awhile, till I saw more of the *fruits;* I resolved to do so; but I soon began to doubt of the *witness,* which, before, I had felt in my heart; and in a little time, I was sensible I had lost both. A second time, after receiving this salvation, I was kept from being a witness for my Lord, by the suggestion, 'Thou art a public character—the eyes of all are upon thee—and if, as before, by *any* means thou lose the blessing, it will be a dishonor to the doctrine of *heart holiness.*' I held my peace and again forfeited the gift of God. At another time, I was prevailed upon to hide it, by reasoning, How few, even of the children of *God,* will receive this testimony; many of them supposing that every transgression of the Adamic law is sin; and, therefore, if I profess to be *free* from sin, *all* these will give my profession the lie; because I am not free in *their* sense; I am not free from ignorance, mistakes, and various infirmities; I will, therefore, enjoy what God has wrought in me; but I will not say, *I am perfect in love.* Alas! I soon found again, He that hideth his *Lord's talent, and improveth it not, from that unprofitable servant shall be taken away even that he hath.*

"Now, my brethren, you see my folly. I have confessed it in your presence; and *now* I resolve before you all to confess my Master. I will confess Him to all the world. And I declare unto you, in the presence of God, the Holy Trinity, I am now *dead indeed unto sin.* I do **DEAD TO SIN** not say, *I am crucified with Christ,* because some of our well-meaning brethren say, by *this* can only be meant *gradual* dying; but I profess unto you, *I am dead unto sin, and alive unto God;* and, remember, all *this is through Jesus Christ our Lord. He* is my Prophet, Priest, and King—my indwelling holiness—my *all in all.* I wait for the fulfillment of that prayer, *"That they all may be one; as thou, Father, art in me, and I in thee, that they also may be one in us: [and] that they may be one, even as we are one."* Oh, for that pure baptismal flame! Oh, for the fullness of the dispensation of the Holy Ghost! Pray, pray, pray for this! This shall make us all of one *heart,* and of one soul. Pray for gifts—for the gift of utterance; and confess your royal Master. A man without gifts is like a king in disguise; he appears as a subject only. You are *"kings and priests unto God!"* Put on, therefore, your robes, and wear on your garter, "Holiness to the Lord."

* * * * *

Holy Spirit, Be My Guide

Mildred Cope, 1924 -   Mildred Cope, 1924 -

1. Ho - ly Spir-it, my heart yearns for Thee; Ho - ly Spir-it, a -
2. Nev - er, nev-er shall I be set free; Nev - er, nev-er, till
3. Ne'er my trust will be in vain, Naught to lose and

bide in me. Make me clean; oh, make me pure!
Thou purg-est me! "Come just now," my cry, my prayer;
all to gain. Take my life, my self, my soul;

REFRAIN

I must know the dou - ble cure!
In - bred sin I can - not bear! Ho - ly Spir - it, be my Guide.
Burn the chaff and make me whole!

Ho - ly Spir - it, my door's o-pen wide. Make me to know Thy

will di - vine; Ho - ly Spir - it, be Thou mine!

* * * * *

Empowerment

To be filled with the Holy Spirit brings added power to conquer sin, to love others, and to witness for Christ.

And, behold, I send the promise of my Father upon you: but tarry ye in the city of Jerusalem, until ye be endued with power from on high (Luke 24:49).

You will receive power when the Holy Spirit comes on you; and you will be my witnesses in Jerusalem, and in all Judea and Samaria, and to the ends of the earth (Acts 1:8, NIV).

I kneel before the Father . . . I pray that out of his glorious riches he may strengthen you with power through his Spirit in your inner being, so that Christ may dwell in your hearts through faith. And I pray that you, being rooted and established in love, may have power, together with all the saints, to grasp how wide and long and high and deep is the love of Christ, and to know this love that surpasses knowledge—that you may be filled to the measure of all the fullness of God (Eph. 3:14, 16-19, NIV).

Sanctifying Power

There is sanctifying pow'r,
Like a sweet, refreshing show'r,
    Waiting for each consecrated heart:
Pow'r to cleanse us from all sin,
Pow'r to keep us pure within,
    Pow'r for service which He will impart.

I'm so glad it reaches me,
All unworthy though I be,
    Overcoming grace made freely mine.
Since the Comforter abides,
And within my heart resides,
    I am walking in the light divine.

                    —LELIA N. MORRIS, 1862-1929

THE HOLY SPIRIT BRINGS POWER[20]

Jesus promised power to His disciples. But be it noticed that their hearts were first cleansed by the Holy Ghost. It is not safe to entrust carnal men with power. It would almost certainly be abused and perverted to selfish ends. . . . Jesus' own disciples would have done it before Pentecost. John and James wanted first and second place in what they supposed would be a material and visible kingdom of God. Had they secured such positions, without an increase of grace, they would most likely have been ruined.

But the great gift of power to the disciples was wisely postponed until their hearts were cleansed by the Holy Spirit. Then they were free from selfishness, and would use their extraordinary power with an eye single to the glory of God. Peter could then preach his moving sermon, not at all for Peter's exaltation, but for the glory of Jesus. The whole apostolic band, suddenly clothed with an unusual power that made men marvel, could remain sweet, humble, and modest without a touch of that sense of self-importance that so often disfigures the character of carnal man. . . .

What then is the power which Jesus gives?

It is a power to bear witness for Jesus. "Ye shall be witnesses unto

---

20. A. M. Hills, *The Secret of Spiritual Power,* 52-58. For biography see 3:334.

me both in Jerusalem, and in all Judaea, and in Samaria, and unto the uttermost part of the earth" (Acts 1:8). It is painful to observe how many professors of religion there are who have no testimony to give for their Lord. They are silent in the prayer meeting . . . silent in the private conversation about their spiritual life. If the world depended upon them for knowledge, it would never hear that it had a Savior. . . .

Dr. Fletcher Wharton, in a published sermon, asks, "What is it, then, to have this spiritual power?" He answers: "Let me answer. Let me answer slowly. It is to have God in our souls. Not some other one's experience of God, but God. Ye shall receive power, after that the Holy Ghost is come upon you."

Mr. Finney said: "No one has at any time any right to expect success unless he first secure this enduement of power from on high. It is the supreme need of today." . . .

But still more dear to God than all our achievements is ourselves, and God gives us not only power *to do* but power *to be.* Multitudes are willing to do great and brilliant things, in contrast to every one who is willing to be like Jesus. People prize notoriety above character, and achievement more than personal worth. God is pleased to have us *like* Him. The Holy Spirit, therefore, coming into the heart in Pentecostal power, cleanses us—in other words, gives us the *power to be holy.* This is the power that will make us pleasing to God, and like God. "He that sanctifieth and they who are sanctified are all of one: for which cause he is not ashamed to call them brethren" (Heb. 2:11).

Oh, how wonderful a feat it is for the Holy Spirit to fix us up so that Jesus shall not be ashamed to own us as kinsfolk in the presence of the Heavenly Father and the holy angels! This is power indeed! power to overcome the world, the flesh, and the devil; power to be "more than conquerors through him that loved us" (Rom. 8:37).

This above all else is dear to God, to have us show to an onlooking universe that "the blood of Jesus Christ his Son cleanseth us from all sin" (1 John 1:7), that we are redeemed from the curse of the fall, and by this redeeming grace can walk the earth in the white robes of righteousness, and remain "unspotted from the world" (James 1:27). "Ye shall receive power, after that the Holy Ghost is come upon you: and ye shall be witnesses" (Acts 1:8).

POWER FOR DAILY LIVING[21]

The majority of people do not have great, romantic experiences in life. Their course leads over a more or less undulating plain. Every

---

21. Chapman, *Holiness, the Heart of Christian Experience,* 48.

day is much like every other day. The necessities of economic life drive them to their hours of labor and of rest. Their occupation brings them the large percentage of contacts with others, and hence their opportunities for doing good. And this is equivalent to saying that what we all need most is grace to live the common life in an uncommon manner. We need wisdom to see God in the circumstances of everyday life, and we need grace to do faithfully the myriad of little things which seem to have no particular connection with our religious profession. To be patient where others would become irritable, to be cheerful where others would be possessed of fear, to be kind when others would be resentful, to be pure when others would break under temptation, to reject all price offered for doing wrong, to just exemplify the spirit of the Master in the common places among common people— this, to the great majority of us, is real victory.

Christlikeness

God offers the ministry of the indwelling Holy Spirit to make us more Christlike.

I have much more to say to you, more than you can now bear. But when he, the Spirit of truth, comes, he will guide you into all truth. . . . He will bring glory to me by taking from what is mine and making it known to you. All that belongs to the Father is mine. That is why I said the Spirit will take from what is mine and make it known to you (John 16:12-15, NIV).

If you have any encouragement from being united with Christ, if any comfort from his love, if any fellowship with the Spirit, if any tenderness and compassion . . . Do nothing out of selfish ambition or vain conceit, but in humility consider others better than yourselves. Each of you should look not only to your own interests, but also to the interests of others.

Your attitude should be the same as that of Christ Jesus (Phil. 2:1, 3-5, NIV).

PRAYER FOR A CHRISTLIKE SPIRIT[22]

Dear Lord, by Your help, and to the best of my ability, I believe that I have met every condition for the sanctification of my spirit. And

---

22. A. F. Harper, "I Would Like to Know God Better."

now I thank You that in keeping with Your promise, the blessed Holy Spirit fills my heart—this very moment.

Make my life and my words a daily witness for You. Out of a heart filled with Your love, let there grow the fruit of the Spirit: love, joy, peace, patience, kindness, goodness, faithfulness, gentleness, and self-control.

> *More love to Thee, O Christ, More love to Thee!*
> *Hear Thou the prayer I make On bended knee.*
> *This is my earnest plea: More love, O Christ, to Thee;*
> *More love to Thee, More love to Thee!*

> —ELIZABETH PRENTISS, 1818-78

A TESTIMONY TO DEEPENED FELLOWSHIP WITH CHRIST[23]

The Spirit of God seemed to take full possession, filled my heart, and lifted me up in my inner life to a new level of joy and blessing. That divinely inspired prayer of Paul in Rom. 15:13 . . . was made a wonderful reality in my experience: "Now the God of hope fill you with all joy and peace in believing, that ye may abound in hope, through the power of the Holy Ghost."

The blessings of heart cleansing and the filling of the Spirit, which I had appropriated in naked faith on God's Word, were . . . made a conscious blessed experience. The result was fullness of joy, which I experienced in the following sevenfold "joy in the Holy Ghost." It is this experience of joy which constitutes some of the riches of holiness.

1. The Joy of the Spirit's Infilling

"He shall baptize you with the Holy Ghost, and with fire" (Matt. 3:11). The indwelling of the Spirit of God became a new and joyous reality. I always love to apply Mal. 4:2 as expressing the effect of the

---

23. Henry Brockett, *The Riches of Holiness*, 38-45.

In the first edition of *The Riches of Holiness* (1936), Brockett described himself as "just a private Christian, one who works in an office in London and engages in Christian service in his spare time."

This spare-time ministry brought invitations to give messages on Christian holiness in churches in the London area. It also brought opportunities to publish those truths in holiness magazines.

Henry's deep and continuing commitment to the message of entire sanctification led to the publication of three volumes, *The Riches of Holiness, Scriptural Freedom from Sin,* and *The Christian and Romans 7.*

baptism of the Spirit on my inner spiritual life. Although I know that verse has a future dispensational meaning, yet it beautifully expresses the manner in which the Spirit of God came upon me and took full possession. The verse says, "Unto you that fear my name shall the Sun of righteousness arise with healing in his wings; and ye shall go forth, and grow up as calves of the stall."

The thoughts of fire, light, warmth, and healing are suggested by that beautiful verse. The blessed Comforter became all that to me. Fire has ever been my favorite symbol of the Holy Spirit. I love the phrase "the baptism of the Holy Ghost and fire." It suggests the immersion of the whole being of the believer in the purifying, glowing love of God. The Spirit of God became very real to me as the fire of God within, "kindling, flaming, burning, flowing." I now began to appreciate more clearly than I had ever done before the meaning of Pentecost. This experience of the infilling of the Spirit was my personal Pentecost, and all the scriptures relating to the glory of the divine indwelling in the heart now became a vivid, conscious, blessed reality to me and filled me with joy in a way they had not done before.

2. The Joy of Deliverance from Sin

"If the Son therefore shall make you free, ye shall be free indeed" (John 8:36). One of the first things that the Holy Spirit did when He took full possession was to glorify Christ. He shone in a new way upon the Cross and Romans 6. He showed me that the blessing of heart holiness had all been provided for me on the Cross. Of course I knew the truth of Romans 6 theoretically, quite well. I had studied it when I had been baptized by immersion three years previously. But as soon as the Spirit came in His fullness He applied Romans 6 and 8:2 in such a way that I was filled with all joy and peace in believing. The painful sense of bondage and corruption within gave way to a blessed experience of freedom and purity.

The Spirit who had previously caused me to groan and say, "O wretched man that I am! who shall deliver me . . . ?" now enabled me to say with joy, "I thank God through Jesus Christ our Lord. . . . The law of the Spirit of life in Christ Jesus hath made me free from the law of sin and death" (Rom. 7:24-25; 8:2). I now knew in power the blessed freedom from sin spoken of in Romans 6 because I saw in the light of the Spirit that my old man was crucified with Him, that the body of sin might be destroyed, that henceforth I should not serve sin. I saw that all that I had asked God to do in me by the baptism of the

Spirit on October 23, 1916, had been provided for me on the Cross. The blessed Son had now made me "free indeed." Oh, the blessed joy of this deliverance from sin!

3. The Joy of Dwelling in Divine Love

"We will come unto him, and make our abode with him" (John 14:23). Another blessed result of the baptism of the Spirit was an inner realization of the love of God which I had not experienced before. How glorious to taste in experience 1 John 4:16! "God is love: and he that dwelleth in love dwelleth in God, and God in him." The love of God, His very inmost nature, seemed to me like a boundless ocean with the rays of the glorious sun shining upon it, and in this ocean of love and light my whole being was immersed, and it filled my heart. I was dwelling in His love, and His love was dwelling in me. I was inwardly satisfied, perfectly satisfied, resting in the boundless love of God. Praise God, there was no painful sense of an aching void that the world cannot fill. The love of God had been poured forth in my heart by the Holy Ghost.

4. The Joy of Christ Within

"I will not leave you comfortless: I will come to you" (John 14:18). Words fail to describe the blessedness of the love of Christ and His indwelling. It "passeth knowledge" (Eph. 3:19). I now knew in a completely new way "Christ in you [me], the hope of glory" (Col. 1:27). At times when all was hushed and quiet, it seemed as if a still small voice within whispered so gently to my heart, "I am here; I have come to abide forever." I was melted with holy joy. The glorious prayer for divine fullness in Eph. 3:14-21, which previously had seemed much too "far away" and "ideal" for me, now began to be realized in my inner life, as the blessed Holy Spirit more and more glorified Christ dwelling in my heart by faith. That wonderful promise of the Lord, "I will come in to him, and will sup with him, and he with me" (Rev. 3:20), was made a wonderful reality, and I tasted something of the blessedness of that experience in 1 Pet. 1:8, "Believing, ye rejoice with joy unspeakable and full of glory."

5. The Joy of Answered Prayer

"Ask, and ye shall receive, that your joy may be full" (John 16:24). My prayer life was deepened and enriched and became a greater joy than ever. One of the blessings the Lord promised as a result of Pentecost was that they should ask and receive, that their joy might be full. The Holy Spirit gave me blessed liberty in access to the Father in the name of the Son, and imparted to me the utmost confidence in asking that I might receive every possible spiritual blessing that the Father had for me in Christ. This Spirit-given sense of heart liberty brought me into a deeper experience of the joy of sonship with the Father, and so I proved the truth of those words, "As many as are led by the Spirit of God, they are the sons of God" (Rom. 8:14), and also, "Where the Spirit of the Lord is, there is liberty" (2 Cor. 3:17). I had the joy of receiving definite answers to prayer for specific blessing for souls. . . .

6. Joy in the Will of God

"The Holy Ghost, whom God hath given to them that obey him" (Acts 5:32). Of course, I had turned from all known sin and yielded to God and desired to know and do His will as a result of the work of the Spirit of God in regeneration. The Word of God says, "Whosoever is born of God does not commit sin; for his seed remaineth in him: and he cannot sin, because he is born of God" (1 John 3:9). I would not, for one moment, underrate the mighty work of grace accomplished by the Holy Spirit in regeneration. But when the Spirit took possession of my heart in His fullness, He produced a deeper, sweeter joy than ever in the will of God.

It was blessed joy indeed to know that the heart, the very secret spring of the being, was cleansed to the depths and the Spirit of God abiding within. The blessed Spirit of Liberty made it a joy and delight to prove what is "that good, and acceptable, and perfect, will of God" (Rom. 12:2). I had been set "free indeed," and yet I felt the willing slave of divine love, as the Psalmist says, "O Lord, truly I am thy servant . . . thou hast loosed my bonds" (Ps. 116:16). Oh, what blessed rest of heart, just to abide in the very center of the will of God and say day by day, and in every circumstance of life, "Thy will—for me—just now!"

7. The Joy of the Manifestation of Christ

"I will love him, and will manifest myself to him" (John 14:21). There are some spiritual experiences that are so precious that one feels reluctant to cast aside the veil and disclose them to others, preferring rather to keep them as a sacred secret between the soul and the Lord. On the other hand, I feel that if the Lord richly blesses us we ought to acknowledge it to His glory, so that the Lord's people may be encouraged and blessed thereby. Our Lord says, "What I tell you in darkness, that speak ye in light: and what ye hear in the ear, that preach ye upon the house tops" (Matt. 10:27). I feel, therefore, that I ought to declare how wonderfully gracious the Lord was to me in manifesting himself to my heart in 1918, nearly two years after my step of faith for entire sanctification. I was still in France on light duty behind the lines, but away from all meetings and with little Christian fellowship. At this time the Spirit of God was working in me a deep love and longing for a further revelation of the person of Christ. He was preparing me for a blessed fulfillment of the Lord's promise in John 14:21: "He that loveth me shall be loved of my Father, and I will love him, and will manifest myself to him." That is what I longed for—a fresh manifestation of Christ in my heart.

About two o'clock one morning I awoke with a strong impression of my mind. The impression was . . . that on the next three consecutive nights I was to awake at midnight, go outside **THE SPIRIT GUIDES US** into a wood nearby, and wait before the Lord in prayer, and that afterward the Lord would manifest himself to me. I wondered at first whether this impression was merely the working of my own mind or whether it was the voice of the Spirit. It is dangerous blindly to follow every impression which may come into the mind. Impressions may emanate from one's own thoughts or from the devil, as well as from the Holy Spirit. If an impression is of the Holy Spirit, He will give time to think and pray about it.

It seemed to me a somewhat strange thing to do, to get up at midnight for three nights in succession and go into a wood and pray. But the Lord told Abraham to do a very strange thing when He bade him offer up Isaac in sacrifice. That act of obedience was to be seen only by the Lord himself. Was the Lord giving me a simple test of obedience, I wondered, by asking me to do an apparently unusual thing which He alone would see? I prayed about this impression and asked that I might not be misled by any foolish workings of my own mind or by the devil. The impression persisted. So the first night I awoke at midnight and crept quietly out of the hut unobserved, went out into a wood, waited, prayed, and then returned. I did the same the second night. The third night, however, as it was pouring rain, I remained where I was for a little time in prayer. Nothing special happened on any of these occasions.

When I awoke in the morning after the third night, I did not think very much about the matter. But just after breakfast I felt that gentle touch upon my spirit, that warmth and unction, which I recognized as of the Spirit. I gradually became conscious in a wonderful way of the Divine Presence, and such was the power that I felt compelled to get right away into a quiet place on my own. Here I lay prostrate on the ground for over half an hour in silent adoration. My whole being was hushed and awed in the consciousness of the presence of the Lord, and, in a way I cannot describe, I was made aware of His presence around me and within me and of my union with Him. . . .

After the time of silent adoration and worship I exclaimed again and again, with a full heart, "My Lord and my God! Holy, holy, holy!" Then the following scriptures were applied with sweet unction and power to my soul: "Both he that sanctifieth and they who are sanctified are all of one" (Heb. 2:11). "The blood of Jesus Christ his Son cleanseth us from all sin" (1 John 1:7). "He that is joined unto the Lord is one spirit" (1 Cor. 6:17). When I rose a deep, sweet rest took possession of my heart, and I was satisfied. I knew that the Lord himself had drawn near and manifested himself to me in accordance with John 14:21. . . .

The next evening, while I was quietly walking, meditating on the things of God, I was powerfully impressed with a thought which I feel was the teaching of the Spirit of God direct to my heart through the Word. The thought was, I must now be content to leave to the Lord himself the manner and occasions of His manifestations of His presence. There is nothing higher for me in this life than to live by faith and walk patiently in love according to 1 Corinthians 13.

*   *   *   *   *

A Heart like Thine

Judson W. Van Deventer, 1855-1939   Judson W. Van Deventer, 1855-1939

1. Give me a love that knows no ill; Give me the grace to
2. On - ly a joy, a few brief years; On - ly a dream, a
3. O - pen mine eyes that I may see; Show me the cross of
4. Pil - low my head up - on Thy breast; Shel - ter my soul and

do	Thy	will.	Par - don and	cleanse this	soul of	mine;
vale	of	tears;	Vain is this	world I	now re	- sign.
Cal	- va -	ry;	There may I	go and	not re	- pine.
give	me	rest;	Fill me with	love as	I re	- cline.

Give me a heart like Thine. Come to my soul, bless-ed

Je - sus. Hear me, O Sav - iour di - vine! O - pen the

foun - tain and cleanse me; Give me a heart like Thine.
a heart like Thine.

A Scriptural Doctrine

We believe the doctrine of entire sanctification is taught in the Bible and is consistent with other salvation truths of Scripture.

They are not of the world, even as I am not of it. Sanctify them by the truth; your word is truth. . . . My prayer is not for them alone. I pray also for those who will believe in me through their message (John 17:16-17, 20, NIV).

May God himself, the God of peace, sanctify you through and

through. May your whole spirit, soul and body be kept blameless at the coming of our Lord Jesus Christ. The one who calls you is faithful and he will do it (1 Thess. 5:23-24, NIV).

*   *   *

I tell you as plain as I can speak, where and when I found this [truth of entire sanctification]. I found it in the oracles of God, in the Old and New Testaments, when I read them with no other view or desire but to save my own soul.—John Wesley.

*   *   *

Q. *How do we know about this blessing of holiness, and about the conditions upon which it may be obtained?*

A. The Bible is our principal Source for knowledge on this subject, and Jesus made reference to this dependable Source of light when He said in His prayer, "Sanctify them through thy truth: thy word is truth" (John 17:17). The Bible requires holiness in its commandments: "Be ye holy; for I am holy" (1 Pet. 1:16). It offers it in its promises: "The very God of peace sanctify you wholly; and . . . [preserve you] blameless unto the coming of our Lord Jesus Christ" (1 Thess. 5:23). It tells how holiness is provided in the atoning work of Jesus Christ: "Wherefore Jesus also, that he might sanctify the people with his own blood, suffered without the gate" (Heb. 13:12). And there are numerous testimonies recorded of those who obtained this grace from God. Surely no one will dispute that to be a Bible Christian one must be holy without and within.—J. B. Chapman, *Holiness, the Heart of Christian Experience*, 58-59.

BIBLE DESCRIPTION OF COMPLETE SALVATION[24]

What terms are commonly used to express full salvation?

The Scripture terms are "perfect love," "perfection," "sanctification," and "holiness." These terms are synonymous, all pointing to the same precious state of grace. While they denote the same religious state, each one of them indicates some essential characteristic, and hence these terms are significantly expressive of full salvation. The word "sanctification" has the double meaning of *consecration* and *purification*—the Old Testament sense of setting apart to a sacred service: "sanctify yourselves . . . and be ye holy" (Lev. 20:7); and the

---

24. J. A. Wood, *Perfect Love*, 9-10.

New Testament sense of spiritual purification: "sanctify them through thy truth" (John 17:17).

The word "sanctify" and its derivatives occur in the Scriptures, with reference to men and things, over 100 times. The term "perfection" signifies completeness of Christian character; it is freedom from all sin, and possession of all the graces of the Spirit, *complete in kind.* "Let us go on unto perfection" (Heb. 6:1). The word "perfection" and its relatives occur 101 times in the Scriptures. In over 50 of these instances it is predicated of human character under the operation of grace.

The term "holiness" is more generic and comprehensive than the **WHOLENESS** others, including salvation from sin, and the possession of the image and spirit of God. To be holy is to be *whole, entire,* or *perfect* in a moral sense, and in ordinary use is synonymous with purity and godliness. "Follow peace with all men, and holiness, without which no man shall see the Lord" (Heb. 12:14). The word "holy" and its derivatives occur not less than 120 times in their application to men and things. The word "justify" and its derivatives occur 74 times in regard to men; and the word "pardon" with its derivatives, in their application to penitent sinners, occur only 17 times.

The phrase "perfect love" is expressive of the spirit and temper, or moral atmosphere, in which the wholly sanctified and perfect Christian lives. "He that dwelleth in love dwelleth in God, and God in him. Herein is our love made perfect" (1 John 4:16-17).

These terms . . . are scriptural and significant, and Christians should not ignore them. No one of them should be employed to the exclusion of the others; nor should other terms be chosen to their exclusion.

CHRISTIAN PERFECTION AND BIBLICAL THEOLOGY[25]

Is there . . . for this Wesleyan doctrine of Christian perfection any support in biblical theology? In Wesley's day there was such an arbitrary and fragmentary and superficial use of Scripture, even by the finest scholars, that many students have gained the impression, if not the belief, that the scriptural argument for Christian perfection cannot endure the test of our modern method of studying the Bible. I am certain that the test can be endured; but, before taking up that matter, I wish to enter a protest against the prevailing notion that before we

---

25. Curtis, *The Christian Faith*, 299-300.

can accept a Christian doctrine every feature of it must have exact scripture proof.

The Bible is not to be used in that hard and fast manner. The Bible is the *normative* authority on Christian doctrine; but we must also provide for the larger and larger interpretations by the developing Christian consciousness. For example, it would be enough to show that Christian perfection is not in contradiction of any scripture, but harmonizes with the *trend of emphasis* in the New Testament upon moral love, and is the loftiest ideal belonging to the most normal and most thoroughly developed Christian consciousness. If we can make it indubitable that the Bible itself never allows the great saints to rest until they hold and experience this doctrine of supreme love, we will have secured quite as good a basis for the doctrine as could be secured by any amount of precise scriptural proof.

THE BIBLE NORMATIVE

John's Doctrine of Love. The essence of the message of John to the Christian man is in this glowing message (1 John 4:16—5:5): "God is love; and he that abideth in love abideth in God, and God abideth in him. Herein is love made perfect with us, that we may have boldness in the day of judgment; because as he is, even so are we in this world. There is no fear in love: but perfect love casteth out fear, because fear hath punishment; and he that feareth is not made perfect in love. We love, because he first loved us. If a man say, I love God, and hateth his brother, he is a liar: for he that loveth not his brother whom he hath seen, cannot love God whom he hath not seen. And this commandment have we from him, that he who loveth God love his brother also.

"Whosoever believeth that Jesus is the Christ is begotten of God: and whosoever loveth him that begat loveth him also that is begotten of him. Hereby we know that we love the children of God, when we love God and do his commandments. For this is the love of God, that we keep his commandments: and his commandments are not grievous. For whatsoever is begotten of God overcometh the world: and this is the victory that hath overcome the world, even our faith. And who is he that overcometh the world, but he that believeth that Jesus is the Son of God?" (ASV).

When we separate the real message of this passage from its rhetorical mannerism, we find the connected points to be these: First, in John's conception of God the finality is love. Second, we make entrance into this love of God by being "begotten of God," and this takes place when we believe "that Jesus is the Christ." Third, we are prepared for the day of judgment by having this love of God made perfect in us; and this perfection of love can be achieved in this life— "because as he is, even so are we in this world." Fourth, the marks of the perfect love are that it "casteth out fear," that it makes a man "love his brother also," and that it enables him to "do his commandments," and to have that perfect faith which "overcometh the world."

HOLINESS IN THE BIBLE[26]

It is our intention to present the proof upon which we rely for the support of the foregoing views [of Christian purity]. And whence shall the proof be derived? "To whom shall we go?" Not to creeds, or decretals, or ecclesiastical canons, or councils! To the Bible!—what saith the Lord? All will admit the propriety of this appeal. . . .

We hope to sustain our position, not by a single and isolated declaration only, or a single inference only, but by a great number of both direct and inferential proofs, of the most unequivocal and irresistible authority: declarations so various contained in commands, promises, prayers, exhortations, statements, and narratives; and inferences so diversified, arising from so many sources, as to convince every candid reader that the doctrine we contend for is not limited to a bare and questionable place, a doubtful and uncertain existence in the holy records, but is repletely and abundantly, explicitly and with great clearness, embodied as a cardinal feature throughout the whole system.

It breathes in the prophecy, thunders in the law, murmurs in the narrative, whispers in the promises, supplicates in the prayers, sparkles in the poetry, resounds in the songs, speaks in the types, glows in the imagery, voices in the language, and burns in the spirit of the whole scheme, from its alpha to omega, from its beginning to its end. Holiness! Holiness needed! Holiness required! Holiness offered! Holiness attainable! Holiness a present duty, a present privilege, a present enjoyment, is the progress and completeness of its wondrous theme! It is the truth glowing all over: webbing all through revelation; the glorious truth which sparkles, and whispers, and sings, and shouts, in all its history, and biography, and poetry, and prophecy, and precept, and promise, and prayer; the great central truth of the system. The won-

---

26. Randolph S. Foster, *Nature and Blessedness of Christian Purity*, 80. For biography see 3:234.

der is, that all do not see, that any rise up to question, a truth so conspicuous, so glorious, so full of comfort.

For All Christians

Entire sanctification is God's call to all Christians.

Sanctify them through thy truth; thy word is truth. . . . Neither pray I for these alone, but for them also which shall believe on me through their word (John 17:17, 20).

Follow peace with all men, and holiness, without which no man shall see the Lord (Heb. 12:14).

Repent and be baptized, every one of you, in the name of Jesus Christ for the forgiveness of your sins. And you will receive the gift of the Holy Spirit.

The promise is for you and your children and for all who are far off—for all whom the Lord our God will call (Acts 2:38-39, NIV).

Q. *Is this blessing of holiness for all Christians?*

A. Yes, it is for all—ministers, missionaries, laymen, adults, and little children. Anyone who has been born again of the Spirit of God, and who desires to be sanctified wholly, may come in the full assurance that God will not deny his prayer or practice any reluctance in fulfilling to him the promise to make him every whit whole. Many people have an exaggerated idea of the force of chronology or geography. They scruple not to say that the baptism with the Holy Ghost was just for the apostles. Or if they allow for any closer approach to our own time than that, they say this is just for those who are called of God to some very special service. But the promise of God is without any such limitations. On the Day of Pentecost, Peter said, "The promise is unto you, and to your children, and to all that are afar off, even as many as the Lord our God shall call" (Acts 2:39). We all need to be holy, no matter what the service we are expected to perform. Sometimes the grace of holiness is as much needed by one whose lot it is to be neglected and overlooked as for one whose place is in the limelight. Humility is as much a fruit of holiness as fluency of tongue or any gift whereby men are made to wonder.[27]

---

27. Chapman, *Holiness, the Heart of Christian Experience*, 64.

"Every Man"—No Limit in Scope[28]

That we may present every man perfect in Christ Jesus (Col. 1:28).

Paul is absolutely sure that "every man" may be made perfect in Christ. The repetition of "every man" in this passage is a challenge to the idea put forward by some teachers in the Early Church, that perfection is the exclusive privilege of an elite group within the community of believers. The apostle is challenging this snobbish idea. The gospel reserves no such exclusive privileges for the select few. *Perfection is within the reach of all, by the power of Christ!*

In the Sermon on the Mount, Jesus commands us to be perfect. "You have heard that it used to be said '*Thou shalt love thy neighbor and hate thine enemy,*' but I tell you, Love your enemies, and pray for those who persecute you, so that you may be sons of your Heavenly Father. For he makes his sun rise upon evil men as well as good, and he sends his rain upon honest and dishonest men alike.

"For if you love only those who love you, what credit is that to you? Even tax collectors do that! And if you exchange greetings only with your own circle, are you doing anything exceptional? Even the pagans do that much. No, you are to be perfect, like your Heavenly Father" (Matt. 5:43-48, Phillips). Every disciple *must* be perfect! Christ's ethic is an ethic of perfection—perfection in love. It is this forgiving, merciful love, this Godlike caring for all men, which is the very badge of our discipleship. Christ makes *no exclusions* when He commands, "You are to be perfect, like your Heavenly Father." The *law* of Christ *requires* perfect love.

---

28. William M. Greathouse, in *The Holiness Pulpit, No. 2*, comp. James McGraw, 10-12.

William M. Greathouse (1919—) is a general superintendent in the Church of the Nazarene. Born in Van Buren, Ark., all of his roots are in the South.

Holding degrees from Lambuth College, Trevecca Nazarene College, and Vanderbilt University, for 23 years he pastored in five churches in Tennessee.

Even while pastoring he joined the faculty of Trevecca in 1946 as a part-time teacher. Elected as dean of religion in 1955, he became Trevecca's president in 1963.

In 1968 Dr. Greathouse was elected president of Nazarene Theological Seminary, and after eight years of this educational ministry was chosen to be a general superintendent.

Amid pastoral, educational, and administrative duties, Dr. Greathouse has carried on a significant writing ministry. His biblical and theological contributions include commentaries on Habakkuk, Zechariah, Malachi, and Romans. He authored *The Fullness of the Spirit* and a historical study of Wesleyan thought, *From the Apostles to Wesley*. He has also coauthored *Introduction to Wesleyan Theology* and *Exploring Christian Holiness, Vol. 2*.

But what about the gospel of Christ? The *gospel* of Christ *promises* perfection. This is clearly Paul's argument in the third chapter of Second Corinthians, where he is showing the superiority of the new covenant over the old covenant given at Sinai. As the mediator of the old covenant, Moses ascended Mount Sinai, where he enjoyed face-to-face communion with the Lord. Coming down from the mount, he put a veil on his face to hide the glory which shone on his countenance. Moses represents a select company of Old Testament worthies who were granted the exceptional privilege of a sanctifying communion with God. Paul vividly contrasts this privileged holiness of the Old Testament with the universal holiness now available to those who worship God through Christ. "*But we all,*" he assures us who know God under the terms of the new covenant, "WE ALL, beholding as in a glass the glory of the Lord, are changed into the same image from glory to glory, even as by the Spirit of the Lord" (2 Cor. 3:18, emphasis mine).

In Old Testament times there was a spiritual aristocracy; a *few* were permitted to ascend the mount of spiritual transfiguration—Enoch, Noah, Abraham, Moses, Isaiah. But in the gospel dispensation we enjoy a spiritual democracy; "*we all*" may climb that mount of face-to-face communion and be transfigured into the likeness of Christ.

Furthermore, in contrast to the *fading* glory which eventually disappeared from Moses' countenance, we may know a *progressively increasing* glory. "We are not like Moses, who veiled his face to prevent the Israelites from seeing its fading glory. . . . But all of us who are Christians have no veils on our faces, but reflect like mirrors the glory of the Lord. We are transfigured by the Spirit of the Lord in ever-increasing splendor into his own image" (2 Cor. 3:13, 18, Phillips). Or as the *Revised Standard Version* renders verse 18, "We all, with unveiled face, beholding the glory of the Lord, are being changed into his likeness from one degree of glory to another; for this comes from the Lord who is the Spirit."

The heights of Christian perfection are within the reach of *every believer,* by the power of the Spirit of Christ!

THE TESTIMONY OF DR. W. L. SURBROOK[29]

God has a sweet, clear, definite second work of grace for every unsanctified soul, and when it comes it will fully satisfy.

---

29. *Flames of Living Fire,* 109-12.

Walter Lewis Surbrook (1891—) is a general superintendent emeritus of the Wesleyan church. Converted and sanctified at 21 years of age, he was ordained in 1920. Dr.

With a background of nearly three generations that were saturated and deeply dyed with the Adventist teaching and stamped by sin, together with gross ignorance of the Scriptures and the way of salvation, there was little or no clear gospel light in my soul.

Born on a farm in Michigan, where I remained quite closely until after having passed the eighth grade, I entered the city high school. This kept me away from home much of my time. During my high school days the Holy Spirit sent a very humble farmer preacher into the community to preach the gospel. The revival was held in the country schoolhouse where I had attended grade school.

With plenty of prejudice, conceit, ignorance, and wariness I attended the meeting on my weekends at home. The minister of the Word was very tender, full of tact, sweetness, and grace; and soon the schoolhouse was filled with hungry, inquisitive listeners. His humble, gracious presentation of truth soon won the confidence of the people.

On Sunday night, March 17, 1912, the first real break came in the meeting, and I was the first soul that night at the altar. It took the Holy Spirit but a few minutes to tender my soul and lead me to genuine godly sorrow and repentance for sin. About 9:20 . . . God for Christ's sake pardoned all my sins, and at a flash I was born again and at once became a new creature in Christ Jesus.

With a background of teaching that the Holy Spirit was merely a divine emanation or influence from the Father and Son, light on His gracious work of cleansing dawned upon me slowly. As the minister preached on the "second rest," "second work of grace," the "carnal nature," and the "old man," I sat with an open heart, wondering whose father he was talking about. Frankly I did not know who the "old man" was.

There was no disposition, however, in my heart to resent the truth. The newfound joy, peace, and victory gave me a hungering thirst for more of what I already possessed. God had given me victory over the world, and my soul was filled with a new warmth, fire, and victory I had neither known nor heard before. "As the hart panteth after the water brooks," so my soul panted after God and righteousness (Ps. 42:1). Except at times of bubbling blessings and spiritual ecstasy, however, my soul thirsted, hungered, yearned, and cried for a "something" I did not possess; yet I was unable to name scripturally or define clearly my need.

HUNGER

Surbrook ministered as pastor, evangelist, college teacher, and president. Then from 1931 until retirement he served in the general superintendency of the Pilgrim Holiness church (later merged with the Wesleyan Methodist church).

There was a constant eagerness in my heart to please God and to walk in all the light He shed upon my path. The Holy Spirit had sent me back over my path to make restitutions and rectify my wrongs. My whole life was changed, for now I was faithfully attending the Sunday School, prayer meetings, and church. The newfound life of joy and peace was now leading me into praying, testifying, and praising God. I had experienced a complete change of heart and life and was now walking with Him, but was not yet sanctified.

As I walked with Him the best I knew how, He gradually deepened the hunger of my soul. To lead me into entire sanctification, He did not bless me more, but rather "unblessed" me or in a measure withheld the blessing, and to that very degree the hunger deepened. Gradually my soul was filled with an insatiable thirst. With the ebb and flow of His blessings, the thirst deepened and the hunger increased.

In response to this hungering and thirsting I was again found at the altar; this time I was not seeking pardon, but purity. My soul was not in the dark, and neither was there any condemnation upon it. I knew I was saved and walking in all the light while fellowshiping with Him and His people, and yet I knew I needed something more. There was no guilt upon my soul, or stain upon my record, but there was inbred sin within my life that needed to be eradicated.

In seeking the fullness of the Spirit in heart cleansing, I knew that the time element did not enter into it. It was not a question of how long I sought but of making a full consecration to God and believing Him to purify my heart. It is very doubtful if I sought at that altar over 20 minutes until every condition was met; and, as faith took hold, the sweet, cleansing Holy Spirit purified my heart. As the quiet, assuring evidence came, a sweet restfulness came over my soul, and at once I knew He had sanctified me.

There was no outward demonstration, but a sweet inward assurance. Since then I have seen many shout and demonstrate hilariously when sanctified, and I have shouted "Amen" with them; but it did not work that way with me. Very few people ever experience this . . . grace in exactly the same manner, and nobody should try to get it the same way or try to imitate others. God has a sweet, clear, definite second work of grace for every unsanctified soul, and when it comes it will fully satisfy.

Some have asked . . . if it is possible for one to have as clear and **ASSURANCE** as definite an experience in entire sanctification as he received when he was converted. Let me assure you, my friend, that it is possible. You may not act the same, nor act like others, but He can and will give you as clear and as definite an experience when sanctified as you received when you were born again.

To support this fact let us quote from John Wesley . . . He declared that "no one ought to think that the work is done until there is added the witness of the Spirit, testifying to his entire sanctification as clearly as his regeneration."

It is now nearly 37 years since God sanctified me, and may I assure you I would not consider living one hour without His sweet, abiding presence in my life, for all these years my soul has been safely anchored.

The Second Blessing

Entire sanctification is experienced as a second blessing of grace subsequent to regeneration.

Therefore leaving the principles of the doctrine of Christ, let us go on unto perfection; not laying again the foundation of repentance from dead works, and of faith toward God (Heb. 6:1).

Draw nigh to God, and he will draw nigh to you. Cleanse your hands, ye sinners; and purify your hearts, ye double minded (James 4:8).

Then Philip went down to the city of Samaria, and preached Christ unto them. . . . When they believed Philip preaching the things concerning the kingdom of God, and the name of Jesus Christ, they were baptized, both men and women. . . . Now when the apostles which were at Jerusalem heard that Samaria had received the word of God, they sent unto them Peter and John: who, when they were come down, prayed for them, that they might receive the Holy Ghost: (for as yet he was fallen upon none of them: only they were baptized in the name of the Lord Jesus.) Then laid they their hands on them, and they received the Holy Ghost (Acts 8:5, 12, 14-17).

THE SECOND BLESSING[30]

We have not spoken in detail of the Wesleyan term "second blessing," a term that Wesley used infrequently. This term, though not found in the Scriptures, is, nevertheless, as we believe, scriptural. Wesley said that sanctification is "a second blessing, properly so-called."

---

30. Chapman, *Terminology of Holiness*, 66.

By this he seemed to mean that it is second to justification, and the only "blessing" in this life that stands on the same level of urgency and meaning with justification. The fact then that there are "thousands of blessings" in the course of the Christian life does in no sense invalidate "the second blessing," as it does not invalidate the first blessing of justification.

The treatment this term has received at the hand of critics has served rather to enhance its value and to increase its usefulness. In their endeavor to demote the term, critics have the more closely identified it with the grace and estate it was invented to describe.

John Wesley did not make extended use of the term "second blessing," and in his day no one seems to have made any special attack upon it. Wesley wisely preferred Scripture terms or terms that are a little better identified with Scripture expressions; and in this, as in many other things, we do well to imitate his example. This we say without intentionally yielding in the least the idea expressed by this term, and with no thought that it shall or should be discarded altogether.

*   *   *

> *Breathe, oh, breathe Thy loving Spirit*
> *Into ev'ry troubled breast!*
> *Let us all in Thee inherit;*
>   *Let us find that second rest.*
> *Take away our bent to sinning;*
>   *Alpha and Omega be.*
> *End of faith, as its Beginning,*
>   *Set our hearts at liberty.*
>   —Charles Wesley, 1707-88

The Double Need and the Double Cure[31]

The penitent convicted of his sins seeks divine forgiveness. The believer convicted of the depravity of his nature sighs for inward purity. The one inquires, How can the sins which are past be forgiven? The other asks, How can I be cleansed from conscious impurity? We are guilty for what we have done, but we were depraved before we were responsible for our doing. The existence of both original and actual sin has always been accepted by the Christian Church as a scriptural doctrine.

---

31. Cook, *New Testament Holiness*, 24-26.

It is because sin exists in this twofold character, as an act and as a state, that salvation assumes a twofold aspect or is applied in two forms. For guilt there is forgiveness, for depravity there is cleansing. Forgiveness is complete forgiveness, but forgiveness can only extend to actual transgression. A mother puts a clean dress on her child and says, "Now, this must not be soiled." But the child disobeys. The mother may forgive the child for her disobedience, but she cannot forgive the dress clean; she must wash it. So God may forgive the wrong we do, but He cannot forgive a depraved heart. Depravity is removed by purgation or cleansing. This is in perfect harmony with the Scriptures. Zechariah represents the fountain of Atonement as opened to meet this double need—pardon for sin (guilt), and the purity for uncleanness (depravity). John's teaching is exactly the same. "If we confess our sins, [God] is faithful and just to forgive us our sins [guilt], and to cleanse us from all unrighteousness [depravity]" (1 John 1:9). . . .

This twofold provision for the two forms in which sin exists runs all through the Scriptures. It was typified in the history of God's ancient Israel when they crossed the Red Sea and the Jordan in leaving Egypt and entering Canaan. We enter the holy place by regeneration, but let us not forget that *after the second veil* is the Tabernacle, which is called the "holy of holies" (cf. Heb. 9:3).

We do not deny that in some instances divine forgiveness and complete inward cleansing may have been experienced at one and the same moment, but certainly that is not the usual order in which God works. Both Mr. Wesley and Dr. Adam Clarke inform us that they never met with a single instance when God both pardoned guilt and purified the heart at the same time. The explanation is that God's work is always in harmony with man's faith. The work wrought and the blessing obtained are in accordance with the faith exercised. God bestows what the soul's intelligence perceives to be its need, and what faith humbly claims.

The faith of the sinner seeking forgiveness is limited by the view his intelligence takes of his necessity. His all-pervading desire is to be pardoned. He is guilty, and must be forgiven. Every other thought is swallowed up in the sense he has of his need of divine mercy. His prayer is, "God be merciful to me a sinner" (Luke 18:13). It is this prayer God hears and answers. All his sins are forgiven, fully forgiven for Christ's sake. He receives according to his faith.

But as yet he knows little of the deep depravity of his heart. God graciously tempers His revelations of our need to our weakness. . . .

It would paralyze the faith and extinguish the hope of many if they had revealed to them their inward corruption when they first see and feel their guilt and danger. Not until the souls can bear the revelation does the Spirit of God reveal "the depths of inbred sin." There is a conviction of our need of cleansing analogous to the conviction of guilt and danger which precedes our pardon and renewal. A painful sense of need is wrought when the Holy Spirit discovers to us the plague of our hearts, the abominations which lurk and fester within the chambers of our souls. Under His all-searching and piercing gaze, the sense of sin within becomes deeper and more poignant, until, deeply humbled we bewail our condition, and cry with the Psalmist, "Create in me a clean heart, O God; and renew a right spirit within me" (Ps. 51:10). It is then, when our intelligence apprehends the soul's deep need of inward purity, that definite prayer is offered, definite faith is exercised, and God speaks the *second* time, "Be clean."

SENSE OF NEED

In a Moment

Because entire sanctification is God's gift in response to faith, it occurs in a moment of time, just as God's forgiveness comes in an instant.

When the day of Pentecost had come, they were all together in one place. And suddenly a sound came from heaven like the rush of a mighty wind, and it filled all the house where they were sitting. . . . And they were all filled with the Holy Spirit and began to speak in other tongues, as the Spirit gave them utterance (Acts 2:1-2, 4, RSV).

While Peter was still saying this, the Holy Spirit fell on all who heard the word. And the believers from among the circumcised who came with Peter were amazed, because the gift of the Holy Spirit had been poured out even on the Gentiles (Acts 10:44-45, RSV).

Is Sanctification Crisis or Process?[32]

Is this death to sin and renewal in love gradual or instantaneous? A man may be dying for some time; yet he does not, properly

---

32. John Wesley, *A Plain Account of Christian Perfection*, 62.

speaking, die, till the soul is separated from the body; and in that instant, he lives the life of eternity. In this manner, he may be dying to sin for some time; yet he is not dead to sin, till sin is separated from his soul; and in that instant, he lives the full life of love. And as the change undergone, when the body dies, is of a different kind, and infinitely greater than any we had known before, yea, such as till then, it is impossible to conceive; so the change wrought, when the soul died to sin, is of a different kind, and infinitely greater than any before, and than any can conceive, till he experiences it. Yet he still grows in grace, in the knowledge of Christ, in the love and image of God; and will do so, not only till death, but to all eternity.

*   *   *

The blessing by faith I receive from above.
Oh, glory! My soul is made perfect in love.
My prayer has prevailed, and this moment I know
The Blood is applied, I am whiter than snow.

—JAMES NICHOLSON, 1828-76

SANCTIFICATION AS A CRISIS EXPERIENCE[33]

As we turn to the testimony of the Word, we find three classes of evidence that entire sanctification is, in fact, instantaneous and not gradual, a crisis experience and not an endless process.

There is, first, the analogy to justification and the new birth. Second, there is the testimony of the terms used to describe the work —terms which customarily refer to actions completed at a given point in time. And, third, there is the logic of example found in the Bible. Let us look briefly at each.

1. *The Analogy with the New Birth.* Consider first the analogy found in the Bible between justification or the new birth and sanctifi-

---

33. W. T. Purkiser, *Conflicting Concepts of Holiness,* 32-42.

Westlake T. Purkiser (1910—) was born to a God-fearing family in Oakland, Calif. He graduated from Pasadena College (now Point Loma Nazarene College). Ordained in 1932, Westlake pastored in southern California for seven years. In 1937 he joined the staff of his alma mater, and from 1948 to 1957 served as president of Pasadena College.

In that year he came to Nazarene Theological Seminary as professor of English Bible. Four years later Dr. Purkiser was elected editor of the *Herald of Holiness,* the official organ of the Church of the Nazarene. Here he served until his retirement.

In 1975 the Christian Holiness Association honored Dr. Purkiser as "Holiness Exponent of the Year." At that time he had written hundreds of editorials and 26 books—most of them dealing with some facet of holy living.

cation or holiness. There are great points of similarity between these two works of divine grace.

Both justification and sanctification are products of divine love: John 3:16, "For God so loved the world, that he gave his only begotten Son, that whosoever believeth in him should not perish, but have everlasting life"; and Eph. 5:25-27, "Husbands, love your wives, even as Christ also loved the church, and gave himself for it; that he might sanctify and cleanse it with the washing of water by the word . . . that it should be holy and without blemish."

Both justification and sanctification are manifestations of God's good, acceptable, and perfect will: 1 Tim. 2:3-4, "For this is good and acceptable in the sight of God our Saviour; who will have all men to be saved, and to come unto the knowledge of the truth"; and Heb. 10:10, "By the which will [that is, the will of God as accomplished by Christ in His atoning death] we are sanctified through the offering of the body of Jesus Christ once for all."

Both justification and sanctification are accomplished through the wonderful light of God's Word: 1 Pet. 1:23, "Being born again, not of corruptible seed, but of incorruptible, by the word of God, which liveth and abideth for ever"; and John 17:17, "Sanctify them through thy truth: thy word is truth."

Both justification and sanctification are wrought in the heart by the effective agency of the Holy Spirit of God: Titus 3:5, "Not by HOLY works of righteousness which we have done, but according to SPIRIT his mercy he saved us, by the washing of regeneration, and renewing of the Holy Ghost," and 2 Thess. 2:13, "But we are bound to give thanks alway to God for you, brethren beloved of the Lord, because God hath from the beginning chosen you to salvation through sanctification of the Spirit and belief of the truth."

Both justification and sanctification are purchased at the cost of Christ's shed blood on Calvary's cross: Rom. 5:9, "Much more then, being now justified by his blood, we shall be saved from wrath through him"; and Heb. 13:12, "Wherefore Jesus also, that he might sanctify the people with his own blood, suffered without the gate."

Both justification and sanctification are brought to the individual believer's heart in response to faith: Rom. 5:1, "Therefore being justified by faith, we have peace with God through our Lord Jesus Christ"; and Acts 26:18, "To open their eyes, and to turn them from darkness to light, and from the power of Satan unto God, that they may receive forgiveness of sins, and inheritance among them which are sanctified by faith that is in me."

Now, virtually all Bible-believing Christians recognize that the new birth, justification, is not gradual but instantaneous. It is an act of God which takes place at a given point in a believer's life. But if both justification and sanctification are products of the same divine love, the same will of God, the same Holy Word, the same blessed Spirit, the same redeeming Blood, and the same human condition, faith—is there any valid reason for supposing that one is instantaneous while the other is gradual? If justification is instantaneous, there is certainly no reason why sanctification, wrought by the same agency, should not be equally the act of a moment.

As a matter of fact, every argument which proves the instantaneity of regeneration is just as forceful when applied to sanctification. If the evidence for the immediacy of sanctification be rejected, there is no logical ground on which to base proof for the immediacy of justification.

2. *The Testimony of the Terms.* We next look briefly at the terms used to describe this second work in the Christian heart. Without exception, the root action is such as to imply that which occurs at a particular point in time.

The verb "to sanctify" is defined in its twofold meaning as "to set apart" and "to make holy." There may, it is true, be a gradual setting apart, a gradual making holy. But the action described is much more naturally thought of as momentary and immediate. Since "to sanctify" in its strictly New Testament sense is always spoken of as a divine act, the burden of proof ought naturally to rest upon those who allege sanctification to be gradual.

Then, this experience is spoken of as a baptism: "John truly baptized with water; but ye shall be baptized with the Holy Ghost not many days hence" (Acts 1:5). Baptism is a term which always implies action at a given point—never that which is drawn out over a long period of time, and perhaps never completed until death. Gradual baptism is an absurdity—whether it be a baptism with water, or the baptism with the Holy Spirit.

It is spoken of as a crucifixion or death. Rom. 6:6: "Knowing this, that our old man is crucified with him, that the body of sin might be destroyed, that henceforth we should not serve sin." Gal. 2:20: "I am crucified with Christ: nevertheless I live; yet not I, but Christ liveth in me: and the life which I now live in the flesh I live by the faith of the Son of God, who loved me, and gave himself for me." Col. 3:5: "Mortify [treat as dead] therefore your members which are upon the earth."

It may be granted that one may be long a-dying. But death always occurs in a moment. Life may wane over a period of time, but it departs the body at a given instant. Gradual death is only a figure of speech for a mortal illness. Death itself is always instantaneous.

Sanctification involves cleansing, purifying. . . . Cleansing and purification may be continuous processes, but the natural meaning of these words indicates that there is always an initial moment when the cleansing and purification begins. To make it gradual is to read into it something which the words themselves certainly do not imply.

This experience is described as a "gift" to be "received." "The gift of the Holy Ghost" is frequently mentioned throughout the New Testament, often as "the promise of the Father." Jesus, in Luke 11:13, said, "If ye, then being evil, know how to give good gifts unto your children: how much more shall your heavenly Father give the Holy Spirit to them that ask him?" Gal. 3:14, ". . . that we might receive the promise of the Spirit through faith." Is it not obvious that a gift is something which passes into the possession of its receiver at some given moment? The gradual giving of a gift is a confusion of terms.

Sanctification is variously described as putting off the old man and putting on the new (Eph. 4:20-24); it is destroying the body of sin (Rom. 6:6); it is being filled with the Spirit (Eph. 5:18); it is to be sealed with that Holy Spirit of promise (1:13).

However, to summarize: "to set apart," "to make holy," "to baptize," "to crucify," "to put to death," "to give," "to receive," "to put off," "to put on," "to destroy," "to be filled," "to be sealed"—these are all verbs describing actions which take place most naturally at a definite time and place, and which do not admit of degrees. They all testify to the fact that sanctification is a crisis experience, not a long-drawn-out and never-completed process of growth.

3. *The Logic of Example.* There is a final line of evidence for the instantaneity of entire sanctification, based upon scriptural examples of this grace.

The experience of Isaiah recorded in Isaiah 6 may be regarded as a type of the believer's experience of entire sanctification. Isaiah had been a prophet of God during part of the reign of King Uzziah, as he tells us in chapter 1. But it was in the year the king died that God's prophet experienced his remarkable cleansing.

In the Temple worshiping, Isaiah saw the Lord high and lifted up, and heard the seraphs' song, "Holy, holy, holy, is the Lord of hosts." That praise of God's holiness found no echo in the prophet's heart, and he who had previously called "woes" on the people now cried out for himself, "Woe is me! for I am undone; because I am a man of unclean lips, and I dwell in the midst of a people of unclean lips."

But the divine response was not long in coming. An angel flew with golden tongs and a live coal from the altar, touched his lips, and said, "Lo, this hath touched thy lips; and thine iniquity is taken away, and thy sin purged." This all took place in less time than it takes to describe. It was not by growth or spiritual development that Isaiah's iniquity was taken away and his sin purged. It was by a divine act at a given time.

In the New Testament, all examples of the baptism with the Spirit and entire sanctification are found in the Book of Acts. They are four in number.

The first involves the disciples of Jesus, whose names were written in heaven (Luke 10:20); who were not of the world (John 14:16-17; 17:14); who belonged to Christ (17:6, 11); of whom not one was lost (v. 12); and who had kept God's words (v. 6). While these clearly justified persons "were all with one accord in one place," "suddenly there came a sound from heaven as of a rushing mighty wind," "and they were all filled with the Holy Ghost" (Acts 2:1-2, 4). There was no gradual growing into this. It came with the unexpected suddenness of a lightning stroke from the skies.

The second example found in the Book of Acts was recorded of the young church in Samaria. Philip had ventured into Samaria after the martyrdom of Stephen. His preaching met with a ready response. The people believed and were baptized in large numbers. Acts 8:8 records that "there was great joy in the city."

Hearing of this revival and the success of the ministry of the Word, the apostles at Jerusalem sent Peter and John to Samaria. When they came, we read that they prayed for these young converts "that they might receive the Holy Ghost: (for as yet he was fallen upon none of them: only they were baptized in the name of the Lord Jesus.) Then laid they their hands on them, and they received the Holy Ghost" (Acts 8:15-17).

It is sometimes fashionable to reject the example of the disciples of Christ as not truly typical, because they lived under two dispensations. Thus, it is claimed, Pentecost was in effect the completion of their regeneration, and every believer now receives the baptism with the Holy Spirit at the moment he first receives Christ as his Savior. How utterly false this argument is, certainly is demonstrated by the example of the Samaritan church.

The Samaritans believed and were baptized in the new dispensation of the Spirit, and they were afterward filled with the Holy Ghost at a given instant of time.

The third example concerns the devout Roman centurion Cornelius, and members of his household. Cornelius is described in no uncertain terms by God's inspired penman. He was a devout man, he feared God with all his house, he prayed constantly, and his prayers were accepted by God (Acts 10:2, 4). Peter, arriving at Cornelius' house, with quick spiritual insight, said: "Of a truth, I perceive that God is no respecter of persons: but in every nation he that feareth him, and worketh righteousness, is accepted with him. The word which God sent unto the children of Israel, preaching peace by Jesus Christ: (he is Lord of all:) that word, I say, ye know, which was published throughout all Judaea" (vv. 34-37).

As Peter continued to speak, suddenly the Holy Spirit fell on those who listened. This was not gradual but instantaneous. That Peter himself regarded the events at Cornelius' home as parallel with and identical to the events at Pentecost is clearly seen in his report to the council at Jerusalem: God, knowing their hearts, bore witness and gave the Holy Spirit, even as He had at Pentecost, purifying their hearts by faith (Acts 15:8-9).

The fourth instance given in the Acts is described in 18:24 to 19:7. It concerns the disciples at Ephesus. . . .

At the close of the apostle Paul's long ministry in Corinth, he, in company with Aquila and Priscilla, his colaborers, crossed the Aegean Sea to the mainland of Asia and the city of Ephesus. Paul himself spent only a brief time preaching in the synagogue at Ephesus; leaving Aquila and Priscilla there, he went on toward Antioch.

While Paul was gone, a man named Apollos came to Ephesus. Apollos is described as eloquent, mighty in the Scriptures, instructed in the way of the Lord, and speaking and teaching diligently the things of the Lord, although, as far as his baptism was concerned, he knew only the baptism of John. Recognizing the potential greatness of Apollos' ministry, Aquila and Priscilla took him and, as we read, taught him the way of God more perfectly (Acts 18:24-28).

Shortly after Apollos left his newfound friends to go to Corinth, Paul came back to Ephesus. Whatever their origin, whether as converts of Aquila and Priscilla, or Apollos, Paul found in Ephesus a nucleus of 12 disciples. Examining them, he learned that they had not received the Holy Ghost, at least in the measure of Pentecost. But after Paul had baptized them in the name of Christ, he prayed, laid hands upon them, and they were filled with the Holy Spirit.

The misunderstanding which surrounds this incident has to do with the spiritual status of the Ephesian disciples. Because they disclaimed knowledge of the Holy Spirit, and because they had received only the baptism of John, some have contended that they were unregenerate persons. However, that these 12 men were genuine children of God, and that this was for them a second instantaneous experience, we firmly believe to be the teaching of this passage. Let us examine the important considerations here.

First, the men are described as disciples (Acts 19:1), and "the disciples were called Christians first in Antioch" (11:26). That is, the designation "Christian" and "disciple" were used interchangeably in the Book of Acts. There is no instance of the use of the term "disciple" in the Acts for any other than true believers in Christ.

Second, Paul did not challenge the fact of their faith. "Have ye received the Holy Ghost since ye believed?" he asked them (Acts 19:2). Whether the original be translated as it is thus in the Authorized Version, or translated as it is in the *American Standard* and *Revised Standard* versions, "Did you receive the Holy Spirit when you believed?" makes not the slightest bit of difference so far as this point is concerned. In either case, it is admitted that they had believed, and it is evident that they had not received the Holy Ghost in the sense in which Paul speaks.

Third, that they were ignorant of the receiving of the Holy Ghost does not mean that they had not been converted. Dwight L. Moody asserted that for many years after his conversion He did not know that the Holy Spirit was a Person, and that many believers today are as ignorant of the person and ministry of the Holy Spirit as these Ephesian believers.[34]

Fourth, that these men had only the baptism of John does not prove that they were unconverted in the full Christian sense of the word. In fact, the baptism of John is spoken of as a "baptism of repentance [unto] the remission of sins" (Mark 1:4). Apollos, instructed in the way of the Lord, fervent in the Spirit, speaking and teaching diligently the things of the Lord, knew only the baptism of John.

---

34. *Secret Power,* 16.

Fifth, that Paul was satisfied with the faith of these disciples is seen in the fact that he rebaptized them in the name of the Lord Jesus Christ before they were filled with the Holy Spirit. If they were only at that time being regenerated in the Christian sense [when "the Holy Ghost came on them" (v. 6)], then Paul was guilty of baptizing a group of unconverted men. . . .

Finally, that receiving the Holy Spirit refers to something more than being born again by the Spirit and led by the Spirit is testified to by no less authority than the Lord Jesus himself. In John 14:15-17, we read: "If ye love me, keep my commandments. And I will pray the Father, and he shall give you another Comforter, that he may abide with you for ever; even the Spirit of truth; *whom the world cannot receive,* because it seeth him not, neither knoweth him: but ye know him; for he dwelleth with you, and shall be in you."

Here Jesus indicates clearly that the world, and those who are of the world, cannot receive the Holy Spirit. One must know Him before receiving Him. One must have the Spirit with him before he can have the Spirit in him. While the word is used only four times in the New Testament (John 14:17; Acts 8:15-17; Acts 19:2; and Gal. 3:14), in each case it is made clear that it is the believer alone who is in a position to *receive* the Holy Spirit.

I would not put too much weight on the argument from analogy, but it is surely no accident that the inspired writers of the New Testament chose the figures *birth* of the Spirit to represent regeneration and *baptism* with the Spirit to describe the "second blessing properly so-called." Obviously, in the order of nature, birth *must* precede baptism . . . a child has to be born before he can be baptized. . . .

Here then is the logic of example. Each instance was characterized by immediacy. Each took place at a given point in the experience of the persons involved. Nowhere is there a trace of sanctification by growth, a long and painful process of self-discipline, never completed until the Rapture. If it is of faith, then it is not of works, lest any man should boast (Rom. 11:6; Eph. 2:9).

*   *   *

> *Blessed be the name of Jesus!*
> *I'm so glad He took me in.*
> *He's forgiven my transgressions;*
> *He has cleansed my heart from sin.*

Refrain:
I will praise Him! I will praise Him!
  Praise the Lamb for sinners slain!
Give Him glory, all ye people,
  For His blood can wash away each stain.
        —MARGARET J. HARRIS, 19th Century

Names

Entire sanctification is also known as Christian perfection, perfect love, heart purity, the baptism with the Holy Spirit, being filled with the Spirit, the fullness of the blessing, full salvation, the deeper life, Christian holiness, scriptural holiness, the rest of faith, and the promise of the Father.

May God himself, the God of peace, *sanctify*[35] you through and through. May your whole spirit, soul and body be kept blameless at the coming of our Lord Jesus Christ. The one who calls you is faithful and he will do it (1 Thess. 5:23-24, NIV).

Be *perfect*, therefore, as your heavenly Father is perfect (Matt. 5:48, NIV).

If we love one another, God dwelleth in us, and his love is *perfected* in us (1 John 4:12).

Blessed are the *pure in heart,* for they will see God (Matt. 5:8, NIV).

But after me will come one who . . . will *baptize you with the Holy Spirit* and with fire (Matt. 3:11, NIV).

When the day of Pentecost came . . . All of them were *filled with the Holy Spirit* (Acts 2:1, 4, NIV).

I know that when I come to you, I will come in *the full measure of the blessing of Christ* (Rom. 15:29, NIV).

I pray . . . that you may be filled to the measure of all the *fullness of God* (Eph. 3:17, 19, NIV).

The Spirit searches all things, even *the deep things of God* (1 Cor. 2:10, NIV).

Make every effort to live in peace with all men and to be *holy;* without *holiness* no one will see the Lord (Heb. 12:14, NIV).

Now we who have believed enter that *rest* (Heb. 4:3, NIV).

---

35. In these scriptures key words have been italicized to show their connection and sequence paralleling the introductory statement.

Wait for *the gift my Father promised,* which you have heard me speak about (Acts 1:4, NIV).

Evaluating a common practice in the Holiness Movement, Dr. J. B. Chapman writes:

It has been the practice all along to allow for certain provincialisms in the terminology of Bible holiness, as the preferences of people have suggested. Therefore people have used the term that best fitted their denominational experience, home training, and other factors that served to give content to their words. We would not criticize, but rather commend this liberality; for in the process of giving content to special terminology the truth is preached, and the reality behind all terminology is made clear.[36]

Dr. A. M. Hills quotes John Wesley:

"Both my brother Charles and I maintain that Christian perfection is that love of God and our neighbor which implies deliverance from all sin. It is the loving God with all our heart, mind, soul, and strength. This implies that no wrong temper, none contrary to love, remains in the soul." "Certainly sanctification (in the proper sense) is an instantaneous deliverance from all sin."

Dr. Hills continues:

Notice during the different years of Wesley's life, what terms he used to express it. 1739, "Renewal of our heart after the image of God." "The mind that was in Christ." 1741, "Deliverance from inward and outward sin." "The evil nature, the body of sin destroyed." 1742, "Cleansed from all the filth of self and pride." "To perfect health restored." "To sin entirely dead." 1757, "Having received the first fruits of the Spirit, patiently and earnestly wait for the great change whereby every root of bitterness may be torn up." 1758, "A heart entirely pure." "Perfected in love and saved from sin." 1761, "Delivered from the root of bitterness." "Cleansed from all unrighteousness." "After being convinced of inbred sin, in a moment they feel all faith and love, no pride, self-will, or anger." 1762, "Full renewal in the image of God." "In an instant emptied of all sin and filled with God." "An instantaneous deliverance from all sin." "Cleansed from sin, meaning all sinful tempers." 1763, "The second blessing." "Destruction of the roots of sin in one moment." "Pure love." 1765, "Love

---

36. *The Terminology of Holiness,* 82-83. For an extended discussion of holiness terminology see pp. 101-15 in this vol. 6 (GHC).

taking up the whole heart, and filling it with all holiness." "The soul pure from every spot, clean from all unrighteousness." "Sin destroyed in a moment." 1768, "The image of God stamped on the heart." "The mind that was in Christ, enabling us to walk as Christ walked." "The perfection I have taught these forty years." "I mean loving God with all our heart and our neighbor as ourselves. I pin down all opposers to this definition; no evasion; no shifting the question." 1770, "An entire deliverance from sin and recovery of the whole image of God." "A second change, whereby we shall be saved from all sin and perfected in love." 1774, "The second blessing, properly so called, deliverance from the root of bitterness, from inbred as well as actual sin." 1781, "Christ in a pure and sinless heart, reigning the Lord of every motion." 1785, "A full deliverance from all sin and a renewal in the whole image of God." "Full salvation now by simple faith." 1789, "The whole image of God wherein you were created." "O be satisfied with nothing less and you will surely secure it by simple faith."[37]

EXPERIENCE MORE THAN A NAME[38]

The greatest need today is not exact definition, but that sacred impulse to claim this blessing that is promised so many times in so many ways in the Bible. The year before he died, Samuel Chadwick wrote: "My guides led me astray . . . it was not a doctrine I was seeking. What I needed was an experience." The conclusion of the matter is that the way for us is to bring in prayer to God any of the great promises, that the Holy Spirit is pressing upon us, maybe for instance, "The blood of Jesus . . . his Son cleanseth us from all sin" (1 John 1:7), and say something like this: "Lord, I do not know exactly what this means, but it suggests something I have not got, and what I need; will You work this work in me?" God will not fail you; "Faithful is he that calleth you, who also will do it" (1 Thess. 5:24). So you will have the experience, and this will give you a more lucid definition, but I doubt if you will ever get a final definition. But the fullness of the blessing is offered to you now by faith.

(2) It is received instantaneously by faith now, but a gradual work of grace often precedes, and always follows. . . . The references to it are copious. We will add one more. Writing to a minister in Sheffield, Wesley said: "The work of God is undoubtedly instantaneous with

---

37. *Scriptural Holiness,* 26-28.
38. J. Baines Atkinson, *The Beauty of Holiness,* 109-10.

regard to sanctification, as well as justification, and it is no objection at all that it is gradual also. Whatever others do, it is our duty strongly and explicitly to exhort the believers to go on to perfection and to encourage them to expect perfect love by simple faith, and consequently to expect it *now*. This is the preaching which God always has blessed, and which He always will bless to those that are upright of heart."[39]

---

39. *Letters,* 7:267.

11

Steps to Seeking and Finding

In chapter 10 we have seen what the Bible and the church teach about God's plan for our sanctification. It is important to know the doctrine, but in following Christ we seek to know in order that our lives may be changed. We want to grasp the doctrine in order to discover the experience for ourselves, and to learn to live the life of holiness. In this chapter we explore how we may find God's grace of entire sanctification. Dr. A. M. Hills gives helpful counsel.

HOW TO BE SANCTIFIED WHOLLY[1]

1. *Believe it is God's will*

Do you, reader, believe that what God says is true? He says, "The promise [of the Spirit] is unto *you*, and to your children, and to all . . . even as many as the Lord our God shall call" (Acts 2:39). He says your sanctification by the Holy Spirit is His will. Do you believe it? He says He hath *called* you to sanctification. Do you believe it? Do you hear the call of the Holy Spirit in your heart now? Will you respond to Him and rise up and claim the blessing? Is this inestimable blessing for one man out of thousands—for Edwards, Finney, Moody, Fletcher, Bishop Simpson, and a few other favored souls—or is it for every regenerated child of God, and so for you? . . .

I wish the readers of these lines would pause a moment and think. Don't hurry. Can you solemnly say with a prayerful heart, "My God, I believe this baptism with the Holy Spirit is for me"?

2. *Be willing that God's blessed will should be done in you—to your sanctification and holiness*

---

1. *Holiness and Power*, 281-83.

Are you *willing* to pray the Lord's Prayer and mean it? "Thy kingdom come [in my heart], thy will be done in earth [in *me*, and by my *will*], as it is in heaven [by the angels of God]." Or are you "willing to be made willing about everything," as F. B. Meyer puts it, "at any cost to yourself"? . . .

3. Said an evangelist: "*We should be willing to forsake every sin that we know, and also the sin that we do not know. . . .*

"No matter what it may be, if there is a touch of sin about it, will you abandon it now? As God searches your heart, if He shall show you anything sinful and impure will you make this pledge to Him, as though you stood in the white light of the judgment, that you will give it up? Can you, reader, say, 'I will'?"

4. *We should be willing to give all our good things to God*

A soul winner said, "I believe a man may forsake every known sin, and pledge himself to give up every unknown sin as well, and still not be qualified for the filling of the Holy Spirit. Oh, so many fail here. There are what we call the neutral things—the *friends*, and the *ambitions*, and the *money*, and the *time*, and the *talents*—all to be turned over to God. Here many fail. . . . Let us bring out the last good thing and lay it on the altar of God.

"I preached six years before I was willing to consecrate the things that were good. Are you willing to do it—to give Him the known things and the unknown? the things that are good—the *money* and the *time*, the *talents* and the *friends*, the *husband* or *wife* or *child*, the *wisdom* and the *ignorance*, the *wealth* and the *poverty*, the *strength* and the *weaknesses*, all that you *know* or *may* know, all that you *have* or *may* have, and say, 'Lord God, it is mine no longer.'"

General Booth says, "Thus consecration has in it the nature of a REAL SACRIFICE. It is the presentation or giving away of all we have to God; a ceasing any longer to own anything which we have hitherto called our own, but all going over into God's hands for Him to order and arrange, and our taking simply the place of servants, to receive back again just what He chooses. This is no easy task, and can only be done in the might of the Holy Spirit; but, when it is done, when all is laid on the altar—body, soul, spirit, goods, reputation, all, *all*, ALL—then the fire descends and burns up all the dross and defilement of sin, and fills the soul with burning zeal and love and power. Consecration is being crucified with Christ; it means dying to all those pleasures and gratifications which flow from the undue love of self, the admiration of the world, the ownership of goods, and the inordinate love of kindred and friends which go together to make up the life and joy of the natural man. This may be painful, but we must be crucified with Christ if we are to live with Him."

Breathe on Me

TRUETT

Edwin Hatch, 1835 - 1889
Alt. by B. B. McKinney, 1886 - 1952

B. B. McKinney, 1886 - 1952

1. Ho - ly Spir - it, breathe on me, Un - til my heart is clean.
2. Ho - ly Spir - it, breathe on me; My stub-born will sub - due.
3. Ho - ly Spir - it, breathe on me; Fill me with power di - vine.
4. Ho - ly Spir - it, breathe on me, Till I am all Thine own;

Let sun-shine fill its in-most part, With not a cloud be - tween.
Teach me in words of liv - ing flame What Christ would have me do.
Kin - dle a flame of love and zeal With - in this heart of mine.
Un - til my will is lost in Thine, To live for Thee a - lone.

REFRAIN

Breathe on me, breathe on me; Ho - ly Spir - it, breathe on me.

Take Thou my heart; cleanse ev-'ry part. Ho - ly Spir - it, breathe on me.

The New Birth

The new birth is a prerequisite to entire sanctification.

Ye must be born again (John 3:7).

Therefore leaving the principles of the doctrine of Christ, let us go on unto perfection; not laying again the foundation of repentance from dead works, and of faith toward God (Heb. 6:1).

IT BEGAN WITH THE NEW BIRTH[2]

I am experiencing life with Christ as a life full of surprises, full of fascination, full of positive challenges.

I believe that the life of holiness is the cause for this experience. Isn't sanctification the highest goal of our Christian life? The goal that stands above all other goals? "Christ . . . is made [our] sanctification" (1 Cor. 1:30)!

I was 15 years of age when, according to my parents' wishes, I was to be confirmed. Brought up in the educational system of Communism, I did not look forward to this day. Neither did our pastor; he did not want to confirm me.

In our church it was customary to recite a verse of a hymn, while kneeling at the altar during the ceremony, as a promise to the Lord. In prayer, my mother had picked the following verse for me:

> *Let me, O Lord, in all things*
> *to Thy will ascribe*
> *and fully dedicate my life to Thee.*
> *Thou givest the will and strength*
> *to dedicate my heart and life to Thee alone.*
> *Take life and soul as sacrifice,*
> *Thou art my all in what I have and feel.*

The day of confirmation arrived, and my mother's verse had stirred up in me a lot of thinking. I then prayed this verse with full intent, and the pastor gave me the following Bible verse: "Blessed are the pure in heart: for they shall see God" (Matt. 5:8).

Later during a counseling session I surrendered my life to Christ. From that time on I consciously followed the Lord Jesus Christ. During this time I experienced many wonderful things. With new Christian friends, it became a very meaningful time, but there were also

---

2. Rose Marie Brasch, *Herald of Holiness*, May 15, 1986. Miss Brasch is a nurse in West Germany and a member of the Nazarene congregation in Stuttgart.

many defeats. My spiritual life was a constant up and down. I put myself under many restraints and asked myself always the question: "What would Jesus have said?" In many ways this was appropriate and good. But for me it became a point of utter defeat and resignation as my behavior and actions did not match my spiritual longings. By nature I am not a bit holy or without blame, as the Bible calls it.

Soon, for the sake of my Christian convictions, I had to flee to the West. Here I experienced loneliness at first because everything was new to me. I encountered many different Christian groups while in the midst of my nurse's training. It was not an easy time to live as a Christian.

I loved the Lord, and my life's desire was to belong to Him. He was to be my Lord, not only my Redeemer, and I wanted to serve Him with all my heart. My life was supposed to be aimed at eternity, and my sincere wish was to obtain a pure heart. But it was all so difficult for me and often against my nature.

HUNGER

Years went by in this struggle. Again and again I asked this question: "What does it mean to seek 'holiness, without which no man shall see the Lord' (Heb. 12:14)?"

I wanted to see Jesus, of course, because I loved Him. Does this mean we have to live a totally perfect life? Without any faults? How could this be possible? For this I consulted the Bible. I had a great urge to find the answer. Many ideas developed in my mind; some I tried, but again I found many to be impractical for daily living.

Today I see that this question of holiness runs through my life like a golden thread. I am convinced that Jesus knew the deepest longings of my heart and that He wanted to fulfill them.

I wanted to learn more English, and this is how I came into contact with holiness teaching. The Lord had more for me than just learning a language. The Church of the Nazarene, I heard, was a holiness church. My initial skepticism was put aside after careful examination of her doctrine. I had to admit that this church had a clear biblical message, that it was truly evangelical. What spoke the most to me was the love of the church members. They did not attend church out of fear or under pressure, and they gave me a warm welcome.

In 1980 the district assembly was held in Hanau, where Dr. Jerry Johnson emphasized the importance of the Holy Spirit for the believer. This message touched me deeply, and I surrendered my life to the work of the Holy Spirit.

Words out of Rom. 6:4 became reality for me for the first time:

"Buried with . . . Christ." This burial of the old life, in which I became conscious of many sins, took many weeks, full of tears and remorse. It seemed necessary in order to become real and not remain an illusion. First Thess. 4:3 says, "For this is the will of God, even your sanctification." I gave the Lord permission to work in me specifically in this direction. I wanted to walk in the light of 1 Thess. 5:23, "And the very God of peace sanctify you wholly."

This experience of sanctification is for me not just a one-time experience but an ongoing process. It is not an experience of constant "hallelujah," but an experience of growth.

I am today at a point where I am in the midst of the sanctified life. It is a growing and deepening experience—"from one clarity to another." Holiness means to accept God's point of view with all my strength and power and to let Him mold my character according to His image—spirit, mind, and body. We should then become one with Jesus!

The work of the Holy Spirit has become increasingly important to me. He convicts of sin, speaks judgment, and justifies. He leads us into the truth as the Comforter, not destroying our personality. Above all He wants to glorify Jesus and leads us ever to praise Him. The most precious moments of my life I spend in contemplation of this fact. Isn't it comforting to know that Jesus is changing my character and life? That He is helping me to love people in practical ways and that all my hours belong to Him. I don't ever want to miss this realization that the Holy Spirit himself is working in and with me.

I am thankful the Holy Spirit challenges me to look at my life under the light of God. Herein I see the path to true fellowship with God, to lasting peace, which the world cannot give. Peace that means a resting in Him, that we may be one with Him. This abiding in Jesus creates not only blamelessness for us but also an inner joy that I may receive His gifts of wisdom, righteousness, holiness, and full redemption.

I want to be molded by Him. I want to stand with joy before the Lord someday and praise Him with those who are pure of heart, who cast their crowns in thankfulness before the Lamb of God.

I am thankful that He has given me brothers and sisters in the local church, all over Germany, and even throughout the world— brothers and sisters who are on the way with me.

It is my desire to follow the Lord faithfully and to walk the way of sanctification until the glorious end. It is my desire to invite others to go with me. It is a precious way, the way of God!

THE NEW BIRTH AND ENTIRE SANCTIFICATION[3]

Regeneration is the beginning of purification. Entire sanctification is the finishing of that work.

Divine forgiveness and the new birth are ever coexistent and inseparable. No man receives the new name of a child of God without at the same time receiving a new nature. He becomes there and then a partaker of the divine holiness. Condemnation is removed, the culprit is forgiven, and as invariably as day follows night, a sublime change is wrought by the Holy Spirit, creating within the soul a new spiritual life, a life of loyalty and love.

The Scriptures describe this work of the Holy Spirit as a new creation, a being "born again," "born of the Spirit"; a passing "from death unto life," "quickened with Christ," and by many like expressions all indicating newness and sanctity. It is such a renewal of the soul as turns the prepondering tendencies toward God; the love of sin is destroyed, the power of sin is broken, and a desire and relish for holiness is begotten.

In a measure and to a certain extent the Christian is sanctified when he is regenerated. He is set apart for God. He is **SANCTIFICATION BEGUN** made a new creature in Christ Jesus. A new and heavenly life is breathed into him by the Holy Spirit. He is translated out of darkness into marvelous light. The dominion of sin is broken. The love of God is shed abroad in his heart; it is the incentive to obedience and [becomes] the germ of holiness. His desires, tastes, impulses, aims, and aspirations are all changed. He no longer lives unto himself; his "life is hid with Christ in God" (Col. 3:3). He has victory over the world and sin, enjoys inward peace, walks before God in newness of life, and loving God, keeps His commandments.

Regeneration is holiness begun. Whatever is of the essence of holiness is found in germ in all who are children of God. But though all the elements of holiness are imparted, the work of inward renewal is only begun, not finished, by regeneration. On this point there is harmony of faith among all the churches. They hold that regeneration does not free the soul from depravity. It introduces a power which checks the outbreaking of depravity into actual sin, but inward corruption remains, manifesting itself in a bias toward evil, in inclinations to sin, in a proneness to depart from God, a "bent to sinning." . . .

---

3. Cook, *New Testament Holiness*, 27-32.

"That a distinction exists," says Richard Watson, "between a regenerate state, and a state of entire and perfect holiness, will be generally allowed. Regeneration, as we have seen, is concomitant with justification, but the apostles, in addressing a body of believers in the churches to whom they wrote their Epistles, set before them, both in the prayers they offered on their behalf, and in the exhortations they administered, a still higher degree of deliverance from sin, as well as a higher growth in Christian virtues. Two passages only need to be quoted to prove this: 1 Thess. 5:23: 'And the very God of peace sanctify you wholly: and I pray God your whole spirit and soul and body be preserved blameless unto the coming of our Lord Jesus Christ'; 2 Cor. 7:1: 'Having therefore these promises, dearly beloved, let us cleanse ourselves from all filthiness of the flesh and spirit, perfecting holiness in the fear of God.' In both these passages deliverance from sin is the subject spoken of; the prayer in the one instance, and the exhortation in the other, goes to the extent of the entire sanctification of the 'soul' and 'spirit,' as well as of the 'flesh' or 'body,' from all sin; by which can only be meant our complete deliverance from all spiritual pollution, all inward depravation of the heart, as well as that which, expressing itself outwardly by the indulgences of the senses is called filthiness of flesh and spirit." . . .

Regeneration is the beginning of purification. Entire sanctification is the finishing of that work. Entire sanctification removes from the soul all the elements which antagonize the elements of holiness planted in regeneration. It is an elimination, as dross is separated from the gold by fire. It is an eradication, the removal of all **ERADICATION OF SIN** roots of bitterness, the seeds of sin's disease. It is a crucifixion, the putting to death of the body or the life of sin. It is such a complete renewal of the heart that sin has no longer any place within, its last remains are scattered, the war within the citadel ceases, and God reigns without a rival. . . .

This teaching is confirmed . . . by the prayer [noted above] which Paul offered for the Thessalonians, "And the very God of peace sanctify you wholly." . . .

Commentators agree that the word translated "wholly" is one of the strongest words that could possibly be used to express complete deliverance from spiritual pollution. Dr. Mahan says it is compounded of two words, one meaning *all,* the other *perfection.* Dr. Adam Clarke says the original word signifies precisely the same as our English phrase, "to all intents and purposes." Luther translates it "through and through." In the Vulgate it is rendered "in your collective powers and parts." Mr. Wesley says it means "every part of you perfectly." If full deliverance from sin is not taught in this prayer, it is not within the power of human language to teach it. Thrice welcome the assurance that follows the prayer: "Faithful is he that calleth you, who also will do it."

Do any ask what is the exact difference between regeneration and entire sanctification? It is this: The one has remaining impurity; the other has none. We do not say that entire sanctification embraces nothing more than complete cleansing from sin—it does. It is the full, gracious endowment of perfect love, and much else, but here . . . it is sufficient . . . to set forth the fact that entire sanctification completes the work of purification and renovation begun in regeneration. . . . We are "delivered out of the hand of our enemies" that we may "serve [God] without fear, in holiness and righteousness before him, all the days of our life" (Luke 1:74-75). The soul then enters upon the Sabbath rest of the love of God, and is filled with perfect peace.

The Cleansing Wave

KNAPP

Phoebe Palmer Knapp, 1839-1908   Phoebe Palmer Knapp, 1839-1908

1. Oh, now I see   the crim-son wave, The   foun-tain deep and wide;
2. I   see the new   cre - a - tion rise;   I   hear the speak - ing Blood.
3. I   rise to walk in heav'n's own light A - bove the world and sin,
4. A - maz-ing grace! 'tis heav'n be - low To   feel the Blood ap - plied,

Je - sus, my Lord, might - y   to save, Points to His wound-ed   side.
It   speaks! Pol- lut - ed   na - ture dies! Sinks 'neath the cleans-ing flood.
With heart made pure, and gar-ments white, And Christ en-throned with - in.
And Je - sus, on - ly Je - sus know, My Je - sus, cru - ci - fied.

REFRAIN

The cleans-ing stream, I see, I see! I plunge and, oh, it cleans - eth me!

Oh! praise the Lord, it cleans-eth me! It cleans-eth me, yes, cleans- eth me!

Hunger

Conviction of need is a condition for the personal quest after holiness.

Blessed are they which do hunger and thirst after righteousness: for they shall be filled. . . .

Blessed are the pure in heart: for they shall see God (Matt. 5:6, 8).

For to be carnally minded is death; but to be spiritually minded is life and peace. Because the carnal mind is enmity against God: for it is not subject to the law of God, neither indeed can be (Rom. 8:6-7).

A PRAYER FOR HOLINESS

"Have mercy upon me, O God, according to thy lovingkindness: according unto the multitude of thy tender mercies blot out my transgressions. Wash me throughly from mine iniquity, and cleanse me from my sin. For I acknowledge my transgressions: and my sin is ever before me. . . . Behold, I was shapen in iniquity; and in sin did my mother conceive me. . . . Purge me with hyssop, and I shall be clean: wash me, and I shall be whiter than snow. . . . Hide thy face from my sins, and blot out all mine iniquities. Create in me a clean heart, O God; and renew a right spirit within me. Cast me not away from thy presence; and take not thy holy spirit from me. Restore unto me the joy of thy salvation; and uphold me with thy free spirit" (Ps. 51:1-3, 5, 7, 9-12).

THE TESTIMONY OF MARY R. DENMAN[4]

I still had a longing in my heart for something more satisfying. . . . *I soon saw there was something more for me and that God was talking to my heart.*

When my pastor asked me, at the age of 15, to be confirmed, I said, "I would like to do so, but have not met with a change of heart." His answer was: "Whence did the desire to become a Christian originate? Certainly it did not come from the evil one." Hence he advised me to join the church. I have always been glad that I followed his advice, for when tempted as a young lady to go into the gaiety of the world I felt restraint, particularly during the season of Lent. As a church member, when the Communion season came around, I must partake of the Lord's Supper, and in some way I always tried to prepare my heart to receive it. After I was married I tried hard to induce my husband to join the church, as I had done, but we were of the world and worldly.

There came a time when I realized that I did not love God with all my heart, as I was taught every Sunday it was my duty to do. I was simple-minded enough to go on my knees and ask God to teach me to love Him with all my heart. He took me at my word and taught me to do so. Soon after this, upon my return to New Orleans, I thought the church members had changed, for they seemed so willing to talk on the subject of religion. The change was with me. This I consider was the date of my conversion. I was soon tested to know if I loved God with all my heart. He took to himself a precious daughter when she was only about four months old. This affliction I bore cheerfully, feeling that God would bless it to my husband, which He did, and when six years afterward, He took him to himself, I claimed the promise given to the widow. He has been true to His promise for over 20 years.

---

4. *Forty Witnesses,* 106-9. Mrs. Denman's testimony to her inner hunger for holiness comes from the latter part of the 19th century. Born in New Orleans, and a lifelong member of the Episcopal church, Mary was most widely known for her leadership in the Women's Christian Temperance Union.

I still had a longing in my heart for something more satisfying.
HUNGER While in this state of mind I learned that a number of Christian people were coming to our city to hold a series of meetings. They were called "higher-life Christians." I heard one minister in these meetings tell of the "rest of faith" he had in his soul. My spirit responded, "This is what I want"; and, knowing that God was not a respecter of persons, I believed He would give it to me if I would meet the conditions. I sought and found this grace.

I delighted in this new joy and desired to meet with Christians who enjoyed the same blessing. But when I was invited to go to a camp meeting, my answer was, "No; I am not a Methodist." The friend replied, "This is not a Methodist camp meeting; it is a national one, where all denominations meet." I concluded to go with my friend, she making all arrangements for me. I praise God for Sea Cliff Camp Meeting. Having the great joy of the Savior in my heart, I did not feel the need of having the roots of bitterness taken out. But I soon saw there was something more for me, and that God was talking to my heart and questioning me, to see if my will was in subjection to His.

One test was, "Would I establish the family altar on my return home?" I was in the habit of praying with my children, but establishing the family altar would involve the cross of praying before visitors, and some very worldly ones. I had already said, "Yes," to this. Then in the night came deeper questions, preparing me for temperance work. "Would I speak for Him before large congregations if my children and every friend on earth turned against me?" This I could not answer, for I felt it would cut me off from all my earthly supports. Still I found it must be answered, or I would never know peace again.

I called Sister Amanda Smith, the colored evangelist, who was in the next tent. She, being awake, put a blanket around her and came to my bedside and prayed with me, making very clear to my mind that God would not ask any thing of me that He would not give me strength to perform. When my will was broken, a wondrous peace came into my soul.

I have often been asked, "Has this peace remained all these 15 years? And how have you kept it?" My answer is, By saying, "I will," to
OBEYING GOD God, and then doing His bidding. Very soon I was called to work for Him in the temperance cause. I began by being willing to lead in ladies' prayer meetings. After seven years' constant work for the Master, when the women would not release me, the dear Lord did, by laying me by with paralysis.

But, oh, how wondrously He has healed me since in answer to prayer! How could I let go my faith in the Almighty arm that did and continues to do so much for me? I do not say that I have been freed from trial or temptation. Those I never expect to be free from while in the body. But I can say, with Paul, that "with the temptation . . . a way of escape" has always been made (1 Cor. 10:13), and I have not lost the deep peace in my soul. I do not remember that I have ever felt power in myself to stand alone, and therefore have always looked to and expected my precious Savior to keep me. He has never forsaken me.

There was a time for about two days when Satan tried to make me think I had not received the baptism of the Holy Ghost, because I had not had just such an experience as another dear friend. But just as soon as I got quiet before God, the Holy Spirit carried me back in mind to that night on Sea Cliff Campground, and I have never doubted since. I do not always experience the same joy, but it is there, down in my heart, like the water in the bosom of the earth waiting the opportunity of the driven well. If I were to be disobedient to His loving command, and leave Him, and look for my pleasures in other fields than He lays out for me, I should expect to lose my peace. But why should I do so, when He is my all and in all?

*   *   *   *   *

Fill Me Now

Elwood H. Stokes, 1815-1895   John R. Sweney, 1837-1899

1. Hov-er   o'er me,   Ho - ly Spir - it, Bathe my trem-bling heart and brow;
2. Thou canst fill me,   gra-cious Spir- it, Though I can - not   tell Thee how;
3. I   am weak-ness, full of weak-ness; At Thy   sa - cred feet I bow.
4. Cleanse and comfort, bless and save me; Bathe, O bathe my heart and brow.

Fill me with Thy hal - lowed pres - ence, Come, O come and fill me now.
But I need Thee, great - ly need Thee; Come, O come and fill me now.
Blest, di - vine, e - ter - nal Spir - it, Fill with love, and fill me now.
Thou art com - fort - ing and sav - ing; Thou art sweet - ly fill - ing now.

REFRAIN

Fill me now, fill me now; Je - sus, come and fill me now.

Fill me with Thy hal - lowed pres-ence; Come, O come and fill me now.

* * * * *

THE HOLY SPIRIT CONVICTS BELIEVERS OF THE NEED OF HOLINESS[5]

The Spirit of God enlightens believers as to their *need* of being sanctified as a means of leading them into the experience. He convicts them of inbred sin, makes them feel and loathe the plague within, and leads them to humble themselves and cry mightily to God for deliverance. Conviction for sanctification is not conviction of guilt for wrong done or for duty neglected. It is not in any sense a conviction of having backslidden from God. On the other hand it presupposes

---

5. Wilson Thomas Hogue, *The Holy Spirit*, 268-70. For biography see 3:306.

present consciousness of walking in the light and enjoying full justification from all past offenses and failures, through faith in the atoning merits of Jesus Christ. But the conviction of which we speak is a painful consciousness that, while we are fully justified from all past transgressions and derelictions, there is a *principle* of sin *within* us, which clings to our very thoughts, tempers, and desires, evermore seeking the ascendancy in outward conduct, defiling the inward man in every part, and from which we should and must be *cleansed* before we can fully glorify God and enjoy uninterrupted communion with Him.

This conviction is accomplished by the Spirit in two ways: first, by those inward operations through which He sheds light upon the soul and reveals to it its own corruptions, still remaining since the **HOW THE** work of regeneration has been effected; and second, by so **SPIRIT** illuminating the Scriptures to the understanding as to make **CONVICTS** these reveal to him the necessity and privilege of being made altogether holy. Sometimes the disclosures thus made of inbred sin are well-nigh overwhelming and cause the soul to doubt for the time being whether it can be possible that he has ever been truly converted. "How can one be a true child of God," he asks himself, "in whom there is so much moral impurity and such a painful sense of unlikeness to the moral character of God?" To be led from the raptures of a sense of reconciliation with God into such a humiliating and painful consciousness of inward unfitness for His holy presence, is, for the time being, a melancholy experience; but by this experience the Holy Spirit is seeking to lead the soul, not to disparage the work already accomplished in its regeneration, but to aspire for and definitely seek after that "higher life" in Christ, that full conformity to the character and will of God that is attainable through faith in the blood of Jesus.

The Holy Spirit not only shows the believer the need of this higher work, but in doing so He likewise reveals the assured possibility of receiving it. He so illuminates the commands, precepts, prayers, promises, and provisions of the Scriptures bearing upon **REVEALS THE** this very point that the conviction of its glorious possi- **POSSIBILITY** bility becomes not only assured, but a mighty incentive to seek it at every cost, and a mighty uplift and inspiration to the faith that is necessary to its attainment. Thus assured, uplifted, and inspired with a vision of the glorious possibility, the soul advances to the realization of the desired object, saying,

The thing surpasses all my thought,
But faithful is the Lord;
Through unbelief I stagger not,
For God has spoke the word.

Faith, mighty faith the promise sees,
And looks to that alone;
Laughs at impossibilities,
And cries, "It shall be done!"

Obedient faith that waits on Thee,
Thou never wilt reprove;
But Thou wilt form Thy Son in me,
And perfect me in love.

Blessed be God! The Comforter who convinces of the *necessity* of this work points us also to the *possibility* of its enjoyment. Our blessed Savior in His intercessory prayer says, "Sanctify them through thy truth: thy word is truth" (John 17:17). So the Holy Spirit who inspired the Word brings to mind the promises and assurances, and reveals the rich provisions of infinite love. Does the child of God groan over his impurities and corruptions? He is pointed to the fountain over which is written, "The blood of Jesus Christ his Son cleanseth us from all sin" (1 John 1:7). Does he sigh over his want of conformity to God? He is assured that, beholding with open face as in a glass the glory of the Lord, he shall be changed into the same image, from glory to glory, even as by the Lord the Spirit (2 Cor. 3:18). Does he doubt whether this is his great privilege? Again the Spirit speaks in His Word, "Faithful is he that calleth you, who also will do it" (1 Thess. 5:24). He is thus led to see that such is the amplitude of the provision, such is the all-cleansing power of the blood of Christ, such is the almightiness of the Eternal Spirit, that no matter what he may be, the work can be done; and whenever, at any stage of the believer's experience, his faith lays hold of these great promises and provisions, the work will be done. According to his faith will it be done unto him.

A Beginning Prayer for Sanctification[6]

Today my prayer is:
I would like to know God better. I recognize that I need His cleansing and controlling power released in my life by the Holy Spirit.

---

6. Harper, "I Would Like to Know God Better."

Lord, I know that I am a Christian, I am trying to please You, and I thank You for all the help You have given me. I believe that You want to fill me with Your Holy Spirit, and I begin now to wait and pray for His coming. I want to receive Him in His fullness and in His cleansing power. In Jesus' name. Amen.

Consecration

Full consecration is both a precondition and a gracious fruit of entire sanctification.

And, behold, one came and said unto him, Good Master, what good thing shall I do, that I may have eternal life?

And he said unto him, Why callest thou me good? there is none good but one, that is, God: but if thou wilt enter into life, keep the commandments. . . .

The young man saith unto him, All these things have I kept from my youth up: what lack I yet?

Jesus said unto him, If thou wilt be perfect, go and sell that thou hast, and give to the poor, and thou shalt have treasure in heaven: and come and follow me (Matt. 19:16-17, 20-21).

Likewise reckon ye also yourselves to be dead indeed unto sin, but alive unto God through Jesus Christ our Lord.

Let not sin therefore reign in your mortal body, that ye should obey it in the lusts thereof.

Neither yield ye your members as instruments of unrighteousness unto sin: but yield yourselves unto God, as those that are alive from the dead, and your members as instruments of righteousness unto God (Rom. 6:11-13).

I plead with you therefore, brethren, by the compassion of God, to present all your faculties to Him as a living and holy sacrifice acceptable to Him—a spiritual mode of worship. And do not conform to the present age, but be transformed by the entire renewal of your minds, so that you may learn by experience what God's will is, namely, all that is good and acceptable to Him and perfect (Rom. 12:1-2, Weymouth).

100% OR NO DEAL[7]

For 15 years, I lived in the land of my birth—Seoul, South Korea.

---

7. Un Chong Yi, *Herald of Holiness*, August 1, 1984. Miss Yi is an advanced student in the conservatory of music and a member of First Church of the Nazarene in Kansas City.

We were Buddhists, but it didn't seem too important to me. The study of music in a private high school I attended was the biggest thing in my life.

At the end of my sophomore year, however, my father decided to move to America, and we settled in Los Angeles. I was very excited. I was sure I would find greater opportunity in America to become a famous pianist.

But the opportunities did not materialize and I became disillusioned. While I was searching for answers I began attending a Korean church. As I sought God in prayer, He proved himself to me again and again.

Through a high school teacher, the door opened for me to go to the University of Southern California for piano studies. It finally seemed I was getting the chance I had been looking for. But just about that time, my father decided to move again. I did not want to move and I resisted strongly. I even prayed for God to change my father's mind. I tried to bargain with God, but it didn't work.

After we moved to Kansas City, I visited many churches. Something was missing. There had to be more reality to this business of being a Christian. Whenever I met happy Christians, I tried even harder to be one. But my pride and anger were too much for me to deal with. The harder I tried, the worse I became.

I entered college in Kansas City, where I found there were others studying music with me who shared the same emptiness I felt. I had thought I was a dedicated Christian, but God began to show me music was really my idol.

I struggled for some time. Finally I reached the place where there was no peace, and I felt that if I didn't find it, I might as well die.

One day when I was browsing in a bookstore, I noticed a book with a wedding couple on the cover. Opening the cover of Ann Kiemel's book *I Gave God Time,* I began to read words that seemed to leap from the page and remind me of my own self-centered ambitions.

What a terrible struggle! I felt like God was asking me to give Him my music. How could I give it up? It was my life! I had been told many times that I showed great talent.

I tried again to bargain with God. On Wednesday, I said to God, "You can have 50 percent of my music." It was not enough. On Thursday, I told Him, "God, You can have 75 percent of my music." But it was "No deal."

That Friday, I returned to the bookstore and this time picked up

Ann's book *YES*. When I opened the book, I read this quote from Betty Scott Stam: "Lord, I give up all my own plans and purposes, all my own desires and hopes, and accept Thy will for my life. I give myself, my time, my all utterly to Thee to be Thine forever. Fill me and seal me with Thy Holy Spirit. Use me as Thou wilt, send me where Thou wilt, work out Thy whole will in my life at any cost, now and forever."

My heart fairly leaped within me. My whole being responded to those words so that I found myself saying right out loud, "Yes, Lord." What a joy filled my heart!

That was the turning point for me. And God has since led in such wonderful ways. Through a student (under God's leadership, I'm sure), I came in contact with the Church of the Nazarene. I was immediately attracted to the church. The people were so enthusiastic and open. They talked so freely about their relationship with God. And I found Truth that meets the need of my heart.

I am still in love with my music, but it belongs to God now. With great joy, I have given it to Him, and I now want His direction as to where and how He wants me to use my talents.

God has blessed in another wonderful way. He has allowed me to be used to show my parents the way. They now know this Christ I serve, as well!

And my church? It's like finding a second home!

What Shall I Give Thee, Master?

What shall I give Thee, Master,
Thou who didst die for me?
Shall I give less of what I possess,
Or shall I give all to Thee?

What shall I give Thee, Master?
Thou hast redeemed my soul.
My gift is small, but it is my all,
Surrendered to Thy control.

Refrain:

Jesus, my Lord and Savior,
Thou hast giv'n all for me;
Thou didst leave Thy home above
To die on Calvary.

What shall I give Thee, Master?
Thou hast giv'n all for me.
Not just a part, or half of my heart;
I will give all to Thee!
—HOMER W. GRIMES

CONSECRATION[8]

Sanctification is both human and divine. Man has always had a part in the application of the atonement of Jesus Christ to himself. Christ's death on the Cross provisionally saved everybody but actually saved nobody except in the case of the irresponsible. The benefits of Christ's death are strictly individual. That is, each individual must make application for those blessings purchased for him by the death of Christ. These blessings are appropriated by the voluntary act of the individual coming to Jesus Christ. "Whosoever will" is the teaching of God's Word. If man does not come to Christ to accept His blessings, the merits of Christ will have no meaning for him so far as salvation is concerned. In order to be converted one must do his part; he must repent and exercise faith in Christ. In order to be sanctified one must do his part.

Thus it is evident that sanctification has both the human element and the divine element. It is both consecration and purification. These two elements combined constitute the great truth of entire sanctification. Consecration is the human element, or man's part. "Sanctify yourselves therefore, and be ye holy," says the Word of CONSECRATION God (Lev. 20:7). In the strictest sense God cannot consecrate a man. Man must do this for himself. God can call, urge, and insist; but in the final analysis man must present himself to God. He must make his own consecration voluntarily. God can and will accept such consecration and use the man thus consecrated for the honor of His own name and the advancement of His kingdom. The act of consecration is man's part and constitutes the human element in sanctification.

We could not stop here and be true to the teachings of the Word of God. . . . If consecration is sanctification or if sanctification is consecration and that only, then it is all purely human, and God has little or nothing to do with it except to accept the work done by man.

---

8. Williams, *Sanctification: The Experience and the Ethics*, 23-25.

This position could never be justified nor defended. The writer of Hebrews says, "He that sanctifieth and they who are sanctified are all of one: for which cause he is not ashamed to call them brethren" (2:11). Here we have the sanctifier, the sanctified, and the relation that exists between the sanctifier and the sanctified. If sanctification is consecration only, how could there be a sanctifier, unless that sanctifier is a man himself? This could not possibly harmonize with the text of scripture under consideration.

Consecration is a part: it is the human element; but there is a divine side to this great truth. Paul prayed that the very God of peace might sanctify us wholly. He also says, "Husbands, love your wives, even as Christ also loved the church, and gave himself for it; that he might . . . cleanse it" (Eph. 5:25-26). It is evident from this statement that God himself is the Sanctifier. This consecration is divinely accepted, the heart is cleansed from all unrighteousness, and man is enabled by the circumcision of his heart to love God with his whole soul, mind, and strength. Man sanctifies himself through consecration. God sanctifies him by the baptism with the Holy Ghost and fire. In this the work is complete.

Man's part is accomplished through consecration, and God's part is accomplished in purification. Man dedicates himself to the Lord, and in answer to a living faith this man receives the baptism with the Holy Ghost and fire by which his heart is purified and he is filled with the love of God. The refining fire is sent through his heart, and the whole nature is purified. What a glorious work! What a marvelous accomplishment! Man lays himself in submission at the feet of God. His all is accepted, he is made a vessel meet for the Master's use. What person could find fault with a perfect consecration? Who would dare state that there could be anything wrong in the consecration of every child of God to the Almighty? Who could find fault with cleansing for the human heart?

A Prayer of Consecration[9]

This is my earnest plea. With the help of the Holy Spirit I now consecrate my whole life to God.

All that I am and all that I have, I lay upon the altar of consecration. You have forgiven my sins. You gave me my life and all that I have.

---

9. Harper, "I Would Like to Know God Better."

I now freely return these gifts to You to be used as You direct. If You take them from me, it is as I have freely given them. If You leave them with me, they shall always be Yours. Accept what I bring, and it shall henceforth be under Your control.

> *All to Jesus I surrender.*
> *Make me, Savior, wholly Thine;*
> *Let me feel the Holy Spirit,*
> *Truly know that Thou art mine.*
>
> —JUDSON W. VAN DEVENTER
> 1855-1939

THE EXPERIENCE OF FRANCES RIDLEY HAVERGAL[10]

I think that the great root of all my trouble and alienation is that I do not now make an unconditional surrender of myself to God; and until this is done I shall know no peace. I am sure of it.

Although Miss Havergal lived a very earnest Christian life and sought to glorify God and serve Him by teaching in Sunday School, singing in churches, and visiting the needy, she felt that she was only a little child in spiritual life, and she longed for a deeper Christian experience. In 1858 she wrote: "Gleams and glimpses, but oh to be filled with joy and the Holy Ghost! Oh, why cannot I trust Him fully?" Later she wrote, "I still wait for the hour when I believe He will reveal himself to me more directly; but it is the quiet waiting of present trust, not the restless waiting of anxiety and danger." That year, at the age of 22, she wrote the well-known hymn "I Gave My Life for Thee." It reveals the deep longings of her heart to be more fully consecrated to Christ.

In 1865, she wrote, "I had hoped that a kind of tableland had been reached in my journey, where I might walk a while in the light, without the weary succession of rock and hollow, crag and morass,

---

10. *Deeper Experiences of Famous Christians,* 222-27.

Frances was the youngest child of Christian parents. She was born in 1836 at Astley, in Worcestershire, England, where her father was the rector.

From the time of her conversion at 14 years of age, Frances lived a very earnest Christian life. She attended schools and colleges in England and Germany. In Germany she was the only truly converted person among the 110 young ladies in her school. She took a firm stand for Christ and suffered much persecution on that account but won the hearts of some of her schoolmates. Returning to England in 1854, she was confirmed in Worcester Cathedral. She began to write hymns and letters in verse at the age of 7 but did not publish anything until 1860. For 19 years she contributed to the hymnody of holiness before she died in Wales in 1879.

stumbling and striving; but I seem borne back into all the old diffi-culties of the way, with many sin-made aggravations. I think that the great root of all my trouble and alienation is that I do not now make an unconditional surrender of myself to God; and until this is done I shall know no peace. I am sure of it."

Later she says, "Oh, that He would indeed purify me and make me *white* at any cost." She prayed regularly three times a day, and every morning she prayed especially for the Holy Spirit. After a season of sickness, she wrote, "Oh, that He may make me a vessel sanctified and meet for the Master's use!"

At last the long-looked-for experience came, and it lifted her whole life into sunshine and gladness. The following account of how she was brought into a Beulah Land experience is from the pen of her sister Maria, who also enjoyed the same experience.

"We now reach a period in the life of dear Frances that was characterized by surpassing blessing to her soul. The year 1873 was drawing to a close. One day she received in a letter from N—— a tiny book with the title *All for Jesus*. She read it carefully. Its contents arrested her attention. It set forth a fullness of Christian experience and blessing exceeding that to which she had as yet attained. She was gratefully conscious of having for many years loved the Lord and de-lighted in His service; but there was in her experience a falling short of the standard, not so much of a holy walk and conversation, as of uniform brightness and continuous enjoyment in the divine love. *All for Jesus* she found went straight to the point of the need and longing of her soul.

"God did not leave her long in this state of mind. He himself had shown her that there were 'regions beyond' of blessed experience and service; He had kindled in her soul the intense desire to go forward and possess them; and now, in His own grace and love, He took her by the hand, and led her into the goodly land."

The sunless ravines were now forever past, and henceforth her peace and joy flowed onward, deepening and widening under the teaching of God and the Holy Ghost. The blessing she had received had "lifted her whole life into sunshine, of which all she had pre-viously experienced was but as pale and passing April gleams com-pared with the fullness of summer glory."

To the reality of this her sister says: "I do most willingly and fully testify. Some time afterwards, in answer to my question, when we were talking quietly together, Frances said, 'Yes, it was on Advent Sunday,

December 2, 1873, I first saw clearly the blessedness of true consecration. I saw it as a flash of electric light, and what you see, you can never *unsee*. There must be full surrender before there can be full blessedness. God admits you by the one into the other. He himself showed me all this most clearly. First, I was shown that "the blood of Jesus Christ his Son cleanseth us from all sin," and then it was made plain to me that He who had thus cleansed me had power to keep me clean; so I just utterly trusted Him to keep me.'"

I Gave My Life for Thee

KENOSIS

Frances R. Havergal, 1836 - 1879   Philip P. Bliss, 1838 - 1876

1. I gave My life for thee; My pre - cious blood I shed,
2. My Fa - ther's house of light, My glo - ry - cir - cled throne,
3. I suf - fered much for thee, More than thy tongue can tell,
4. And I have brought to thee, Down from My home a - bove,

That thou might'st ransomed be, And quick-ened from the dead.
I left for earth - ly night, For wan - d'rings sad and lone.
Of bit - t'rest ag - o - ny, To res - cue thee from hell.
Sal - va - tion full and free, My par - don and My love.

I gave, I gave My life for thee. What hast thou giv'n for Me?
I left, I left it all for thee. Hast thou left aught for Me?
I've borne, I've borne it all for thee. What hast thou borne for Me?
I bring, I bring rich gifts to thee. What hast thou brought to Me?

I	gave,	I gave	My	life	for thee.	What hast	thou giv'n	for	Me?
I	left,	I left	it	all	for thee.	Hast thou	left aught	for	Me?
I've	borne,	I've borne it	all	for thee.	What hast	thou borne	for	Me?
I	bring,	I bring rich	gifts	to thee.	What hast	thou brought	to	Me?

THREE PRAYERS OF CONSECRATION

Andover, February 10, 1859

This day I make a new consecration of my all to Christ.

Jesus, I now forever give myself to Thee; my soul to be washed in Thy blood and saved in heaven at last; my whole body to be used for any purpose to Thy glory; my feet to carry me where Thou shalt wish me to go; my heart to be burdened for souls, or used for Thee anywhere; my intellect to be employed at all times for Thy cause and glory. I give to Thee my wife, my children, my property, all I have, and all that ever shall be mine. I will obey Thee in every known duty.

—A. B. Earle[11]

Dr. Philip Doddridge (1702-51), famous English preacher, is remembered for his hymn "O Happy Day." It was he who wrote the following form of consecration:

This day do I, with the utmost solemnity, surrender myself to Thee. I renounce all former lords that have had dominion over me; and I consecrate to Thee all that I am, and all that I have; the faculties of my mind, the members of my body, my worldly possessions, my time and my influence over others; to be all used entirely for Thy glory, and resolutely employed in obedience to Thy commands, as long as Thou continuest me in life; with an ardent desire and humble resolution to be Thine through the endless ages of eternity; ever holding myself in an attentive posture to observe the first intimations of Thy will, and ready to spring forward with zeal and joy to the immediate execution of it.

To Thy direction also I resign myself, and all I am and have, to be disposed of by Thee in such a manner as Thou shalt in Thine infinite

---

11: *The Rest of Faith.*

wisdom judge most subservient to the purposes of Thy glory. To Thee I leave the management of all events, and say without reserve, NOT my will but Thine be done.[12]

As a result of that unreserved consecration, Philip Doddridge could sing in his much-loved hymn:

> *Now rest, my long divided heart;*
> *Fixed on this blissful center, rest;*
> *Nor ever from my Lord depart,*
> *With Him of ev'ry good possessed.*

Another helpful form of consecration and pledge of faith was drawn by Rev. Isaiah Reid.

Consecration for Holiness

Text: Rom. 12:1-2. O Lord, in view of this thing Thou hast besought me to do, I hereby now do really consecrate myself unreservedly to Thee for all time and eternity. My time, my talents, my hands, feet, lips, will, my all. My property, my reputation, my entire being, a living sacrifice to be and to do all Thy righteous will pertaining to me. . . . Especially at this time do I, Thy regenerate child, put my case into Thy hands for the cleansing of my nature from the inherited taint of the carnal nature. I seek the sanctification of my soul.

Pledge of Faith

Now, as I have given myself away, I will, from this time forth, regard myself as Thine. I believe Thou dost accept the offering that I bring. I put all on the altar. I believe the altar sanctifieth the gift. I believe the Blood is applied now as I comply with the terms of Thy salvation. I believe that Thou dost now cleanse me from all sin.

Vow

By Thy grace, from this time forth, I promise to follow Thee, walking in the fellowship of the Spirit, perfecting holiness in the fear of the Lord.

Name _____

Date _____[13]

---

12. *The Rise and Progress of Religion in the Soul,* chap. 17.
13. Brown, *The Meaning of Sanctification,* 183-84.

Faith

Faith, grounded on the full-orbed purpose of Christ's death and the fullest consecration of which we are capable, is the human condition for entire sanctification.

God, who knows the heart, showed that he accepted them by giving the Holy Spirit to them, just as he did to us. He made no distinction between us and them, for he purified their hearts by faith (Acts 15:8-9, NIV).

And without faith it is impossible to please God, because anyone who comes to him must believe that he exists and that he rewards those who earnestly seek him (Heb. 11:6, NIV).

Come in Faith

Are you longing for the fullness Of the blessing of the Lord
In your heart and life today?
Claim the promise of your Father; Come according to His Word,
In the blessed, oldtime way.

Like the cruse of oil unfailing Is His grace forevermore,
And His love unchanging still;
And according to His promise, With the Holy Ghost and pow'r
He will ev'ry vessel fill.

—LELIA N. MORRIS, 1862-1929

THE OPERATION OF FAITH[14]

Have you a definite view of holiness? Do you realize your need of it? Are you willing to receive it? Is it your desire and purpose to persevere until you obtain it; and, in order thereto, do you realize a readiness to give up all to God, in entire consecration? If this should be your mind, one thing more and the work will be done; "Believe on the Lord Jesus Christ, and thou shalt be saved" (Acts 16:31).

Faith . . . is the only condition upon which the blessings of the gospel are offered. "Justification" is by faith; "regeneration" is by

BY FAITH faith; "sanctification" is by faith; "glorification" is by faith— by faith as the instrument, and by the blood of Jesus as the merit, and by the Spirit as the Agent. Whenever faith is exercised, the

---

14. Foster, *Christian Purity*, 130-32.

work will be done. The preceding advices are only prescribed as means of assisting—as cooperating with the grace of God to bring the mind up to the point of faith—to prepare us for this saving exercise. And let it not be supposed that a long and tedious process is necessary, in order to this preparation. With diligent application, and by divine assistance, the work may soon be accomplished.

And now we again distinctly repeat, "It is by simple faith." "Believe . . . and thou shalt be saved." But how and what are you to believe? If the previous advices have been complied with, this is soon and easily answered; but if not, it is vain to talk to you of faith; for . . . without a proper state of mind and the affections, faith is impossible. However directly faith is wrought in the soul, and however sudden the work of sanctification, still intervening is this preparation of mind, which goes before, or if not before, along with faith. But now do you see the prize—holiness? Do you feel your need of it? Are you willing to receive it? More, are you desirous to obtain, and resolved not to stop short? Are you enabled to consecrate your all to God—to give up all for this blessing? Is this your feeling? Is it? Are you willing now? Then believe! The work will be done. Believe what? Believe in the Lord Jesus Christ as your Savior. Trust Him to do the work now, just as you are!

STEPS IN BELIEVING It may be important to be still more explicit at this point. Faith includes the ideas both of "belief and trust," and exists in various stages.

1. A general belief in Christ, as the Savior and Sanctifier.
2. Belief that He is able to sanctify us.
3. Belief that He is willing to do it.
4. Belief that He is able and willing to do it now, not tomorrow.
5. Belief that He has promised to do the work, and that His promise will not fail.
6. Belief that if I now have faith, He will now, this moment, do it.
7. Reliance, or trust in Him now, this moment, to do, accompanied with a belief that He does it. Mark, that He now, when I believe according to His promise, does it; not a belief that it is done, but, accompanying my faith, it being a sound faith, that He does the work.

These, as we believe, are the almost invariable stages, or progressive steps of faith; the mind is thus led along, by an easy and regular process, to that reliance—to that taking God at His Word, which brings the promised blessing. These various and successive grades of faith may not indeed sensibly take place in the soul; the mind may not detect their existence as elements; but they are, nevertheless, included in the faith that sanctifies.

Let it be remembered that when this exercise of faith takes place, it is not a mere intellectual calculation, but it occurs when the soul is travailing for sanctifying power; when it is groaning for deliverance from distressing sinfulness; when it is giving up all to Christ; when it is feeling that "it is worse than death its God to love, and not its God alone"; when it is purposing to claim and obtain holiness, at all hazards. That is the state of the soul: It is now agonizing at God's altar; it is pleading for salvation—looking at the promises; the Holy Spirit is helping, imparting illumination, and strengthening the faltering faith.

Now comes the moment when sanctification is about to be imparted. Now the soul believes it will be done, just now; taking firmer hold of the promises, and looking steadfastly upon the atoning sacrifice . . . it believes it is being done; the refining fire touches it, as the coal Isaiah's lips, it yields, it trusts—the work is done; and now the soul, sanctified, believes it is done. The belief that it will be done—that it is being done—is the trust that brings the blessing. The belief that it is done follows after. They are each distinct, though all may occur in the interval of a minute.

FAITH WITHOUT FEELING[15]

F. B. Meyer says, "As once you obtained forgiveness and salvation by faith, so *now* claim and receive the Spirit's fullness. Fulfill the conditions already named, wait quietly but definitely before God in prayer; for He gives the Holy Spirit to them that ask Him: Then reverently appropriate this glorious gift, and rise from your knees, and go on your way reckoning that God has kept His Word, and that you *are filled* with the Spirit. Trust Him day by day to fill you and keep you filled. There may not be at first the sound of rushing wind, or the coronet of fire, or the sensible feeling of His presence. Do not look for these, any more than the young convert should look for feeling as an evidence of acceptance. But BELIEVE *in spite of feeling* that YOU ARE FILLED. Say over and over, 'I thank Thee, O my God, that Thou hast kept Thy word with me, though as yet I am not aware of any special change.' And the feeling will sooner or later break in upon your consciousness, and you will rejoice with exceeding joy, and all the fruits of the Spirit will begin to show themselves."

---

15. Hills, *Holiness and Power,* 285.

A PRAYER OF FAITH[16]

O Savior, I believe that Your promise to send the Holy Spirit is meant for me personally.

As far as I know, I have consecrated my whole life to You. I am waiting and believing for "the promise of the Father." I want to be filled with the Holy Spirit more than anything else in this world. By faith in Your promise, I accept Your Gift. I believe that You do now cleanse me from all sin. In that faith my glad heart cries:

I rise to walk in heav'n's own light
Above the world and sin,
With heart made pure, and garments white,
And Christ enthroned within.
—PHOEBE PALMER KNAPP, 1839-1908

*   *   *   *   *

Whiter than Snow
FISCHER

James Nicholson, 1828-1876   William G. Fischer, 1835-1912

1. Lord Je - sus, I   long   to be per - fect - ly whole; I   want Thee for-
2. Lord Je - sus, look, down from Thy throne in the skies, And help me   to
3. Lord Je - sus, for   this   I most hum -bly en - treat. I   wait, bless - ed
4. Lord Je - sus, Thou se -   est I   pa - tient - ly wait. Come now, and with-
5. The bless-ing by   faith   I re - ceive from a - bove. Oh, glo - ry! My

ev-er to   live in my soul. Break down ev - 'ry   i - dol, cast out   ev - 'ry
make a complete sac-ri - fice. I   give   up my - self, and what -ev -. er   I
Lord, at Thy cru-ci -fied feet. By   faith, for my cleans-ing I   see Thy blood
in me a   new heart cre-ate. To   those who have sought Thee Thou never saidst
soul is made perfect in love. My   prayer has pre-vailed, and this mo - ment I

16. Harper, "I Would Like to Know God Better."

REFRAIN

```
foe.   Now wash  me  and  I  shall  be whit - er than snow.  Whit - er than
know.  Now wash  me  and  I  shall  be whit - er than snow.  Whit - er than
flow.  Now wash  me  and  I  shall  be whit - er than snow.  Whit - er than
no.    Now wash  me  and  I  shall  be whit - er than snow.  Whit - er than
know   The Blood is ap - plied, I     am whit- er than snow.  Whit - er than
```

```
   snow, yes, whit-er  than  snow; Now wash me and  I  shall be  whit-er than snow.
5. snow, yes, whit-er  than  snow; The Blood is ap - plied; I  am whit-er than snow.
```

Assurance

God gives the witness of His Spirit when we are sanctified wholly.

God, who knows the heart, showed that he accepted them by giving the Holy Spirit to them, just as he did to us. He made no distinction between us and them, for he purified their hearts by faith (Acts 15:8-9, NIV).

The Spirit himself testifies with our spirit that we are God's children (Rom. 8:16, NIV).

This then is how we know that we belong to the truth, and how we set our hearts at rest in his presence whenever our hearts condemn us. For God is greater than our hearts, and he knows everything. Dear friends, if our hearts do not condemn us, we have confidence before God (1 John 3:19-21, NIV).

The fruit of the Spirit is love, joy, peace, patience, kindness, goodness, faithfulness, gentleness and self-control. Against such things there is no law. Those who belong to Christ Jesus have crucified the sinful nature with its passions and desires. Since we live by the Spirit, let us keep in step with the Spirit (Gal. 5:22-25, NIV).

Blessed Assurance

Blessed assurance, Jesus is mine!
Oh, what a foretaste of glory divine!
Heir of salvation, purchase of God,
Born of His Spirit, washed in His blood!

Refrain:

This is my story, this is my song,
Praising my Savior all the day long.
This is my story, this is my song,
Praising my Savior all the day long.

—FANNY J. CROSBY, 1820-1915

WITNESS OF THE SPIRIT[17]

It is the uniform testimony of those who believe and teach the Wesleyan doctrine of Christian perfection, that the Spirit bears witness to this work of grace in the heart, exactly as He bears witness to Christian sonship. "None, therefore, ought to believe that the work is done," says Mr. Wesley, "till there is added the testimony of the Spirit witnessing his entire sanctification as clearly as his justification." "We know it by the witness and by the fruit of the Spirit" (Wesley, *Plain Account*, 79, 118).

Dr. J. Glenn Gould says that "this inner assurance is made up of three distinct phases. That is, they are logically distinct, though the [seeker's] experience of them may seem to be instantaneous. They are (1) the witness of the seeker's own heart; (2) the witness of God's Word; and (3) the inner illumination of the Holy Spirit" (Gould, *The Spirit's Ministry*, 8). The sanctified soul may know by the testimony of his own spirit, and the witness of the Holy Spirit, that the blood of Jesus Christ has cleansed him from all sin. Here we have the testimony of consciousness, which we can no more doubt than our own existence. And in addition to this, there is the direct and positive testimony of the witnessing Spirit.

CHRISTIAN ASSURANCE[18]

Aunt Julia was serving God the best she knew, but she was troubled. She came to her pastor and asked: "Can I be sure that I am among God's elect?"

---

17. H. Orton Wiley, *Christian Theology*, 2:514-15. For biography see 3:371.
18. Harper, "I Would Like to Know God Better," 14-17.

Her pastor replied, "I feel sure for myself, but I cannot tell you that you can be sure." A sincere Christian deserves a better answer than that.

We Need Assurance

We need to be sure of our standing before God. We long to know that our lives are wholly pleasing to Him; and it is reasonable that we should be assured. If we fall in love, we know it. If we are hungry to be sanctified wholly, we know that. Is it not, therefore, reasonable that when the Holy Spirit fills our hearts, we should also know it? Wesley prayed:

> *I want the witness, Lord,*
> *That all I do is right,*
> *According to Thy will and Word,*
> *Well-pleasing in Thy sight.*

God Gives Assurance

Who can read the Scriptures and doubt that God plans to assure us that our hearts are perfect before Him? Paul testifies: "The Spirit itself beareth witness with our spirit, that we are the children of God" (Rom. 8:16). Peter describes this assuring work when he reports the experience at the house of Cornelius: "And God, which knoweth the hearts, bare them witness, giving them the Holy Ghost, even as he did unto us" (Acts 15:8).

The Bible teaches that Christian holiness is a matter of conscious experience within the reach of all Christ's followers. . . . "Entire sanctification is provided by the blood of Jesus, is wrought instantaneously by faith, preceded by entire consecration; *and to this work and state of grace the Holy Spirit bears witness*" [*Manual*, Church of the Nazarene]. Wesley taught that "none therefore, ought to believe that the work is done till there is added the testimony of the Spirit, witnessing his entire sanctification as clearly as his justification."

The assurance of full salvation is like a river with four tributary streams: (1) the witness of God's promises in the Bible, (2) the assurance of our own sincerity before God, (3) the direct witness of the Holy Spirit to our hearts, and (4) the testimony of a changed life.

The Witness of Scripture

Dr. Orval J. Nease tells of his mother's experience as she sought to be sanctified wholly. He writes: "Mary Storey, wise altar worker that she was, began to quote scripture to aid Mother's faith. Putting an Old Testament portion with a New Testament selection, she quoted: 'Whatsoever toucheth the altar is holy . . . the altar . . . sanctifieth the gift.' It was the avenue of assurance Mother needed, and with firm confidence she said, 'That being true, on the authority of God's Word I am sanctified.'"

One of God's clear and blessed promises is: "If we walk in the light, as he is in the light, we have fellowship one with another, and the blood of Jesus Christ his Son cleanseth us from all sin" (1 John 1:7). When we boldly claim the promise and assert our faith, we have the witness of God's Word that the work has been accomplished. With George Keith we exult:

> *How firm a foundation, ye saints of the Lord,*
> *Is laid for your faith in His excellent Word!*

The Witness of Sincerity

The second stream of assurance flows into our spirits as we complete and maintain our consecration. A young man testified: "At that moment there came the peace of God that passeth all understanding. Quiet, but oh how sweet! I knew in my heart that I had said the last yes to all of God's will."

This experience of saying an unconditional yes brings what may be called the witness of sincerity. In this moment we have the witness of our hearts that every condition of consecration has been met. It is a long step toward assurance when with inner honesty we can say, I have met God's requirements. The Bible tells us, "Beloved, if our heart condemn us not, then have we confidence toward God" (1 John 3:21). This certainty of our own sincerity is a prelude to, and joins with the witness of, the Holy Spirit. Paul declares, "When we cry, 'Abba! Father!', it is this Spirit *testifying along with our own spirit* that we are children of God" (Rom. 8:15-16, Moffatt).

The Witness of the Holy Spirit

The ultimate witness that we are wholly sanctified must be the witness of God himself. The Bible assures us, "Hereby know we that we dwell in him, and he in us, because he hath given us of his Spirit" (1 John 4:13).

Wesley taught: "By the testimony of the Spirit, I mean an inward impression on the soul, whereby the Spirit of God immediately and directly witnesses to my spirit that I am a child of God. The child of God can no more doubt this evidence than he can doubt the shining of the sun, while he stands in the full blaze of its beams." We know that we have been sanctified wholly when, in answer to our prayer, the

Holy Spirit reveals himself directly to our consciousness.

The Assurance of a Changed Life

The fourth tributary to the stream of assurance is the witness of a changed life. When the Holy Spirit comes in sanctifying power, His love motivates all our impulses, thoughts, and attitudes. He changes us at depths that lie beyond conscious control, but that transformation gloriously influences all of our conscious experiences.

It was this confirming witness of changed attitudes to which a young lady testified. With radiant face she rose from the altar and exclaimed, "Oh, I love everybody!"

The Continuing Witness

It is glorious to know God's gracious assurance, but that experience is not always equally strong. Wesley says Christian assurance is sometimes greater, sometimes less, sometimes absent. What, then, shall I do when assurance grows dim?

We may thank God that all of the tributary streams are still open channels; all can flow again. If a stream has dried up, we may go to its source and ask God for renewal. To review the promises of God brings fresh assurance. To reaffirm my consecration lifts my confidence. To declare my faith in the present indwelling Holy Spirit brings His responding touch on my soul.

Does the manifestation of my love seem to fall somewhat short of perfection? I confess it to God, I ask for His continued cleansing and for Christ's help in this special need. As He answers my prayer, I know that He is with me. I am again at rest—

> *A rest where all our soul's desire*
> *Is fixed on things above;*
> *Where doubt and pain and fear expire,*
> *Cast out by perfect love.*
>
> —Wesley Hymns

HOW HOLINESS AND ASSURANCE MAY BE REGAINED[19]

As soon as you return heartily to God, He will return to you: but it must be a full, hearty, entire return. . . . You must come as first you came, with an entire offering, and God will accept it.

---

19. Foster, *Christian Purity,* 171-74.

We consider now the question, How may one who has enjoyed the grace of entire sanctification, and lost it, be restored? It is obvious,

DEGREES OF BACKSLIDING reference must be had to the extent of his lapse—the condition into which he has fallen. Much more may be necessary for one than for another—a different kind and amount of effort. One has fallen from the summit of a mountain into a deep gulf at its base; another has just perceptibly declined slightly down its slope: one will need much more to regain the apex than the other.

Has one who was evidently a truly sanctified child of God, fallen entirely away, become sevenfold more the child of the devil than he was before? In addition to the enormity of his sins, has he continued long in this state? How dreadful his condition! One is almost ready to conclude there is no mercy, no salvation for him; that to renew him again to repentance is impossible. We would not go so far; yet we think the chances are, he never will be restored. Should he, however, in his abyss of sin, ever awake, and think of returning to his injured and dishonored Savior, deep and painful will be his conviction; broken, indeed, will be his heart; his cry will ascend as from the very belly of hell.

The probabilities are, he will find trouble and sorrow. Not because the Savior will be less merciful; but because the man will find it hard to confide in mercy that has been so much abused. Not because the blood of Jesus will be ineffectual to wash away his sins; but because he will find it difficult to avail himself, by faith, of that Blood that has been trampled beneath unhallowed feet.

Should one who has fallen so deplorably chance to read this page, we would speak to him in behalf of his abused Lord; and yet, our words shall be kind. See what you have done! How great is your sin! Look back to other days. Call to mind the goodness of God. Behold yourself now! How sad! But what then? Are you overwhelmed? filled with shame and sorrow? It is well.

Will you return? Will you come back to the arms of your slighted Savior? Do you say, How can I?—there is no mercy. Say not so. There

RETURN TO THE SAVIOR is mercy, if you have a heart to seek it. Come as first you came. The same Savior can still save; His blood will still be efficacious. You need to commence again at the beginning, to lay again the foundations; but do this, and all will be well. The cup is bitter, but you need to drink it; the path thorny, but you must travel it. It may be your sorrows will be greater than before; you must suffer them. But this one thing remember, and let it sustain you: If you will retrace your steps, if you will make the needful efforts, you may again be happy.

But [suppose] your case is not that which is described above; the advice does not meet your particular want. You have not entirely forsaken the Savior. You are still a Christian, in the enjoyment of a good hope, outwardly witnessing a good profession, and inwardly enjoying some of the sacred influences of the Spirit; but you are not in the high grace of a former experience.

The love of the world in an undue measure, yielding to the force of some temptation, neglect of some duty, want of watchfulness, has laid waste your confidence. You have departed in some degree from God; your thoughts, or your affection, have been given to an improper object, you have preferred your own will to the will of God in some particular, you have let in vanity or sloth, pride or impatience, uncharitableness or selfishness; you have ceased to be entirely the Lord's; guilt has ensued, condemnation is upon you. You feel it; you are unhappy. You do not doubt your relation, but all is not right within.

Humble yourself before God, confess your fault, return; wherein you have departed in thought, affection, volition, or deed, at once correct the wrong, and expect God to renew you again. There may be times and circumstances when the confession of your departure to the church may be necessary. If your failure has been manifest, it will bring your profession into discredit, and violate your own sense of propriety, should you continue the profession, without an admission of your temporary departure.

Soon as you return heartily to God, He will return to you: but it must be a full, hearty, entire return; not a mere desire, not a convulsive **WHOLEHEARTED** effort, not a declaration, not a semisincere and half-**RETURN** earnest thing; you must come as first you came, with **ESSENTIAL** an entire offering, and God will accept it. If you find great difficulty, as perhaps you may—it is possible even more than at first, for your reproof—you must overcome, overcome as at first, not in your own strength, but in the strength of God, which will become yours, by the use of the means, with which you are sufficiently acquainted.

And should any who have relapsed from this blessed experience

chance to read these pages, we would say to them, Return; retrace
TAKE your steps. You cannot, whatever other Christians may do,
IMMEDIATE find rest in an inferior state. You know the more excellent
ACTION way. Duty calls you with a 10-fold voice: Do not turn away,
be not overcome with discouragement, let not self-upbraidings hinder
you. You now know the cause of your loss; you may succeed better—
try again. Privilege invites, duty points the way, your unsatisfied heart
urges, the Spirit moves—do not delay.

Whatever be the extent of your departure, whether of long or
short duration, into more grievous or less guilty backslidings; whether
you have lost all, or only a part of your religious character—stop now.
Go not one step further. Turn at once to your dishonored Savior; bring
back your heart, guilty as it may be, and become His again. Think not
your case is hopeless. It may be deplorable—dreadful. You may have
deeply grieved the Spirit, reproached the Redeemer, insulted the Father; still, if you will return, there is no occasion for despair. See how
much is involved, and, as you would not risk your undoing, make
haste to find what you have unhappily forfeited.

Look before you. It is high time that you awake out of sleep.
What you do must be done now. A moment, and it may be too late.
Oh, that we might feel how much and earnestly we are called to work
now, and to work diligently, seeing that "the night cometh, when no
man can work" (John 9:4)!

* * *

When my inner assurance begins to grow faint I resolve to pray, to
obey, and to trust God until the assurance is strong again.[20]

---

20. Harper, *Holiness and High Country,* 194.

Since the Holy Ghost Abides

Rev. F. E. Hill, 20th Century

Mrs. F. E. Hill, 20th Century

1. Peace, blessed peace is   fill-ing now my soul, Since He pardon'd all my sin;
2. Rest, per-fect rest now   all my na-ture stills, Since His promis'd grace is mine;
3. Fire, ho - ly fire   is   burning in my heart, And the glo-ry rolls in tides;
4. Light, perfect light shines on this ho - ly way; Twice He touch'd my blinded eyes.

Love, per-fect love, in bil-lows o'er me roll, Since He cleans'd my heart with-in.
Joy, per-fect joy   my hap - py spir-it thrills, Since the day I said, "I'm Thine."
Pow'r, ho-ly pow'r is fill - ing ev - 'ry part, Since the Ho - ly Ghost a - bides.
Sight, perfect sight my vi - sion has to-day, Healed by Blood that sanc-ti- fies.

REFRAIN

Peace, per-fect peace! Love, perfect love! Sweeping o'er my soul in heav'n-ly tides!

Rest, per-fect rest!   Joy, per-fect joy! is mine since the Ho-ly Ghost a-bides.

12

Living the Life of Holiness

Entire sanctification is an experience to be received as the gracious gift of God. But it is also a life to be lived—a life filled with the Spirit of God.

The living of the sanctified life is usually referred to as the holy life, or the life of holiness. Here we are concerned with Christian growth that is maximized as we are daily guided by the Holy Spirit within. We grow as He gives us added knowledge of God's will for us; and we grow as we respond, through the power that He gives, to each new duty that He makes clear. Living the life of holiness is to be illumined by the Holy Spirit to see the holy way, and to be empowered by the Holy Spirit to walk in the paths that He shows to us.

* * *

"The steps of a good man are ordered by the Lord," said the Psalmist (37:23). George Müller added, "And the stops also."

Growth

Christians grow in likeness to Christ, both before and after entire sanctification. Successful growth requires obedience, trust, deep devotion, and personal discipline.

If we live in the Spirit, let us also walk in the Spirit (Gal. 5:25).

Just as you once accepted Christ Jesus as your Lord, you must continue living in vital union with Him, with your roots deeply planted in Him, being continuously built up in Him, and growing stronger in faith (Col. 2:6-7, Williams).

More like the Master

More like the Master I would ever be,
More of His meekness, more humility;
More zeal to labor, more courage to be true,
More consecration for work He bids me do.

Refrain:

Take Thou my heart; I would be Thine alone.
Take Thou my heart and make it all Thine own.
Purge me from sin, O Lord, I now implore.
Wash me and keep me Thine forevermore.

More like the Master is my daily prayer;
More strength to carry crosses I must bear;
More earnest effort to bring His kingdom in;
More of His Spirit, the wanderer to win.

More like the Master I would live and grow;
More of His love to others I would show;
More self-denial, like His in Galilee;
More like the Master I long to ever be.

—CHARLES H. GABRIEL, 1856-1932

MOMENT-BY-MOMENT CLEANSING[1]

"The blood of Jesus Christ . . . cleanseth us from all sin" all the time by cleansing us every now.

Holiness is both a *crisis* and a *process*. As Bishop Moule would say, "It is a crisis with a view to a process." A crisis is undoubtedly reached when, after full surrender of all we have, and are, to the Lord Jesus, we venture out upon the promise with an appropriating act, "the blood of Jesus Christ his Son cleanseth *[me, even me]* from all sin" (1 John 1:7). When we believe this, the Holy Spirit comes to our hearts in sanctifying power, excluding all the evil, and filling us with divine love, just as He came to our hearts in regenerating power when we believed for forgiveness and were adopted into the family of God. The heart is only cleansed from all sin by the Holy Spirit taking full possession of it, and it is only kept clean by His remaining in full possession. We teach, therefore, not a *state of purity,* but a *maintained condition of purity,* a moment-by-moment salvation

HOLY SPIRIT

---

1. Cook, *New Testament Holiness,* 43-45.

consequent upon a moment-by-moment obedience and trust. "The blood of Jesus Christ . . . cleanseth us from all sin" *all the time* by cleansing us every *now.*

Blessed word, *"cleanseth"* —present progressive tense—it goes on cleansing. Does it not teach, as Miss Havergal puts it, "a continual present, always a present tense, not a present which the next moment becomes a past, not a coming to be cleansed in the fountain only, but a remaining in the fountain"? It means ever-present provision for ever-present need; Christ is always a present Savior. We are kept clean like the eyes of a miner who is working all day amid the flying coal-dust. When he emerges into daylight his face is grimy enough, but his eyes are clear and lustrous, because the fountain of tears in the lachrymal gland is ever pouring its gentle tides over the eyes, cleansing away each speck of dust as it alights. Our spirits need a similar cleansing, and this is what our blessed Lord does for us, as we believe moment by moment that the Blood cleanseth.

The habit of faith must be acquired. Faith in the spiritual world has been compared to breathing in the physical. We breathe this moment and receive the oxygen into our lungs, it purifies the blood which goes coursing through the system, carrying life and nutriment to all the tissues; but when another moment comes we must breathe again. Life is made up of successive acts of breathing. We breathe moment by moment, and live moment by moment. If we cease to breathe, we cease to live. In like manner, we trust the blood of Jesus for cleansing this moment, and it cleanseth from all sin; another moment comes, and we trust again, and another moment yet again. We are thus kept clean exactly as we are made clean, through a constant succession of acts of faith in the cleansing Blood. But this habit of faith requires time to establish. Every habit grows out of a succession of little acts. The faith that cleanses our hearts from sin requires a definite effort at first, but repeated moment by moment it becomes spontaneous, and by and by, as natural as breathing. The habit becomes a necessity and easier as it grows.

DAILY FAITH

But only as we walk in the light does the blood of Jesus cleanse from all sin. Should there be a moment's hesitation about yielding, obeying, or trusting, communion with God will be broken, and darkness and sin will return. We must not only maintain a perpetual attitude of self-surrender and abandonment to the will of God, but our consecration must keep pace with the ever-widening circle of illumination. Most believers over whom Satan gets

DAILY YIELDING

an advantage are either disobedient to one of God's written commands or to the inward promptings of the Holy Spirit. The Blood, however, never loses its virtue, and whenever, in our walk in the light, we are sensible of the least soil of evil, we may wash again and be clean.

As already explained, holiness expresses that state of soundness in the spiritual part of man which corresponds to health in the physical part of man; but our souls, like our bodies, are liable to disease, though at present they may be in perfect health. Just as to maintain bodily health we must observe the laws of health, so to maintain spiritual health, we must moment by moment trust and obey.

How Holiness May Be Retained[2]

If holiness be worth possessing, it is worthy of the effort requisite to its attainment and preservation.

It is not sufficient that we know how to obtain; it is not sufficient that *we have obtained;* we must know, also, how to keep when we have made the acquisition. The secret of its preservation is not less important than the secret of its possession.

A greater mistake could not be committed, than to suppose that religion, when gained in any of its degrees, will be retained without effort—remain with us, as a thing of course, without care. **EFFORT REQUIRED** Character is eminently . . . liable to change; and to be perpetuated in one form, requires nurture and vigilance. Surrounded, as all of us necessarily are in this state, with countercurrents of influence, all acting upon us ceaselessly, with greater or lesser force, and, in their degree, having a tendency to leave their impression—to impart their tone and coloring, nothing can be more obvious than the absolute importance of constant attention and activity.

These influences need not, indeed, act upon us fatally, but they will act upon us certainly, unless restrained—resisted. A man enters upon the day with unsullied honor; he is tempted; he yields; his honor is in the dust. A Christian goes forth to duty, with a conscience void of offense—with a heart pure: evil presents itself; he is overcome; his purity is marred; his conscience is violated. Not a day passes in which there are not some such liabilities. What, under these circumstances . . . must be done in order that a sanctified soul may preserve its state and character; that it may be in the evening what it was in the morning;

---

2. Foster, *Christian Purity,* 162-66, 169-70.

this week, what it was last; this year, what it was the former year? . . .

We should never, when contemplating the subject of actual salvation, lose sight of the fact that we are coworkers with God; He works,

COWORKERS
WITH GOD

and we work with Him. It is so in the incipient motions, it is so throughout; so in the beginning, so in the progress; so in attaining, and so in maintaining our state. . . . But the question recurs—What must we do?

1. We answer, first: We must acquire the habit of constant watching against sin. The tempter is a vigilant and insidious foe, ever on the alert, ever cunning, and full of artifice. We need to be as wakeful and vigilant. There is no place where he may not approach us, no place so sacred that he will not dare to intrude himself. Even in the privacy of the closet, at the Communion, in the sanctuary, when alone, when in society, when musing, when conversing, when preaching, when praying, when praising, when engaged in business, when seeking pleasure, when employed, when idle; he ever lurks near us and seeks our ruin.

He often disguises his true character; sometimes appearing to us as an angel of light, using the honeyed tones of friendship, professing love, assuming a meek and suppliant air, consulting our good, wearing the mien of disinterestedness, extremely conscientious, employing plausible agents, not infrequently using our friends, recommending courses not decidedly sinful, proposing compromises, flattering, that we may become vain, persuading, that we may conciliate, raging, that we may yield, and with a thousand other modes, seeking either to surprise, conciliate, or overwhelm us.

Our only safety is in watching against him; guarding, with sleepless vigilance, the sacred precincts of the soul, that, if he enter, he be

GUARDING
OUR THOUGHTS

not entertained; nay, that he be refused an entrance— repulsed at the portal. This will require watching over our thoughts, that they be not idle, empty, vain, improper—on improper subjects, at improper times, in improper measure; over our motives, that they be not sinful, carnal, selfish, worldly; over our affections, that they do not wander, fix on wrong objects, exist in an inordinate degree, seek sinful indulgence or gratification.

Let it not be supposed that this would engross one's entire time —that it is requiring too much. By the grace of God, and the *instincts*, if I may employ the term, of a sanctified soul—by which I mean no more than its ready, almost spontaneous effort—it may be done, and done with ease. This is not our rest: and if holiness be worth possessing, it is worthy of the effort requisite to its attainment and preservation; and such effort is neither impracticable, in any state of circumstances, nor excessive.

2. Would you maintain a sanctified state? Then must there be on your part an absolute refusal to comply with temptation, under any **RESIST TEMPTATION** circumstances, to *any degree*. The slightest compliance is death. We would impress this deeply upon your minds. It is a very different thing from the watchfulness advised above. A sentinel may be very watchful, but not faithful: he may see the enemy, but not sound the alarm; nay, may make terms with him. You are not only to watch the approach of sin, but absolutely and totally to resist it!

It matters nothing though the temptation be powerful, though the indulgence be venial, you may not yield. You may not parley if the case is unequivocal. You may not go one step even toward apologizing for rudely repelling the unworthy seducer. Treat him with no tenderness when you repulse him; show no pity. Civility encourages him, and kindness begets intimacy. Let the purpose be firmly inflexible, whatever may be the hazard, that you will not go one step—not even look with a desire toward the path of the transgressor; "avoid it, pass not by it, turn from it, and pass away" (Prov. 4:15). This is your only safety, if you would maintain your relation to God—the state of your own soul.

If you . . . compromise, if you cannot consent to exercise such firmness of purpose, you need not calculate upon success; it is out of the question. It may require strength. You will have it. As your day is, so your grace will be. God will not leave you to struggle alone. If you use what you have, you shall never lack for whatever more may be needful. Remember this. And be not dismayed though your foes gather upon you like the tempest; though their name be legion; though you seem to be helpless in their hands. Trust in God, be of good courage; greater is He that is for you, than all they that are against you. . . .

6. Acquire the habit of living by the minute. Learn the secret of that wise counsel, when properly understood, "Be careful for noth-
MOMENT ing" (Phil. 4:6). Not that you are to be careless; but let each **BY** minute provide for itself. Let it not be supposed that you are **MOMENT** not to act for the future, but act by the minute. Take care of this moment now, while you have it, and the next when it comes; you will not then neglect any. You can live this minute without sin! Is it not so? Do it, then. Never mind what is before you. Do not sin now. When

each successive minute comes, do likewise. If you will do this, you will not sin at all. Days are made up of minutes; if each one is sinless, the day will be so. Now try this. Nothing is easier, nothing is more wise. Live by the minute. Carry on your business, trade, labor, study, plan for the future; but in all, act for the present, and do not sin now. Trust in God now; do God's will now; do not offend God now. If you will observe this simple rule, you will not fail to succeed. And now, what more need we add? Surely, if these advices be followed, and they certainly are practicable, you will not come short, you will ever prevail. May heaven prosper you!

The Testimony of Gen. Albert Orsborn[3]

Nothing is clearer to me than that the sanctification of my spirit has been conditional on continuous obedience.

My sanctification was a sweet and gracious experience. The work was accomplished in me, by God's Holy Spirit, when in my early teens. Through the influence of a Salvation Army officer's homelife, together with the formative effects of the meetings I attended, I was quite susceptible to religious appeals, from a tender age. I cannot remember the time when I did not earnestly covet goodness; yet all the while, evil had a tempting relish for me, and perhaps this was even accentuated by my closely guarded innocence of the world's ways.

God very clearly and convincingly revealed how perilously easy it had become for me to be insincere, and I became careful not to testify beyond my actual experience. This occasioned me many and bitter revelations and not a few confessions, for I failed again and again, in my secret heart experience. Consequently, my testimony was a very guarded and incomplete thing, "sometimes joyful, sometimes sad."

One day, in a flood of light, I saw myself and the "way of holiness," and God sanctified me for Christ's sake—body, soul, and spirit. With this experience came a new vision of Christ, and power to serve Him.

---

3. *Flames of Living Fire*, 89-91.

Albert William Orsborn (1886-1967) was the son of Salvation Army parents. Educated in boarding schools, he became an officer at age 22. He early served in New Zealand as chief secretary of the Salvation Army work, and later in the International Salvation Army Training College.

Elected territorial commander of the work in Scotland and Ireland, he served as British commissioner from 1940 to 1946. In 1942 his nation conferred on him the honor Commander of the British Empire. In 1946 Commissioner Orsborn was elected the sixth general of the Salvation Army, where he served until retirement in 1954.

His publications were mostly poetry and songs in Salvation Army periodicals.

Nothing is clearer to me than that the sanctification of my spirit has been conditional on continuous obedience. I did not then understand all that would be implied in my sanctification for the future, but I could say then, as I can say now, "He sanctifies." In this sense it is perhaps true to speak of our complete and continuous sanctification. The continuation of the divine favor is, I realize, the first essential of my officership in the Salvation Army. It is to me more than a delightful privilege; it is an absolute necessity. Continuation of divine favor has most certainly been conditional on my response to progressive revelation of ideals and of duty. More than once my feet have faltered. More than once my heart has almost deceived me. More than once, in temptations of fierce heat, I have had to fly to the Blood and cry, "Save me, Jesus, or I die!"

You who have passed this way will understand. Surely, God is glorified even in this! He is pleased to work more through our conscious weakness than through our conscious strength.

Satan has attacked me with the peril of the cold heart! At times I was concerned, moved by the mood of the moment; but the deep and abiding instincts and impulses of the soul winner I knew **CONCERN FOR SOULS** not. I humbled myself before the Lord, and by waiting at Calvary I saw and felt that elemental passion for saving others which burned itself into my inmost being, and is to this day the central fire of my spirit. Satan attempted to smother the flame. His assault has moved not so much on the more obvious lines as by the subtleties of transvaluation in life's plans and purposes. His strategy has been directed against the hidden thoughts and intents of my heart. As a rule, things which are in themselves good have been used as weapons against my soul.

God has permitted me to be tried through the very work of the King. It is so easy to get into the heat of the conflict, putting one's whole soul into the day's task, unconscious of the expenditure of one's spiritual resources. It has been truly said, "The evangelical worker is always on the edge of the abyss." It is so easy to get taken up with the Kingdom more than the King. No, my soul! The King first, always!

The purification of motive is another way in which God is always trying and proving my heart. Is it not the fact that our opportunities expose us to countless temptations in the direction of mixed motives?

When I laid aside sin and self and pride, the change was immediate. In my religion came sincerity; in my character, the discovery of weaknesses and the victory to conquer them; in my service, a delight.

PRAYER FOR A SPIRIT-LED LIFE[4]

Father in heaven, from this day forward I offer myself afresh to be led by Your Spirit. My prayer is and shall daily be:

Holy Spirit, be my Guide.
Holy Spirit, my door's open wide.
Make me to know Thy will divine;
Holy Spirit, be Thou mine! *

—MILDRED COPE, 1924—

*© 1963 by Lillenas Publishing Co. All rights reserved.

Attitudes

Being filled with the Spirit makes a difference in a Christian's attitudes.

Do not grieve the Holy Spirit of God, with whom you were sealed for the day of redemption. Get rid of all bitterness, rage, and anger, brawling and slander, along with every form of malice. Be kind and compassionate to one another, forgiving each other, just as in Christ God forgave you (Eph. 4:30-32, NIV).

The fruit of the Spirit is love, joy, peace, longsuffering, gentleness, goodness, faith, meekness, temperance (Gal. 5:22-23).

A NEW SPIRIT[5]

A new spirit will I put within you (Ezek. 36:26).

My spirit is seen in my basic attitudes, and those attitudes faithfully reflect the kind of person that I am.

If I am selfish, can I become generous? If I am critical, can I become appreciative? If I was born in a negative mood and have all of my life lived in reverse gear, can my spirit be changed so that I have a helpful, positive attitude? Although it seems too good to be true, God's answer to all of these questions is a glad yes.

The people to whom this promise was first made had a bad spirit. They defiled the land "by their own way and by their doings." They had oppressed their neighbors to the point of bloodshed. They were so indifferent to God that they had set up idol worship (Ezek. 36:17-18)—and yet God gave them this promise.

---

4. Harper, "I Would Like to Know God Better."
5. Harper, *Holiness and High Country*, 303.

If God can remake such lives as these, surely there is help for me also. This is the good news of the gospel. God not only forgives our past sins; He also changes our bad attitudes. But how?

It is through His indwelling presence. God's Spirit has always been with His people in some measure. But since Pentecost that Presence has been unique. Jesus said of the Holy Spirit, "Ye know him; for he dwelleth with you, *and shall be in you*" (John 14:17). From the inside God can and does work to make us like himself. We may have new spirits when we accept His Spirit.

> *Thou canst fill me, gracious Spirit,*
> *Though I cannot tell Thee how.*
> *But I need Thee, greatly need Thee;*
> *Come, oh, come, and fill me now!*
> —ELWOOD H. STOKES, 1815-95

SOMETHING MORE[6]

A Life Changed Because Spirit-filled

Sitting on the beach during the summer holidays, I had a chance to chat in relaxed circumstances with a Salvation Army bandsman. He is exemplary in attendance at band practice and meetings. He practices daily, so he is skilled in musicianship; and having been brought up in a Salvationist home, we would call him a good Salvationist, together with his wife and two children. But his "inner man" was spiritually hungry. "After 39 years," he said, "what have I got?"

His frank evaluation of his own knowledge of God reminded me of the late Bandmaster Tom Rive. Although God works in many different ways to call us into a vital relationship with himself, Bandmaster Rive says there are definite similarities or steps in our spiritual pilgrimage. First, there seems to be a realization of spiritual drought and then a seeking to see if there is, indeed, "something more." When one is convinced that there is, then comes the time of decision when one asks, accepts, and believes. Then, under the Spirit's tuition, there is a daily conversation with God which leads to a change of life-style in a continuing, maturing process.

The sense that something was missing from my Salvationist testimony became real to me between the ages of 15 and 18.

HUNGER It was when I heard clear preaching on holiness and began reading books and asking questions of both my contemporaries and

---

6. Testimony of Mrs. Stanley Walters, *The War Cry*. Printed in "The Sounding Board," Spring 1985. Used by permission.

my elders that I realized what that "something missing" was. In different generations different words are used to describe it. For me it was "the blessing of holiness." Today I usually speak of being "filled with the Spirit." But I agree with Col. John Larsson who suggests that we might again use the early Army term of "full salvation" because, although we often speak of salvation and holiness as two separate experiences, both are open to us because of the crucifixion and resurrection of Jesus Christ.

When I had gone through the stages of hungering for something more, and being convinced that what I needed was both available and promised, I knelt alone by my bedside and, with the help of a little booklet called *A Ladder to Holiness,* I made a commitment of my life to Christ. There was no question that I had been converted 11 years earlier, but I had grown up physically since then, and my spiritual development had not kept pace. I did not experience any great emotion, but I was sincere and knew that I wanted only what God wanted for me and was willing to forgo anything that did not meet with God's approval.

Having made that commitment once and for all, I pointed to the promises in 1 Thess. 5:23-24 and thanked God for doing the work of sanctification in my life. For a few days I had no inward assurance of ASSURANCE the fullness of the Spirit, but I kept thanking God for what I believed He had done in accordance with His promise; and then, as I was telling my girlfriend about my commitment, a wonderful knowledge that He had indeed accepted and sealed my offering came over me, and I knew I had been sanctified!

What does this "something more" mean in everyday practical words? I will try to tell you what it has meant in my life over these last 30 or more years.

New Reality

There were obvious things in the beginning. I found a new reality in my personal devotional life, as Paul promised would happen in 2 Corinthians 3. At that time I was a bank teller, and I would spend my lunch hour in a nearby park, delighting in reading the Bible and talking with God in prayer. How well I remember the strength that came to me through reading Psalm 27 before I opened a letter which I had guessed would contain unpleasant news of a teenager.

Joyful Service

My service in the corps became a joy rather than a duty. Several pleasures and habits I had been beginning to enjoy, although I knew they were questionable for Salvationists, were dropped without any sense of loss. I had a new direction to my life and a new satisfaction.

Vital Witnessing

A Spirit-filled life is attractive, and the "experience" is contagious. I spent that summer with a number of other young Salvationists. Most of us came alive spiritually together, and I can look at corps right across Canada today and point out those good friends of long ago, still happily and reliably serving the Lord.

Facing Selfish Ambition

But what of long-range, continuing effects of the blessing of holiness? Two verses in Psalm 118 put my description of a sanctified life in a biblical, picture language. Verse 19 asks God to "open to me the gates of righteousness." To me that depicts the seemingly narrow entrance into the beautiful life of holiness. Gates are narrow, and we cannot carry through with us any selfish ambitions or concealed doubtful actions if we long for righteousness. Yet once we commit ourselves in glad and binding abandonment to the doing of God's will, we find the truth of verse 5 which says, "The Lord answered me, and set me in a large place." Surprisingly the narrow gates of righteousness lead to a large place of opportunity for service, self-fulfillment and development.

Freedom

Because my whole being has been securely tied at the center to Christ and His will, I have felt able to venture out in all directions to study, investigate, feel, and relate. I can do this because the Holy Spirit empowers or restrains me inwardly, as promised in Jeremiah's vision of the new covenant (Jer. 31:33).

It reminds me of the tennis practice ball I used years ago. On an elastic string, but securely fastened to a central rock, it could be hit in any direction, for it would safely return to the center when it had reached the end of the safe periphery. What wonderful freedom and liberty I have—freedom from traits of character that would pull me down, and liberty to grow in the likeness of Jesus into the image of God which was His original plan for mankind—all this through the power of the Holy Spirit, and the result of walking in obedience to and dependence upon Him.

Change of Motivation

Because I had been brought up in a Christian home and became converted as a child, there were no drastic changes in my life-style. It was, rather, a change in motivation. There was a cleansing of the inner life, and the result of this has been a transparency or openness in my living. Because every action is lined up by the plumb line of whether or not it pleases God, I am not tied (too much, anyway) by the fear of what others think or say. The time I arise, the way I spend free time, the way I work at the office or at home, how much I get accomplished each day, are open to everyone's view. My thoughts and actions are quite open to question and discussion, for they are under my Master's jurisdiction, and therefore I am happy and relaxed in my life-style. This way of living has been tested in the cloisterlike setting of the training college and a boys' secondary boarding school in Africa where, naturally, we all seemed to live on top of one another.

Peace

One other attribute of the life of holiness stands out in my mind, and that is peace. Consistently throughout the years I have found that the Holy Spirit will not allow broken relationships in my life. If there have been disagreements or harsh words, I have not been able to spend many hours before I have had to be the activator in the process of reconciliation. No price is too much to pay for the peace of the Holy Spirit who acts as umpire in my life (Col. 3:15).

Then there is peace in my work. Since my ultimate goal in life is to please God and work for Him, no job or position is too lowly, for there is no task where we cannot witness for Him, either in word or in doing gladly the set work, for Jesus' sake. There is also peace from a restless spirit and a craving to justify oneself when maligned. God will prove our righteousness (Ps. 37:6), and it is to Him that we must answer (Rom. 14:4). Although by nature I am a worrier, I find that searching in the Scriptures for promises that speak of my immediate concern, brings peace to my anxious, edgy spirit.

Do you say, you make it seem all bright and rosy, so simple and easy? Once the initial dedication has been made, there is no need for struggle and defeat. But we are all human, and there have been times when I have made the wrong decisions or dabbled in things that were not helpful or had to work hard at keeping a right attitude or when busyness has made me physically exhausted and therefore spiritually weak. But the Holy Spirit has always gently prodded me, and the knowledge of the peace I had been missing has quickly brought me back to a renewed submission and dedication.

So my path has been similar to that of Bandmaster Rive—a need, a seeking, a claiming, and a daily walking. I would say to the bandsman I met on the beach, "It's obvious that the Lord has led you to the first step, for you have a sense of 'something missing.' Do press on till you prove for yourself that there is 'something more.'"

ATTITUDES OF LOVE[7]

Love is the distinguishing feature of the Christian life. Other religions say much about sacrifice, but they put little emphasis on love. No man can be a Christian who has not the love of God in his heart. "He that loveth not knoweth not God; for God is love" (1 John 4:8). This divine love enters our heart at conversion, when we are born again of the Spirit of Christ (John 3:3). "We know that we have passed from death unto life, because we love the brethren" (1 John 3:14).

At conversion, we become partakers of the divine nature, which is love. But there still remains in the heart of the saved man a love of self and of the world. Therefore, the love of God cannot be *perfectly* expressed in him. The old self-life will at times resist the gentle promptings of the new life of love within his heart. Thus it is that Christians will often think and say and do things that are not loving or Christlike. They need to be "made perfect in love" (1 John 4:18). In other words, they need to be perfectly filled and controlled by the Christ love within them.

God's love is always perfect, but it cannot find perfect expression in a heart that is not fully cleansed from sin and emptied of self. God's love, being perfect, cannot increase in quality; but it must ever grow within our hearts, increasing in quantity. In the parable of **FRUIT OF THE SPIRIT** the vine (John 15) Jesus tells us that we must bear fruit, then much fruit, and always more fruit. The fruit of the Spirit is love, and from the day of conversion there should be the fruit of love. As we grow in grace there should be an increasing abundance of love, and then as we come to the life of full surrender, there should be a

7. Maj. Allister Smith, *The Ideal of Perfection*, 55-59.

Allister Smith was born in South Africa of missionary parents. Converted in his teens at Cape Town, he later studied law and graduated from Pretoria University. After 13 years in government service, following a deep spiritual experience, he heard God's call to full-time service. Resigning from government work, he became a Salvation Army officer in Britain in 1929. Since 1937 he has campaigned continually in Britain and other lands.

fullness of love, or what John Wesley calls perfect love. By this he means that our love to God is now perfectly free from sin and from self.

In Gal. 5:22-23, we read that "the fruit of the Spirit is love, joy, peace, longsuffering, gentleness, goodness, faith, meekness, temperance." It will be noticed the text speaks of *fruit*, not fruits. In other words, all these virtues are different aspects of love. The well-known holiness writer S. D. Gordon says, "Joy is love singing; peace is love resting; longsuffering is love enduring; gentleness is love's touch; goodness is love's character; faith is love's habit; meekness is love forgetting itself; temperance (or self-control) is love holding the reins."

This perfect love of the sanctified Christian is beautifully expressed in 1 Corinthians 13, which has been called the love song of the Christian. It may seem to be an impossible ideal for us who are so human and so weak. In our own strength it is unattainable, but "with God all things are possible" ([Matt. 19:26; Mark 10:27] see Luke 1:37). This holiness, or perfect love, is simply Christ filling our lives, and living His life of love in us and through us. This love chapter of Paul's is in fact a portrait of Christ. Where the word "love" occurs in the chapter, we may put the word "Christ." Thus, Christ in us suffers long and is kind; Christ envies not; Christ is not easily provoked; Christ thinketh no evil; and so on.

CHRIST IN US

This wonderful chapter shows us the secret of holiness. It is something more than sacrifice, or service, or talents, or gifts, important though these may be. It is the divine nature completely possessing us to the exclusion of all sin and self. It is the music of God in the soul, the beauty of the Lord shining out of us, the fullness of Christ flowing through us. We will not be conscious of this, but others will see Christ in us.

Divine love in us helps us to love the unlovable, the degraded, the drunkards, the lowest men and women. It helps us to see good in the worst. It makes us willing to forgive those who hurt us, and to love our enemies. It is the greatest power in the world. It makes sacrifice easy and gives joy in suffering. It keeps us from impatience and resentment.

This life of perfect love is only possible while there is daily surrender and daily faith. If, for a moment, the sanctified man should fail in his surrender, or falter in his faith, he will fail in this matter of love. He will think, or say, or do something which is not loving and kind. Then he must confess this and seek the cleansing of the blood of Christ, also confessing to others when necessary. It is a moment-by-moment experience, calling for a close walk with Christ. If we are to bear this fruit of love all the time, we must constantly abide in Christ, as the branch does in the vine. If the union is broken for a moment, we must restore it (John 15:5).

SEARCH ME, O GOD[8]

I open my heart to You, Lord. Show me any attitude that is unchristlike. I now offer my prayer:

> *Search me, O God, and know my heart today.*
> *Try me, O Savior, know my thoughts, I pray.*
> *See if there be some wicked way in me;*
> *Cleanse me from ev'ry sin, and set me free.*
>
> —J. EDWIN ORR, 1912—

Wholeness

Holiness tends toward fulfillment of life and wholeness of personality.

I have come that they may have life, and have it to the full (John 10:10, NIV).

Since the day we heard about you, we have not stopped praying for you and asking God to fill you with the knowledge of his will through all spiritual wisdom and understanding. And we pray this in order that you may live a life worthy of the Lord and may please him in every way: bearing fruit in every good work, growing in the knowledge of God, being strengthened with all power according to his glorious might (Col. 1:9-11, NIV).

Ho! Every One That Is Thirsty

> *Ho, ev'ry one that is thirsty in spirit!*
> *Ho, ev'ry one that is weary and sad!*
> *Come to the fountain; there's fullness in Jesus,*
> *All that you're longing for. Come and be glad.*

Refrain:

> *"I will pour water on him that is thirsty;*
> *I will pour floods upon the dry ground.*
> *Open your heart for the gift I am bringing.*
> *While ye are seeking Me, I will be found."*

---

8. Harper, "I Would Like to Know God Better."

Child of the Kingdom, be filled with the Spirit!
Nothing but fullness thy longing can meet;
'Tis the enduement for life and for service.
Thine is the promise, so certain, so sweet.
—LUCY J. RIDER, 20th Century

HOLINESS AS SOUL HEALTH[9]

What is holiness? Well, holiness is that state of heart which results from being sanctified wholly by the power of the Holy Spirit. Sanctification is the crisis; holiness is the result following the crisis. Such a state is that of moral purity. The will is completely adjusted to the will of God, and the affections are purified, alienated from sin and the world, and exalted to a supreme love for God. It is not a negative state, implied simply by freedom from sin; it is also a positive condition in which the heart is filled with perfect love of God, which enables one to love God with all his heart and his neighbor as himself.

Holiness and health come from the same root word in the Anglo-Saxon. That is, holiness is soul health. Holiness is to the soul what health is to the body. Health is that state of the body in which there is freedom from disease and in which there is general and complete soundness of organs and tissues. It is not easy to describe the symptoms of health. Perhaps it is best to think of it as the state in which one is enabled to live from day to day without pain or tormenting weariness and with a minimum of thought and care concerning himself. And holiness is like that to the soul. Sin is abnormal, like disease in the body. It is likened to a thorn in the side or to a broken foot. It brings uneasiness and strain and burden. Holiness removes the thorn, cures the broken foot, and makes the Christian life a joy.

INTEGRATED PERSONALITY[10]

The person who is entirely sanctified begins the life of holiness
with a spiritual wholeness or integration of personality that those who
have not been sanctified do not know.

The experience of entire sanctification and the life of holiness does not impersonalize or dehumanize its possessor. Rather through

---

9. Chapman, *Holiness, the Heart of Christian Experience,* 19-20.

10. Corlett, *Meaning of Holiness,* 86-88.

the cleansing and the spiritual wholeness brought about in entire sanctification, the true self is freed from many former lim-
SPIRITUAL
WHOLENESS itations, and the result is a truly normal expression and
development of the personality. Paul expressed this freedom thus: "The law of the Spirit of life in Christ Jesus hath made *me*
free from the law of sin and death" (Rom. 8:2). And he further stated
that through the crucifixion of the old self, the true self was made to
live: "I am crucified with Christ: nevertheless I live; yet not I, but
Christ liveth in me" (Gal. 2:20). A sanctified person is just as human as
an unsanctified man, but he is aware of an inner freedom of which the
unsanctified person knows nothing. He enjoys freedom from impurities of sin, his heart is cleansed. He has freedom from the inner
strain caused by the presence of the carnal mind. That which "is
enmity against God . . . not subject to the law of God, neither indeed
can be" (Rom. 8:7) has been removed. He has a freedom in the fullness
of the Holy Spirit which gives power in service and victory in conflict.
He is human, but he is devoted to God and filled with His Spirit.

Holiness as devotedness to God brings a dominant purpose to
life. In this sense holiness is conceived as love to God and devotion to
His will, or as perfect love. "Love is in a sense perfect or all-inclusive,
when it rules all the life and embraces all people, as the Father's love is
perfect or all-inclusive because it encircles all men (Matt. 5:44-48).
Love is complete to a certain limit when it . . . pervades the whole
conscious life and has in a large measure reorganized character around
itself as the dominating principle."[11] Speaking of the sanctified person,
Dr. Daniel Steele says, "However fractional the man may be in all other
respects, he is in one sense an integer: love pervades the totality of his
being."[12]

This phase of holiness and that of spiritual wholeness corresponds greatly to what psychologists call personality integration, the
term which a modern psychologist defines as "the achieve-
BLENDED
IMPULSES ment of that harmonious development of one's personality
which makes possible a sense of ease and facility in meeting
the issues of life. It is free from disturbing inner conflicts that try the
souls of men and render them ineffective in their daily tasks. Unbridled appetites do not dominate, violent emotions do not un-
expectedly break through and take control. . . . The emotional
attitudes, the desires, the impulses and propulsions of the individual

---

11. Curtis, *An Epoch in the Spiritual Life*, 201.
12. *Milestone Papers*, 32.

have been so blended as to permit him to direct his energies toward one end." What this writer suggests as the achievement of a person, Dr. Daniel Steele says is "the great work of the Sanctifier," which "by His powerful and usually instantaneous inworking, is to rectify the will, poise the passions aright, hold in check all innocent and eradicate all unholy appetites, and to enthrone the conscience over a realm in which no rebel lurks."[13]

Another writer expresses this phase of holiness in these words: "The goal of Christianity is to bring men into perfect communion with God. . . . When Christ has been accepted as the Lord of the life and perfect relationship with God through Him has come to be the master sentiment, all other sentiments become coordinated in their expression to help toward the [realization] of the master sentiment. . . . His energy is no longer wasted in activity which is unrelated to the ultimate goal of his life. Everything he does is an aid to the realization of that goal. Abundant life for him means life that is spent in fellowship with God."[14]

This devotedness to God as a dominant force in life is of great practical benefit in the life of holiness. The inner unanimity gives a poise to life, an abiding peace in the heart, and a disposi-

INNER UNANIMITY tion to face life's conditions and battles with courage and fortitude. Evelyn Underhill says: "Indeed, it is a peculiarity of the great spiritual personality that he or she constantly does in the teeth of circumstances what other people say cannot be done. He is driven by a total devotion which overcomes all personal timidity, and gives a power unknown to those who are playing for their own hand or carving their own career."[15]

The person who is entirely sanctified begins the life of holiness with a spiritual wholeness or integration of personality that those who have not been sanctified do not know.

*　　*　　*

W. E. McCumber reminds us that this wholeness and integration of personality is one of the common denominators of entire sanctification.

In 1 Thess. 5:23 the apostle prays that the believer may be put and kept in a condition of blamelessness, body and soul and spirit

---

13. Ibid., 134.
14. Clifford Barbour, *Sin and the New Psychology.*
15. *The Spiritual Life,* 96.

made holy and governed by God. Man's physical, mental, and moral faculties are to be properly oriented to each other, and all to God.

The prayer for the Hebrews (13:21) that the God of peace would make them perfect, is [also] a prayer for this beautiful harmony of all that constitutes man and manhood. The word perfect . . . suggests the mending of a net or the setting of a dislocated member, that their original purpose may be accomplished. It unfolds the wonderful possibility of being completely adjusted to and harmonized with the will of God, for doing God's will is man's business in life. The appetites, faculties, and passions which were deranged and degraded by sin are to be cleansed and controlled by God.

In all three viewpoints [faith, goodness, and wholeness], the negative implications are too patent and strong to be ignored. Faith is not completed until unbelief is destroyed. Goodness is not satisfied until badness is mortified. Personality is not integrated until carnality is eradicated. The prayers are for an experience of entire sanctification that makes one holy by the utter extirpation of all that is unholy. The "carnal mind," the "evil heart of unbelief," is to be dealt with decisively and ruthlessly. It is to be abolished.[16]

Satisfied

All my life-long I had panted
For a draught from some cool spring
That I hoped would quench the burning
Of the thirst I felt within.

Well of water, ever springing,
Bread of life, so rich and free,
Untold wealth that never faileth,
My Redeemer is to me.

Refrain:

Hallelujah! I have found Him—
Whom my soul so long has craved!
Jesus satisfies my longings;
Through His blood I now am saved.

—CLARA TEAR WILLIAMS, 1858-1937

Humanity

Though sanctified wholly, men and women are still limited by

---

16. *Holiness in the Prayers of St. Paul*, 104-5.

their imperfections in judgment, personality, and conduct; they are still subject to all sorts of temptations.

The eyes of the Lord run to and fro throughout the whole earth, to shew himself strong in the behalf of them whose heart is perfect toward him (2 Chron. 16:9).

He said unto me, My grace is sufficient for thee: for my strength is made perfect in weakness (2 Cor. 12:9).

We have this treasure in earthen vessels, that the excellency of the power may be of God, and not of us.

We are troubled on every side, yet not distressed; we are perplexed, but not in despair;

Persecuted, but not forsaken; cast down, but not destroyed;

Always bearing about in the body the dying of the Lord Jesus, that the life also of Jesus might be made manifest in our body (2 Cor. 4:7-10).

JOHN WESLEY'S VIEW[17]

We . . . believe that there is no such perfection in this life as implies an entire deliverance, either from ignorance or mistake, in things not essential to salvation, or from numberless infirmities wherewith the corruptible body more or less presses down the soul. We cannot find any ground in Scripture to suppose, that any inhabitant of a house of clay is wholly exempt, either from bodily infirmities, or from ignorance of many things; or to imagine any is incapable of mistakes, or falling into diverse temptations.

THE HUMAN AND THE CARNAL[18]

We admit that the physical phases of the consequence of sin may properly be included under a general name like depravity. And when such general terms are used, a broad claim that depravity is separable [from human life] is not valid. It is only the moral taint, the virus in the bloodstream of the spiritual man, which is included in the promise, "The blood of Jesus Christ his Son cleanseth us from all sin" (1 John 1:7). The holiness which is commanded and promised for this life is a wholeness of spirit, not a wholeness of the complete personality. Dr. Wiley is undoubtedly correct when he says, "Since mental strain often weakens the physical constitution, and physical weakness in turn

---

17. "Principles of a Methodist," *Wesley's Works,* 14:364.
18. Chapman, *The Terminology of Holiness,* 29-30.

clouds the mind and spirit of man, there is ever needful, a spirit of charity toward all men."[19] And to this we would add, what I think Dr. Wiley implies, that this charity should not exclude ourselves. There are many sincere people who very much need their own mercy to save them from unnecessary torment because of their weaknesses and tendencies that are involuntary and which are of the physical rather than of the moral nature.

Because of the delicate measure of the line which divides the physical and the moral, the human and the carnal, it is not always possible to distinguish the one from the other. And while we need charity for ourselves and for others that we may not call human weakness sin, we also need to be exceedingly careful (especially when appraising ourselves) that we do not call that which is sinful and carnal by some softer name. To do so would compromise the fundamentals of holiness on the altar of a misplaced charity.

But however difficult it may be to distinguish the human and the carnal, it is the obligation of every Christian to do so within himself. Having made the distinction, human weakness remains as a badge of his humiliation, but sin is to be completely destroyed through faith in our Lord Jesus Christ. In thought, and so far as possible in word, the term sin should be applied only to the carnal and separable. That which is only human and inalienable should be known as weakness or infirmity. Such an observance of terms would save much misunderstanding.

HOLINESS AND TEMPTATION[20]

It is not temptation, but the yielding to it, that is sinful.

It is a mistake to suppose that there is any state of grace this side of heaven which puts a Christian where he is exempt from temptation. So long as a soul is on probation it will be tested by solicitations to sin.

It is true, when the heart is cleansed from all evil, the warfare *within* ceases. The struggle with the flesh, or inbred sin, or depravity, by whatever name it may be called, comes to an end when all antagonisms to God are expelled from the soul, and Christ reigns without a rival. But there are other enemies than those which exist within, against whom we shall have to fight strenuously to the end. "We wrestle not against flesh and blood, but against principalities, against pow-

---

19. *Christian Theology,* 2:140.
20. Cook, *New Testament Holiness,* 12-15.

ers, against the rulers of the darkness of this world, against spiritual wickedness [wicked spirits] in high places" (Eph. 6:12). This implies temptation, but temptation cannot be inconsistent with holiness, because Jesus "was in all points tempted like as we are, *yet without sin*" (Heb. 4:15).

The Christian life is a long battle, but that fact does not imply that we are sinful, or inclined to sin. The nearer we live to God, the thicker and faster will Satan's arrows fly. Some Christians do not live near enough to God to be the subject of a downright spiritual struggle. There is no better evidence of grace and progress than that we are much harassed by Satan's emissaries. He does not need to employ his forces against nominal and inconsistent professors of religion. Severe temptation often precedes or follows special and signal blessing.

JESUS WAS TEMPTED   Christ's great battle with Apollyon occurred immediately after the descent of the Holy Ghost at His baptism. As soon as He had received the signal anointing, which was to prepare Him for His great mission, "then was Jesus led up of the Spirit into the wilderness to be tempted of the devil" (Matt. 4:1). His temptation was evidently a part of the divine plan, not only permitted, but arranged for. Experience was gained in His conflict with Satan, which could not have been obtained in any other way. Having *"suffered* being tempted, he is [now] able to succour them that are tempted" (Heb. 2:18) as would have been impossible had He not resisted Satan's fiery darts himself.

Temptations are permitted for a purpose. None can come without divine permission. Did not Satan complain that God had set a hedge about Job which he could not pass without a special permit? The Indians say that when a man kills a foe, the strength of the slain enemy passes into the victor's arm. In that weird fancy lies a great truth. Each defeat leaves us weaker for the next battle, but each conquest leaves us stronger.

"Did Jesus Christ know that Judas was a thief?" was a question asked at one of our recent holiness meetings. The reply was in the **STRENGTH THROUGH TESTING**   affirmative. "Then why did the Master, if He knew that, give him the bag?" continued the interrogator. The reply was: God allows the bag to be put in every life—by the bag is meant that which is constantly testing our loyalty to Him—and usually the temptation comes in the weakest place of our character. God permits this because He knows we can only gain strength in the weak place by overcoming temptation at that point. Each new triumph brings an increase of moral power and makes victory the next time easier. This is probably the reason why Bunyan places nearly all the great combats which Christian fought with Satan early in his journey. The first years of Christian life are the formative period of Christian character when the assaults of the tempter are fullest of possibilities of benefit to the believer. . . .

Some sincere souls are in constant bondage because they have never been taught to discriminate between *evil thoughts* and *thoughts about evil.* We must discern between things that differ. So long as we are in this world, and so long as we have five senses coming in contact with a world abounding with evil, Satan will be sure to use these as avenues of temptation. But no taint comes on the spirit from temptation which is at once and utterly rejected. It may and should be instantly repelled.

Milton says:

> *Evil into the mind of God or man*
> *May come and go, so unapproved, and leave*
> *No spot or blame behind.*

It may seem difficult to some to ascertain whether certain states of the mind are the result of temptation, or the uprisings of evil in their own nature. But when suggestions of evil awaken no response and kindle no desire, when they cause a shudder and a recoil, when they are opposed to our usual inclinations and desires, and cause pain, we may safely conclude that they are from without and not from within, and no self-reproach need ensue.

An evil thought springs from evil existing in the heart, but a thought about evil is a suggestion, flashed upon the mind by what we see or hear, or by the law of association, or by the enemy of our souls. Those who are holy have no evil within, consequently no evil thoughts; but intruding thoughts and whispers of evil will often need to be resisted. These are an unchangeable condition of probation. Provided proper caution has been used to avoid occasion of temptation, "no spot or blame" is left behind, any more than the shadow of a cloud passing over a beautiful lake disturbs or defiles it. It is not temptation, but the yielding to it, that is sinful, and there is a condition in which we may, with Paul, always triumph.

Temptation is first presented to the intellect, flashed it may be in a moment, the thoughts are appealed to—this is the earliest stage of temptation. Thence it is transmitted to the sensibilities, in which region it operates upon the senses, appetites, passions, or emotions.

There is danger lest these be excited with a desire for gratification. A critical stage of temptation is now reached, but no guilt is necessarily contracted. In the case of those whose hearts are not entirely cleansed from sin, the temptation finds more or less inward sympathy, but there is no guilt incurred unless the evil suggestion is cherished or tolerated. The will has yet to be challenged, and upon its decision depends entirely whether the tempter is to be successful or not. If the will says, "No," to the temptation, the tempter is foiled and defeated, and the soul comes off more than conqueror.

Though it is possible for the fully cleansed soul to listen to Satan, and to reason with him until he again injects sin into the heart as of old—he "beguiled Eve through his subtilty" (2 Cor. 11:3), whose heart was perfectly pure—still it is not so likely that he will be successful as before the heart was cleansed from sin. . . . Holiness makes none so secure as that they cannot sin, but it gives them to possess all the elements of strength and stability. Though the warfare be long and severe, yet, by abiding in Christ, victory may be constant and complete; and as storms help to root the trees, we shall find that the best helps to growth in grace are the affronts, the crosses, and the temptations that befall us.

Yield Not to Temptation

Yield not to temptation, For yielding is sin.
Each vict'ry will help you Some other to win.
Fight manfully onward; Dark passions subdue.
Look ever to Jesus; He'll carry you through.

Refrain:
Ask the Savior to help you, Comfort, strengthen, and keep you.
He is willing to aid you; He will carry you through.

—HORATIO R. PALMER, 1834-1907

Dangers

Dangers to which the sanctified are especially vulnerable include spiritual pride and setting standards too high.

Abide in me, and I in you. As the branch cannot bear fruit of itself, except it abide in the vine; no more can ye, except ye abide in me.

I am the vine, ye are the branches: He that abideth in me, and

I in him, the same bringeth forth much fruit: for without me ye can do nothing.

If a man abide not in me, he is cast forth as a branch, and is withered; and men gather them, and cast them into the fire, and they are burned (John 15:4-6).

Spiritual Pride[21]

It must be clear by now that the sanctified life is basically life lived utterly under the control, moment by moment, of the Holy Spirit. How can we know when we have crossed the line . . . from self-respect to pride? . . .

An infinite amount of trouble and misunderstanding among Christians arises out of this persistent temptation to judge others, imputing motives which we have no right to impute. It is true that we are to exercise righteous judgment and that the power to weigh evidence and choose the good and reject the bad, the critical faculty, is a part of the equipment God has given us. With this, evil may be cut off from the church. But here is one more case where a legitimate, God-given quality can become the agent of self. What is there which is so ready to Satan's hand with which to pull at the vanity of our minds as the pride of our opinions and judgments?

It has not yet dawned in the minds of many Christians that the pride of opinion is just as damning and must be dealt with just as decisively as any other sin. Of course the answer always is, "But I am right!" That is the way we always feel about our judgments. It is in the very nature of judgment that it should carry with it an emotional tone which we call conviction or certainty. But suppose two sanctified people hold opposite judgments. Each feels the other is wrong. Actually both are wrong if there is not a disposition to yield! So I must stop passing judgment on whether my brother is sanctified when he wears things I cannot wear without pride, or speaks more explosively than I would let myself under provocation, or seems too sensitive about the criticisms I have given for his good. I just do not know whether he has crossed his line in these matters or not, and he is not judged before God by my line.

*   *   *

Wesley asks, "How shall we avoid setting perfection too high or too low?"

---

21. Everett L. Cattell, *The Spirit of Holiness*, 49-50.

He answers, "By keeping to the Bible, and setting it just as high as the Scripture does. It is nothing higher and nothing lower than this— the pure love of God and man; the loving God with all our heart and soul, and our neighbor as ourselves. It is love governing heart and life, running through all our tempers, words, and actions."[22]

A Charge to Keep I Have
BOYLSTON

Charles Wesley, 1707-1788   Lowell Mason, 1792-1872

1. A   charge to keep   I   have,   A   God to glo - ri   - fy;
2. To   serve the pres - ent   age,   My   call - ing to   ful - fill;
3. Arm me   with jeal - ous   care,   As   in Thy sight to   live;
4. Help me   to watch and   pray,   And on thy-self re -   ly,

A   nev - er - dy - ing   soul to save, And   fit it for   the   sky.
Oh,   may it   all   my   pow'rs en - gage To   do my Mas - ter's will!
And,   oh, Thy ser - vant, Lord, pre - pare A   strict ac-count to   give!
As - sured if   I   my   trust be - tray I   shall for - ev - er   die.

---

22. *Wesley's Works*, 11:397.

13

Witnessing and Proclamation

God has planned that the good news of salvation through Christ shall spread by word of mouth and by example of life from us who have found Him to those who yet need to know Him. We believe this method of witnessing is as true for full salvation as for the message of forgiveness. Jesus said, "When the Holy Spirit comes on you . . . you will be my witnesses" (Acts 1:8, NIV).

Christ wants the message proclaimed by His preachers, testified to by those who have received sanctifying grace, and exemplified in daily conduct by all who seek to "walk in the Spirit" (Gal. 5:16, 25).

By every available channel of human communication we seek to spread the full gospel to the whole world until our Lord returns to this earth.

Witnessing

Testifying to God's work of entire sanctification honors God and spreads the truth.

You will receive power when the Holy Spirit comes on you; and you will be my witnesses in Jerusalem, and in all Judea and Samaria, and to the ends of the earth (Acts 1:8, NIV).

When they saw the courage of Peter and John and realized that they were unschooled, ordinary men, they were astonished and they took note that these men had been with Jesus. . . . Then they called them in again and commanded them not to speak or teach at all in the name of Jesus. But Peter and John replied, "Judge for yourselves whether it is right in God's sight to obey you rather than God. For we cannot help speaking about what we have seen and heard" (Acts 4:13, 18-20, NIV).

Of the several paradoxes in the Christian gospel, one is this: It characteristically produces both *humility* and *testimony*. A Christianity so humble that it does not testify is false to the New Testament. On the other hand, a Christianity that gives its personal witness in terms or tones that exalt oneself is likewise alien to the New Testament.[1]

* * *

Testimony is an indispensable factor and an effective force in the propagation of the doctrine and the promotion of the experience of holiness among the people of God.

In giving personal testimony it is always best to use forms that exalt Christ and not ourselves. The vast majority of intelligent people are offended if anyone says, "I am sanctified," or, "I am holy." This sounds like holiness is an accomplishment bringing merit to the possessor. The proper form is, "God has graciously sanctified me," or, "The abiding Holy Spirit keeps my heart clean from sin." Here the emphasis is on the divine grace, where it actually belongs.[2]

SPOKESMEN OF THE SPIRIT[3]

"We cannot but speak" (Acts 4:20).

The Spirit came to inspire witness. The repeated references to *speaking* establish a motif in this chapter (Acts 4). From Peter and John we learn what it means to be spokesmen of the Spirit.

A. *They Spoke to the People*

"They were speaking to the people" (v. 1, RSV used in this section), the crowd attracted by the boisterous rejoicing of a healed beggar. They seized every chance to make Christ known!

---

1. Paul S. Rees, in *Flames of Living Fire*, 95.

2. Chapman, *Terminology of Holiness*, 78.

3. W. E. McCumber, in *Proclaiming the Spirit*, comp. Harold Bonner, 79-81.
William E. McCumber (1923—) has been editor of the *Herald of Holiness* since 1976. Born in Wheeling, Mo., he was converted in 1940 and called to preach.
He holds the M.A. from Point Loma Nazarene College and an honorary D.D. from Trevecca Nazarene College. After pastoring for 27 years, Dr. McCumber taught for 9 years at Point Loma and Eastern Nazarene colleges before his present assignment.
Among his books are *Holiness in the Prayers of St. Paul, Preaching Holiness from the Synoptic Gospels,* and editor of *Great Holiness Classics,* vol. 5, *Holiness Preachers and Preaching.*

Many "believed" (v. 4)! Indeed, "about five thousand" men were converted on this occasion. This was harvest even greater than at Pentecost. Why should we not believe that our mightiest results always lie in the future, since the power of the Spirit and the Word never diminish?

But others were "annoyed" (v. 2), namely, the religious leaders of Jerusalem (v. 5). The successes of the gospel posed a threat to their vested interests, and they reacted swiftly to protect themselves by arresting Peter and John (v. 3). There is risk and cost involved in being a witness for Christ!

B. *They Spoke to the Court*

"Peter, filled with the Spirit, said to them" (v. 8). The Spirit supplied "uneducated, common men" (v. 13) with boldness to speak out in the council as freely as they had in the Temple!

They spoke out, *exalting the authority of Jesus.* The council demanded, "By what power or by what name did you do this?" (v. 7). And the instant response was "By the name of Jesus . . . this man is standing before you well" (v. 10). The dauntless apostles proclaimed the crucified and risen Jesus as the one Way to God (vv. 9-12). "By what . . . name? . . . By the name of Jesus . . . There is no other name"!

They spoke out, *defying the authority of the court!* The angry and frustrated council, unable to deny the miracle, sought to silence the witnesses (vv. 14-18). They "charged them not to speak"! But they were under orders to speak and chose to obey God rather than men. Of such courageous witnessing has been the Church's advance throughout history.

C. *They Spoke to the Lord*

Released under threat, they joined the Church in prayer, and "lifted up their voices together to God." Whoever would speak *for* Him must speak *to* Him!

They *acknowledged His sovereignty.* The leaders who conspired to oppose Christ were unwittingly fulfilling what the sovereign Maker and Ruler of men "had predestined to take place" (vv. 24-28). God, and not human power structures, controls history!

They *implored His support.* "Lord, look upon their threats, and grant to thy servants to speak thy word with all boldness" (v. 29). Not in their human bravery could they dismiss the threats and renew the mission. They knew their weakness and sought that strength from God which is perfected in weakness.

They *received the Spirit.* "They were all filled with the Holy Spirit and spoke the word of God with boldness" (v. 31). Courage to stand up and speak out for Christ in the face of threat is the gift of the indwelling Spirit. He will not be silenced when men desperately need to hear the judging, saving Word of God, nor will those in whom He lives and rules. Speak to God, and you can speak to men!

"We cannot but speak"! The people need to hear; therefore we go on speaking! We are under orders to witness; therefore we go on speaking! The Spirit within us makes proclamation irrepressible; therefore we go on speaking!

SANCTIFIED THROUGH A PERSONAL WITNESS[4]

It was so unmistakably real that I can do no other than bear my witness.

It is a joy for me to tell what happened in this deeper relationship with God, and what it has meant to me.

It happened a long time ago; but the memory of it is so fresh and the results have been so lasting that it is still gloriously up-to-date, affecting my entire Christian life—past, present, and future.

From that first moment of the realization of saving grace, I wanted all that God could give me, and soon found myself yearning for a deeper life in Him. It was not long before I began to feel that, glorious as my new experience in conversion had been, God was now holding before me something of a deeper nature than that which I already enjoyed.

While my love for Christ was such that it pained me to know that

---

4. Harry E. Jessop, *I Met a Man with a Shining Face,* 14 ff.

Harry Edward Jessop (1884-1974) was one of the ablest expositors of Christian perfection to come from the British Holiness Movement.

Converted at 17, Harry later "met a man with a shining face" (his own expression) who led him into the experience of entire sanctification. He joined the Church of the Nazarene in 1916 and pastored the Morley church.

In 1920 Jessop was invited to pastor the Holiness Mission Tabernacle in Manchester and to serve as president of the International Holiness Mission in the north of England.

He left England in 1929 to become guest pastor of the Northwest Tabernacle in Chicago. The following year he became pastor of the Chicago Austin Church of the Nazarene. While there he was invited to teach at the Chicago Evangelistic Institute (now Vennard College, University Park, Iowa). Jessop's gifts soon led to his election as dean, and later as president of C.E.I. He was awarded the honorary D.D. by Asbury College.

Author of many tracts and a dozen books, three titles indicate the emphasis of his ministry: *The Heritage of Holiness, We the Holiness People, The Consecrating Believer and the Sanctifying God.*

I had grieved Him, my spiritual life was far from constant, and my communion was not sustained. Frequently, the conflicts into which I came did not end in such a manner as to bring glory to the Lord. I was conscious of a lack of power in service, and of a strange inward conflict which did not seem to be consistent with New Testament standards.

One day, however, an unexpected thing happened: I met a man whose face shone with something I had never seen before. It was a heavenly radiance betokening a real soul satisfaction and suggesting a deep inward rest. As I looked at him, my heart was filled with an unspeakable longing to have what he possessed; but the longer I looked, the more puzzled I became. As he looked at me, he evidently read the longing of my hungry heart, for he startled me with a strange question:

"Brother," said he, "have *you* been baptized with the Holy Ghost and with fire?"

My reply must have sounded simple, but it came from my heart as I answered:

"I don't know what you mean by being baptized with the Holy Ghost and fire; but if that is it that shines out of your face, I want it."

He was not long in telling me that the radiance on his countenance was the result of a definite spiritual experience, a baptism with the Holy Spirit. Wesley called it *the second blessing;* and this, said my newfound friend, is for *you,* and for every child of God who will seek it today. He began to give me some simple instructions as to how I might receive it, showing me the need of a complete consecration, my entire life with all its reaches being demanded as a living sacrifice to God. When that consecration was complete, a simple act of faith would bring the blessing.

It is a joy to testify that the consecration was made and the faith exercised; and, blessed be God, the blessing came!

The question now comes, and rightly so: Just what did this do for you; what were the immediate results; and what have been the lasting benefits as the years have passed?

There have been definite results, both immediate and abiding. The phases have been many. Here, however, I shall mention only three as they now occur to me, believing as I do that such an experience is within reach of all who will seek it.

First of all, this baptism with the Holy Spirit brought a consciousness of *deep inward cleansing.* When God saved me, there was, of course, some measure of cleansing; but in this further experience the work was deeper. It went further and did more.

In that first work of grace, which was glorious indeed, the inwardness of it had to do with the assurance of salvation. The Spirit answered to the Blood, and told me I was born of God. Here, however, that same Spirit, exercising an entirely different office, seemed to deal more directly with *me*—with my innermost being, cleansing the depths of my nature as with a purging by fire. I do not pretend to understand it, much less to explain it. All I know is that, as I opened my inmost being to the Holy Spirit, He came in as a fiery energy, bringing a sense of cleanness into the very depths of my nature. It was so unmistakably real that I can do no other than bear my witness.

A second feature of this experience was a *deep sense of release*. You will notice that again I am using that word *deep*, for that is exactly what it was—deeper down than anything I had yet known. It seemed to reach the very depths of my being. Inward bands were broken and fetters snapped, so that whereas there had been a measure of bondage to people, their opinions and views, there was now a glorious liberty in the service of God and in the doing of His will.

A further result of this spiritual baptism has been a *deep inward illumination*. Again I am constrained to use that word *deep*, for the light seemed to break way down in the inner recesses of my being. It was as though subterranean passages, hitherto dark and unexplored, had been suddenly lighted up and their darkness chased out by a divine glory which surged through them. These divinely illuminated parts have showed no tendency to darken again; for as the Holy Spirit has been recognized and obeyed, the blessing has remained.

Of the abiding peace, the power for service, the periods of exultant joy, and so many other glorious accompaniments, time forbids me to speak, except to say that every day the marvel grows, and every day I am increasingly perplexed as to why the Lord should have been so good to me. But what is best of all, this experience is not for special individuals; it is for all who will honestly seek it.

"If ye then, being evil, know how to give good gifts unto your children: how much more shall your heavenly Father give the Holy Spirit to them that ask him?" (Luke 11:13).

BLESS THE LORD, O MY SOUL[5]

We are his witnesses of these things; and so is also the Holy Ghost, whom God hath given to them that obey him (Acts 5:32).

---

5. Harper, *Holiness and High Country*, 377.

It is always fitting that our testimony to the experience of entire sanctification be given with a deep sense of indebtedness to God. We are finders, not because we are such great seekers, but because God is such a great Giver. I testify today to the wonder of this free gift of God's grace.

Sixty years ago I was a young man beginning my junior year in college. I felt my deep need to be cleansed from sin and to be filled with the Holy Spirit. I knelt at the altar in a college chapel and earnestly sought this blessing. At the altar God graciously dealt with my soul and helped me to reach a place of utter commitment to Him, but the assurance of full salvation did not come immediately. I sought on for a day or two. One morning in my dormitory room as I knelt by my window in meditation and prayer, it happened. Just as the first rays of the rising sun touched the building and lighted up my windowpane, the Holy Spirit came to my soul and illuminated all of my life.

I cannot yet testify to the end of my days, but I can testify that for these 60 years He has been with me. There have been some days of uncertainty, but He has remained. He has made me a better man than I was then. He has led me into paths of Christian service of which I did not dream. The prospect has not always been bright, but the retrospect has always been luminous. In the light of this faith and with the assurance of His presence I propose to journey until traveling days are done.

Bless the Lord, O my soul: and all that is within me, bless his holy name (Ps. 103:1).

* * * * *

I Will Praise Him

Margaret J. Harris, 19th Century   Margaret J. Harris, 19th Century

1. When I saw the cleansing foun-tain   O-pen wide for all my sin,
2. Tho' the way seem'd straight and narrow, All I claimed was swept a-way;
3. Then God's fire up-on the al-tar   Of my heart was set a-flame.
4. Bless-ed be the name of Je-sus!   I'm so glad He took me in.

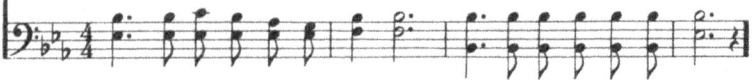

I o-beyed the Spir - it's woo - ing When He said,"Wilt thou be clean?"
My am- bi - tions, plans, and wish - es At my feet in ash - es lay.
I shall nev - er cease to praise Him. Glo - ry, glo - ry to His name!
He's for - giv - en my trans - gres - sions; He has cleansed my heart from sin.

REFRAIN

I will praise Him! I will praise Him! Praise the Lamb for sinners slain!
for sinners slain!

Give Him glo-ry, all ye peo-ple, For His blood can wash a - way each stain.

* * * * *

Preaching

The truth of entire sanctification and a holy life is to be proclaimed through preaching.

And he said unto them, Go ye into all the world, and preach the gospel to every creature. . . .

And they went forth, and preached every where, the Lord working with them, and confirming the word with signs following (Mark 16:15, 20).

Whosoever shall call upon the name of the Lord shall be saved.

How then shall they call on him in whom they have not believed? and how shall they believe in him of whom they have not heard? and how shall they hear without a preacher? (Rom. 10:13-14).

PREACHING HOLINESS[6]

It is the duty of all who are chosen to preach holiness to qualify themselves for such a high calling.

All who effectively preach this message must be fully persuaded in their own minds that holiness is a sound Bible doctrine. An honest student of the Word of God should find no difficulty in arriving at that conclusion if he approaches the study of the Holy Scriptures with an unprejudiced mind. It is a great advantage for the preacher to be able to acquire a sufficient knowledge of philosophy and psychology to assure himself that holiness doctrine is philosophically and psychologically sound. And it is the privilege of every Christian believer, through the witness of the Spirit, to possess a perfect persuasion of the truth as it is in Jesus. This will mean that he enjoys the "full assurance of understanding" (Col. 2:2); "the full assurance of hope" (Heb. 6:11); and the "full assurance of faith" (10:22).

This certainty will save the preacher from speculation. He can say, "I know and therefore I speak." He will never feel that he must make a defense for the message he declares or the people who have embraced it. He will not often feel that he must preach controversially. He, being in the light himself, will preach with the assumption that his hearers accept this glorious truth as they do the fact that the sun

---

6. G. B. Williamson, *Preaching Scriptural Holiness*, preface.

Gideon B. Williamson (1898-1982) was a general superintendent in the Church of the Nazarene. Born near New Florence, Mo., Gideon grew up in the Midwest. He testified that, though converted as a child, he became a settled Christian at 18, and was sanctified wholly at 21.

A graduate of John Fletcher College (now Vennard), Dr. Williamson pastored for 16 years in Iowa, Illinois, Ohio, and Missouri.

From 1936 to 1945 he served as president of Eastern Nazarene College, Wollaston, Mass. Resigning from the college in 1945, he came to Kansas City to pastor the First Church of the Nazarene. The following year he was elected as a general superintendent, where he served until his retirement.

For 11 years after retirement in 1968 both Dr. and Mrs. Williamson taught at Nazarene Bible College in Colorado Springs.

Always a strong holiness exponent, 3 of Dr. Williamson's 10 books focus sharply on the truths of Christian holiness.

shines to illuminate and warm the earth. The preacher who is constantly debating the issue gives the impression that he is seeking to persuade himself. He should preach with such conviction that those who hear the truth will be eager to embrace it.

The importance of preaching holiness can hardly be exaggerated. When considered in all its aspects and with all its implications, holiness includes the whole gospel message. If it be preached scripturally it will give opportunity to emphasize every vital truth of the divine revelation. To be sure, if one takes only some one phase of the message of holiness he will become eccentric. He will go off on a tangent which can lead only into a dead-end street. But taking holiness as the major thesis of the gospel of full redemption from sin will mean that one has in clear perspective the entire scope of revealed truth.

THE TESTIMONY OF DWIGHT L. MOODY[7]

I took the old sermons that I had preached before without any power; it was the same old truth, but there was a new power. Many were impressed and converted. This happened years after I was converted.

At the summer school for Bible study, held at Mount Hermon, Moody addressed the boys' class and answered questions. The subject of "Enduement of Power" was before the class; the necessity of it for service was urged. Moody's explanation follows:

No need to stop your work in order to wait for this enduement of power, but do not be satisfied until you get it.

Let it be the cry of your heart day and night . . . Young men, you will get this blessing when you seek it above all else. There will be no trouble about knowing when you have got it.

SEEK IT

---

7. Taken from *The Christian*, London, Aug. 26, 1886.

Dwight Lyman Moody (1837-99) was born in Northfield, Mass. As a young man clerking in a Boston shoe store, Dwight was converted through the personal witness of a Christian friend. He united with the Mount Vernon Congregational Church of Boston in 1850 but settled in Chicago in 1856.

There Moody built up a mission Sunday School of more than 1,000 pupils; it later became a congregation known as the Chicago Tabernacle, and still later as the Moody Church.

In 1873 the pastor began evangelistic work with Ira D. Sankey. Six years later, in Northfield, he founded a school for poor girls. The school later grew into the widely known Northfield and Mount Hermon institutions. In 1886 he also founded the school that eventually became known as the Moody Bible Institute of Chicago.

Although living before the invention of radio or television, it is estimated that Moody preached to more than 50 million persons.

We should not have to wait long for this baptism of the Spirit if we did not have to come to the end of ourselves. This sometimes is a long road.

If God were to endue us with power when we were full of conceit we should become vain as peacocks, and there would be no living near us. [Mr. Moody then told his experience—a thing which he was not greatly given to do.]

This blessing came upon me suddenly, like a flash of lightning. For months I had been hungering and thirsting for power in **IN A MOMENT** service. I had come to that point that I think I would have died if I had not got it. I remember I was walking the streets of New York. I had no more heart in the business I was about than if I had not belonged to this world at all. Right there, on the street, the power of God seemed to come upon me so wonderfully that I had to ask God to stay His hand. I was filled with a sense of God's goodness, and felt as though I could take the whole world to my heart. I took the old sermons that I had preached before without any power; it was the same old truth, but there was a new power. Many were impressed and converted. This happened years after I was converted myself.

It was in the fall of 1871. I had been very anxious to have a large Sunday School and a large congregation, but there were few conversions. I remember I used to take a pride in having the largest congregation in Chicago on a Sunday night. Two godly women used to come and hear me. One of them came to me one night after I had preached very satisfactorily, as I thought. I fancied she was going to congratulate me on my success; but she said, "We are praying for you." I wondered if I had made some blunder, that they talked in that way.

Next Sunday night they were there again, evidently in prayer while I was preaching. One of them said, "We are still praying for you." I could not understand it and said, "Praying for me! Why don't you pray for the people? I am all right."

"Ah," they said, "you are not all right; you have not got power; there is something lacking, but God can qualify you." I **POWER IN PREACHING** did not like it at first, but I got to thinking it over, and after a little time I began to feel a desire to have what they were praying for.

They continued to pray for me, and the result was that at the end of three months God sent this blessing on me. I want to tell you this: I would not for the whole world go back to where I was before 1871. Since then I have never lost the assurance that I am walking in communion with God, and I have a joy in His service that sustains me and makes it easy work. I believe I was an older man then than I am now; I have been growing younger ever since. I used to be very tired when preaching three times a week; now I can preach five times a day and never get tired at all. I have done three times the work I did before, and it gets better and better every year. It is so easy to do a thing when love prompts you. It would be better, it seems to me, to go and break stone than to take to preaching in a professional spirit.

I Surrender All

SURRENDER

Judson W. Van Deventer, 1855-1939   Winfield S. Weeden, 1847-1908

1. All to Je - sus I sur - ren - der; All to Him I free - ly give.
2. All to Je - sus I sur - ren - der; Hum - bly at His feet I bow,
3. All to Je - sus I sur - ren - der, Make me, Sav - iour, whol - ly Thine;
4. All to Je - sus I sur - ren - der; Lord, I give my - self to Thee.
5. All to Je - sus I sur - ren - der. Now I feel the sa - cred flame.

I will ev - er love and trust Him, In His pres - ence dai - ly live.
World - ly pleas-ures all for -sak - en. Take me, Je - sus, take me now.
Let me feel the Ho - ly Spir - it, Tru - ly know that Thou art mine.
Fill me with Thy love and pow-er; Let Thy bless-ing fall on me.
Oh, the joy of full sal - va - tion! Glo -ry, glo - ry to His name!

REFRAIN

I sur - ren - der all. I sur -ren - der all.

All to Thee, my bless - ed Sav - iour, I sur - ren - der all.

Teaching

Understanding the truth of Christian holiness and hunger for the experience are communicated through teaching.

They that be teachers shall shine as the brightness of the firmament; and they that turn many to righteousness as the stars for ever and ever (Dan. 12:3, marg. reading).

All power is given unto me in heaven and in earth.

Go ye therefore, and teach all nations, baptizing them in the name of the Father, and of the Son, and of the Holy Ghost:

Teaching them to observe all things whatsoever I have commanded you: and, lo, I am with you alway, even unto the end of the world (Matt. 28:18-20).

> *Lord, speak to me, that I may speak*
> *In living echoes of Thy tone;*
> *As Thou hast sought, so let me seek*
> *Thy erring children lost and lone.*
>
> *Oh! teach me, Lord, that I may teach*
> *The precious things Thou dost impart;*
> *And wing my words, that they may reach*
> *The hidden depths of many a heart.*
>
> —FRANCES R. HAVERGAL, 1836-79

USE CLEAR LANGUAGE[8]

Our interest in the terminology of Bible holiness is twofold. In the first place, we want to know what terms men of the past used in expressing the truths they held and propagated. We want to know

---

8. Chapman, *Terminology of Holiness*, 14-15.

these words both for the assurance such knowledge will give us that their users did indeed hold the views we have heard they held, and then we want to know them that we may include them in our own list of words for the sake of variety and fullness.

In the second place, we are interested in terminology for practical purposes, for we want to tell others of the treasure we have found in language that is both accurate and adequate. This practical interest suggests that we shall do well to major on perspicuity rather than on plentitude. We shall do well, both personally and as a people, to use a few terms until they are well known and clearly understood, and then keep on using them because they are well known and clearly understood. Distinctions that are not based on real differences are not only wearisome but misleading as well. An old book on homiletics, that dignified itself with the title *Sacred Rhetoric,* gave the example of a novice who referred to Moses as "the peerless son of Amram," more to the muddling than to the enlightening of his hearers.

Language, to serve its full purpose, must be clearly understood by both speaker and hearer or writer and reader. Serious speakers strive earnestly to master the tongue of their hearers, and are never content until this end is gained. One well-known preacher said that if he planned to use a word and then discovered that 20 people in his audience did not understand that word, he would cross it out. But it is not enough for the Christian teacher to use the words his people already know. It is also his duty to give content to words in order that he may use them to convey his message. The Christian teacher is like the traveler who must build roads, as well as travel roads that already exist, because the language of secular and worldly life is but partially adapted to the purpose of bearing the full message of the gospel.

We find, then, that we must not only learn what terms mean to others; we must also be clear that they have definite meaning to us. And if some would entrap us by defining our words for us, we must not give way to the pressure. The ideas are ours, and it is ours to find terms for their expression. If existing words do not convey the idea, then we must burden words with the content we have in mind, and then make these words mean this to others.

A SUNDAY SCHOOL TEACHER SEEKS AND FINDS[9]

Eleven years after graduating from Pasadena College, I joined the

9. *Herald of Holiness,* Sept. 1, 1981.
George J. Reed is now retired from public service and operates an avocado ranch in Escondido, Calif.

cabinet of the newly elected governor of Minnesota as deputy direc-
tor of the Department of Youth Corrections.

After two years of gratifying success, everything blew up. We had
a suicide at one of our reformatories, and reporters also found evidence of several bodies buried in the yard at the St. Cloud Re-
formatory. These horrible crimes by guards had occurred many years
before I came to Minnesota, but that did not deter the press and the
governor's political enemies from requesting an investigation by the
state legislature. Only a few days earlier I had presented an enlarged
budget to the legislature to increase our diagnostic and treatment
centers, and to build two juvenile forestry camps to get these young
men out doing constructive reforestation work in northern Minnesota. In late April 1951, it began to look like our political enemies
would prevail and that the whole program Governor Youngdahl and
George Reed had put together could be wiped out.

I was teaching the Young Married Couples Class in Minneapolis
First Church of the Nazarene. Beginning in April, the Sunday School
lesson quarterly started a series of lessons on sanctification.

Up to that point in my Christian life I had always argued, because
of my training in criminology and human behavior, that I did not
understand sanctification. The first Sunday the lesson was on the
theology of sanctification. Because of my Pasadena College classes
under Dr. H. Orton Wiley and Dr. Olive Winchester, the first lesson
went well. However, by the third lesson on experiencing heart holiness, I found myself before a large class of couples, fumbling my way
through an unending hour of attempting to tell my class about experiencing sanctification. Although I had always enjoyed public speaking,
and teaching my class, on that Sunday morning I experienced total
defeat. At the close of the class, bathed in sweat and embarrassed over
my failure, I hurriedly left the room.

En route home after church, I told my wife, Lois, about my
horrible experience and told her that I would never again attempt to
teach a Sunday School class or hold an official church office until I
personally had experienced heart purity through entire sanctification.
That evening we did not attend the service, and I slept very little
during the night.

Monday morning broke cloudy, damp, and cold for May 15.
With a heavy heart and carrying the entire state of Minnesota on my
back, I started for the office at the Capitol in St. Paul. By the time I
arrived at the Wold-Chamberlain Airport, I could no longer carry the
load alone, not even a mile farther. I turned my car off the highway by

the airport and broke into sobbing. I cried out to God, asking Him for relief from my convicted heart.

All my life, up to that hour, I had felt that there was nothing that George Reed could not handle. However, that morning I honestly confessed to God that the department's budget, even the program itself, was in grave danger of being wiped out. I told God that as important as all this was to me, far more important than "all these things" was the great heart void and ache that must first be filled lest I die.

I told God that if He would cleanse my self-centered, proud heart, and give me the Holy Spirit as my Comforter, I would do His will and serve Him in any capacity or job to which He would lead me. My professional pride was placed upon God's altar and my future placed at His disposal. After crying out my need for the Holy Spirit's presence in my heart, and after some two hours of struggling, a still small voice quietly said, "Why don't you let Me take full charge of your life?"

Whereupon I said, "Yes, Lord, I surrender George Reed and his future totally to Your control for this hour and forever." At that moment the heavy burden lifted; the Holy Spirit hovered over my car and took residence in the throne room of my heart. I began to laugh and praise God for giving me "my Comforter" and Senior Partner for life.

Two weeks later, the legislature closed its hearings on our program, and the new budget was passed without losing one dime of our request. I served two more years in Minnesota. During the next 23 years I had the honor of serving five presidents and eight attorneys general as chairman or vice chairman of the United States Board of Parole. My Helper and Senior Partner has also given me opportunity to serve my church in a small way over these years.

I testify that the Holy Spirit abides in my heart today. I am rejoicing and praising God for His precious presence. My future was never brighter, and my daily prayer is that my church will continue her God-given mission of proclaiming Christian holiness.

*   *   *

If I can help reveal Thy truth
To other hearts, dear Lord;
If through Thy help I can impart
The beauty of Thy Word,
I shall be giving back to Thee
Something that has been given to me.

—GRACE NOLL CROWELL, 1877-1969

Writing

The truth of Christian holiness is spread through written testimony, exposition, and exhortation.

I beseech you therefore, brethren, by the mercies of God, that ye present your bodies a living sacrifice, holy, acceptable unto God, which is your reasonable service.

And be not conformed to this world: but be ye transformed by the renewing of your mind, that ye may prove what is that good, and acceptable, and perfect, will of God (Rom. 12:1-2).

My dear children, I write this to you so that you will not sin. But if anybody does sin, we have one who speaks to the Father in our defense—Jesus Christ, the Righteous One. He is the atoning sacrifice for our sins, and not only for ours but also for the sins of the whole world.

We know that we have come to know him if we obey his commands (1 John 2:1-3, NIV).

THE MINISTRY OF WRITING

The apostle Paul testified, "I have become all things to all men so that by all possible means I might save some. I do all this for the sake of the gospel" (1 Cor. 9:22-23, NIV). And he lived by his principles. More than any other New Testament person Paul wrote in order to promote the gospel.

In the 20th century the six volumes of *Great Holiness Classics* testify to the extent to which men and women of God have relied on the written word to spread the good news of entire salvation. Also the testimonies of Christians who have been led into full salvation through a printed message give witness to the effectiveness of written communication.

Wherein lies the unique power of the printed word?

1. When I read a book or an article on holiness, the setting finds me with a readiness to receive the message. I have seen the title and I am interested. Or I have chosen the book because I wanted to learn more about God's plan for full salvation. I am thus open to receive the truth.

2. A written message lets me proceed at my own pace. If the thought is not clear, I can go back and read again until I understand the idea. If I am hesitant to accept what I understand, I can raise my

questions. The Holy Spirit has a way of using this honest dialogue to open my spirit to His answers.

3. When reading, I am usually alone, undistracted by other persons. I focus full attention on the message. As the truth convinces me, I am free to respond with yearning and prayer. I do business with God best when He and I are thus alone, confronting each other face-to-face.

I thank God for Christian writers and for their written words. I am grateful for every faithful servant of God who has recorded his experience of God's sanctifying grace. My life has been enriched and my spirit has often been blessed by the words of one of God's children who has shared in writing the work of God's Holy Spirit in his life. *Editor.*

HOLINESS LITERATURE[10]

[The year] 1725 may be circled as the inaugural of holiness literature. That was the year in which William Law published the little book *A Serious Call to a Devout and Holy Life.* The book compelled Wesley to drive a probe deep into his soul, examine the motives of his life, and scrutinize his intentions. That book has been a conscience goad and a life guide for serious-minded Christians for over 250 years. In its many editions it has been a serious call to a devout and holy life to thousands of people. . . .

Wesley never flagged in what he understood to be a crucial part of his work, namely the production and sale of religious literature. He wrote books and pamphlets by the score; he borrowed, edited, and circulated the writings of others; his saddlebags symbolize the Methodist publishers and all later holiness publishing houses. He appointed, supervised, and guided editor after editor. When he died he left, as probably the liveliest and most enduring resource of a holiness preacher, the Methodist Publishing House. Since his death, the offspring of Methodism—Primitive Methodists, Free Methodists, Wesleyans, United Methodists, Nazarenes, and others—have given priority to the terribly decisive matter of Christian literature. Wesley died at the end of the 18th century; the 19th became undoubtedly the most fruitful and crowded period of the production of substantial writings on "second blessing holiness."

---

10. T. Crichton Mitchell, ed., *The Wesley Century,* in *Great Holiness Classics,* 2:18-19.

HELPED BY HOLINESS WRITERS[11]

As far back as when I was a student in Oberlin College, my beloved classmate, the now well-known faith missionary in Bulgaria, Mrs. Anna V. Mumford, had received the baptism with the Spirit and urged me to seek it. She presented me a volume of President Mahan's *Baptism of the Holy Ghost.* The book has inspired many another to seek and find the blessing, but somehow it did not make the matter plain to me *how* to take the blessing in simple faith. I went to President Finney, who tenderly prayed with me but gave me no light. I was thoroughly persuaded that there was such a blessing for men. Indeed, all these years I have felt that a dozen unanswerable arguments could be made that would satisfy any logical mind of the attainability of holiness.

I soon after went to Yale Seminary to study theology, and there, I confess it now with shame and sorrow, like many another theological student does, I suffered a decline in spirituality and lost much of the heart hunger for holiness. I have deserved all I have received, and much more, of sorrow and disappointment at the hands of a grieved and patient God, who lovingly chastised His child that he might become a partaker of the divine nature.

God gave me revival after revival in my pastorates, gracious harvests of souls, and I had more calls to help pastors in revival work outside of my own pulpit than I could fill. But I was a slow, dull pupil of grace, and God permitted my pride to be wounded, and my ambitions to be crushed, till I cried out in agony, "Oh, my Father, dost Thou not care for Thy child?" But through it all, He was bringing me to himself, driving me, I might say, by a whip of love, to His very bosom, and awaking again the deep and abiding heart hunger for holiness and Spirit power.

After two long pastorates, lasting 16 years, followed by two short pastorates . . . and nearly 2 years' service as state evangelist of Michigan, I moved to Oberlin to enter general evangelistic work, with my humbled soul hungering for God. My constant reading, outside of the busy work of preaching 15 times a week and writing *The Life and Labors of Mary A. Woodbridge,* was all on the precious theme of the Holy Spirit.

In such a frame of mind I was invited to lead a revival in Oberlin in January of 1895. I preached in the afternoon meetings a full salvation; I dared not preach anything else. Months afterward the leader of

---

11. Hills, *Holiness and Power,* 292-96.

the holiness band of Oberlin . . . loaned me some books of Wood and Garrison and Steele and Mahan that fed all the more the consuming flame of my soul.

I was providentially invited to assist Rev. G. S. Butler of Three Rivers, Mass., who with his wife had received the baptism with the Spirit, and who had much literature on the subject in his library. Among other things I there found an address by Brother Torrey, of Chicago, and the address of another man . . . I took down the outlines of them in my notebook. On the famous hilltop back of the parsonage, overlooking 11 cities and villages, under a tree I knelt in prayer and gave myself away to God anew for the baptism with the Spirit, and wrote in my book, "Oh, my God, Savior, sanctifying Spirit, I receive Thee. Come in now and fill my soul. A. M. Hills, May 29, 1895."

The influence of that act was a refreshing blessing to my soul all the summer through, and had I then believed with all my heart, I might have received the blessing at once; but I retained a lingering doubt. However, in the month of December in that same dear parsonage, I read an address of Varley on "The Sin of Unbelief," that went to my heart. I determined not to be shut out of the blessing any more by a wicked unbelief so cruel and so dishonoring to Jesus. I went to the Thursday evening meeting and publicly confessed my sin, and declared I would take God for a full salvation.

I had read previously in Keene's *Faith Papers:* "Are you a child of God seeking FULL SALVATION? Seize upon some declaration of God's Word, such as 'The blood of Jesus Christ his Son cleanseth from *all* sin'; apply it to your heart; confess to yourself, to Satan, and to God, that it is true to *you*, because the Lord hath spoken it; refuse to listen to the lying voice of Satan that it is not so. Let no inward feeling or outward sign dissuade you from your voluntary choice to count God's Word true to yourself. And according to such a faith it shall be done unto you. Have you given all to Christ? Are you now longing to be *fully* saved? Are you persuaded that

> *'Tis the promise of God full salvation to give*
> *Unto him who on Jesus, His Son, will believe?*

You may at once begin to sing:

> *I* CAN, *I* WILL, *I* DO *believe,*
> *That Jesus saves me now.*"

The next day I said over and over again, "I will believe; I will believe." At night I walked the park in the darkness, saying:

I CAN, *I* WILL, *I* DO *believe,*
That Jesus saves me NOW.

With such a persistent determination of faith I retired. The next morning (December 7) before I rose it occurred to me to thank God for the blessing as a thing received, just as F. B. Meyer advises. I began to do it, when speedily the Spirit came to bring the witness that God is true. A tide of joy swept into my soul, and I cried out, "O bless the Lord! Praise the Lord! He does come and fill my spirit!" From that hour my life has been consciously changed.

Oh, that Christians would learn this simple lesson of *believing,* of simply taking God at His word without evidence! We should soon have "the oil of joy for mourning, the garment of praise for the spirit of heaviness" (Isa. 61:3); and the Church, no longer bowed down in weakness and sorrow and doubt and sin, would arise and shine, her light having come, and the glory of the Lord having risen upon her (cf. 60:1).

"The method of faith," says Dr. Keene, "is for the soul to recognize that *it can believe* God's Word, then *choose to believe* it, which always carries it over to the consciousness: '*I do believe.*' Believing is our part, and is antecedent; saving is God's part, and is consequent. All the blessed effects of faith—pardon, adoption, entire sanctification— are the Lord's doings, and are marvelous in our eyes; and they are all possible to him who believes on the Son of God."

Dear reader, as you lay down this paper, say: "Lord, I believe."

Thou dost this moment save,
With full salvation bless.

Ethics

We document and prove holiness by living holy lives and by Christian ethical behavior.

Wherefore by their fruits ye shall know them.

Not every one that saith unto me, Lord, Lord, shall enter into the kingdom of heaven; but he that doeth the will of my Father which is in heaven (Matt. 7:20-21).

Since we live by the Spirit, let us keep in step with the Spirit (Gal. 5:25, NIV).

Put on the new self, created to be like God in true righteousness and holiness.

Therefore each of you must put off falsehood and speak truthfully to his neighbor, for we are all members of one body. "In your anger do not sin": Do not let the sun go down while you are still angry; and do not give the devil a foothold. He who has been stealing must steal no longer, but must work, doing something useful with his own hands, that he may have something to share with those in need (Eph. 4:24-28, NIV).

* * *

When I need help, I shall get alone and let God speak to me.

PERFECT LOVE, THE TOUCHSTONE OF CHRISTIAN ETHICS[12]

The validity of doctrine and the reality of experience can be proved only by a Christian life. Doctrine and ethics without experience have no point of meeting. They stand unsteadily like two shafts pivoted in uncertain balance. They are sure to fall. Likewise experience and ethics are insufficient without the foundation which doctrinal truth affords for a faith that produces vital knowledge of God and a life consistent thereto.

Mark Hopkins said, "Religion without morality is a superstition and a curse. And morality without religion is impossible." This is the equivalent of saying that if religion does not transform the life and regulate conduct in harmony with moral principles and ethical ideals, it is a burden instead of a blessing. . . .

The scope of Christian ethics is outlined by Paul. In his letter to Titus he wrote, "For the grace of God that bringeth salvation hath appeared to all men, teaching us that, denying ungodliness and worldly lusts, we should live soberly, righteously, and godly, in this present world" (Titus 2:11-12). The term *Christian ethics* includes conduct in three relationships: to self, to other men, and to God.

To Self

In relation to self, the Christian is to live "*soberly.*" He must live a self-disciplined life. Many declare that what they do with regard to personal habits is their own business and that no one has a right to interfere. But the Word of God teaches us that in body, mind, and spirit the Christian is to live a holy life. The body is the temple of the

---

12. Williamson, *Preaching Scriptural Holiness* (1976), 42-43, 45-48, 51-53, 59.

Holy Ghost. Therefore, anything that defiles or degrades the body is sinful. All depraved habits must be broken by the power of God's grace. All the appetites acquired by wicked practice must be cleansed away. All the natural desires that have been perverted in sinful living must be sanctified. Peter sets the ideal before us clearly. He says: "Wherefore gird up the loins of your mind, be sober, and hope to the end for the grace that is to be brought unto you at the revelation of Jesus Christ; as obedient children, not fashioning yourselves according to the former lusts in your ignorance: but as he which hath called you is holy, so be ye holy in all manner of conversation" (1 Pet. 1:13-15). . . .

To Other Men

. . . In relation to others the Christian is to live *"righteously."* . . .

Righteous living takes in all conduct toward personal friends and acquaintances. It includes social, professional, business, and all community contacts. It includes also the obligations of citizenship. It places the Christian under duty to his city, his state, his nation. He is to honor and respect those upon whom responsibility for government rests. He must also have Christian attitudes toward people of all nations and races. He cannot excuse the sins of a nation more than his own sins. Christian principles must be applied in sharing all material and spiritual blessings with all men. This is the basis of missionary activity. We are debtors to all men to give them the gospel with all its glorious by-products.

To God

The Christian must also live *"godly."* Right ethical conduct includes worship. This means private and family prayers, attendance upon the means of grace offered in the services of the church, reverence toward life itself, toward all the creation, and toward the Creator.

Fellowship with God and in the Christian community is both an obligation and a privilege to those who desire right relations to God. This entails membership in the church and participation in its service for the building of God's kingdom among men.

Partnership with God in business and faithful stewardship of all He entrusts to our care is also a duty toward God. This will mean that all our business practices are carried on with His knowledge and approval; that profits are shared with employees; that God is honored with tithes and with offerings and praise is given unto Him as the Giver of every good. . . .

Ethics as a Witness

By the practice of Christian ethics we represent Christ among men. The breakdown of Christianity has been in its failure to demonstrate its virtue and its power in Christlike lives. Christ is the Ideal but we follow Him afar off. The Bible is our Rule of practice but we come far short of it. To make the Christian religion what it ought to be in the world, namely, a light to all in darkness, the saving salt to preserve the Church in holy character, we must translate our ideals into action. The solution to this fundamental problem is not in the legalistic approach. We cannot enforce the law and the varied rules of thumb which men would multiply. We must begin at the center of the personality, not at the circumference of conduct. The springs of life must be purified that sweet waters may flow forth. The tree must be made good that the fruit may be holy. We cannot gather figs of thistles.

Right conduct is fundamental but it cannot be enforced upon those whose lives have not been transformed by regenerating and sanctifying grace. Let us lead men into the experience of spiritual transformation by the renewing of the mind. Then conformity to the Christian concepts of life will be desired, and rules of conduct will be cheerfully obeyed. The discipline of a sanctified soul is easy. He desires to do the will of God, and does his best to gain all the light God's holy Word affords him. He will with pleasure and profit walk in the light. Then his own life will be a light to guide others on the shining pathway. Therefore, when God said, "Be ye holy; for I am holy" (1 Pet. 1:16), He gave us the summation of the whole code of Christian ethics. Holy conduct can proceed only from holy character.

The Touchstone

Perfect love, then, is the touchstone of Christian ethics. This is a scriptural term. It was a favorite with John Wesley. Dr. J. B. Chapman places it next to the term *holiness* as a desirable designation of the state of the entirely sanctified. Certainly it expresses the heart of the teaching of Christ. He said when asked what is the great commandment in the law: "Thou shalt love the Lord thy God with all thy heart, and with all thy soul, and with all thy mind. This is the first and great commandment. And the second is like unto it, Thou shalt love thy neighbour as thyself. On these two commandments hang all the law and the prophets" (Matt. 22:37-40). . . .

This royal law of love is the criterion, the standard by which all our conduct is measured. We are to check our thoughts, words, and deeds against the standard of perfect love.

Furthermore this perfect love of God shed abroad in our hearts by the Holy Ghost is the source of grace and power by which men are enabled to live according to the royal law of love. The great ideals of the Sermon on the Mount and the 13th chapter of First Corinthians are out of reach of all who have not received entire sanctification and the fullness of the Spirit. Aiming at these standards is good, but attaining them is impossible without the mighty power of God's Spirit to enable one. But in the reality of the experience of entire sanctification, attainment is within reach. . . .

Entire sanctification cleanses the fountain of life. Out of the heart are the issues of life. God fills the soul with perfect love. This means the motives and intentions are good and holy. But limited knowledge, imperfect judgment, human frailty may cause one to err many times. When he sees his mistake, he is quick to rectify it. He will try never to repeat it. This means that the image of God in the soul is perfect, [even when] the picture presented by the life is faulty. But God looks upon the heart, not on the appearance.

The differential between the perfect intention of the heart and the best performance of fallen man, even when sanctified, often seems great. That difference is made up by the precious blood of Christ. John said, "My little children, these things write I unto you, that ye sin not. And if any man sin, we have an advocate with the Father, Jesus Christ the righteous: and he is the propitiation for our sins: and not for ours only, but also for the sins of the whole world" (1 John 2:1-2).

When holy people look at one another, they look through eyes of love and charitable understanding. They refrain from judgment of others. They seek to know the truth that makes men free and holy. They obey it to the best of their ability.

ETHICAL DIMENSIONS OF HOLY LIVING[13]

No one has ever questioned that there are ethical dimensions to the holiness experience. We have always assumed that the relationship was there. But I am reasonably sure that the specifics of that relationship have not always been spelled out in concepts that are suf-

---

13. Laurence K. Mullen, in *Wesleyan Theological Journal* 14, no. 2 (Fall 1979): 92-95.

Dr. Mullen is associate professor of Bible and philosophy, Houghton College, Houghton, N.Y.

ficiently clear. The thesis that I wish to defend is that the experience of holiness meets the criteria that are demanded of an adequate ethic. . . . Let me point out three essential characteristics of Christian holiness that confirm its adequacy for practical ethics.

1. Christian holiness offers to each of us the personal guidance of the Holy Spirit. Jesus said, "Howbeit when he, the Spirit of truth, is come, he will guide you into all truth" (John 16:13). . . . The Christian has been given the Scriptures and the guidance of the Holy Spirit to direct him in his quest to know the good.

2. Christian holiness deals realistically with the nature of man. It recognizes his sinful nature for what it is, and deals with it efficaciously. Philosophical ethics, on the other hand, has failed consistently at this point. The blanket assumption has always been made that man is basically good, that he is naturally capable of altruism, and that no innate condition hinders his quest for virtue, perfection, and peace of mind. . . .

What does Christian holiness offer as an alternative? The answer lies in the adequacy of divine grace to deal radically with the problem of sin. The sanctified heart is a healed heart, a united heart, a heart set free—free to love, to serve, to praise. God, in His infinite wisdom, knew what was in man, and knowing, He acted graciously in Christ to release us from our sinful natures and to re-create us in the image of His Son. Christ's cross signaled the ultimate triumph of God over Satan's kingdom, the prince of this world was judged, and we share by faith in that mighty victory!

3. Christian holiness brings to us the enabling power of the indwelling Spirit. "Not I . . . but Christ" (Gal. 2:20) speaks of an inner dynamic that surpasses all human effort and inclination. Philosophical ethics has not been short on ideals and programs for human betterment. Where then lies the flaw? The answer lies in man's constitutional inability to actualize the very ideals that he strives to realize. Why should I pursue the good of the greatest number? The utilitarianism of Bentham and Mill did not [give] a good answer. Their grand dreams of equity and justice, in a new world of peace, were shattered by innate selfishness and naked greed. . . .

In summary then, it is in the Holy Spirit that we find the uniqueness and the adequacy of Christian holiness ethics. God, in the person of the Holy Spirit, chooses to indwell the hearts of His children—to guide them into truth, thus enabling them to *know* the good; to purify them from sin, thus enabling them to *will* the good; and to empower them for service, thus enabling them to *do* the good.

KNOWLEDGE GUIDES CONDUCT[14]

The sanctified man in reality faces but one vital question, namely, What is the will of God for me?

People are not equally well informed. Some have greater light than others, some have keener powers of discrimination. This fact must be again and again emphasized. Quality and quantity of light or knowledge will have a bearing upon what we do, and our ability to distinguish between right and wrong will determine the nature of our conduct. It is difficult to imagine how our ethics can rise higher than our knowledge. Imperfect knowledge will likely result in an imperfect system or code of ethics.

God commands us to walk in the light; that is, to do the best we know, and live up to the extent of our information. We are to bring up **LIVE UP TO KNOWLEDGE** the "bottom of our lives to the top of our light." The higher the light, the greater distance the bottom will have to come if the two are to meet. No man can live beneath his light and stand justified before God and the bar of his own conscience. But he must not be too readily condemned if he is doing the best he knows.

[Ignorance, however,] is no excuse for us to hide behind. We should not only strive to walk in the light we have, but we should endeavor to become better and better informed each day. We should grow in the knowledge of the Lord Jesus Christ. It is not enough to walk in the light we possess, but moral responsibility enforces upon us the necessity of striving for additional light, energetically and conscientiously. Thus, knowledge is a factor in any code of ethics.

Concerning knowledge, there are two facts that must be kept in mind continuously. First, that it is enjoined upon us by the Word of God to walk in all the light we have in order to be justified before the Bible, before the conscience, and before God. Second, it is obviously our duty to seek light, to increase in knowledge each day in order that **SEEK MORE KNOWLEDGE** we might approach nearer and nearer toward the standard of perfect ethics. At the present moment lack of knowledge might be an excuse for faulty ethics, but if the power lies within us, and the opportunity is presented to us to increase our stock of knowledge, and acquire more light in order that we might take from our ethics the faults and shortcomings, we are then forced to put forth every effort possible to measure up to this tremendous

---

14. Williams, *Sanctification: The Experience and the Ethics*, 52-55.

responsibility. We must walk in the light we possess and continually seek additional light and [thus] raise the standard of our ethics.

Conscience, the other factor in ethics, or that function of conscience that we call impulse, can be perfect and must be **THE IMPULSE TO DO RIGHT** perfect. The power to discriminate may be imperfect, but impulse must be perfect. No man can rightly claim any degree of grace in his heart who does not accept right, willingly and gladly when it is presented to him and he perceives it as right. No man can claim the possession of religion who knows the wrong and yet hesitates to take sides against it. Conscience must say "Yes" to right and "No" to wrong. There is no middle ground and no time for argument. The soul that hesitates at this point immediately enters the fogs and haze of doubt and disobedience, and loses his bearing and also his favor with God. When right is perceived it must be immediately accepted and defended with determination; and when wrong is perceived, it must be immediately rejected, condemned, and opposed.

The sanctified man in reality faces but one vital question, namely, What is the will of God for me? To always know the will of God is not an easy matter, but to do the will of God when once it is known is the outstanding duty and joy of every consecrated soul. Many of us have spent sleepless nights and feverish days trying to decide what the will of God is concerning many of the details of our lives; but it is difficult to imagine how any conscientious child of God could weep and struggle to get the consent of his own mind to do the will of God when once he knows the divine plan and purpose for him.

It is evident that we can have a perfect conscience if conscience is to be defined purely as impulse, but if discrimination is to be attributed to conscience, then conscience is not perfect and not likely will it ever be. In this case its perfection would depend upon its education.

Our difficulty lies in the fact that conduct or ethics is based not only on impulse, which is accepting right and rejecting wrong when it appears, but it is based upon discrimination, or knowledge, as well. Knowledge may be imperfect and naturally is, therefore our ethics may show imperfections, which fact accounts for much we see in people that we deplore.

Take My Life, and Let It Be

Frances R. Havergal, 1836-1879

HENDON

Henri A. Cesar Malan, 1787-1864

1. Take my life, and let it be Con-se-crat-ed, Lord, to
2. Take my feet, and let them be Swift and beau-ti-ful for
3. Take my lips, and let them be Filled with mes-sag-es for
4. Take my will and make it Thine; It shall be no lon-ger
5. Take my love; my God, I pour At Thy feet its treas-ure

Thee. Take my hands, and let them move At the
Thee. Take my voice, and let me sing Al-ways,
Thee. Take my sil-ver and my gold; Not a
mine. Take my heart; it is Thine own! It shall
store. Take my-self and I will be Ev-er,

im-pulse of Thy love, At the im-pulse of Thy love.
on-ly, for my King; Al-ways, on-ly, for my King.
mite would I with-hold, Not a mite would I with-hold.
be Thy roy-al throne. It shall be Thy roy-al throne.
on-ly, all for Thee; Ev-er, on-ly, all for Thee.

Appendix

Holiness in the 20th Century

How influential is the Holiness Movement in the late 20th century? One measure is the number of church bodies that hold to the doctrine as a major tenet of their Christian faith.

Very possibly we have missed some groups, especially in overseas countries, who share our faith in God's sanctifying grace. Below, however, we have listed official statements of belief from 15 English-speaking holiness bodies known to us in the United States, Canada, and England. Most of these groups are affiliated with the Christian Holiness Association, successor to the National Holiness Association; the latter was founded in 1867 for the specific purpose of promoting the doctrine and experience of entire sanctification among Christians in Protestant churches.

The careful reader will detect minor differences in understanding and emphasis. But a study of these statements will reveal the unanimous agreement on the central issues of the biblical teaching of Christian holiness.

Christian Holiness Association

CHA Center
P.O. Box 100
Wilmore, KY 40390

STATEMENT OF FAITH

The Christian Holiness Association is a body of churches, organizations, and individuals who accept the inspiration and infallibility of sacred Scripture and the evangelical doctrine that pertains to divine revelation, the incarnation, the resurrection, the second coming of Christ, the Holy Spirit, and the Church as affirmed in the historic Christian creeds. The particular concern of this fellowship is the biblical doctrine of sanctification identified historically in what is known as the Wesleyan position.

The Association believes that personal salvation includes both the new birth and entire sanctification wrought by God in the heart by faith. Entire sanctification is a crisis experience subsequent to conversion which results in a heart cleansed from all sin and filled with the Holy Spirit. This grace is witnessed to by the Holy Spirit. It is maintained by that faith which expresses itself in constant obedience to God's revealed will and results in a moment by moment cleansing.

Wesleyan Theological Society
215 E. 43rd St.
Marion, IN 46952

PURPOSE:
To encourage exchange of ideas among Wesleyan-Arminian theologians; to develop a source of papers for CHA seminars; to stimulate scholarship among younger theologians and pastors; and to publish a scholarly Journal.

DOCTRINAL POSITION:
We believe in the salvation of the human soul, including the new birth; and in a subsequent work of God in the soul, a crisis, wrought by faith, whereby the heart is cleansed from all sin and filled with the Holy Spirit; this gracious experience is retained by faith as expressed in a constant obedience to God's revealed will, thus giving perfect cleansing moment by moment (1 John 1:7-9), as taught by John Wesley.

The Bible Holiness Movement
P.O. Box 223, Postal Stn. A
Vancouver, B.C. V6C 2M3

The Bible Holiness Movement . . . insists that it is the duty and privilege of every believer to be sanctified wholly, and to be preserved blameless unto the coming of the Lord Jesus Christ. Every one who is received into full connection, either professes to enjoy that perfect love which casts out fear, or promises diligently to seek until he obtains it.

*   *   *

8. It is the duty and privilege of all believers to be wholly or entirely sanctified. Regeneration is the deliverance from the guilt, condemnation, and power of sin; and the corruption acquired by actual transgression. This saves one from sinning. Entire Sanctification is the total destruction of sin from within the heart of a justified person and an entire renewal in love instantaneously effected by the Holy Ghost

through the merit of the cleansing blood of Jesus Christ. This experience of heart holiness is received by the people of God when they so repent of inbred sin as to hate, loathe, and abhor it and believe in Jesus for full redemption. The Spirit bears direct witness to this work. No one need seek this experience who has not the direct witness of sonship. Without holiness no man shall see the Lord.

Rom. 6:13-14; 1 Thess. 4:3; 1 Thess. 5:23; 1 John 1:7; 1 John 1:9; 2 Tim. 2:19, 21-22; Rom. 12:1; Titus 2:14.

—*The Discipline of the Bible Holiness Movement,* 1985, 5, 9-10

Bible Missionary Church

1524 W. Platte Ave.

Colorado Springs, CO 80904

XI. ENTIRE SANCTIFICATION

15. We believe that entire sanctification is that act of God, subsequent to regeneration, by which believers are made free from original sin, or depravity, and brought into a state of entire devotement to God and the holy obedience of love made perfect.

16. It is wrought by the baptism with the Holy Ghost and comprehends in one experience the cleansing of the heart from sin and the abiding, indwelling presence of the Holy Ghost, empowering the believer for life and service.

17. Entire Sanctification is provided through the blood of Jesus; is wrought instantaneously by faith, preceded by entire consecration; and to this work and state of grace the Holy Spirit bears witness (Rom. 12:1; Rom. 6:11, 13, 22; Rom. 6:6; Gal. 2:20; Rom. 15:16; Heb. 13:12-13; Heb. 10:14-15).

18. This experience is also known by various terms representing its different phases, such as "Christian Perfection," "Perfect Love," "Heart Purity," "The Baptism with the Holy Ghost," "The Fullness of the Blessing," and "Christian Holiness."

—*Manual of the Bible Missionary Church,* 1983, 12-13

Brethren in Christ Church

P.O. Box 245

Upland, CA 91785

ARTICLE VII

SANCTIFICATION

Sanctification throughout the Word of God is used with various meanings: to declare holy,[1] to set apart,[2] and to cleanse.[3]

As a Christian experience, sanctification embodies the setting apart of the believer in entire consecration[4] and the cleansing of the believer's heart from carnality,[5] accompanied by the baptism of the Holy Spirit.[6]

The sanctification of the believer is required by God,[7] provided for by Christ in His atonement,[8] and divinely wrought by the Holy Spirit.[9]

When the believer led by the Spirit becomes aware of an inner conflict of flesh and Spirit,[10] loathes his condition, confesses his state and need; makes an unreserved consecration,[11] and exercises a living faith in the work of Christ on Calvary, he is definitely cleansed from the carnal mind. Thus the work of holiness which was begun in regeneration is perfected, and the believer is "sanctified wholly."[12]

This experience for believers is obtained instantaneously and subsequent to the new birth.[13] The scriptural terms used to describe the cleansing of the believer's heart imply the same: purifying the heart;[14] crucifixion of the old man;[15] body of sin destroyed;[16] circumcision of the heart;[17] deliverance;[18] creation.[19]

Even though it is possible for a sanctified believer to fall into sin,[20] Scriptures reveal that by giving heed to the Word,[21] being devoted in prayer,[22] and by rendering loving and obedient service to Christ[23] he is kept from willful transgression by the power of God.[24]

Although sanctification perfects the motives and desires of the heart, the expression of these in terms of accomplishment is a progressive growth in grace until the close of this life.[25]

---

1. Gen. 2:3; Ex. 29:43, 44. **2.** Ex. 13:2; Jno. 17:19. **3.** Ex. 19:10; Eph. 5:26, 27. **4.** Rom. 12:1, 2; Jno. 17:17. **5.** Acts 15:8, 9; Eph. 5:26. **6.** Matt. 3:11; Acts 2:1-10. **7.** Rom. 8:5-8; Heb. 12:14. **8.** Heb. 10:10; Heb. 13:12. **9.** Heb. 10:14, 15; Acts 15:8, 9. **10.** Gal. 5:17; Rom. 7:14-24. **11.** Rom. 6:13-16; Rom. 12:1. **12.** II Cor. 7:1; I Thess. 5:23. **13.** Acts 8:14-17; Jas. 4:8. **14.** Acts 15:8, 9. **15.** Rom. 6:6. **16.** Rom. 6:6. **17.** Col. 2:11. **18.** Rom. 7:24. **19.** Psa. 51:10. **20.** Jno. 15:6; II Pet. 2:20-22. **21.** I Tim. 4:15, 16. **22.** Heb. 4:15, 16. **23.** Rom. 6:16. **24.** Jude 20-24. **25.** II Tim. 3:16, 17; II Pet. 3:18.

—*Manual of Doctrine and Government,* 1961 and 1984, 13-14

Churches of Christ in Christian Union

1426 Lancaster Pike
Circleville, OH 43113

VIII. SANCTIFICATION

A. *Entire sanctification is a second, definite work of God's grace.*

By this act of grace the heart of a child of God is cleansed from what is known as "original sin" and is also filled with the Holy Ghost. We use the words "entire" or "wholly" with sanctification to designate it from the sanctification that every Christian possesses when he is born again. Note I Thessalonians 5:23.

B. *All sanctification involves separation from sin to God.*

When we are regenerated, we are given power to cease from our past habits of the practice of sin. This may be gradual as God gives light. When we are entirely sanctified, a second work of grace, we are immediately or instantly cleansed from all sin (I John 1:7).

C. *Sanctification enables us to live above sin.*

We maintain that while all *may* sin, sin is not a necessity. We do not become infallible, however, any more than Adam was infallible when God created him. Though he was created perfect, he fell into sin.

D. *Sanctification involves specific conditions.*

Since God commands us to be holy (I Peter 1:16-17) and willed and called us to sanctification and holiness (I Thessalonians 4:3, 7-8), it becomes our responsibility to acquire this grace. The conditions for this are also clear.

There must be complete consecration to the will of God (Romans 6:13; 12:1-2). In this sense we sanctify ourselves, since we must certainly provide the willingness to be sanctified (I John 3:3).

Faith is a must. Note in Acts 15:8-9 where Peter makes clear that the hearts of those who receive[d] the Holy Ghost at Pentecost were purified by faith. Note also in Acts 26:17-18 where Jesus spoke to Paul about an "inheritance among them which are sanctified by faith that is in me." See Hebrews 13:12.

—Manual, 1985, 13

Church of God

1200 E. 5th St.
Anderson, IN 46018

NATURE OF ENTIRE SANCTIFICATION

. . . Sanctification may be described as being a cleansing from the depravity of the nature; or to state it more liberally, it is a restoration of the nature from its deranged condition. If depravity is largely a perversion of the affections, then sanctification must be principally a restoration of them. The effects of sanctification are the absence of the effects of depravity. That the second cleansing taught in the Scriptures is a restoration from depravity is evident from the fact that this is according to man's need. In the very nature of the case it is impossible that a cleansing of the heart subsequent to justification could be a cleansing from those sins which are already forgiven.

Sanctification does not effect an eradication of any essential qualities of human nature as originally constituted, but only of the evil dispositions resulting from its perversion. When God created man he endowed him with a certain natural pride, commonly known as self-respect, which is very desirable in that it causes one to seek to be agreeable and pleasing to his fellow men. This natural pride is perverted through moral depravity to such an extent that men in their sinful condition desire, not only to be well thought of by their fellows, but to be esteemed more highly than any one else. They come to have an unduly exalted estimation of themselves. This perversion of a natural and proper disposition is the result of selfishness and is sinful. Sanctification results simply in the restoration to the natural condition where one is free from sinful pride, yet is possessed of a proper self-respect.

—Russell R. Byrum, *Christian Theology*, rev. ed. Arlo F. Newell (Anderson, Ind.: Warner Press, 1982), 380-81. (The above is not an official statement but has been commended as an indication of the position of the Church of God.)

Church of the Nazarene

6401 The Paseo
Kansas City, MO 64131

13. We believe that entire sanctification is that act of God, subsequent to regeneration, by which believers are made free from original sin, or depravity, and brought into a state of entire devotement to God, and the holy obedience of love made perfect.

It is wrought by the baptism with the Holy Spirit, and comprehends in one experience the cleansing of the heart from sin and the abiding, indwelling presence of the Holy Spirit, empowering the believer for life and service.

Entire sanctification is provided by the blood of Jesus, is wrought instantaneously by faith, preceded by entire consecration; and to this work and state of grace the Holy Spirit bears witness.

This experience is also known by various terms representing its different phases, such as "Christian perfection," "perfect love," "heart purity," "the baptism with the Holy Spirit," "the fullness of the blessing," and "Christian holiness."

14. We believe that there is a marked distinction between a pure heart and a mature character. The former is obtained in an instant, the result of entire sanctification; the latter is the result of growth in grace.

We believe that the grace of entire sanctification includes the impulse to grow in grace. However, this impulse must be consciously nurtured, and careful attention given to the requisites and processes of spiritual development and improvement in Christlikeness of character and personality. Without such purposeful endeavor one's witness may be impaired and the grace itself frustrated and ultimately lost.

Jeremiah 31:31-34
Ezekiel 36:25-27
Malachi 3:2-3
Matthew 3:11-12
Luke 3:16-17
John 7:37-39; 14:15-23; 17:
6-20
Acts 1:5; 2:1-4; 15:8-9
Romans 6:11-13, 19; 8:1-4,
8-14; 12:1-2

2 Corinthians 6:14—7:1
Galatians 2:20; 5:16-25
Ephesians 3:14-21; 5:17-18,
25-27
Philippians 3:10-15
Colossians 3:1-17
1 Thessalonians 5:23-24
Hebrews 4:9-11; 10:10-17;
12:1-2; 13:12
1 John 1:7, 9

"Christian perfection," "perfect love"
Deuteronomy 30:6
Matthew 5:43-48; 22:37-40
Romans 12:9-21; 13:8-10
1 Corinthians 13

Philippians 3:10-15
Hebrews 6:1
1 John 4:17-18

"Heart purity"
Matthew 5:8
Acts 15:8-9

1 Peter 1:22
1 John 3:3

"Baptism with the Holy Spirit"
Jeremiah 31:31-34
Ezekiel 36:25-27
Malachi 3:2-3

Matthew 3:11-12
Luke 3:16-17
Acts 1:5; 2:1-4; 15:8-9

"Fullness of the blessing"
Romans 15:29

"Christian holiness"
Matthew 5:1—7:29
John 15:1-11
Romans 12:1—15:3
2 Corinthians 7:1
Ephesians 4:17—5:20
Philippians 1:9-11; 3:12-15
Colossians 2:20—3:17

1 Thessalonians 3:13; 4:7-8; 5:23
2 Timothy 2:19-22
Hebrews 10:19-25; 12:14;
13:20-21
1 Peter 1:15-16
2 Peter 1:1-11; 3:18
Jude 20-21

—*Manual,* 1985, 28-30

Evangelical Christian Church

P.O. Box 277
Birdsboro, PA 19508

ENTIRE SANCTIFICATION

Every child of God is commanded to be sanctified wholly. Entire sanctification is an instantaneous work of grace, subsequent to regeneration obtained by faith in God's promise. The experience is wrought by baptism of the Holy Spirit at which time the believer is cleansed from original sin, filled with perfect love, empowered for service, established spiritually and enabled to live a holy life. Jesus provided for our sanctification—we may experience it now, the Holy Spirit will bear witness to it and spiritual growth results from it. It is obtained when the believer *completely* presents himself to God.

—The *Manual*, 1986

The Evangelical Church of North America

7525 S.E. Lake Rd., Suite No. 7
Milwaukie, OR 97222

ARTICLE VIII. SANCTIFICATION

¶108. The Holy Scriptures declare that sanctification begins in the new birth and is the work of God's grace through the Word and the Holy Spirit, by which those who have been born again and delivered from the wilful practice of sin are enabled to live in accordance with God's will,[1] and to seek earnestly for holiness without which no one will see God.[2]

Entire Sanctification is that second definite, instantaneous work of God, wrought in the heart of the believer, subsequent to regeneration, by which God cleanses the heart from all inherited sin and fills the soul and spirit with the person of the Holy Spirit, thus enabling us to love God with all of our heart, soul, mind, and strength and to love our neighbor as ourselves.[3] This gracious work is conditioned upon total consecration of the whole self to God, total death to all inherited sin and faith in the sacrifice of Jesus Christ on Calvary.[4]

There is a clear distinction that must be made between consecration and entire sanctification. Consecration is that more or less gradual process of devoting oneself wholly to God, consumating in the crucifixion of the old self or death to the Adamic nature, by the help of the Holy Spirit which comes to a completion at a point in time. Total consecration of necessity precedes and prepares the way for that definite act of faith which brings God's instantaneous sanctifying work to the soul.

This gracious work does not deliver us from the infirmities, ignorance and mistakes common to man, nor from the possibility of further sin. A person is freed so that he may experience a continued growth in divine knowledge, spiritual strength and good works to the glory of God.[5] The Christian must continue to guard against the temptation to spiritual pride and seek to gain victory over this and every temptation to sin.[6] There also follows a life of Christian perfection which consists in a purity such as that of Jesus,[7] resulting in the same mind which was also in Him, and enabling us to walk even as He walked.[8]

1. Acts 15:9; Rom. 8:1-4; 6:6; I Thess. 5:23, 24
2. Heb. 12:14
3. Matt. 22:37; Gal. 5:22, 23; I Peter 1:22; I John 1:9
4. Rom. 6:1, 2, 11-14; 12:1, 2
5. Heb. 12:10-15; Phil. 2:1-5
6. Col. 1:9-14
7. I John 3:3
8. Phil. 2:2

—*The Discipline of the Evangelical Church*, 1982, 5

Evangelical Friends Church
Eastern Region
(Formerly Ohio Yearly Meeting of the Friends Church)

1201 30th St., N.W.
Canton, OH 44709

43.   SANCTIFICATION: We believe that children of God at the moment of their conversion do receive the Holy Spirit[15]. As they trust in Him and obey His will, they manifest more and more of the fruit of the Spirit and conform more and more to the likeness of God and thus are being continuously sanctified[16].

44.   It is also the will of God that believers receive the fullness of the Spirit[17] which He will graciously grant in response to their full consecration to His will and their faith in Christ's promises and in His atoning death[18]. Sanctification is thus a process in which the Holy Spirit continuously disciplines the believer into paths of holiness and an act in which He cleanses the heart from an imperfect relationship and state[19].

45.   We further believe that the fullness of the Holy Spirit does not make believers incapable of choosing to sin, nor even from

completely falling away from God, yet it so cleanses and empowers them as to enable them to have victory over sin, to endeavor fully to love God and man, and to witness to the living Christ[20].

15. Romans 8:14; I Cor. 12:13
16. Galatians 5:22-25
17. Acts 2:38, 39; Eph. 5:18
18. Exodus 32:29; Romans 5:8; Romans 12:1, 2
19. John 17:17; Romans 6:1, 2, 22, 23; I John 3:5, 6
20. I Cor. 9:27; II Cor. 7:1; II Peter 2:20-22

—*Faith and Practice, the Book of Discipline,* 1981, 15-16

The Evangelical Methodist Church

3000 W. Kellogg Dr.
Wichita, KS 67213

XXVI. PERFECT LOVE*

¶46. Perfect love is that renewal of our fallen nature by the Holy Spirit, received through faith in Jesus Christ, whose blood of atonement cleanseth from all sin; whereby we are not only delivered from the guilt of sin, but are washed from its pollution, saved from its power, and are enabled, through grace, to love God with all our hearts and to walk in His holy commandments blameless.

*Explanation: Christian perfection is a state of righteousness and true holiness, which every regenerate believer may obtain. It consists in being cleansed from all sin, loving God with all the heart, soul, mind, and strength, and loving our neighbor as ourselves. This gracious state of perfect love is obtainable in this life by faith, both gradually and instantaneously, and every child of God should earnestly seek to grow in grace. It does not deliver us from temptations, infirmities, ignorance, and mistakes which are common to man. We accept as our doctrinal interpretation *Wesley's Sermons, Wesley's Notes On The New Testament, Wesley's Journal,* and *Wesley's A Plain Account of Christian Perfection.*

—*Discipline of the Evangelical Methodist Church,* 1985, 44-45

The Free Methodist Church

901 College Ave.
Winona Lake, IN 46590

XIII. ENTIRE SANCTIFICATION

¶119. We believe entire sanctification to be that work of the Holy Spirit, subsequent to regeneration, by which the fully consecrated believer, upon exercise of faith in the atoning blood of Christ, is cleansed in that moment from all inward sin and empowered for service. The resulting relationship is attested by the witness of the

Holy Spirit and is maintained by faith and obedience. Entire sanctification enables the believer to love God with all his heart, soul, strength, and mind, and his neighbor as himself, and it prepares him for greater growth in grace.

—*The Book of Discipline*, 1979, 16-17

The Missionary Church

3901 S. Wayne Ave.

Fort Wayne, IN 46807

d. *Sanctification and Filling with the Holy Spirit.* We believe that sanctification is the work of God in making men holy. It is the will of God. It is provided in the atonement, and is experienced through faith by the operation of the Holy Spirit through the Word and the blood. While the divine work of making men holy begins in repentance and regeneration, yet through a subsequent crisis experience the believer is to die to self, to be purified in heart, and to be filled with the Holy Spirit so that he may be separated wholly unto God to serve Him in righteousness and holiness. After the crisis experience, the believer is to be perfected in holiness in the fear of God and to grow in grace and in the knowledge of our Lord and Saviour Jesus Christ.

Ps. 4:3; I Thess. 5:23; I Pet. 1:15, 16; Heb. 12:14; I Thess. 4:3; II Thess. 2:13; John 17:17; Eph. 5:26; I John 5:6; I Pet. 1:2; Gal. 2:20; 6:14; Col. 3:3; Rom. 6:19, 22; 12:1, 2; Acts 15:8, 9; II Cor. 7:1; II Pet. 3:18

—*Manual and Constitution*, 1985, 4

The Salvation Army

101 Queen Victoria St.

London, England

We believe that it is the privilege of all believers to be "wholly sanctified," and that their "whole spirit and soul and body" may "be preserved blameless unto the coming of our Lord Jesus Christ" (1 Thess. 5:23). . . .

The experience of holiness involves both a crisis and a process—the initial dedication when the commitment is made, and the process or subsequent action by which the implications of this commitment are worked out in every department of life (2 Cor. 7:1).

—*The Salvation Army Handbook of Doctrine*, 1969, 145, 159

The Wesleyan Church
Box 2000
Marion, IN 46592

· XIV. SANCTIFICATION: INITIAL, PROGRESSIVE, ENTIRE

117. We believe that sanctification is that work of the Holy Spirit by which the child of God is separated from sin unto God and is enabled to love God with all his heart and to walk in all His holy commandments blameless. Sanctification is initiated at the moment of justification and regeneration. From that moment there is a gradual or progressive sanctification as the believer walks with God and daily grows in grace and in a more perfect obedience to God. This prepares for the crisis of entire sanctification which is wrought instantaneously when the believer presents himself a living sacrifice, holy and acceptable to God, through faith in Jesus Christ, being effected by the baptism with the Holy Spirit who cleanses the heart from all inbred sin. The crisis of entire sanctification perfects the believer in love and empowers him for effective service. It is followed by lifelong growth in grace and the knowledge of our Lord and Savior, Jesus Christ. The life of holiness continues through faith in the sanctifying blood of Christ and evidences itself by loving obedience to God's revealed will.

Gen. 17:1; Deut. 30:6; Ps. 130:8; Isa. 6:1-6; 35; Ezek. 36:25-29; Matt. 5:8, 48; Luke 1:74-75; 3:16-17; 24:49; John 17:1-26; Acts 1:4-5, 8; 2:1-4; 15:8-9; 26:18; Rom. 8:3-4; I Cor. 1:2; 6:11; II Cor. 7:1; Eph. 4:13, 24; 5:25-27; I Thess. 3:10, 12-13; 4:3, 7-8; 5:23-24; II Thess. 2:13; Titus 2:11-14; Heb. 10:14; 12:14; 13:12; James 3:17-18; 4:8; I Peter 1:2; II Peter 1:4; I John 1:7, 9; 3:8-9; 4:17-18; Jude 24.

—The Discipline, 1985, 26

Bibliography

We have included here only works quoted or cited in volume 6. A comprehensive bibliography titled *Holiness Works: A Bibliography*, compiled in 1986, is available from Beacon Hill Press of Kansas City.

Agnew, Milton S. *More than Conquerors.* Kansas City: Beacon Hill Press of Kansas City, 1977.

Arthur, William. *The Tongue of Fire.* Nashville: Publishing House M.E. Church, South, 1888.

Atkinson, J. Baines. *The Beauty of Holiness.* New York: Philosophical Library, 1953.

Barbour, Clifford Edward. *Sin and the New Psychology.* New York: Abingdon Press, 1930.

Bassett, Paul, and Greathouse, William M. *The Historical Foundations.* Vol. 2 of *Exploring Christian Holiness.* Kansas City: Beacon Hill Press of Kansas City, 1984.

Bonner, Harold, comp. *Proclaiming the Spirit.* Kansas City: Beacon Hill Press of Kansas City, 1975.

Brockett, Henry. *The Riches of Holiness.* Kansas City: Beacon Hill Press, 1951.

———. *Scriptural Freedom from Sin.* King's Highway Press, 1941. Reprint. Kansas City: Beacon Hill Press, 1951.

Brown, Charles Ewing. *The Meaning of Sanctification.* Anderson, Ind.: Warner Press, 1945.

Cattell, Everett Lewis. *The Spirit of Holiness.* Kansas City: Beacon Hill Press of Kansas City, 1977.

Chapman, J. B. *Holiness, the Heart of Christian Experience.* Kansas City: Beacon Hill Press, 1943.

———. *The Terminology of Holiness.* Kansas City: Beacon Hill Press, 1947.

Clarke, Adam. *Commentary on the Holy Bible,* vol. 6. New York: Abingdon Cokesbury, n.d.

Comfort, William Wistar. *Stephen Grellet.* New York: Macmillan Co., 1942.

Cook, Thomas. *New Testament Holiness.* London: Epworth Press, 1902.

Corlett, D. Shelby. *The Meaning of Holiness.* Kansas City: Beacon Hill Press, 1944.

Curtis, Olin Alfred. *The Christian Faith.* Grand Rapids: Kregel Publications, 1905. Reprint. 1956.

Davies, E. *Life and Journal of Mrs. Hester Ann Rogers.* Reading, Mass.: Holiness Book Concern, 1882.

Doddridge, Philip. *The Rise and Progress of Religion in the Soul.* Boston: Kimball and Johnson, 1831.

Earle, A. B. *The Rest of Faith.* Boston: James H. Earle, Publisher, 1878.

Foster, Randolph S. *Nature and Blessedness of Christian Purity.* New York: Carlton and Porter, 1857.

Garrison, S. Olin. *Forty Witnesses.* 1888. Reprint. Freeport, Pa.: Fountain Press, 1955.

Geiger, Kenneth, comp. *Further Insights into Holiness.* Kansas City: Beacon Hill Press, 1963.

———. *Insights into Holiness.* Kansas City: Beacon Hill Press, 1962.

Godet, F. *Epistle to the Romans.* Edinburgh: T. and T. Clark, 1894.

Gordon, A. J. *The Ministry of the Spirit.* New York: Fleming H. Revell Co., 1894.

Gould, J. Glenn. *The Spirit's Ministry.* Kansas City: Nazarene Publishing House, 1941.

Harper, A. F. *Holiness and High Country.* Kansas City: Beacon Hill Press, 1964.

———. "I Would Like to Know God Better." Manuscript.

Hills, A. M. *The Secret of Spiritual Power.* Kansas City: Beacon Hill Press, 1952.

———. *Holiness and Power.* Cincinnati: M. W. Knapp, 1897. Reprint. Jamestown, N.C.: Newby Book Room, n.d.

Hogue, Wilson T. *The Holy Spirit.* Chicago: William Rose, Agent, 1916.

Ironside, H. A. *Lectures on the Epistle to the Romans.* New York: Loizeaux Bros., 1942.

Jessop, Harry E. *Foundations of Doctrine.* Chicago: Chicago Evangelistic Institute, 1938.

———. *The Heritage of Holiness.* Kansas City: Beacon Hill Press, 1950.

———. *I Met a Man with a Shining Face.* Chicago: Chicago Evangelistic Institute, 1941.

Joad, Cyril Edwin Mitchenson. *God and Evil.* New York: Harper and Brothers, 1943.

Jones, E. Stanley. *A Song of Ascents.* Nashville: Abingdon Press, 1968.

Kelly, Thomas R. *A Testament of Devotion.* New York: Harper and Row, 1941.

Laurin, Roy L. *Romans, Where Life Begins.* Wheaton, Ill.: Van Kampen Press, 1948.

Lawson, James Gilchrist. *Deeper Experiences of Famous Christians.* Anderson, Ind.: Warner Press, 1911.

Lowrey, Asbury. *Possibilities of Grace.* New York: Phillips and Hunt, 1884.

McCumber, W. E. *Holiness in the Prayers of St. Paul.* Kansas City: Beacon Hill Press, 1955.

———. *Preaching Holiness from the Synoptic Gospels.* Kansas City: Beacon Hill Press of Kansas City, 1972.

McGraw, James, comp. *The Holiness Pulpit, No. 2.* Kansas City: Beacon Hill Press of Kansas City, 1974.

Mitchell, T. Crichton, ed. *The Wesley Century.* Vol. 2 of *Great Holiness Classics.* Kansas City: Beacon Hill Press of Kansas City, 1984.

Moody, Dwight L. *Secret Power.* Chicago: Bible Institute Colportage Assn., 1908.

Morrison, H. C. *The Baptism with the Holy Ghost.* Louisville, Ky.: Pentecostal Herald Press, 1900.

Oehler, Gustave Friedrich Von. *Theology of the Old Testament.* New York: Fleming H. Revell Co., 1896.

Purkiser, W. T. *Conflicting Concepts of Holiness.* Kansas City: Beacon Hill Press, 1953.

Robertson, Archibald Thomas. *Word Pictures in the New Testament*, vol. 4. Nashville: Broadman Press, 1931.

Simpson, A. B. *Christ in the Bible*. Vol. 2, *Romans*. New York: Christian Alliance Publishing Co., 1894.

Smith, Allister. *The Ideal of Perfection*. London: Oliphants, 1963.

Smith, Bernie. *Flames of Living Fire*. Kansas City: Beacon Hill Press, 1950.

Steele, Daniel. *Milestone Papers*. New York: Eaton and Main, 1878.

Talbot, Louis T. *Addresses on Romans*. Wheaton, Ill.: Van Kampen Press, 1937.

Taylor, J. Paul. *Holiness, the Finished Foundation*. Winona Lake, Ind.: Light and Life Press, 1963.

Taylor, Richard S. *The Theological Foundations*. Vol. 3 of *Exploring Christian Holiness*. Kansas City: Beacon Hill Press of Kansas City, 1985.

Thomas à Kempis. *The Imitation of Christ*. Rev. trans. New York: Grossett and Dunlap, n.d.

Underhill, Evelyn. *The Spiritual Life*. New York: Harper and Bros., n.d.

Vine, W. E. *The Epistle to the Romans*. London: Oliphants, 1948.

Watson, George Douglas. *Coals of Fire*. Cincinnati: God's Revivalist, 1894.

Wesley, John. *A Plain Account of Christian Perfection as believed and taught by the Reverend Mr. John Wesley from the year 1725 to the year 1777*. New York and Cincinnati: Methodist Book Concern, n.d.

———. *Sermons on Several Occasions*. New York: Lane and Scott, 1884.

Wesleyan Theological Journal: Bulletin of the Wesleyan Theological Society 14 (Fall 1979), no. 2.

Wiley, H. Orton. *Christian Theology*. 3 vols. Kansas City: Nazarene Publishing House, 1942.

Wilkes, A. Paget. *The Dynamic of Redemption*. England, 1924. Reprint. Kansas City: Beacon Hill Press, 1946.

Williams, R. T. *Sanctification: The Experience and the Ethics*. Kansas City: Nazarene Publishing House, 1928.

Williamson, G. B. *Preaching Scriptural Holiness*. Kansas City: Beacon Hill Press, 1953. Reprint. Kansas City: Beacon Hill Press of Kansas City, 1976.

———. *Roy T. Williams, Servant of God*. Kansas City: Nazarene Publishing House, 1947.

Wood, J. A. *Perfect Love*. Chicago: Christian Witness Co., 1880.

———. *Purity and Maturity*. North Attleboro, Mass.: Published by the author, 1882.

Author Index

Agnew, Col. Milton S. 140
Arthur, William 43, 47
Atkinson, J. Baines 294
Barbour, Clifford 353
Boone, Brindley 156
Booth, Gen. William 297
Bottome, Frank 82
Brasch, Rose Marie 299
Brockett, Henry 243, 264
Brooks, Phillips 45
Brown, Charles Ewing 116, 321
Burpo, Mrs. Loyd 248
Cattell, Everett L. 161, 360
Chambers, Oswald 181
Chapman, James B. 66, 234, 246,
255, 262, 271, 275, 280,
293, 351, 355, 363, 374
Comfort, William Wistar 189
Cook, Thomas 248, 250, 256,
281, 302, 336, 356
Cope, Mildred 259, 343
Corlett, D. Shelby 225, 242,
246, 351
Crosby, Fanny 109, 327
Crowell, Grace Noll 377
Curtis, Olin A. 237, 272, 352
Davies, E. 257
Denman, Mary R. 306
Doddridge, Philip. 59, 320
Dunham, E. S. 253
Earle, A. B. 109, 320
Eckhart, Meister 59
Faber, Frederick William 252
Finney, Charles G. 262
Fletcher, John 255, 257
Foster, Randolph S. . . .274, 322, 330,
338
Fox, George 61, 62, 169
Gabriel, Charles H. 336
Gordon, A. J. 44
Gordon, S. D. 349
Gould, J. Glenn 327
Greathouse, William M. 276
Greenlee, Harold J. 196, 250

Grellet, Stephen 189
Grimes, Homer W. 315
Harper, A. F. 263, 311, 316, 325,
327, 333, 343, 350, 367
Harris, Margaret J. 292, 368
Hatch, Edwin 298
Havergal, Frances R. . .243, 317, 319,
337, 374, 390
Heber, Reginald 232
Hill, F. E. 333
Hills, A. M. 237, 261, 293,
296, 324, 380
Hogue, Wilson Thomas 309
Jessop, Harry E. 365
Joad, C. E. M. 119
Johnston, Julia H. 244
Jones, E. Stanley 209
Keene, S. A. 381, 382
Keith, George 329
Kelly, Thomas R. 57
Knapp, Phoebe Palmer 234, 325
Lange, J. P. 253
Lowrey, Asbury 103, 236
McCumber, William 353, 363
Martin, I. G. 111
Mason, Lowell L. 156
Meyer, F. B. 147, 324
Mitchell, T. Crichton. 379
Moody, Dwight L. 290, 371
Morris, Lelia N. 261, 322
Morrison, H. C. 23
Mullen, Laurence K. 386
Müller, George 154, 335
Nease, Orval J. 328
Nicholson, James 150, 284, 325
Oehler, Gustave F. Von 130
Orr, J. Edwin 241, 350
Orsborn, Gen. Albert 150, 341
Owen, John 42
Palmer, Horatio R. 359
Pennington, Isaac 58
Prentiss, Elizabeth 264
Purkiser, W. T. 284

Reed, George J. 375
Rees, Paul S. 363
Reid, Isaiah 321
Rider, Lucy J. 351
Robertson, A. T. 157
Rogers, Hester Ann 257
Simpson, A. B. 149, 154
Smith, Maj. Allister 348
Smith, Hannah Whitall 212
Stam, Betty Scott 314
Steele, Daniel 352, 353
Stites, Edgar Page 113
Stokes, Elwood H. 308, 344
Surbrook, W. L. 277
Talbot, Louis T. 143, 147, 149
Thomas à Kempis 137, 233
Toplady, Augustus M. 245
Tracy, Ruth 156
Underhill, Evelyn 353

Van Deventer, Judson W. . . . 269, 317,
373
Vanderpool, D. I. 238
Vine, W. E. 148
Walters, Mrs. Stanley 344
Watson, G. D. 130
Watson, Richard 303
Wesley, Charles . . .151, 254, 281, 361
Wesley, John 237, 242, 271, 280,
283, 293, 294, 327,
328, 329, 355, 360
Wharton, Fletcher 262
Wiley, H. Orton 327, 355
Wilkes, A. Paget 247
Williams, Clara Tear. 354
Williams, R. T. 48, 315, 388
Williamson, G. B. 49, 370, 383
Wood, J. A. 103, 271
Woolman, John 61
Yi, Un Chong 312

Subject Index

Abandoned to God 64
Adamic nature 398
Agapē 250
Alive to God 154
Aorist tense 154, 205-7, 237
Appeals 64, 74, 81, 101, 296,
332, 340, 381
Assurance 279, 326, 330, 345
Atonement 84, 98, 245
Attitudes. 165, 176, 182,
301, 343, 348
Backsliding 331, 338
Baptism with the Holy Spirit 24,
135, 255, 256
Beauty of holiness, the 231
Carnality/Cleansing. 35, 71,
171, 211
Choice. 80
Christian Holiness Association . . . 391
Christian perfection 61, 106, 202,
250, 400
Christlikeness 217, 227, 263, 349
Christ's example. 88
Cleansing 202, 213, 237, 247

Cleansing and discipline 175
Consecration 60, 80, 312, 315,
316, 320
Conviction for carnality 310
Cornelius's experience . . 32, 216, 289
Courage. 136, 362
Courtesy 55
Coworkers with God. 339
Daily faith. 337
Daily fellowship 193
Daily yielding 337
Dangers. 85, 187, 244, 360
Death to self. 168
Decision and sanctification. 168
Deeper spiritual life 367
Depravity 118
Die to sin 147, 150, 152, 153,
154, 259, 265
Effort required 338
Emblems of the Spirit 126
Empowerment 260
Envy 173
Ephesian Pentecost 289
Eradication 167, 188, 214,
236, 303, 354

Ethics 50, 86, 92, 99, 382
Evil thoughts 358

Faith 44, 81, 83, 98, 152, 322
Faith and feeling. 324
Fall, the. 120, 122
Figurative terms . .110, 169, 235, 248
For all Christians 26, 30, 41, 75, 100, 275, 392, 398
Freedom from sin. 159, 166
Freedom in the Spirit. 346
Fruit of the Spirit 348

Godly life 86
God's moral standards. 229
Grace. 43, 79, 99, 106, 230, 242
Growth 52, 133, 162, 335
Guidance of the Spirit . .91, 177, 179, 188, 189-95, 268, 387

Hagios. 198, 200, 204
Holiness and common people. 262, 275
Holiness commanded 63
Holiness is love 230
Holiness of God. 199, 201, 227
Holy in this life 72
Holy Spirit 29, 38, 83, 104, 108, 126, 165, 255, 285, 301
Humanity . . . 79, 132, 148, 170, 213, 243, 354, 396
Hunger . .34, 62, 63, 64, 73, 80, 139, 278, 300, 305, 307, 344

Image of God 121, 122
In a moment. . . 29, 37, 78, 149, 206, 213, 283, 372
Indwelling sin 119, 124, 214
Influence. 51
Integration of life 168, 351

Joy in the Holy Spirit. 264-67

Keep open to God 62

Law in the heart. 252
Love gives 251

Moment-by-moment cleansing. . .336, 340, 392

Names. 95, 292
New birth 299
Now is the time 98, 101

Obeying God 307, 337, 341
Old man, the 145

Opposed to sin. 228

Patience. 183
Pentecost 256, 257
Perfect love 55, 86, 105, 249, 250
Philos 250
Power 37, 39, 65, 129, 216, 261, 372, 387
Preaching 51, 68, 89, 207, 369, 372
Pride 179, 187, 360

Rejection of the Holy Spirit 40
Rest of faith 109, 307

Samaritan Pentecost. . . . 32, 280, 288
Sanctification as relationship 178
Sanctification begun 302, 402
Sanctification of sex 184
Sanctified human nature 172
Sanctified speech 174
Sarx. 234
Scriptural 83, 97, 205, 270, 272, 274
Second blessing 31, 96, 97, 201, 280, 281
Seeking 46, 253, 371, 375
Selfish ambition 346
Self-pity. 173
Sense of need 283
Sin principle, the 141
Sinful nature 123, 171
Sinful self crucified . . . 147, 150, 167
Soul winning. 342
Spirit-filled 108, 164, 256
Steps to sanctification . 323, 344, 394
Subconscious, the 211, 213
Subsequent to regeneration. . 31, 393, 396
Suppression. 167, 215, 236
Surrender to God. 155, 168, 317

Teaching 374
Temper 181, 238
Temptation 170, 340, 356
Terms. 108, 345
Testimonies. 23, 48, 67, 137, 147, 154, 211, 233, 238, 257, 264, 277, 299, 306, 312, 317, 328, 341, 344, 365, 371, 375, 380

Unsurrendered will. 166

Victorious life 135, 163

Wesleyan Theological Society.... 392
Whole message of the Bible 204, 208
Wholeness 75, 104, 214, 219, 272, 350, 351, 365

Witness of the Spirit 327
Witnessing 33, 68, 76, 104, 106, 136, 138, 239, 258, 346, 362, 363, 385
Writing 212, 318, 378

Index of Scripture References

Genesis
1:2 126
1:26-27 120
1:28 120
1:31 120
2:7 127
2:17 122
5:3 123
6:3 42
6:5-6 125
8:21 125
9:6 122

Exodus
3:2-4 128
21:2, 5-6 158
33:11 137

Leviticus
19:2 226
20:7-8 225, 271, 315
20:26 226
21:8 226

Deuteronomy
6:5 249
18:15 137

Joshua
24:19 226

1 Samuel
6:20 226

1 Kings
18:21 155

1 Chronicles
28:9 47

2 Chronicles
16:9 355

Job
33:4 127

Psalms
24:3-4 228
25:14 34
37:6 347

37:23 335
40:8 252
42:1 278
51:1-3 306
51:5 125, 306
51:7 71, 306
51:9-12 306
51:10 283
73:25 62
103:1 368
116:16 267
118:5, 19 346
119:165 136

Proverbs
4:15 340
15:8 33
28:9 33

Ecclesiastes
7:29 120

Isaiah
6:1, 3 226, 228
6:1-7 287
6:5 62, 228
6:6-7 129
30:21 194
42:8 181
44:3-4 129
60:1 382
61:1 130
61:3 382
62:4 112

Jeremiah
31:33 346

Ezekiel
1:4 128
18:4 229
36:17-18 343
36:25-28 233, 235, 343
37:9 127

Daniel
12:3 374

Hosea
6:3 115

Zechariah
13:1 71

Malachi
3:2-3 117, 128, 235
4:2 264

Matthew
1:21 93
3:11-12 26, 27, 129, 144, 235, 255, 264, 292
4:1 357
4:21 203
5:3 219
5:6 34, 305
5:8 292, 299, 305
5:13 87
5:23-24 176
5:43-48 276, 352
5:48 202, 292
6:24 159
7:7-8 34
7:11 125
7:20-21 382
8:2 202
10:27 268
12:19 137
12:35 214
13:8 133
14:36 144
15:19 125
16:24 146
19:16-17, 20-21 312
19:26 349
22:37-40 385
23:25-26 202
23:33 176
24:44 94
24:46 221
27:37 217
27:46 229
28:18-20 26, 88, 374

Mark
1:4 290
1:19 203
3:10 144

10:27 349
15:34 229
16:15-20 88, 218, 369

Luke
1:37 349
1:73-75 79, 87, 304
6:40 203
10:20 31, 288
11:9-13 34, 287, 367
11:25 108
11:34 61
17:21 39
18:13 282
23:43 146
24:49 135, 242, 260

John
1:11 40, 46
1:14 227
1:18 226
1:29 235
1:33 219
2:6 204
2:17 173
3:3 60, 145, 348
3:5-8 125, 127, 299
3:16 285
3:30 27
7:37-39 28, 35, 43, 217
8:23 125
8:36 151, 265
8:42 151
8:46 151
8:47 34
9:4 333
9:34 124
10:10 109, 127, 154, 350
10:27 190
12:32 51
13:33 39
13:34 251
14:8 266
14:15-17 28, 34, 39, 288, 291, 344
14:18 266
14:21 267, 268, 269
14:23 266
14:26 28, 40
15:2 202
15:4-6 243, 350, 360
16:7 26
16:8 127, 145
16:12-15 40, 263, 387
16:24 266
17:6 288
17:9 73
17:11-12 31, 288
17:14-15 152, 288

17:16 31, 270
17:17 83, 97, 270, 271, 272, 275, 285, 311
17:20 73, 270, 275
17:26 250
18:23 176
20:22 256
20:28 61

Acts
1:4-5 28, 144, 145, 255, 286, 293
1:7-8 37, 129, 135, 136, 216, 221, 260, 262, 362
2:1-4 29, 30, 127, 128, 255, 283, 288, 292
2:11 217
2:38-39 30, 101, 275, 296
4:1-31 363
5:32 267, 367
8:5-8 32, 280, 288
8:12 32, 280
8:14-17 280, 288, 291
8:23 35
10:2-4 32, 289
10:34-37 33, 289
10:38 131
10:44-45 283
11:24 89
11:26 290
15:8-9 37, 216, 289, 322, 326, 328
16:31 322
17:16 183
18:24—19:7 289
19:2 30, 45, 290, 291
23:1-5 176
26:17 215
26:18 79, 83, 103, 111, 152, 285

Romans
1:4 204
1:11-12 29
2:12 144
3:3 148, 203
3:10 126
3:23 76
3:31 148
5:1 141, 285
5:5 164, 250
5:9 285
5:12 120, 123
5:14 123
5:15-16 124
5:20 142
5:21 231

6:1-7 142
6:4 300
6:6 203, 235, 236, 237, 247, 286, 287
6:8-14 99, 150, 151, 203, 265, 312
6:15-23 157, 160, 166, 236
7:2 203
7:9 125
7:17 125
7:19 159
7:20 125
7:21-24 35, 36, 125, 146, 159, 265
7:25 265
8:1 166
8:2 93, 125, 142, 265, 352
8:3-5 166, 247
8:6-9 233, 305
8:7 36, 125, 166, 305, 352
8:9 145, 166, 235
8:11 169
8:12-13 166
8:14 189, 194, 267
8:15-16 326, 328, 329
8:23 122
8:37 262
10:13-14 370
11:6 291
11:14 234
12:1-2 155, 267, 312, 321, 378
13:10 105
13:13 174
14:4 347
14:17 39
15:13 264
15:16 83, 215
15:29 109, 292

1 Corinthians
1:30 299
2:6 202
2:10 292
3:1-3 36, 233
3:16 38
6:17 269
6:19 38
7:14 200
9:22-23 378
9:27 185
10:12 100
10:13 308
12:11 217, 218
12:13 144

12:29-30   217
13:4-8   173, 183, 203, 249
15:22   124
15:26   203
15:45   124
15:49   125
15:56   124

2 Corinthians
3:13   277
3:17   267
3:18   277, 311
4:7-10   355
5:17   60
5:19   230
6:6-7   219
7:1   201, 206, 303
7:11   173
9:8   43
11:3   359
12:9   355
13:9   203

Galatians
2:20   61, 145, 160, 286, 352, 387
3:14   287, 291
3:17   203
5:11   203
5:16-17   149, 212, 362
5:22-23   218, 326, 343, 349
5:24-25   150, 326, 335, 362, 382
6:17   158

Ephesians
1:3   114
1:13   287
2:3   125
2:9-10   244, 291
2:12   126
3:14-21   206, 261, 266, 292
4:3   243
4:4-6   143
4:12   203
4:20-28   121, 163, 166, 181, 236, 287, 383
4:30-32   343
5:18   287
5:25-27   94, 130, 245, 246, 285, 316
6:1   90
6:12   38, 114, 357

Philippians
2:1   263
2:3-5   263
4:6   340

Colossians
1:9-11   43, 350
1:27   266
1:28   202, 276
2:2   370
2:6-7   335
3:3   162, 168, 302
3:5   286
3:9   236
3:10   121
3:15   347
4:6   129

1 Thessalonians
3:10   203
3:13   204
4:3   207, 301
4:3-7   207
4:4   204
5:19-22   206
5:23-24   97, 201, 205, 271, 292, 294, 301, 303, 311, 345, 353

2 Thessalonians
2:13   204, 285

1 Timothy
1:5   105
2:3-4   285
2:15   204

2 Timothy
1:7   129, 137
2:21   236
4:10   159

Titus
2:11-14   72, 86, 160, 236, 242, 246, 383
3:5   84, 244, 285

Hebrews
1:3   204
2:11   262, 269, 316
2:14   148
2:18   357
4:3   292
4:11   113
4:12   78
4:15   357
5:14   202
6:1   272, 280, 299
6:11   370
7:26   227
8:10   252
9:3   282
9:13   204
9:14   202, 246
9:22   202
10:10   285

10:22   370
10:38   41
11:6   322
12:1   235
12:14-15   101, 235, 272, 275, 292, 300
13:12   83, 93, 97, 245, 246, 271, 285
13:13   245
13:21   203, 354

James
1:8   167
1:14-15   125
1:27   262
3:9   122
4:8   280

1 Peter
1:8   266
1:13-16   79, 97, 225, 226, 229, 271, 384, 385
1:23   285
5:10   203

2 Peter
3:9   231

1 John
1:7   72, 74, 202, 205, 242, 262, 269, 294, 311, 329, 336, 355
1:8   126
1:9   93, 202, 205, 282
2:1-3   157, 379, 386
2:27   130
3:1-3   94, 250
3:9   267
3:14   348
3:19-21   326, 329
4:4   38, 72
4:6   34
4:8   348
4:12-13   292, 329
4:16-17   266, 272
4:16—5:5   273
4:18   252, 348
5:3   99

Jude
5   41

Revelation
1:6   131
2:14   88
3:20   165, 266
20:6   94
22:1   43